NEW LE.

New Lefts

THE MAKING OF A
RADICAL TRADITION

TERENCE RENAUD

PRINCETON UNIVERSITY PRESS
PRINCETON & OXFORD

Published by Princeton University Press
41 William Street, Princeton, New Jersey 08540
6 Oxford Street, Woodstock, Oxfordshire OX20 1TR

press.princeton.edu

All Rights Reserved
ISBN 978-0-691-22079-6
ISBN (pbk.) 978-0-691-22081-9
ISBN (e-book) 978-0-691-22080-2

British Library Cataloging-in-Publication Data is available

Editorial: Priya Nelson and Thalia Leaf
Production Editorial: Jenny Wolkowicki
Cover design: Pamela L. Schnitter
Production: Brigid Ackerman
Publicity: Alyssa Sanford and Amy Stewart
Copyeditor: Maia Vaswani

Cover image: Street art. Paris, France / Alamy Stock Photo

This book has been composed in Arno Pro

10 9 8 7 6 5 4 3 2 1

For Ruth

This superficial rabble, crazy for novelties
Which never wears its boot soles out
Never reads its books to the end
Keeps forgetting its thoughts
This is the world's
Natural hope.
And even if it isn't
Everything new
Is better than everything old.

—BERTOLT BRECHT,
"EVERYTHING NEW IS BETTER
THAN EVERYTHING OLD"

CONTENTS

ABBREVIATIONS

AFGF   American Friends of German Freedom

Antifa   Antifascist Committee (Antifaschistischer Ausschuss) (Germany)

APO   Extraparliamentary Opposition (Außerparlamentarische Opposition) (Germany)

BdS   League of Democratic Socialists (Bund demokratischer Sozialisten) (Thuringia, occupied Germany)

BLM   Black Lives Matter (USA)

BOC   Catalan Workers and Peasants' Bloc (Bloc Obrer i Camperol) (Spain)

BPI   Berlin Psychoanalytic Institute

BRSD   German League of Religious Socialists (Bund religiöser Sozialisten Deutschlands)

CDG   Council for a Democratic Germany (USA)

CDU   Christian Democratic Union (West Germany)

CGT   General Confederation of Labor (Confédération générale du travail) (France)

Comintern   Communist International

CRS   Republican Security Companies, specialized force of the French National Police (Compagnies républicaines de sécurité)

CSU   Christian Social Union (Christlich-Soziale Union) (West Germany)

EDC   European Defense Community

F-Course   Org Advanced Course (Fortgeschrittener Kursus)

FDJ   Free German Youth (Freie Deutsche Jugend)

GL   Justice and Liberty (Giustizia e Libertà) (Italy)

ISK   International Socialist Militant League (Internationaler Sozialistischer Kampfbund) (Germany)

JCR   Revolutionary Communist Youth (Jeunesse communiste révolutionnaire) (France)

KAPD   German Communist Workers' Party (Kommunistische Arbeiterpartei Deutschlands)

KPD   German Communist Party (Kommunistische Partei Deutschlands)

KPO   German Communist Party–Opposition (Kommunistische Partei Deutschlands–Opposition)

LBC   Left Book Club

LSI   Labour and Socialist International

NATO   North Atlantic Treaty Organization

NKVD   People's Commissariat for Internal Affairs (Naródnyy Komissariát Vnútrennikh Del) (USSR)

Org   Leninist Organization (Leninistische Organisation) (Germany)

OSS   Office of Strategic Services (USA)

PCE   Spanish Communist Party (Partido Comunista de España)

PCF   French Communist Party (Parti communiste français)

POUM   Workers' Party of Marxist Unification (Partido Obrero de Unificación Marxista) (Spain)

PSOE   Spanish Socialist Workers' Party (Partido Socialista Obrero Español)

PSU   Unified Socialist Party (Parti socialiste unifié) (France)

RDR   Revolutionary Democratic Assembly (Rassemblement démocratique révolutionnaire) (France)

RPF   Assembly of the French People (Rassemblement du peuple français)

RSD   German Revolutionary Socialists (Revolutionäre Sozialisten Deutschlands)

SA   Subversive Action (West Germany)

SAJ   Socialist Worker Youth (Sozialistische Arbeiter-Jugend) (Germany)

SAP   German Socialist Workers' Party (Sozialistische Arbeiterpartei Deutschlands)

SDS   Socialist German Student League (Sozialistischer Deutscher Studentenbund)

SDS   Students for a Democratic Society (USA)

SED   East German Socialist Unity Party (Sozialistische Einheitspartei Deutschlands)

Sex-Pol   German Association for Proletarian Sexual Politics (Deutscher Reichsverband für Proletarische Sexualpolitik)

SFIO   French Section of the Workers' International (Section française de l'Internationale ouvrière)

SMAD   Soviet Military Administration in Germany (Sowjetische Militäradministration in Deutschland)

SOPADE   German Social Democratic Party in Exile (Vorstand der SPD im Exil)

SouB   Socialism or Barbarism (Socialisme ou barbarie) (France)

SPD   German Social Democratic Party (Sozialdemokratische Partei Deutschlands)

UDSO   Union of German Socialist Organizations in Great Britain (Union deutscher sozialistischer Organisationen in Großbritannien)

NEW LEFTS

The Origins of Neoleftism

THE WHITE-HAIRED German theorist Herbert Marcuse, whom the *New York Times* labeled foremost philosopher, hero, idol, and prophet of the New Left, took the stage at the Fillmore East in New York City on December 4, 1968, to deliver a talk titled "On the New Left." Addressing a packed theater, he began by disowning those labels: "I never claimed to be the ideological leader of the left and I don't think the left needs an ideological leader. And there is one thing the left does not need, and that's another father image, another daddy."[1]

Marcuse sympathized with the student activists and other youth militants around the world who rallied under the banner of the New Left in the 1960s. His philosophy of revolution inspired many of them to devise alternatives to the repressive politics and culture of advanced capitalism during the Cold War era. But he refused to play the role of intellectual leader for an anti-authoritarian movement that was in principle leaderless. Activists of the New Left, he claimed, must behave as "models of what may one day be a human being" in a liberated society. That meant their mode of organization had to anticipate or prefigure the kind of social relations that they desired

---

1. Marcuse, "On the New Left," 469. For coverage by the *New York Times* of Marcuse and the New Left, see Andrew Hacker, "Philosopher of the New Left," March 10, 1968, BR1; Philip Shabecoff, "The Followers of Red Rudi Shake Up Germany," April 28, 1968, SM26; Lionel Abel, "Seven Heroes of the New Left," May 5, 1968, SM30; and the interview by Jean-Louis Ferrier, Jacques Boetsch, and Françoise Giroud, "Marcuse Defines His New Left Line," trans. Helen Weaver, October 27, 1968, SM29. The young lawyer and US New Left activist Bernardine Dohrn introduced Marcuse at the December 4 event by claiming that the *Times* had called him "the ideological leader of the New Left," an exact phrase that the newspaper seems never to have used. The event commemorated the twentieth anniversary of the US radical left paper the *Guardian* (originally *National Guardian*). Murray Schumach, "Guardian Marks 20th Birthday: Radical Publication Looking for Ways to Grow," *New York Times*, December 6, 1968, 26.

for the future. Marcuse noted the difficulty of persuading a majority of people to join the revolution, since industrial workers had become ideologically and materially integrated into the system and mass media remained outside activists' control. There were no revolutionary masses, so it made no sense to organize a centralized revolutionary mass party. Because the capitalist state had at its disposal such overwhelming military and police force, the New Left should stop dreaming of a revolutionary seizure of power. At the same time, activists should expect nothing from popular parties that played the electoral game of liberal democracy, which in his view served to reinforce the system.

Instead, Marcuse called for a "diffuse and dispersed disintegration of the system, in which interest, emphasis and activity [are] shifted to local and regional area[s]." Riots, uprisings in poor urban neighborhoods, and grassroots action of all sorts would produce a new sensibility to counter the conformism of existing society. Unlike the parties and unions of the old left, the New Left of the 1960s had "an entirely overt organization, diffused, concentrated in small groups and around local activities, small groups which are highly flexible and autonomous." These autonomous groups functioned as a "political guerrilla force in peace or so-called peace." In their abolition of hierarchy and institution of direct democracy, Marcuse likened these networked small groups to the councils or soviets that sprang up during the Russian and Central European revolutions. They shared an evanescent form of (dis)organization, embodying what he called organized spontaneity.[2]

He was correct to link the 1960s New Left organizational form of anti-authoritarian and extraparliamentary opposition to the council form that peaked in the revolutionary years 1917–23. In fact, sixties militants young and old recognized an affinity between their decentralized alternatives to seemingly obsolete party politics—whether electoral or vanguardist—and earlier moments of nonparty left activism. In terms of organization and aspiration, a continuity existed between new lefts present and new lefts past. As a young man, Marcuse himself had participated in a soldiers' council in Berlin at the end of World War I. He became a philosopher during Germany's tumultuous Weimar Republic, witnessed the rise of fascism, was betrayed by his doctoral supervisor Martin Heidegger (who joined the Nazi Party), and emigrated after the Nazi seizure of power, fearing for his life as a person of Jewish descent. The solidarity between Marcuse and the militant youth who set the world on fire in the late 1960s symbolizes this book's long-term, multigenerational history of new lefts.

2. Marcuse, "On the New Left," 472.

The origins of neoleftism as a distinct organizational phenomenon date to the two decades following the end of World War I, when Western Europeans and particularly Germans developed a radical left politics on the margins of mainstream Social Democratic and Communist parties. Germany was for various reasons a cradle of new lefts. Germans had created the first socialist mass party between 1863 and 1875. Their capitalist class and aristocratic elite helped engineer two world wars. The Nazi regime turned fascism into an existential threat for the left everywhere. Afterward, divided Germany functioned as the main European front in the Cold War, freezing already frigid relations between Social Democrats and Communists. A densely organized German workers' movement endured two totalitarian dictatorships in the shape of a fascist racial state and a communist authoritarian state. And according to neoleftists, postwar West Germany endured an authoritarian restoration of capitalism. German philosophy had moreover produced Karl Marx and inspired so-called Western Marxism, which provided the theoretical impetus behind so many new lefts.[3]

The German group New Beginning serves as this book's main case study. It was founded in Berlin around 1930, when fascism was on the rise and the global economic crisis had just begun. Back then the city was a hotbed of revolt and cultural experimentation. Nazis and Communists fought street battles by day, while by night wild parties at jazz clubs raged into the small hours. Social misery coexisted with sexual freedom. Forming a coalition government for the Weimar Republic was like a game of musical chairs. Social Democrats struggled to maintain a moderate position, while everybody talked about the crisis of democracy. The workers' movement and the political left were divided, and the right only gained momentum. A circle of renegade Communists and frustrated Social Democrats began meeting in secret to discuss what could be done to unite the left and seize the opportunity for a new revolution. They called themselves the Org, short for Leninist Organization, which owed to their strategy of using a conspiratorial vanguard to infiltrate the major left parties and unions. In that way they hoped to steer the left toward united action. Beyond subterfuge, however, members of the Org hoped to fundamentally reshape left politics for the better. They thought that Social Democrats limited themselves to piecemeal reforms within parliament and placed too much faith in existing institutions. They thought that Communist apparatchiks wielded too much authoritarian control over the rank and file, subordinating workers

---

3. Possibly the first person to identify a Western Marxist tradition in contrast to Soviet Marxist orthodoxy was the French phenomenologist Maurice Merleau-Ponty in his book *Adventures of the Dialectic*, ch. 2.

and the party to the caprice of Moscow. They also thought that Communists' theory of "social fascism," which treated moderate socialists and actual fascists as objectively the same, was tragically stupid. Other left tendencies such as anarcho-syndicalism, the Org thought, misunderstood immediate political tasks and had no realistic long-term strategy. The Org carefully recruited the brightest young workers and intellectuals, training them in revolutionary Marxist theory and preparing them for the coming struggle to define a new left for Germany and Europe.

The sudden Nazi takeover at the end of January 1933 complicated their plan, to say the least. Under increasing pressure and police surveillance, the Org nonetheless wove a transnational web of resisters in multiple cities, industries, and social milieus, all committed to forging an antifascist new left. The group's founder Walter Loewenheim wrote an illegal pamphlet under the pseudonym Miles in late 1933. Titled *Neu beginnen!*, it called on the young generation to wrest control over what remained of left party and union organization from the older, discredited leaders. Within circles of resistance underground and in exile, many heeded that call and imagined themselves as linked, at least in spirit, to the New Beginning group.

This book identifies an overlooked current of interwar German and Western European antifascism. New Beginning belonged to a cohort of small groups on the fringes of mainstream labor organizations, a cohort that often cooperated to reorganize the left under the banner of radical antifascism and a revolutionary new culture. Organizational problems preoccupied these militants in Germany, France, Spain, and elsewhere. They suspected that the hierarchical party and union structures themselves might pose an obstacle to grassroots mobilization. So they experimented with alternative forms: councils, assemblies, action committees, discussion circles, networks, and even militias. Interwar neoleftists were not pacifist and did take up arms against fascism, for example, during the Spanish Civil War. But usually their small size and internal ends within the workers' movement precluded violent means. Their activities varied from country to country, but in general these neoleftists disrupted the monopoly over progressive politics exercised by the Social Democratic and Communist old left.

Compared to the wholesale organizational realignment of the left caused by the Bolshevik Revolution and the spread of communism, the neoleftist realignment in the 1930s was marginal. Even the Popular Front, which unified diverse currents of the left against fascism, did not satisfy neoleftists' niche desire to break with all existing party and union forms. That desire would survive World War II and grow in the context of the postwar welfare state. In West Germany and throughout Western Europe, left socialists from the late 1940s through the early 1960s challenged the "modernized" parties of the center left. By the time an anti-authoritarian movement emerged in the late 1960s among militant youth who openly identified as the New Left, neoleftism had moved from a marginal to a central phenomenon of antisystemic opposition in the advanced capitalist world.

In reverse gear, this book could operate as a prehistory of the sixties New Left. It traces the phenomenon of neoleftism back to its origins in the 1920s and 1930s and chronicles the most creative attempts to sustain democracy within socialist organizations. It also unearths some of the past century's most radical attempts to transcend capitalist, imperialist, and authoritarian domination. For midcentury new lefts, the form your organization took determined the fate of your politics.

Fundamentally this is a book about form, and about leftists who grappled with it. Through a collective biography of New Beginning and its Western European counterparts, the book offers the first long-term history of neoleftism. The proper name New Left went mainstream only in the 1960s, but a succession of lowercase new lefts had been confronting the same problem for decades: How does one sustain the dynamism of a grassroots social movement without succumbing to hierarchy, centralized leadership, and banal political routine? For radical small groups, that problem translated into how to prefigure within their own ranks the kind of participatory democracy and popular control that they expected from a future, postcapitalist society. Keeping radical politics forever young is a problem that I call the neoleftist dilemma.

From around 1918 to around 1968, several generations of German and Western European activists rejected the party structures of Social Democracy and Communism. They self-consciously rebelled against what the sociologist Robert Michels dubbed the iron law of oligarchy, or the supposedly inevitable process by which democratic movements harden into elitist cartels. Their chief opponents were fascists, conservatives, and authoritarians, but as new lefts they also opposed reactionary tendencies within the labor and progressive movements themselves. Eventually, however, each neoleftist generation would experience the irony of backing institutions and values that a younger generation of radicals wished to subvert. Formerly radical organizations thus became institutionalized as part of the existing system.[4] Meet the old left, once the same as the new left.

---

4. On processes of rationalization, bureaucratization, and homogenization within social organizations, see Paul J. DiMaggio and Walter W. Powell, "The Iron Cage Revisited: Institutional Isomorphism and Collective Rationality in Organizational Fields," *American Sociological Review* 48, no. 2 (1983): 147–60.

This book explores the intersection of class and generation in the history of radical politics. It focuses on milieus that the German poet Bertolt Brecht once styled a "superficial rabble, crazy for novelties."[5] At first still bound to the industrial working class, neoleftist demographics gradually shifted over the mid-twentieth century into an affair of the educated middle-class youth. This change owed in large part to the material transformation of advanced capitalism into a postindustrial society, a transformation that the final chapter will survey through the lens of neoleftist sociology. At historical neoleftism's decisive moments, however, generational consciousness tended to outweigh class consciousness.

The Hungarian sociologist Karl Mannheim, whose 1929 book *Ideology and Utopia* served as an inspiration for New Beginning, published an essay one year earlier on "The Problem of Generations." He started by pointing out the weaknesses of two prevailing approaches to understanding generations: the positivist-biological school and the Romantic-historical school. The former approach tried to quantify a regular rhythm in human group reproduction that broke down into fifteen- to thirty-year intervals. The latter tried to qualify the spiritual essence of a given age group, linking it to national awakenings or great cultural achievements. According to Mannheim, neither school alone could account for the decisive role of social forces. In emphasizing the social construction of generations, he drew on his characteristic synthesis of Max Weber's positivist sociology and Marx's critical social theory.

Mannheim developed his conception by analogy to class formation. A generational unit forms when individuals not necessarily of the same background are galvanized by some historical event or common experience that has a strong age component—like, for example, going to war. Generational consciousness functions like class consciousness, he argued. Just as individuals who have jobs in different industries may nevertheless join the same union and recognize one another as fellow workers, so individuals from different class backgrounds may join organizations or movements based on a shared generational consciousness. He observed that "it may sometimes happen that a feeling for the unity of a generation is consciously developed into a basis for the formation of concrete groups, as in the case of the modern German Youth Movement."[6] New Beginning and the plethora of midcentury new lefts

---

5. Bertolt Brecht, "Everything New Is Better than Everything Old" [1929], trans. Christopher Middleton, in *Poems, 1913–1956*, ed. John Willett and Ralph Manheim (New York: Methuen, 1979), 159–60.

6. Karl Mannheim, "The Problem of Generations" [1928], in *Essays on the Sociology of Knowledge*, ed. Paul Kecskemeti (New York: Oxford University Press, 1952), 276–320 (at 288). The historian Robert Wohl argued that Mannheim's concept of generation was irreconcilable with

constituted just such groups. Generational units could attract earlier or later age cohorts to their ideological message and political style. Mannheim advanced a concept of generation that was not age-determinist. Accordingly, while it focuses on young radicals at several historical moments, this book never excludes neoleftists at heart.

Class, generation, and ideology blend in the composition of social movements, especially the labor movement. Mannheim recognized the link between the physical rejuvenation of a movement's personnel and the intellectual revitalization of its theory. But young versus old did not always map stereotypically onto progressive versus conservative: the European far right between the world wars was a case in point. The youth's "being young" and the "'freshness' of their contact with the world," he wrote, "manifest themselves in the fact that they are able to reorient any movement they embrace, to adapt it to the total situation." Young socialists thus always sought an up-to-date formulation of socialism, while young conservatives sought a renewal of conservatism.[7] It is worth noting here an analytic and historical difference between new lefts and new rights. While similar in terms of their rebellious style and counterculture, only new lefts have sought out democratic forms that contradict the hierarchical, inegalitarian, and disenfranchising institutions of existing society. New rights can mimic external hierarchies within their own organization without contradiction. Unlike new lefts, they face no dilemma of prefiguring or sustaining new forms. They are "new" only by virtue of articulating views of natural inequality and ethnic difference historically after the defeat of old nationalisms or fascisms.[8]

Usually, youth have provided the energy behind new lefts. Although not yet identifying as "Sixty-Eighters," the young radicals of the late 1960s did

---

class analysis. Wohl, *The Generation of 1914* (Cambridge, MA: Harvard University Press, 1979), 73–84.

7. Mannheim, "Problem of Generations," 297n1. Translation revised slightly. For a generational history and collective biography that partly inspired my own, see Shore, *Caviar and Ashes*. See also Hartmut Berghoff, Uffa Jensen, Christina Lubinski, and Bernd Weisbrod, eds., *History by Generations: Generational Dynamics in Modern History* (Göttingen: Wallstein, 2012).

8. See Terence Renaud, "Leftist Guys on the Right: From National Bolshevism to the Post-'68 New Right," paper delivered at the annual conference of the German Studies Association in Portland, OR, October 2019, accessed May 2020, https://www.academia.edu/40560262/Leftist_Guys_on_the_Right_From_National_Bolshevism_to_the_Post-_68_New_Right. On the difference between left subversion and right "eversion" of existing institutions, see Agnoli, *Subversive Theorie*, 14–15. On the related Frankfurt School concept of conformist rebellion, see Max Horkheimer, *Eclipse of Reason* [1947] (London: Bloomsbury, 2004), ch. 3. See also Kołakowski, "Concept of the Left," and Weiß, *Die autoritäre Revolte*.

think of themselves as a generational force that threatened all institutions of the adult world.[9] The American mantra "Don't trust anyone over thirty" expressed a fear shared by European militants that existing institutions and outside forces might co-opt the energy of the nascent movement. The militants' new culture had to stay forever young. This politics of youth went beyond shortsighted ageism. Youthfulness in body or spirit did conceptual work. It foregrounded consciousness of new forms and the difficulty of sustaining them. It turned ephemerality itself into a political problem—or even a conscious goal.[10] For anti-authoritarians in the 1960s as well as for radical antifascists in the 1930s, this temporal consciousness influenced neoleftist strategy and tactics.

Not only people in power but also abstract social structures exuded oldness. Everything about capitalist market logic, technocratic administration, and middle-class conformity struck sixties rebels as antiquated and repressive. A new society required permanent revolution, or what Marcuse called the Great Refusal: no to institutions, no to bureaucratic rules, no to fixed social relations, and no to any compromise with existing reality.[11] As a result, Western European neoleftists viewed traditional parties and trade unions as obstacles to change. In order to transform society, the left first had to transform itself.

The Sixty-Eighters rebelled against their parents' generation, just as some of those same parents had rebelled in their youth against an old left incapable of combatting fascism. Both generations learned the hard way that formal political organizations often betray the original goals of grassroots movements. In that disjuncture between political representation and social forces, antifascist and anti-authoritarian new lefts invented strategies for breaking the deadlock of the capitalist state. They perceived that even existing organizations of the left had succumbed to bureaucratic sclerosis. Neither Social Democratic reformism nor Communist dictatorship held much appeal for them. Instead, neoleftists tried to form nonhierarchical associations based on direct democracy. Sustaining internal democracy over time constituted their main challenge, a dilemma without a solution.

Permanent renewal on the left could degenerate into compulsive repetition of past defeats, as if no lessons were learned. However, new lefts during the antifascist era and later on combined their desire for new beginning with an

9. On the contested nature of that generational consciousness, see Von der Goltz, *"Talkin' 'bout My Generation."*

10. See Scott, *Younger than That Now*, and Nehring, "'Generation' as Political Argument." For a political theory perspective, see Elizabeth F. Cohen, *The Political Value of Time: Citizenship, Duration, and Democratic Justice* (Cambridge: Cambridge University Press, 2018).

11. Marcuse, *One-Dimensional Man*, 256–57.

effort to work through the tradition of past defeats. Anti-authoritarian and nonhierarchical ways of organizing cropped up alongside reinterpretations of the young Marx, Rosa Luxemburg, Wilhelm Reich, and other theoretical lodestars. But the "new" for midcentury new lefts was never static. It shifted constantly and produced scenes that pitted former neoleftists from older generations against the latest avant-garde, which rejected all previous definitions of the new. Each moment in this book's fifty-year history had its own material conditions, yielding new lefts that looked different from one another across time. For example, in contrast to the antifascist new left, the sixties New Left introduced new ways of being political on the terrain of everyday life, ways that derived from the arts, youth culture, and consumer culture characteristic of the postwar decades. Such epiphenomenal differences in content belonged nonetheless to the same formal dialectic of renewal, which often devoured its children.

In order to weave the moments of radical antifascism, left socialism, and anti-authoritarianism together into a continuous narrative, this book combines methods of intellectual history, social history, and critical theory. It intervenes in four areas of scholarship. The first three are historical fields, while the final area concerns the political theory of left organization.

The first and most obvious area is the history of the European left, which tends to be overly compartmentalized. Historians have studied either interwar antifascism or sixties anti-authoritarianism or, less often, postwar left socialism, but almost never all at once. A few large syntheses exist, such as the landmark histories by Geoff Eley and Donald Sassoon, but these books privilege mass movements and the electoral politics of Social Democratic parties. They rarely emphasize the role of marginal groups, extraparliamentary action, or new lefts. For example, Sassoon dismisses out of hand "small organizations and sects" that never had to face "the problems and constraints of political power."[12] New Beginning was one such small organization, and my book uses it and other Western European examples as case studies in an alternative history of socialism. Organizational creativity took place on the periphery of mainstream Social Democratic and Communist politics, and a fixation on elections or seizing state power obscures that phenomenon.

There is another reason to address the subject of interwar antifascism now. Antifascism's legitimacy as a political cause has fallen under suspicion. Long

---

12. Sassoon, *One Hundred Years of Socialism*, xxiv. Eley includes more nonparty examples, especially the women's movement, but his book nevertheless favors mainstream left parties. Eley, *Forging Democracy*. For what he does say about marginal groups, cf. Eley, "Reviewing the Socialist Tradition."

after the Cold War, debates about antifascism still revolve around whether physical resistance can ever be justified, even to counter violent provocation by the far right. That question presupposes liberal norms of behavior: peaceful, orderly, electoral, and at most "progressive." So, many commentators today banish antifascists and far-right activists together from the realm of acceptable politics. Seen as morally equivalent, the left and right extremes supposedly meet.[13]

Such an equation of fascism and its opposite is both politically irresponsible and historically inaccurate. The global resurgence of the far right in the early twenty-first century has enabled the worst sort of neo- or quasi-fascist adventurism, racism, Holocaust denial, and complacency about social injustice. At the end of May 2020, amid national protests against the racist police killing of George Floyd, the US president even declared the loosely affiliated antifascist network Antifa a terrorist organization.[14] In association with Antifa or not, antifascism draws on a legacy with great emancipatory potential. Its occlusion by decades of Cold War posturing, liberal myopia, and conservative fearmongering ought to end. As the editors of a recent volume argue, we have now reached a point where it has become necessary to rethink antifascism "not in terms of what it turned into after 1945, but as the various things that it was, and the ways in which it was perceived and lived, at the different times and places in its evolution since the 1920s."[15] A return to the sources of antifascism parallels this book's fresh look at neoleftism.

From the other direction, this book revises standard accounts of the sixties anti-authoritarian left. Recently, the fiftieth anniversary of the French uprising of May 1968 and the world events symbolized by that year prompted reassessments by a diverse array of commentators.[16] A frequent observation about the New Left was that it played a central role in fashioning the Global Sixties. In that decade, neoleftists raised public awareness of the Third World and Europe's global entanglements. Young militants criticized imperialism and the Vietnam War at every opportunity. As studies by Christoph Kalter, Timothy S. Brown, Quinn Slobodian, and others have shown, neoleftists actively sought out revolutionaries from Africa, Asia, and Latin America. In the process they

---

13. For example, see Will Yates, "America's Extremist Battle: Antifa v Alt-Right," *BBC News*, February 20, 2017, http://www.bbc.com/news/blogs-trending-39004753. For the classic historical treatment, see Sternhell, *Neither Right Nor Left*.

14. Nicholas Bogel-Burroughs and Sandra E. Garcia, "What Is Antifa, the Movement Trump Wants to Declare a Terror Group?" *New York Times*, May 31, 2020.

15. García et al., *Rethinking Antifascism*, 3.

16. For scholarly reassessments, see for example "*AHR* Reflections: 1968," *American Historical Review* 123, no. 3 (2018).

forged transnational alliances. The historians Jeremy Varon, Gerd-Rainer Horn, and Martin Klimke have demonstrated how a network of mutual aid and influence formed between radical students in West Germany, the Netherlands, France, Italy, Britain, and the United States.[17]

Together these examples represent a spatial turn in scholarship on the sixties. While I welcome that turn, I worry about what gets lost if we focus on transnational connections at the expense of long-term continuities in midcentury left politics. My book argues instead for a temporal turn in our understanding of the New Left in particular, one that goes beyond forays into the so-called Long Sixties, a periodization that expands the decade from the late 1950s through the mid-1970s. What I propose also goes beyond identifying an overlooked "first new left," as Michael Kenny and others have done.[18] By exploring the pre–World War II origins of neoleftism and the formation of an antifascist new left in the 1930s, my book reveals the structural dynamics of new lefts in general. Over the long term, neoleftism describes a formal process that generated nonparty theory and practice in a discrete historical moment, then negated that theory and practice in the next moment. More than simply a series that repeated the same phenomenon, midcentury new lefts involved a self-reflexive and critical overcoming of past organizational forms: each new left abolished new lefts past and prefigured new lefts future. This is what I mean by a temporal turn, which technically speaking is a dialectical turn in the history of the sixties New Left. My book dwells on the irony of situations in which old radicals ended up defending the very establishment that their younger selves would have rejected. That irony comes to the fore in the history of left socialism, a political tendency in between Social Democracy and Communism that dated back to the interwar years but really took shape in France, Britain, and West Germany during the 1950s. With the notable exceptions of Gregor Kritidis and Sean Forner, historians have mostly ignored the role of left socialists as mediators between the antifascist and anti-authoritarian generations.[19]

The second area of scholarship to which this book contributes is German intellectual history. Several books have appeared in recent years that challenge the conventional timeline over which modern German ideas about politics

17. Kalter, *Discovery of the Third World*; Brown, *West Germany and the Global Sixties*; Slobodian, *Foreign Front*; Varon, *Bringing the War Home*; Horn, *Spirit of '68*; and Klimke, *Other Alliance*. See also Chen et al., *Routledge Handbook of the Global Sixties*.

18. Kenny, *First New Left*.

19. Kritidis, *Linkssozialistische Opposition*, and Forner, *German Intellectuals*, ch. 8. For France, see also Kalter, *Discovery of the Third World*, and for Britain, see Kenny, *First New Left*, and Hamilton, *Crisis of Theory*.

developed. In popular memory the year 1945 has long served as zero hour for contemporary German history, or the rupture between the Nazi regime and the postwar reconstruction of two separate states in the East and West. Through the work of historians such as Udi Greenberg and Noah B. Strote— despite their disagreements—we can see important continuities between interwar political thought and postwar ideologies. German history did not start from scratch in 1945, a fact that is evident in the history of concepts such as responsible elites, militant democracy, totalitarianism, and social market economy.[20] Neoleftism counts as another theory and practice that had interwar roots.

Recent histories have also emphasized the role of exile and transnational knowledge exchange in the construction of German political thought. Scholars such as Forner and Daniel Bessner highlight the importance of social networks for the dissemination of midcentury ideas.[21] Their studies emphasize the institutional reception of ideas and alter our assumptions about the type of intellectuals who gained the most influence. Instead of "great thinkers" working in isolation, we see how ideas were made within concrete institutions, such as university institutes or the national defense establishment. Often it was not the famous philosophers who succeeded in implementing the most consequential ideas about the German social order. What I call insider intellectuals did the majority of mental labor by publicizing political ideas, writing constitutions, founding radical groups, and constructing the ideologies and counterideologies that shaped, among other things, the history of new lefts in Western Europe.[22]

From the perspective of insider intellectuals who were engaged in politics, the development of leftist theory in Europe looks different. My book's third area of intervention is the history of Western Marxism. Scholars such as Susan Buck-Morss, Martin Jay, and Enzo Traverso have defined Western Marxism as that alternative body of cultural and aesthetic theory that grew chiefly under the aegis of the Frankfurt School. Philosophers associated with that school include Marcuse, Walter Benjamin, Max Horkheimer, and Theodor W. Adorno. Besides the Frankfurt School, other Western European intellectuals

---

20. Greenberg, *Weimar Century*, and Strote, *Lions and Lambs*. On his disagreements with Greenberg, see Noah Benezra Strote, "The Intellectual Migration and the 'Other Weimar,'" *Modern Intellectual History* 14, no. 2 (2017): 597–606. See also Chappel, *Catholic Modern*, and Nicholls, *Freedom with Responsibility*. On the problematic concept of "zero hour" and the need to treat the mid-1940s as a broader transition period, see Hoffmann, "Germany Is No More."

21. Forner, *German Intellectuals*, and Daniel Bessner, *Democracy in Exile: Hans Speier and the Rise of the Defense Intellectual* (Ithaca, NY: Cornell University Press, 2018).

22. Renaud, "Insider Intellectuals."

experimented with nonconformist Marxism, such as the Italian Communist theorist Antonio Gramsci and the French existentialist Jean-Paul Sartre. Conventionally, histories of Western Marxism present us with a narrative of defeat: In the wake of failed revolutions, Western Marxists studied authoritarian reaction, psychological repression, alienating effects of mass culture, and strategies for building an alternative culture (e.g., what Gramsci understood as counterhegemony or Marcuse as a new sensibility). The Germans in particular operated in a melancholy mode, reassembling the pieces of the great historical catastrophe caused by industrial modernity, the world wars, and the Holocaust.[23] In the 1930s and again in the 1960s, Western Marxism served as a beacon for new lefts. But the standard narrative of defeat does not do justice to the breadth of experience among militant leftists. Insider intellectuals succumbed less often to despair than the high theorists, so they continued actively to combat the tide of reaction. For them, defeat always generated something new. My book highlights the resilience of neoleftist theory and practice in moments of crisis, without of course ignoring the real losses suffered. Instead of just melancholy, I perceive among neoleftists a recurrent alternation between revolutionary hope and despair.

Finally, my book engages with political theorists who have moved the question of organization back to the center of debates about democracy. The catalyst for this renewed interest in organization was the 2008 financial collapse and the remarkable series of popular uprisings that followed around 2011: the Arab Spring, Indignados in Spain, anti-austerity protests in Greece, riots in London, Occupy Wall Street, and so on. Observers noted that the uprisings lacked recognizable leaders and much prior organization. They looked like spontaneous assemblies of the multitude, as Michael Hardt and Antonio Negri would put it. Some commentators spoke of horizontalism, a concept that arose from the alter-globalization efforts of the late 1990s and early 2000s and refers to social movements that resist vertical hierarchies. But the problem with such movements is that they disappear as suddenly as they appear.

Some commentators, like Joshua Clover and the late David Graeber, have celebrated the riotous ephemerality of the 2011 uprisings and various disruptive actions since. Others want to find ways to sustain their antisystemic energy and build a new left that lasts. Neocommunist theorists like Slavoj Žižek, Alain Badiou, and Jodi Dean call for a return to the centralized vanguard party.

---

23. Traverso thinks that melancholia lay at the root of Western Marxism and its concern with the cultural and psychological mechanisms of counterrevolution. Traverso, *Left-Wing Melancholia*. See also Jacoby, *Dialectic of Defeat*, 4–5, and P. Anderson, *Considerations on Western Marxism*, 42–43.

The sociologist Manuel Castells believes that social media could be a techno-logical solution to the problem of horizontalist organization. Meanwhile, Chantal Mouffe and her late partner Ernesto Laclau have demanded a robust left populism. All of these theorists agree that the big question facing the anti-capitalist movement of the early twenty-first century is which organizational form it should take: party, union, council, assembly, *rassemblement, Sammlungsbewegung,* or something else. Which form could channel the move-ment's radical democratic content while still offering the best chance at suc-cess? And does anything below the high bar of seizing state power qualify as success? Just as neoleftists did in the middle of the last century, radicals today face the internal dilemma of how to break free from modes of left politics that preserve rather than transform existing society.[24]

If fascism, imperialism, and authoritarianism were the main targets of new lefts past, then now it is neoliberalism. A strange symmetry exists between the phenomena of neoleftism and neoliberal capitalism. Neoleftist-style for-mations such as Occupy always end in entropy and decline, much as neolib-eralism has atomized social communities and decimated public services around the world. Every radical magazine, study group, and encampment devolves into its own idiosyncratic new left, much as neoliberalism lionizes the solitary, entrepreneurial self. Sooner or later, every new left succumbs to the assimilatory new spirit of capitalism. Just as entrepreneurs disrupt mar-kets with new products, neoleftism ironically turns back on itself, creatively destroying its prior forms. Advanced capitalism demonstrates a remarkable ability to reinvent itself in response to new challenges, and new lefts have responded by reinventing left politics. Transcending capitalism may actually require a strategic mimicry of capitalism's own structural logic. Yet a contra-diction arises between new lefts' planned mimicry of creative destruction and their unplanned obsolescence, a contradiction that makes neoleftism some-times look like self-indulgent rebellion. While neoliberal and neoleftist goals differ considerably, anxiety about whether neoleftism subverts or sustains the dynamics of advanced capitalism animated the work of many protagonists in this book.

New lefts' self-defeating yet perennially hopeful dynamic is expressed by Brecht in the playful lines quoted in this book's epigraph, "Everything new / Is better than everything old." The dilemma of new lefts lay precisely in their unplanned obsolescence: against intentions, everything new becomes some-thing old. New lefts strove to break this vicious cycle of innovation and

---

24. For a compelling defense of the council form as a solution to this dilemma, see Popp-Madsen, "Constituent Power and Political Form."

assimilation. Thus we might judge neoleftism according to a different metric of success than we usually apply to electoral politics and mass movements. Achieving power or governmental control was never new lefts' chief aim. Instead, they looked inward in an attempt to maintain their own capacity to begin anew. The theorist Hannah Arendt may have been correct when she observed that beginning anew is what saves human affairs from natural ruin.[25]

The primary sources for this book consist of personal papers of New Beginning members; meeting minutes, memos, and other internal documents of diverse radical groups; official records of state security services; university archives; newspaper reports; leaflets and other movement ephemera; published and unpublished memoirs; and the many books and articles written by neoleftist intellectuals. I draw on sources in German, French, Spanish, and English, and I rely on translations of material from wherever else my subjects operated. My geographical focus is Germany, but just the history of New Beginning alone requires a transnational framework: its members regularly crossed borders, either voluntarily or involuntarily, and they always conceived of their project in international terms. Beyond the inherent transnationalism of New Beginning, I have added as many Western European comparative cases as possible without disrupting the narrative or exceeding the scope of a monograph.

The first chapter begins by dividing the concept of a new left into its constituent parts, each with its own history: newness and leftism. Notable attempts to conceptualize radical newness occurred at the turn of the twentieth century. The young Georg Lukács, a Hungarian Marxist whose ideas exerted an outsized influence on later new lefts, wrestled with the problem of creating new forms that were uncorrupted by the existing bourgeois society. Bureaucracy, institutionalization, and cultural stagnation were his bogeymen. He and his friends in the Budapest avant-garde explored the theme of radical newness in art before transposing it into politics. For a brief period, leftists like the early Lukács fixated on workers' and soldiers' councils as an alternative to party politics. They faced their first serious criticism from within the international left in the form of Lenin's 1920 pamphlet *"Left-Wing" Communism: An Infantile Disorder*. That pamphlet provided a blueprint for all subsequent criticism of neoleftists as childish, immature, individualistic, inexperienced, romantic, and naïve. Even before the novelty of the Soviet experiment had worn off, European leftists in the early 1920s sensed that official Communism might pose an obstacle to radical politics in the future.

---

25. Arendt, *Human Condition*, 247. For a postmodern take, cf. Groys, *On the New*. See also Bürger, *Theory of the Avant-Garde*, 59–63.

The German group New Beginning appears on the scene in the second chapter. New Beginning would come to embody the élan of the antifascist new left. That current resided on the fringes of mainstream antifascism, which we typically associate with the Popular Front and its appeals to reason, democracy, freedom, and human dignity in the face of fascist oppression in Europe. Mainstream antifascists were sincere in their politics. The Popular Front did improve everyday life for millions of workers and expand the horizon of possibility for progressive social change in the future. From a neoleftist perspective, however, mainstream antifascists made a troubling compromise with liberal democrats, moderate socialists, and Stalinists that postponed revolutionary tasks until after fascism's defeat. Radical antifascists believed that the twin crisis of democracy and capitalism, of which fascism was only a symptom, offered a unique chance to reshape left politics. Defeating fascism required nothing less than new revolution, they believed. Around 1933, when fascism grew into a general European and global threat, New Beginning joined other experimental small groups like Socialist Battle in France, Justice and Liberty among Italian émigrés, and the Left Book Club in Britain to form a loose network across national borders. Through this network, novel ideas entered left politics that pushed the boundaries of traditional working-class concerns. Wilhelm Reich's theory of sexual revolution, for example, made private life into a terrain of social contestation: the personal became the political. Neoleftist small groups sought to understand why the masses, including many workers, had been won over by fascism, a movement that contradicted their own class interests. Charismatic leaders like Karl Frank and Marceau Pivert emerged from the shadows cast by the paralyzed left parties. The antifascist new left that they represented agonized over organizational forms. With its analysis of historical antifascism, this chapter provides some context for debates today about how to resist racism and far-right violence.

In the third chapter, the book turns to the organizational experiments conducted by neoleftists in the émigré capitals of Prague, Paris, Barcelona, and London. Exile politics provided the impetus for sizeable neoleftist formations, such as the Spanish Workers' Party of Marxist Unification (POUM). New Beginning's influence increased considerably in exile. The Spanish Civil War gave antifascists an opportunity to expand left politics beyond the working class and forge the international solidarity of marginalized groups. Spain functioned as a sort of Third World unto itself, a proxy for Europe's colonial periphery and a laboratory for a new culture. Radical democracy was palpable within the POUM and anarchist militias. As a neoleftist microcosm, the militia form resisted incorporation into the disciplined army system. There women especially experienced liberation to an unprecedented degree, which contributed to a neoleftist feminism during the interwar years.

The fourth chapter recounts the dramatic break with Soviet Communism undertaken by New Beginning and other neoleftist small groups in the latter half of the 1930s. They tried out different ways of working productively with the Communists, such as Popular Front collaborations and various iterations of a left united front. But the murder of dissidents by Soviet agents in Spain, the Moscow show trials in 1936–38, and the infamous Nazi-Soviet Pact in 1939–41 proved to the antifascist new left that Stalin had betrayed the revolution and threatened the survival of the international labor movement. This break with Communism proved essential for future new lefts and their ability to imagine radical democracy apart from existing pseudorevolutionary organizations. Left-wing anti-Communism had less to do with opposing the Russians than with rejecting the authoritarian party form. During World War II, New Beginning members stayed active in British and American exile. As they provided invaluable services to the Western Allied war effort, however, they assimilated into the genteel liberal democracy of their host countries. So began the internal and external taming of the antifascist new left, which transformed it into a pillar of reconstruction in postwar Europe.

Many neoleftists survived in Europe for the duration of the war. The fifth chapter returns to their stories, reconstructing their hopes and uncertainties during those first few months after the fall of Nazism. For example, New Beginning survivors maintained an underground network in Berlin that emerged from the ruins to play a key role in the struggle against the Communist effort to forge a Socialist Unity Party. They retained their commitment to internal democracy and a radical new culture. But in their increasing identification with anti-Communism, German neoleftist survivors lost sight of revolutionary goals. Like their counterparts in British and American exile, they soon assimilated into a democratic establishment that aimed to reform rather than abolish capitalism. Circumstances were different in France, where small groups such as David Rousset and Jean-Paul Sartre's Revolutionary Democratic Assembly now came to the fore. During the late 1940s and early 1950s, radical journals like Cornelius Castoriadis and Claude Lefort's *Socialism or Barbarism* appeared that altered the intellectual terrain of the left in Western Europe. They tested new theories of bureaucracy and subjected all forms of left organization to critique.

The flipside of neoleftism in the 1950s was social democratic modernization. Many veterans of the antifascist new left now assumed leading positions in the reconstructed center-left parties. Against neoleftist visions of a new culture, they fashioned a rival aesthetic of modernization in order to appeal more to middle-class voters in a growing consumer society. Former New Beginning members such as Fritz Erler and Richard Löwenthal rose to prominence in the German Social Democratic Party, lobbying for pivotal reforms at the Bad

Godesberg party convention in 1959. There it became clear that social democratic modernization would require abandoning Marxism for good. A similar process occurred in France around Édouard Depreux and the Unified Socialist Party, which after the collapse of the social democratic French Section of the Workers' International as a result of Guy Mollet's vacillating Algeria policy became that country's most important current of moderate socialism. The sixth chapter demonstrates what happens when left renewal takes place without enough attention to organizational form, prefigurative politics, and internal democracy. Despite using the rhetoric of modernization, this left renewal occurred only at the level of ethical ideals and electoral messaging. As the price paid for political success especially in West Germany, social democratic modernization conformed to advanced capitalism and the postwar welfare state.

The seventh chapter concentrates on the chief opponents of both Stalinism and social democratic modernization in the 1950s and early 1960s. Those whom I call left socialists, such as the social scientists Wolfgang Abendroth and Ossip K. Flechtheim, reluctantly broke with the postwar parties of the old left, which at first they viewed optimistically. In France, a *Nouvelle gauche* formed as early as 1954 in reaction to existing left parties' failure to oppose imperialism in any meaningful way. British Marxists who went on to found the *New Left Review* likewise broke with Communism after observing in 1956 the Soviet repression of the Hungarian Uprising and their own government's invasion of Egypt to secure the Suez Canal. Both French anti-imperialists and the British New Left belonged to a transnational current of left socialists who functioned as transmitters of the antifascist tradition and mentors of the rebellious youth. Together with left socialists in West Germany, they bridged the divide between antifascists and a new generation of discontents. Universities became a battleground for radical politics because the postwar youth came to see them as factories for the reproduction of middle-class consumers and managerial elites. At issue for left socialists in the late 1950s was the welfare state's ability to "deliver the goods." How should the left respond to the prospect of a postscarcity economy based on capitalist consumption? Why did existing parties and unions of the left continue to prop up the system? Abendroth insisted that visions of a leveled middle-class society obscured real social antagonisms, while Flechtheim urged the West German youth to look to the US civil rights movement and Third World anticolonial struggles for models of decentralized, grassroots action. In the early 1960s, breakaway new lefts evolved into the anti-authoritarian core of the coming insurrection. During this transition period, usage of the term "new left" shifted from an indefinite noun (a new left) to a proper name (the New Left).

The final chapter unpacks the older radical currents and Third World liberation struggles that made up the sixties New Left. Works by interwar theorists such as Lukács, Reich, and Gramsci were rediscovered. From Rudi Dutschke to Daniel Cohn-Bendit, young activists all attempted to keep fluid neoleftism from hardening into fixed organizations or dogmas. The group to which Dutschke belonged, Subversive Action, assumed leadership of the Socialist German Student League, paving the way for radical campus politics in 1967–68. And Cohn-Bendit helped steer a movement of student rebels in Paris that sparked the street battles and general strike of May 1968, a high point of European neoleftism. Characteristic of that revolutionary month was the proliferation of action committees, a nonparty form of organization that briefly exercised direct and radically democratic control over everyday life. The history of new lefts came full circle: Cohn-Bendit could now subvert Lenin's critique of leftists' "infantile disorder" in a book called *Leftism: Remedy for the Senile Disorder of Communism*. The extraparliamentary opposition was the New Left's answer to the sclerosis of party politics. Like the antifascist new left, however, activists of the anti-authoritarian New Left again confronted the same dilemma. The exuberance of the action committees could not last, and the history of new lefts once again ended in defeat.

But defeat was always relative for midcentury new lefts, not absolute. It inhered already within the neoleftist dilemma. The epilogue brings this book's history up to date. After the French general strike of May 1968, which eroded the postwar welfare consensus, the cycle of new lefts broke down. In the 1970s people on the left grew weary of radical experiments, which sometimes devolved into isolated acts of terrorism. While neoleftism continued to thrive in theory if not in practice, neoliberalism was ascendant as both a structural change in advanced capitalism and a hegemonic ideology. New social movements such as environmentalism, feminism, human rights, and the Greens gave up on building a revolutionary new society, focusing instead on equality and participatory democracy within the existing system. In the 1980s and 1990s, membership in left parties and unions declined, and postmodern apathy wormed away at militancy. Left-alternative lifestyles kept radicalism alive, but it was only after the 2008 financial crisis that a large number of people again mobilized against social inequality and corporate power. The defunct parties of the old left were ill equipped to mobilize this discontent. Instead, an incredible series of popular uprisings, anti-austerity actions, and wildcat strikes began around 2011. Various left populist and democratic socialist movements have cropped up since then. Starting in 2018, further antisystemic mobilization has occurred in the name of climate justice. Can this anti-capitalist energy be sustained, especially against a rising authoritarian tide? Will it catalyze a new left for the twenty-first century? Either way, mobilizing the left today requires serious thought about organization. The radical question of form is back on the agenda.

Drawing on select examples, this book presents a historical interpretation of new lefts and the organizational continuities that existed between interwar antifascism, postwar left socialism, and sixties anti-authoritarianism. The book's focus on insider intellectuals and "low theory" makes it accessible to people who have only a basic familiarity with Marxism and the history of the left. Anyone who is curious about what can be done now to combat neoliberalism, capitalist-driven climate change, and right-wing authoritarianism would do well to explore the history of European new lefts. The past is rich in examples of inspired protest, perhaps especially those that failed in their immediate goals. Walter Benjamin once urged historians to redeem the vanquished by brushing history against the grain. The historian Reinhart Koselleck even thought that "if history is made in the short run by the victors, historical gains in knowledge stem in the long run from the vanquished."[26] This book strives mainly for historical gains in knowledge. However, as the last century's most vanquished radicals, new lefts perhaps also deserve a redemption song.

26. Benjamin, "Theses on the Philosophy of History," 257, and Reinhart Koselleck, "Transformations of Experience and Methodological Change: A Historical-Anthropological Essay," in *The Practice of Conceptual History: Timing History, Spacing Concepts* (Stanford, CA: Stanford University Press, 2002), 45–83 (at 76).

1

Leftism and the New

ACTUAL USAGE of the term "new left" to describe a current of radical politics began in the 1950s. In these first few chapters, I look beyond the term itself at the patterns of behavior, forms of organization, and recurrent theoretical problems that lay behind it. A helpful way of introducing this long-term history of new lefts is to analyze the term's two constituent parts: leftism and newness.

The left has been around since the French Revolution, when the antimonarchist members of the National Assembly took their seats on the left side of the chamber.[1] Two centuries later, people casually call leftist anything that has to do with social justice, from wealth redistribution to racial and gender equality. Conservatives often use it as a term of abuse. Particularly in the United States, leftist typically means anyone whose politics are left of center, a fuzzy category that includes liberals and much of the Democratic Party. But I mean something else. Unlike today's so-called leftists, historical leftists practiced a specific kind of revolutionary politics that rejected electoral parties altogether.

Leftism, *gauchisme*, or *Linksradikalismus* emerged at the turn of the twentieth century in conjunction with European anarcho-syndicalism. The word implied a commitment to direct action and a maximalist stance on every issue. This tendency drew on a diverse array of theories and strategies, from the French philosopher Georges Sorel's myth of the general strike to the Dutch theorist Anton Pannekoek's council communism. Reaching peak influence

---

1. Marcel Gauchet claims that despite their origin in the French Revolution, "right" and "left" became cemented as primary terms of political identity in France only between 1900 and 1914 as a result of the Dreyfus affair. Gauchet, "Right and Left," 257. For the historian Geoff Eley, by contrast, the left in Europe was defined starting in the 1860s in association with liberal constitutionalism, voting rights, and socialist mass parties. But he agrees that the period 1905–14 saw "a new series of radicalized conflicts" that dissolved the nineteenth-century framework for popular politics and set the scene for the later "polarized politics of revolution and counterrevolution that generated fascism." Eley, *Forging Democracy*, 4–5.

during Europe's revolutionary crisis of 1918–21, leftists championed the raw spontaneity of worker- and soldier-led uprisings. They refused to compromise with bourgeois society and demanded immediate and permanent revolution: against capitalism, against the state, against bureaucracy, and against hierarchical institutions as such. Anarchists formed one important leftist camp, but in the immediate wake of the Bolshevik Revolution in Russia, it was left-wing Communists who bore the torch of leftism in Central and Western Europe. The end of the crisis and Europe's economic stabilization in the mid-1920s lessened the appeal of leftism. Established trade unions and official Communist and Social Democratic parties reasserted control over left politics. But historical leftism survived for decades as an underground current.[2]

The idea of newness, or the revolutionary *novum*, is harder to pin down. Its roots go back to religious origin stories and millenarian prophecies. The Christian conception of newness begins with the world's creation out of nothing and ends with the messianic transcendence of that world.[3] Europe's transition to industrial modernity in the eighteenth and nineteenth centuries gave newness a social dimension, as many people dreamt of a new society that was achievable by collective action in this world. Like the Jewish and Christian messiahs, the worldly novum promised redemption. But secular newness posed a challenge for revolutionary politics, which took place within existing social contexts. How could one create conditions for the new society while still beholden to the old society's customs and prejudices? How did one even know what the New should look like? Answers varied over the nineteenth century, with utopian socialists offering the most imaginative visions and Social Democrats the most pragmatic plans.[4]

Karl Marx rejected the possibility of defining the New in advance. In an early letter, he stated that "we do not anticipate the world with our dogmas but instead attempt to discover the new world through the critique of the old." Instead of dreaming up fantasies, "we shall develop for the world new principles

2. See Bourrinet, *Dutch and German Communist Left*; Bock, *Geschichte des "linken Radikalismus"*; and Gombin, *Origins of Modern Leftism*.

3. See Warren Breckman, "Creatio ex nihilo: Zur postmodernen Wiederbelebung einer theologischen Metapher," trans. Cordula Grewe, *Zeitschrift für Ideengeschichte* 1, no. 2 (Summer 2007): 13–28. On the distinct meaning of creation in the Hebrew Bible, cf. Alter, *Genesis: Translation and Commentary*.

4. See Peter Beilharz, *Labour's Utopias: Bolshevism, Fabianism, Social Democracy* (London: Routledge, 1992); Bronisław Baczko, *Utopian Lights: The Evolution of the Idea of Social Progress* [1978] (New York: Paragon, 1989); and Frank E. Manuel, *The Prophets of Paris* (Cambridge, MA: Harvard University Press, 1962).

from the existing principles of the world."[5] Marx's method owed its supposedly scientific character to its denial of utopianism and reliance on determinate
negations of the present. That is, only by exposing the contradictions of existing
social relations, locating the causes of economic misery, and grasping capitalism's dynamics could one infer the next stage of historical development. Instead
of a ready-made plan for the postcapitalist future, Marx offered an immanent
critique of the capitalist present. Only revolutionary practice, he believed,
would make the contours of the new society visible.[6]

At the turn of the twentieth century, leftists ignored Marx's method and
tried again to design the New. Their main issue was the proper form of revolutionary organization. In France and Italy, where trade unions or syndicates
operated with a great deal of autonomy, theorists such as Sorel argued that the
form of revolutionary movements must correspond to the form of their desired
future society. Today people refer to that idea as prefigurative politics. If workers
want freedom from bourgeois oppression, Sorel thought, then they must shed
all vestiges of bourgeois tradition, including reliance on electoral politics. Breaking free from the bourgeoisie required a new way of life. Only through direct
action, the general strike, and indeed violence could the oppressed masses overthrow capitalism and establish a free syndicalist community.[7]

In Germany, the socialist cause was increasingly bound up with voting in
elections and concrete gains through parliamentary legislation. The largest
socialist organization in the world, the Social Democratic Party (SPD), had
hundreds of thousands of members and millions of voters. It served as the
archetype of the democratic working-class party. Eduard Bernstein was the
leading Social Democrat in favor of revising Marxism in order to account for
the success of welfare legislation and the improved living standards that workers had attained within the capitalist system. For him, the ultimate goal of
socialism was unimportant compared with the really-existing movement—
that is, the well-being of the socialist party, the unions, and their members.[8]
Critics such as Rosa Luxemburg warned that the economic boom of the 1890s

---

5. Karl Marx, "For a Ruthless Criticism of Everything Existing" (letter to Arnold Ruge)
[1843], in Tucker, *Marx-Engels Reader*, 12–15.

6. Only in *The German Ideology* (posth. 1932), the *Critique of the Gotha Program* (posth.
1891), and fragments of the *Grundrisse* (posth. 1941) did Marx offer previews of a communist
future. Cf. Friedrich Engels, *Socialism: Utopian and Scientific* (1880).

7. Sorel, *Reflections on Violence* and "Syndicalisme révolutionnaire." Of course, Sorel's belief
that violent means alone could achieve a harmonious end contradicted the principle of prefigurative politics. See Boggs, "Marxism."

8. Bernstein, *Preconditions of Socialism*. On Bernstein's ambivalent legacy, see Riley, "Bernstein's Heirs."

and early 1900s depended on a momentary expansion of overseas colonial markets that would not last forever. As for parliament, she believed that it functioned under restraints imposed by the ruling class. Sooner or later the SPD's gains through welfare legislation would be erased.[9]

The most trenchant critique of Social Democratic modes of organization came from Robert Michels, a German sociologist with ties to the Italian anarcho-syndicalist movement. Michels predicted that democratic class parties like the SPD, which began as emancipatory movements, would succumb eventually to an "iron law of oligarchy": over time, leaders of the movement would accrue power within the party apparatus, create a hierarchy of loyal subordinates, and betray the movement's original goal of democracy. Michels's iron law stipulated that fluid social movements would harden into fixed elite organizations.[10]

Leftists evoked Michels's iron law when they criticized the bureaucracy of socialist mass parties, be they the German SPD or the French Section of the Workers' International. As leftists witnessed those supposedly democratic organizations degenerate into oligarchies, their unease with electoral politics grew. Party bosses and socialist members of parliament sporting top hats and tails seemed indistinguishable from the bankers, factory owners, aristocrats, and other elites that composed the ruling class. To bitter workers and leftist intellectuals, the very act of casting a vote seemed to compromise the whole revolution. Especially after World War I, mere voting did not meet the apocalyptic expectations of many Europeans. Although democratic class parties succeeded in channeling the energy of revolutionary movements into concrete reforms, they also produced conformist modes of behavior. If by their very nature political parties could not transcend the old society, then what other forms of organization might enable the realization of the New? How could one sustain the revolutionary movement without some kind of authority, leadership, hierarchy, and rules of order—that is, without a disciplined party structure? These questions constituted the leftist dilemma in the early twentieth century.

Tragedy of Culture in the Early Work of Georg Lukács

The person at the center of this chapter articulated the leftist dilemma perhaps more clearly than anyone. The Hungarian Marxist philosopher Georg Lukács exerted an outsized influence on the history of new lefts. Neoleftist

9. Rosa Luxemburg, "Social Reform or Revolution?" [1899], in *Rosa Luxemburg Reader*, 128–67, and *Accumulation of Capital*.

10. Michels, *Political Parties*.

resurgences in the 1950s and 1960s often took their inspiration from pirated copies of his early works. I regard his identification of the organizational problem endemic to leftism as the Lukácsian moment for new lefts in Europe.[11] Lukács's eclectic blend of aesthetics, literary criticism, and political theory burst on the scene in the years surrounding World War I and the Russian Revolution. The development of his thought from about 1910 to 1924 provides a key to understanding the fruitful but ultimately tragic intersection of leftism and newness.

Lukács is usually credited with having inspired the intellectual current known as Western Marxism, a less dogmatic and culturally more sophisticated alternative to the Stalinist orthodoxy of the East.[12] The concepts of totality and class consciousness guided his thought. Gained through collective action, workers' practical awareness of their class position within the social whole was for him the real fruit of Marxist method. He understood totality both spatially, in terms of the dense web of class relations that determined power across the globe, and temporally, in terms of past trends and future prospects. Lukácsian totality was open-ended, because only the conscious action of the most oppressed class could decide the story's ending. Totality, variously conceived, served as the chief weapon in Western Marxists' conceptual arsenal against liberalism, positivism, Social Democratic reformism, and bureaucratic Communism alike.

Another concept associated with Lukács is thingification (*Verdinglichung*), more commonly known as reification. He considered reification the distinctive feature of modern life, where we experience everything in the form of a commodity. Because capitalism turns all objects including laboring humans into things to be bought and sold, we develop a feeling of estrangement (*Entfremdung*), or alienation, from one another and our environment. Reality under capitalism is mediated entirely by fungible commodities. Direct, meaningful relationships between individuals become impossible once we lose the ability to perceive the conscious and collective practices that constitute our reified world. Capitalism engenders a sense of individual powerlessness within a complex and inscrutable system.[13] Through the undeniable progress in

---

11. Cf. J.G.A. Pocock's study of the republican dilemma, *The Machiavellian Moment: Florentine Political Thought and the Atlantic Republican Tradition* (Princeton, NJ: Princeton University Press, 1975). A collection of 1960s German pirate editions of Lukács's work can be found in HIS, Graue Literatur.

12. See the classic accounts: Jay, *Marxism and Totality*; Jacoby, *Dialectic of Defeat*; Arato and Breines, *Young Lukács*; and P. Anderson, *Considerations on Western Marxism*.

13. According to some interpreters, Marx's phenomenological aim in *Capital* was to explain why capitalism appears to us as an objectively detached system. See Michael Heinrich, *An*

technology made by capitalism, humans gain power over nature but lose control over their social world.

Lukács's emphases on totality, reification, and alienation preceded by several years the posthumous publication of Marx's *Economic and Philosophical Manuscripts*. It is largely owing to the prescient alignment of his thought with that of the young Marx more than a half century before that Lukács earned his reputation as arguably the greatest Marxist philosopher of the twentieth century.[14]

In his earliest political texts, written in 1918–19, he sketched out a social, cultural, and political theory of newness. These writings on tactics and organization examined how to harness the creative power of revolution for the construction of a new culture that would be resistant to institutionalization, stagnation, and decline. Lukács treated radical experimentation and permanent revolution as the only ways to sustain newness. After converting to Communism, he sought to implement a fluid form of popular mobilization that could realize a new culture. He put his ideas into practice while serving as deputy commissar of education and culture under the short-lived Hungarian Soviet Republic. Before that dramatic phase of Lukács's career, however, he meditated on the leftist dilemma in the realm of aesthetics. An examination of his work from before and during World War I reveals that his later leftism transposed into a political key what he had written earlier about art and cultural forms.

Lukács's biography is well documented.[15] He was born in 1885 into a wealthy family of assimilated Jews, and he grew up among the cultural elite of Budapest at the height of the Austro-Hungarian Empire. He spoke German and Hungarian at home and learned French and English at school. At the University of Budapest he studied philosophy and, at his father's behest, law. But his passion was for literature. In 1904 he and some like-minded friends founded an avant-garde theater company called Thália. They produced modernist plays by the likes of Henrik Ibsen, August Strindberg, and Maxim Gorky, all in an

---

Introduction to the Three Volumes of Karl Marx's "Capital" [2004], trans. Alexander Locascio (New York: Monthly Review Press, 2012), and Moishe Postone, *Time, Labor, and Social Domination: A Reinterpretation of Marx's Critical Theory* (Cambridge: Cambridge University Press, 1993). For a phenomenological reading of Lukács that emphasizes forms of objective reality (*Gegenständlichkeitsformen*), see Westerman, *Lukács's Phenomenology of Capitalism*.

14. On the general importance of Lukács, see Feenberg, *Philosophy of Praxis*, and Michael Thompson, ed., *Georg Lukács Reconsidered: Critical Essays in Politics, Philosophy and Aesthetics* (London: Continuum, 2011).

15. See Arpad Kadarkay, *Georg Lukács: Life, Thought, and Politics* (Cambridge, MA: Blackwell, 1991); Gluck, *Georg Lukács*; Congdon, *Young Lukács*; G.H.R. Parkinson, *Georg Lukács* (London: Routledge and Kegan Paul, 1977); and Lichtheim, *George Lukács*.

effort to reinvigorate what they considered a moribund Hungarian culture.[16] Lukács's earliest writings concerned modern drama and its use for cultural renewal.

Like many intellectuals of his time and milieu, he went to Germany to study philosophy. In Berlin he met Georg Simmel, the unorthodox sociologist who introduced him to an idea that would permeate his early thought: the tragedy of culture. The leitmotif of Simmel's 1900 book *The Philosophy of Money* was "the growing preponderance of quantity over quality, the tendency to dissolve the latter into the former and to replace every specific, individual, and qualitative determination by simply numerical determination." Although Simmel associated this phenomenon with the rise of capitalist society, he also linked it to an essential human tragedy: "the estrangement of objective from subjective culture, the rise of the culture of things and the decline of the culture of persons."[17] Put another way, a person must express her spiritual yearnings through externalized objects: artwork, religion, language, custom, and so on. But she will immediately feel alienated from the objects she has created, and even more alienated from the mass of inherited culture into which she was born.

In his 1910 essay "Aesthetic Culture," Lukács explored this tragic condition as it manifested in artistic forms. His main target of criticism was turn-of-the-century aestheticism, a movement known by its slogan "Art for art's sake." Aestheticism had given up on the task of creating new forms, he claimed, and instead indulged in a mélange of old forms. The aesthete wanted to set a mood, not to break new ground: style trumped substance.[18] Lukács thought that while the art of Claude Monet and others offered novelties, such "impressions" lacked deeper meaning. In a related essay, he explained his critique of aestheticism explicitly in terms of newness:

> If there only exist moods and sensations, only their freshness and power distinguishes them from each other. And everything new and everything interesting, in the very moment that it exists, is already less new and less interesting. And with every moment, every analogy and repetition it becomes less new and less interesting, until finally it loses all the character

---

16. Gluck, *Georg Lukács*, 62–64, and José Ignacio López Soria, "L'expérience théâtrale de Lukács," *L'homme et la société* 43, no. 1 (1977): 117–31.

17. Löwy, *Georg Lukács*, 43–44. See Simmel, "Concept and Tragedy of Culture," and Anna Wessely, "Simmel's Influence on Lukács's Conception of the Sociology of Art," in *Georg Simmel and Contemporary Sociology*, ed. Michael Kaern, Bernard S. Phillips, and Robert S. Cohen (Dordrecht: Springer Netherlands, 1990), 357–73.

18. Lukács, "Aesthetic Culture."

of a sensation; it ceases to have an effect, it is dead, and no longer in existence.[19]

Everything new and interesting, treated as an end in itself rather than a means to a new culture, grows dull after a while. Lukács likened this kind of superficial novelty to consumer fashion. Innovation for innovation's sake could easily serve capitalist interests. As a fetishization of the New, the exotic only reproduced the totality of the old culture.[20]

The burning question at the center of his first book, *Soul and Form* (1910 in Hungarian, 1911 in German), was "How is authentic culture possible?" He tried to answer it by tracing the history of art forms as they emerged to define new spiritual contents. The philosophical or literary essay emerged to give form to inchoate expressions of life, he claimed, just as revolutionary forms might organize spontaneous social movements. Unlike a past-oriented epic or a complete system of philosophy, the essay prophetically announced a momentous thing to come, some great hope. "The essayist," wrote Lukács, "is a John the Baptist who goes out to preach in the wilderness about another who is still to come [i.e., Christ]. . . . And if that other does not come—is not the essayist then without justification?"[21] There is a striking analogy between his treatment of the essay form and what he would later write about political forms. Without a real connection to life (like a social base), the essay (like a revolutionary organization) lacked justification. It had no reason for existing other than its anticipation of a new world. Once the great thing arrived (like the revolution), the transitional form of the essay (like the organization) would become obsolete.

He chose another literary genre for the subject of his next book, *The Theory of the Novel* (1916). Lukács later remarked that he wrote this book "in a mood of permanent despair over the state of the world,"[22] which was an understandable sentiment in the middle of the Great War. He had escaped military conscription owing to an apparently unhealthy physique, but in 1915–16 he fulfilled his civilian duty as post office censor in Budapest, "a task we may assume he interpreted in a liberal spirit."[23] He opposed the war on ethical grounds, but

19. Georg Lukács, "The Ways Have Parted" [1910], trans. George Cushing, in *Between Worlds: A Sourcebook of Central European Avant-Gardes, 1910–1930*, ed. Timothy O. Benson and Eva Forgács (Cambridge, MA: MIT Press, 2002), 125–29 (at 127).

20. Lukács, "Old Culture and the New Culture," 24.

21. Lukács, *Soul and Form*, 16. See also Tom Huhn, "Lukács and the Essay Form," *New German Critique*, no. 78 (Autumn 1999): 183–92.

22. Lukács, preface (1962) to *Theory of the Novel*, 12.

23. Lichtheim, *George Lukács*, 38.

the war alone did not account for his despair. Influenced by Sorel's skepticism of modernity and the vitalist philosophies of Henri Bergson and Wilhelm Dilthey, he hoped that "a natural life worthy of man can spring from the disintegration of capitalism and the destruction . . . of the lifeless and life-denying social and economic categories." *The Theory of the Novel* was an attempt to synthesize socialist politics and conservative cultural pessimism.[24] Accordingly, scholars have labeled his prewar and wartime writings "romantic anticapitalism," a term that Lukács himself coined.[25]

The nineteenth-century Romantics did inspire one of his key concepts: second nature, or the world of man-made structures.[26] The progress of civilization meant an increasing technical mastery over first nature, or the indigenous environment of earth, plants, and animals. But human artifice and culture constituted another, synthetic nature that imposed new constraints on life. This second nature was filled with dead content, the now-expired creations of dead souls. We do not create society ourselves, Lukács observed: we inherit it from our ancestors.

He believed that all the novels of Leo Tolstoy presented a conflict between first and second nature. Primary naturalness was Tolstoy's ideal, which was set in opposition to custom, convention, and dead culture. The Russian writer's final novel, *Resurrection* (1899), railed against the injustice of established religion and the artificiality of human laws. But Lukács considered Tolstoy's opposition between first and second nature an insoluble problem. The novelist had failed to understand that a "totality of men and events is possible only on the basis of culture, whatever one's attitudes towards it." In order to solve that problem, the artist would have to produce something greater than a novel, something like "a new form of artistic creation: the form of the renewed epic." According to Lukács, the ancient Greek epic had emerged from a historical stage in which individuals belonged to integrated communities and therefore did not experience modern alienation. Drawing on the sociologist Ferdinand Tönnies's distinction between organic community and modern society, Lukács announced a sort of postmodern homecoming: the return of the epic as the expression of a reintegrated community. By contrast, the older form of the novel embodied a

24. Lukács, *Theory of the Novel*, 20–21.

25. Michael Löwy, "Naphta or Settembrini? Lukács and Romantic Anticapitalism," *New German Critique*, no. 42 (Autumn 1987): 17–31.

26. Lukács, *Theory of the Novel*, 63. Jean-Jacques Rousseau, that eccentric forerunner of Romanticism, offered perhaps the earliest critique of second nature in his *Discourse on Inequality* (1754).

transcendental homelessness, which "must remain the dominant form so long as the world is ruled by the same stars."[27]

A glint from a different star shone on the book's conclusion. Lukács dedicated his remarkable last paragraph to the Russian writer who haunted all his meditations on the tragedy of culture. Fyodor Dostoevsky was originally his subject for a big unfinished project, to which *The Theory of the Novel* would have served as an introduction.[28] Dostoyevsky fascinated him because in his novels, or antinovels, one caught a glimpse of a "new world, remote from any struggle against what actually exists." Characters like Prince Myshkin in *The Idiot* (1874) and Alyosha Karamazov in *The Brothers Karamazov* (1880) were truly good people who gave readers hope for a more generous, beautiful, and authentic community. Lukács wondered in his final line "whether the New has no other herald but our hopes: those hopes which are signs of a world to come, still so weak that it can easily be crushed by the sterile power of the merely existent."[29] Dostoyevsky's renewed epics epitomized the hope for a new beginning that animated Lukács during his early phase of romantic anti-capitalism.

Upon returning to Budapest in 1917 after spending a year in Max Weber's Heidelberg study circle, Lukács and several friends founded the Free School of the Humanities as a forum for philosophical and cultural exchange outside the confines of the university system. The Free School presented lecture series to a small but dedicated audience of young intellectuals who felt stranded by the war and the desultory spirit of the times. Lukács's partner in this venture was Karl Mannheim, the later sociologist of knowledge.

To introduce the lecture series for 1918, Mannheim delivered the programmatic talk "Soul and Culture," which pretty well summarized Lukács's own position. Mannheim interpreted the Free School as an institution for the new generation of artists and scholars poised to renew European culture. "Firmly grounded in our similar subjective cultures," he said, "we have set ourselves the task of turning this school into a unified manifestation of objective culture,

27. Lukács, *Theory of the Novel*, 146–47 and 152–53. See Tönnies, *Community and Society*. On another revolutionary idea of community, the league (*Bund*), see Eugene Lunn, *Prophet of Community: The Romantic Socialism of Gustav Landauer* (Berkeley: University of California Press, 1973). See also J. M. Bernstein, *The Philosophy of the Novel: Lukács, Marxism, and the Dialectics of Form* (Minneapolis: University of Minnesota Press, 1984).

28. See Löwy, *Georg Lukács*, 117–20; Arato and Breines, *Young Lukács*, 69–71; and Congdon, *Young Lukács*, 100–108.

29. Lukács, *Theory of the Novel*, 153. See Richard Westerman, "From Myshkin to Marxism: The Role of Dostoevsky Reception in Lukács's Revolutionary Ethics," *Modern Intellectual History* 16, no. 3 (2019): 927–60.

so that it may gather all who feel solidarity with it." This remark showed the influence of Simmel, who had highlighted the opposition between subjective soul and objective forms. In the act of externalizing our spiritual strivings in artwork, language, and religion, Mannheim claimed, "culture comes to life, as an independent reality, and sets out like a golem . . . on a path of its own." He extended the analogy, describing golem-like individuals who "merely follow a road to its end, actualizing the possibilities revealed to them by beginnings that had once been meaningful." Thus old forms become alien to us once they have been realized, while new spiritual contents, still formless, "flash on the horizon."[30]

Revolutionary Forms

Lukács and Mannheim soon transposed their insights about culture into a political key. Socialist mass parties had thrived in the late nineteenth century, they claimed, but now they plodded along like golems. New flashes on the horizon came from the Russian Revolution and the chaotic end of the Great War. The solution to both the tragedy of culture and the alienation of workers from lifeless party organizations was leftism. From early on, Lukács expressed sympathy for socialism. His Thália theater company collaborated with the Hungarian Social Democratic Party to put on plays especially for workers. He placed modest hope in the working class as an agent of cultural renewal. As the proletarian masses smashed the petrified bourgeois culture, "the force of the revolutionary spirit" might in turn create new forms.[31]

One lecture on the Free School's program was Ervin Szabó's "On the Ultimate Issues of Marxism." A decade older than Lukács, Szabó had years of experience as a left-wing Social Democrat and anarcho-syndicalist agitator. In 1902 at the University of Budapest, he had cofounded the first socialist student organization in Hungary. According to one account, the teenage Lukács was a charter member.[32] In 1909–10, it was Szabó's edition of the *Selected Works of Marx and Engels* that gave him his first real taste of Marxism. More significantly for the development of Lukács's leftism, however, Szabó also introduced him to the work of Sorel. For a while Lukács deemed French revolutionary syndicalism "the only oppositional socialist movement that could be taken

30. Mannheim, "Soul and Culture," 286–301 (at 292–93). Löwy speculated that Mannheim based his later figure of the "free-floating intellectual" on the illustrious crew gathered at the Free School (Béla Balázs, Béla Bartók, Zoltán Kodály, Arnold Hauser, et al.). Löwy, *Georg Lukács*, 82–85.

31. Lukács, "Aesthetic Culture," 373.

32. Lichtheim, *George Lukács*, 31.

seriously."[33] Ideas that he shared with Sorel included "the dislike of liberal bourgeois democracy [and] of positivist science"; "the critique of bureaucracies or of parties likely to become self-perpetuating repressive structures"; and "the emphasis on action, on militancy, [and] on the need to liberate the creative forces of the proletariat."[34] Toward the end of his life, while reminiscing about the Hungarian cultural scene of his youth, Lukács supposedly remarked that Szabó (and through him, Sorel) "was the spiritual father of us all."[35]

In 1917–18, Szabó helped coordinate the schedules of the Free School and the more established Social Science Society.[36] A fascinating debate between representatives of the two groups occurred in the spring of 1918 on the theme of "conservative and progressive idealism." Lukács's young disciple Béla Fogarasi delivered the main talk, which defended a progressive form of idealism— understood as the study of objective cultural forms—against both Platonic idealism and crude materialism. A progressive idealist commitment to how things ought to be rather than how they contingently are, Fogarasi argued, was the only means of transcending existing customs, laws, and culture.[37]

Lukács's subsequent remarks refined Fogarasi's argument. Progressive idealism yielded two possibilities, he claimed: either "ethical *action directe* [i.e., Sorel's option] ... which 'pays no heed to the detour of [electoral] politics' and immediately sets out 'to change men's souls'"; or "political action, conceived as an ethical instrument whose only aim is 'to create institutions corresponding as far as possible to ethical ideals, and to bring about the disappearance of those which hinder the realization of such ideals.'"[38] Either direct action or the long march through the institutions: those were the two options for people who wanted to change the world. But relying on institutions was risky. "Every institution, once it becomes an end in itself," Lukács warned, "has a conservative character. . . . [M]ovements that are initially very progressive stagnate as soon as the institutions they created as a means become independent of the end." He cited German Social Democracy as an example. To prevent such a

---

33. Lukács, *Record of a Life*, 41.

34. Rodney Livingstone, introduction to Lukács, *Tactics and Ethics*, xii.

35. Quoted in Goldberger, "Ervin Szabó," 452. Despite their regular encounters, shared acquaintances, and occasional collaborations, Lukács never got along personally with Szabó. His debt was solely intellectual. Lukács, *Record of a Life*, 51–52.

36. Goldberger, "Ervin Szabó," 454.

37. Gluck, *Georg Lukács*, 95–96, and Lee Congdon, *Exile and Social Thought: Hungarian Intellectuals in Germany and Austria, 1919–1933* (Princeton, NJ: Princeton University Press, 1991), 24–25. I have been unable to find a full translation of this Hungarian debate, so I have relied on partial translations in secondary sources.

38. Löwy, *Georg Lukács*, 126.

conservative institutionalization of an originally emancipatory movement one needed "a permanent revolution against what exists" predicated on a refusal to compromise. Only such ethical maximalism could sustain the momentum of progressive politics. Lukács's version of permanent revolution resembled Marx's and Auguste Blanqui's earlier versions and Leon Trotsky's later version. For Lukács in the spring of 1918, however, the concept corresponded to his emergent leftism, or as one scholar has put it, his "dazzling and moving *revolutionary radicalism*."[39] The historian George Lichtheim went so far as to claim that after Szabó's untimely death in September of that year, Lukács inherited his position as "chief theorist of the Hungarian ultra-left."[40] Leftism determined his ethics and politics during the chaotic final months of World War I.

The Austro-Hungarian Empire collapsed in October 1918, and the ensuing revolutions laid the groundwork for a democratic republic in Hungary. Events in Russia over the previous year, however, had shown the world how Communism could overtake an originally democratic revolution. Militant intellectuals in Central Europe feverishly debated whether the cultural and economic conditions there permitted Bolshevik-style action. In his last essay before joining the Communist Party that December, Lukács probed the ethics of this question. The present moral dilemma, he wrote, lay in the fact that while choosing Communism meant accepting the "dictatorship, terror, and the class oppression that goes along with it," not choosing Communism meant a possibly infinite delay of the new society.[41] The first option required a blind faith that the dictatorship of the proletariat would abolish all forms of oppression. The second option ran the risk of tactical compromises turning into ends in themselves—that is, the institutionalized politics that Lukács detested in Social Democracy. Drawing on a distinction between the ethics of conviction and the ethics of responsibility, he opted at that moment for democratic responsibility instead of the Bolsheviks' "metaphysical assumption that the bad can engender the good."[42] Not that Lukács intended to join the Social Democrats: he only thought that, for lack of a better option, it was morally preferable

---

39. Löwy, *Georg Lukács*, 126–27. Emphasis in original.

40. Lichtheim, *George Lukács*, 31.

41. Lukács, "Bolshevism as a Moral Problem," 422.

42. Lukács, 424. While participating in Max Weber's Heidelberg Circle in 1912–15, Lukács helped the German sociologist develop his ideal-type ethics of conviction and of responsibility. The two men continued to correspond afterward. Zoltán Tarr, "A Note on Weber and Lukács," *International Journal of Politics, Culture, and Society* 3, no. 1 (Autumn 1989): 131–39. See M. Weber, "Politics as a Vocation."

to sacrifice the purity of one's convictions by accepting compromise with moderates than to betray ethics altogether by enabling terrorism.

But he soon changed his mind and joined the Communist Party. The first article he published after that, "Tactics and Ethics" (1919), has been the subject of much scholarly debate, not least because Lukács's exact reasons for becoming a Communist remain unclear. In the article he argued that the moral dilemma of Bolshevism could be resolved only by sacrificing one's individual ethic for the sake of a higher, collective ethic: the emancipation of the proletariat.[43] Over the course of 1919, he wrote a series of essays that explained his position in terms of the leftist dilemma of sustaining new forms.

The relatively bloodless founding of the Hungarian Soviet Republic that March along with his new job as deputy commissar of education and culture added a fresh, practical dimension to his writing. He opened a workers' theater whose productions of Gogol, Molière, Ibsen, Shaw, and others combined "classicism and revolutionary boldness." As part of his commissarial duties, Lukács also launched a sex education campaign, which provoked so much controversy that it had to be shut down.[44] And his provocations were not limited to subversive sex ed. When the Hungarian Red Army fought for the survival of the Republic that summer, he served as political commissar to the Fifth Division facing off against Czech forces. One time, a soldier had to interrupt Lukács's speech and pull him down into the trench to avoid sniper fire. Lukács explained his brazenness by saying, "there must be no rift between theory and practice."[45]

Behind the front lines, he delivered a pair of speeches that demonstrated continuity between his earlier aesthetic concerns and his present political engagement. The old culture faced imminent destruction, he declared, and a new culture would rise from the ruins. Whereas all previous cultures developed under the control of the ruling class, Communist culture by its very nature would be open to all. The new culture would liberate itself from domination by exchange value. De-commodified culture would yield artworks "in which the whole genesis of the work is exclusively the result of the artist's labor and each element of the work is conditioned by his individual qualities," not by market forces. If capitalism fragmented art production by imposing an anarchic succession of detached forms, then Communism would reintegrate it into an organic continuum in which "the linkage to another's work, the continuation of another's work . . . again becomes possible." This creative transformation could result only from the abolition of economic misery and material

43. Georg Lukács, "Tactics and Ethics" [1919], in *Tactics and Ethics*, 3–11.

44. Löwy, *Georg Lukács*, 150–51. See Kettler, *Marxismus und Kultur*.

45. Quoted in Löwy, *Georg Lukács*, 153.

scarcity. Dismantling the old society would provide material for constructing the new.[46]

Lukács steered between a classical defense of bourgeois culture and a destructive nihilism that never created anything new. In the essay "Party and Class," he applied his analysis of cultural forms to the problem of revolutionary organization. Szabó and Sorel had taught him that political parties modeled on Social Democracy would corrupt the revolutionary movement and ultimately stabilize the old society. But not long before, in March 1919, the Hungarian Social Democratic Party had endorsed the Communist Party program in a gesture of left unity. It was this decision that had made the Soviet Republic possible. Lukács praised the unity program, which called for a proletarian dictatorship "exercised through councils of workers, soldiers and peasants."[47] To leftists like him, councils were the revolutionary organizational form par excellence. Finally a new alternative had arrived that rendered both the Social Democratic mass party and the Communist cadre party obsolete, or at least shifted them into auxiliary roles. For a brief period, the council form was his answer to the leftist dilemma.

Councils, or soviets, had entered the left's repertoire during the Russian Revolution of 1905. They reappeared in dramatic fashion during the Russian period of "dual power" between February and October 1917 and again during the Central European revolutions of 1918–19. A council consisted of anywhere from a dozen to several hundred people from a local factory, military unit, school, or agrarian estate. It would assume direct control over the administrative, managerial, and police functions for its locality. A council usually belonged to a federation of municipal councils that in turn constituted regional and national councils. Councils differed from the representative institutions of a liberal democracy insofar as they were composed of ordinary people rather than professional politicians. Often council membership was identical to the workforce itself, but in larger enterprises delegates were elected. They served unfixed terms, always subject to recall. For the existing social hierarchy the councils substituted a spontaneous and decentralized power apparatus. They deliberately bypassed the procedures of the official trade unions and political parties, although sometimes they did form alliances with those organizations. The historian Geoff Eley has described the councils of 1917–23 as a "new medium of working-class activity" that "articulated extraparliamentary, direct-democratic, self-consciously class-based alternatives to the labor movement's existing strategies and institutions." Workers, soldiers, and peasants

46. Lukács, "Old Culture and the New Culture," 23 and 28–29.
47. Quoted in the editor's note to Lukács, "Party and Class," 28n2.

took the branches of government into their own hands, practicing the most autonomous form of direct democracy. Councils have never lasted long, but their rare germinations have coincided with the most exciting revolutionary moments of the twentieth century.[48]

Lukács greeted the development of a council system in Hungary as proof that alongside the destruction of the old regime, the proletariat also laid the foundation for a new regime. Destruction and construction, he wrote about the councils, "are just as organically connected and inseparable as life and death." The formation of workers', soldiers', and peasants' councils showed the creativity and "the highest and purest constructive powers" of the revolutionary classes. Here he echoed Sorel when the latter praised the inventiveness of workers on the shop floor.[49] But Lukács also criticized French and Italian syndicalists for failing to recognize the necessary if auxiliary role of parties. In the revolutionary crisis, party and class must work together.

The workers still needed a party because existing power relations demanded it. At the same time, "those same power relations made of this party organization an element which hindered the actions of the proletariat." Lukács concluded that it was necessary to build a party of a new type. Even if it arose out of a crisis within the Social Democratic mass party, the Communist cadre party actually constituted a radical break from all previous party forms. It functioned as a sort of antiparty, he explained, because in the revolution's final phase, "the proletarian movement [will have] outgrown the organizational framework of the party."[50] Thus according to Lukács's leftist argument, spontaneous mass action would gestate within and alongside the Communist Party but outgrow it over time. The abolition of the party form was the logical result of direct workers' control.

48. Eley, *Forging Democracy*, 160–64 (at 160 and 161). The Soviet Union would have a council system in name only. Scholars usually define its mode of government as party dictatorship. On the formation of soviets and other popular initiatives during the Russian Revolution itself, see Christopher Read, *From Tsar to Soviets: The Russian People and Their Revolution, 1917–21* (London: UCL Press, 1996); S. A. Smith, *Red Petrograd: Revolution in the Factories, 1917–1918* (Cambridge: Cambridge University Press, 1983); Diane Koenker, *Moscow Workers and the 1917 Revolution* (Princeton, NJ: Princeton University Press, 1981); and Anweiler, *Soviets*. On the councils during the Central European revolutions, see M. Jones, *Founding Weimar*; Hoffrogge, *Working-Class Politics*; Carsten, *Revolution in Central Europe*; and Broué, *German Revolution*. On the fate of the council form after Communism fell in Eastern Europe, see Jay, "No Power to the Soviets."

49. Lukács, "Party and Class," 29, and Sorel, *Reflections on Violence*, 244 and 248–49. In his 1918 defense of Lenin, Sorel had written that "the bolsheviks are obliged to destroy and to reconstruct." Appendix to *Reflections on Violence*, 283–93 (at 288).

50. Lukács, "Party and Class," 33. Emphasis removed.

The unity pact between Social Democrats and Communists in Hungary had created a situation in which both parties lost their reason to exist, Lukács thought. The dictatorship of the proletariat, as administered through the councils, represented the new revolutionary form in politics analogous to Dostoyevsky's renewed epic in literature. Even the meaning of the word "party" had changed. As Lukács somewhat ambiguously explained, the word now meant "the executive organ of the will that is developing in the new society from new sources of strength." He claimed moreover that the Hungarian workers accomplished on their own what the Russian workers had done only with the guidance of a vanguardist cadre party and all the factional strife that came with it. Of great significance for socialism in Europe, he declared that "the Hungarian revolution has demonstrated that this revolution is possible without fratricidal struggles among the proletariat itself. The world revolution is thereby carried another stage further."[51] Given his later fealty to Moscow, Lukács would have reason to regret those lines. They implied nothing less than that the Central European revolutions superseded the Russian Revolution.

Lukács later claimed that the essay "Party and Class" displayed the last "vestiges of Ervin Szabó's syndicalism" in his thought.[52] But that essay also owed its leftist brand of communism to his intense study of Lenin's works during the early months of 1919. In *What Is to Be Done?* (1902), Lenin had proposed forming a conspiratorial band of professional revolutionaries that would provide the proletariat with a correct class consciousness. Most scholars now consider the work a classic expression of Leninist vanguardism. But that particular tract was virtually unknown to Lukács and other European socialists at the time.[53] They were more likely to have read the Bolshevik leader's most leftist work, *The State and Revolution* (1917). In the words of one scholar, the latter text "outlines the incompatibility of Leninism and Western democracy. According to Lenin, Leninists cannot participate in democracy for any purpose other than to destroy it. Parliamentary government must be swept away. The non-Leninist state must be shattered and utterly destroyed."[54] Lenin argued that the only purpose of electoral democracy was to neutralize class antagonisms. Electoral democracy peacefully reconciled the oppressors and the oppressed, all while preserving the structure of oppression itself. In such a situation, there could be no question of organizing the revolutionary class according to any

51. Lukács, 36.

52. Lukács, *Record of a Life*, 59.

53. For a masterful debunking of the myth of *What Is to Be Done?* as well as a new translation of the text, see Lih, *Lenin Rediscovered*.

54. Henry M. Christman, editor's note to Lenin, "The State and Revolution" [1917], in *Essential Works of Lenin*, 271–364 (at 271).

preexisting political form, be it a democratic working-class party or a vanguardist cadre party. To be sure, the proletariat must temporarily co-opt state power in order to crush capitalist resistance and spearhead a socialist economy. But Lenin claimed that this state would wither away as it yielded to a new form, the dictatorship of the proletariat. During the transition period, "the state must inevitably be a state that is democratic *in a new way* (for the proletariat and the propertyless in general) and dictatorial *in a new way* (against the bourgeoisie)." Proletarian democracy would entail the abolition of electoral liberalism and all forms of bureaucracy.[55]

For all its administrative centralism and contempt for anarchist adventures, Lenin's *State and Revolution* hardly mentioned a vanguardist cadre party. During the period following the February Revolution, the Bolshevik leader dreamt of a party of a new type: "Wider! Raise up new elements! Awaken a new initiative, new organisations in all sections, and *prove* to them that peace will be brought only by an armed Soviet of Workers Deputies, if it takes power."[56] So, a leftist like Lukács might be forgiven for interpreting the Lenin of 1917 through early 1918 as a supporter of grassroots workers' control.[57] After the success of the October Revolution and the ensuing civil war, however, Lenin shifted to his more familiar stance in favor of vanguardist party dictatorship.

The intersection of leftism and newness continued to preoccupy Lukács during the heady days of the Hungarian Soviet Republic and its chaotic aftermath. In August 1919, after a four-and-a-half-month existence and a series of foreign policy mistakes, the Republic fell as its Red Army succumbed to counterrevolutionary forces backed by the Entente powers. The soviets gave way to Miklós Horthy's military dictatorship. Communists faced violent reprisals, went underground, or fled into exile—a pattern of left defeat that would repeat itself during the coming age of fascism. Briefly Lukács tried to run the Communist Party's illegal network in Budapest, but he was forced into hiding. In October, he escaped to Vienna in hopes of carrying on the struggle from abroad.[58]

55. Lenin, "State and Revolution," 288, 295, and 303. Emphasis in original.

56. Lenin to Alexandra Kollontai, March 17, 1917, in *Collected Works*, 35: 297–99 (at 299). To my knowledge, this letter is the only place that Lenin used the term "party of a new type." Stalin later appropriated it.

57. Although he did not focus on it in that text, Lenin did occasionally praise workers' control and the council system (*Collected Works*, 35: 339, 345–49, and 363). He even defended the council communist Pannekoek against criticism from a leading theorist of German Social Democracy, Karl Kautsky (357–61).

58. Congdon, *Young Lukács*, 166–67.

Creative Destruction

Upon arriving in Vienna, Lukács briefly assumed leadership of the Hungarian Communist Party in exile. He collaborated with other militant intellectuals there such as Gerhart Eisler and Josef Révai on the journal *Kommunismus*, which they designed as a forum for theoretical debate about communism in Central and Southeastern Europe. This journal represented a leftist viewpoint—ultraleft, in the parlance of the time—that was shared by an impressive range of oppositional currents: the Dutch *Tribune* circle around Pannekoek, Herman Gorter, and Henriette Roland-Holst; the British Workers' Socialist Federation led by the radical suffragette Sylvia Pankhurst; the Italian left-communist followers of Amadeo Bordiga; and the German Communist Workers' Party (KAPD) led by Otto Rühle among others, which had a mass following in the tens of thousands. This loose coalition of leftists challenged Lenin and the Bolsheviks' growing insistence on maintaining party discipline and bourgeois legality. To them, as Rühle put it, the revolution was not a party affair.[59]

Nearly all Lukács's contributions to *Kommunismus* in 1920–21 dealt with organizational problems. As his earlier writings indicated, organization for him was never simply a matter of tactics. Whether party, union, council, or something else, the form of political organization certified the authenticity of the revolutionary goal and the realizability of the new society. His article "The Question of Parliamentarism" caused an uproar in Communist circles when it appeared in March 1920. Its refusal to compromise with existing political forms gave a preview of new lefts to come.

When workers found themselves on the defensive, Lukács admitted, they must adapt to liberal norms by sending representatives to parliament. But while on the offensive during a revolutionary situation, any insistence on electoral procedure or legality would weaken class consciousness. "Parliament, the bourgeoisie's very own instrument," he wrote, "can therefore only ever be a *defensive weapon for the proletariat*." Even when Communists had no choice but to work through representative institutions, they must use their position to "fight parliament within parliament itself." Communist members of parliament should provoke the representatives of bourgeois parties into taking actions that exposed the violence of class rule and the charade of electoral democracy. Lukács claimed that such subversive participation could shield the Communist Party against co-optation or assimilation. Still, using

---

59. Rühle, *Die Revolution ist keine Parteisache*. For another KAPD tract on the leftist dilemma, see Schröder, *Vom Werden der neuen Gesellschaft*.

electoral tactics required accepting "that revolution is unthinkable in the fore-seeable future."[60] Writing in the spring of 1920, Lukács himself was not ready to admit defeat.

Central Europe still found itself in a revolutionary situation, he thought. A focus on electoral campaigns in such a situation was dangerous. Echoing the rhetoric of leftist organizations such as the KAPD, he claimed that casting a vote was "sham action" that served to suppress class consciousness. Campaign slogans encouraged "the sham unity of the old parties" rather than the new unity of the proletariat in the council system. Unlike parliamentary factions, "the workers' councils by their mere existence point the way forward beyond bourgeois society. . . . [T]hey are the true index of the progress of the revolution." The councils functioned as both an extraparliamentary opposition and a creative anticipation of the new society. Legality, understood as an adherence to bourgeois democratic norms, "is the death of the workers' council." Lukács believed that the mere possibility of a council system rendered parliamentarism obsolete.[61] From the economist Joseph Schumpeter, who coincidentally worked in Vienna at that time, I borrow the idea of creative destruction to describe Lukács's expectation that councils would disrupt all established political forms.[62]

Members of the councils, he continued, had to defend themselves against bourgeois reactionaries as well as their own former leaders in the left parties. In a revolutionary situation, therefore, it was the task of the revolutionary movement to combat the old left as relentlessly as it did the forces of capitalism. Lukács targeted Social Democracy in particular, but the implications for the Communist Party were obvious. "The workers' council spells the death of social democracy," he wrote, no less than of the vanguardist cadre party.[63]

To be clear, he did not throw in his lot entirely with leftists such as the Dutch Tribunists or Italian Bordigists. If the purpose of articles like "The Question of Parliamentarism" was to discourage blind obedience to the party

60. Lukács, "Question of Parliamentarism," 55, emphasis removed.

61. Lukács, "Question of Parliamentarism," 59, 61, and 63. Emphasis removed.

62. Schumpeter, *Capitalism, Socialism, and Democracy*, 81–86. Schumpeter used the term to describe the disruptive effect of entrepreneurial innovation on established businesses.

63. Lukács, "Question of Parliamentarism," 63. Emphasis removed. Lukács wrongly assumed that the new institutions of the Soviet Union would be immune to the bureaucratic tendencies of modern industrial society. Still, he warned that Communism too might "degenerate or ossify even before [it has] had a chance to develop properly." Lukács, "The Moral Mission of the Communist Party" [May 1, 1920], in *Tactics and Ethics*, 64–70 (at 68–69).

form, elsewhere he defended the role of parties and criticized pure leftism.[64] Because anarchists, syndicalists, and other leftists remained "the unconscious but really revolutionary elements," the party had to ensure that those elements developed a correct consciousness. In return, leftists had to ensure that party Communists did not succumb to oligarchy like the Social Democrats.[65] This mutual obligation bound councils and the Communist Party together, but that bond proved unstable. Soon Lukács himself ran afoul of the Communist Party.

Responding directly to the article on parliamentarism, Lenin judged Lukács's analysis "very Left-wing, and very poor. Its Marxism is purely verbal."[66] As mentioned earlier, Lenin had a complex take on revolutionary forms. In his 1919 pamphlet *A Great Beginning*, he praised the heroism of Russian workers who had volunteered for Communist Saturdays, or days of unpaid labor for the benefit of the revolution. One needed to foster those and other "young shoots of the new," he wrote.[67] Already by the late spring of 1920, however, Lenin saw fit to prune back those shoots.

The pamphlet *"Left-Wing" Communism: An Infantile Disorder* was Lenin's most important intervention in international Communist debates at the time, and the most important for Lukács's own development. The Russian word *levizny* (левизны) in the title translates more accurately as "leftism" rather than "left-wing," and only the standard French title of the pamphlet (*Gauchisme*) truly captured it. Lenin first used the word in 1908–9 to criticize the alleged recklessness of the Social Revolutionaries and the Bolshevik faction known as the Otzovists (Recallists).[68] Those groups refused on principle to participate in the parliamentary Duma, while Lenin favored a more flexible approach. Bolshevism, he wrote in 1911, "has 'got over' the otzovist sickness, the sickness of revolutionary phrase-mongering, the playing at 'Leftism,' the swinging from Social-Democracy to the left."[69] By 1915, he

---

64. For example, see Georg Lukács, "Opportunism and Putschism" (August 17, 1920), "The Crisis of Syndicalism in Italy" (October 16, 1920), and "Spontaneity of the Masses, Activity of the Party" (*Die Internationale*, March 15, 1921), all in *Tactics and Ethics*, 71–79, 80–90, and 95–105. See also Feenberg, "Post-Utopian Marxism."

65. Lukács, "Moral Mission of the Communist Party," 69.

66. Lenin, *Collected Works*, 31: 165.

67. Lenin, "A Great Beginning" [July 1919], in *Collected Works*, 29: 409–34 (at 425). In the third volume of *Capital*, Marx had similarly described producer cooperatives as representing "within the old form the first sprouts of the new." Marx, *Capital: A Critique of Political Economy*, vol. 3 [posth. 1894], ed. Friedrich Engels (New York: International Publishers, 1967), ch. 27.

68. Lenin, *Collected Works*, 15: 148 and 357–58.

69. Lenin, 17: 277.

regularly labeled council communists such as Pannekoek "extreme Leftists" and accused them of "pseudo-Marxist and pacifist distortions."[70] Before long, any position to the left of Bolshevism earned Lenin's sobriquet "leftism": from Trotsky's early Menshevik internationalism to Rosa Luxemburg's critique of party dictatorship.

In *"Left-Wing" Communism*, Lenin specifically targeted German leftists in the KAPD and British leftists in Pankhurst's Workers' Socialist Federation. He ensured that every delegate to the Second Congress of the Communist International in the summer of 1920 received a copy. The pamphlet's rhetoric contrasted the older and more experienced Bolsheviks with the younger and less experienced purists. The main reason why the Bolsheviks had succeeded in Russia, he claimed, was their "most rigorous and truly iron discipline." No other revolutionary organization in the world could match the Bolsheviks' wealth of experience accumulated during the years 1903–17, which saw a "rapid and varied succession of different forms of the movement—legal and illegal, peaceful and stormy, underground and open, local circles and mass movements, and parliamentary and terrorist forms." Overcoming the entrenched resistance of the bourgeoisie required "a long, stubborn and desperate life-and-death struggle which calls for tenacity, discipline, and a single and inflexible will."[71] Those were not qualities that one typically found among romantic young idealists who played at revolution.

An effective revolution demanded total centralization, not a decentralized free-for-all. According to Lenin, people who rejected compromise on principle smacked of "childishness, which it is difficult even to consider seriously." He actually described quite well the patterns of behavior that would later coalesce into neoleftism: "It all adds up to that petty-bourgeois diffuseness and instability, that incapacity for sustained effort, unity and organised action." By giving free rein to all creative impulses, leftists made the mistake of thinking they could invent new structures of workers' control overnight. Lenin reminded his readers that the spadework of communism took many years: "To attempt in practice, today, to anticipate this future result of a fully developed, fully stabilised and constituted, fully comprehensive and mature communism would be like trying to teach higher mathematics to a child of four."[72] In their youthful impatience, leftists mimicked the actual immaturity of the proletariat. The adults in the room knew better.

70. Lenin, 21: 213.

71. Lenin, "'Left-Wing' Communism: An Infantile Disorder" [June 1920], in *Collected Works*, 31: 17–118 (at 23–26).

72. Lenin, 37, 43–44, and 49–50.

The only thing that leftists had proven, Lenin continued, was "that they are not a party of a class, but a circle, not a party of the masses, but a group of intellectuals and of a few workers who ape the worst features of intellectualism." Such anti-intellectualism would persist in later attacks on neoleftism, by socialists and conservatives alike. Once confronted with "the actual state of the class-consciousness and preparedness of the entire [working] class," Lenin wrote, true revolutionaries recognized the usefulness of electoral participation. Communist members of parliament had a platform for exposing bourgeois hypocrisy and "educating the backward strata" of the population.[73] Every tactic had its right time and place. Leftists' uncompromising stance ruled out a range of useful tactics.

Communists had to have "the ability to effect all the necessary practical compromises, tacks, conciliatory manoeuvres, zigzags, retreats and so on." Extraparliamentary opposition may look good on paper, Lenin implied, but it must be treated as a primordial communism "that has not yet matured to the stage of practical political action." And although leftists claimed to prefer the newest forms of organization, they actually clung to obsolete forms of syndicalist agitation. "Our work today has such a durable and powerful content," Lenin countered,

> that it can and must manifest itself in any form, both new and old; it can and must regenerate, conquer and subjugate all forms, not only the new but also the old—not for the purpose of reconciling itself with the old, but for the purpose of making all and every form—new and old—a weapon for the complete and irrevocable victory of communism.

As this passage shows, Lenin sometimes couched his own arguments in the radical language of leftism. Social Democrats fetishized the old forms of bourgeois democracy without recognizing the revolutionary new content unleashed by imperialism and the world war. Leftists, on the other hand, fetishized new forms of spontaneous working-class action without seeing how old forms had changed their function and therefore might be used again by the proletariat. Communists should be formally omnivorous. They had a duty "to master all forms," switching rapidly from one to another as the situation demanded. He concluded this incendiary pamphlet with "hope for a rapid and complete recovery of the international communist movement from the infantile disorder of 'Left-wing' communism."[74] Little did he know that the neoleftist era had only just begun.

73. Lenin, 57–59. Emphasis removed.
74. Lenin, 94–98 and 103–4.

Lenin's pamphlet made leftism look like the easy route, whereas a successful revolution was hard. His portrayal of leftists' impotence, instability, and eclecticism highlighted the destructiveness of the phenomenon. Leftism allegedly caused organizational splintering and divided the working class. While that same charge would be hurled at new lefts again and again, it obscured the creative side of leftist and neoleftist politics. One can see in Lenin's pamphlet the seed of future conflict between old lefts and new lefts. His polemic provided a lexicon of antileftist insults: selfish, individualistic, inexperienced, ridiculous, adventurist, romantic, naïve, childish, young, and so on. By contrast, the old left valued sobriety, objectivity, and maturity. Such rhetoric expressed more than just a generational divide: "if youth [alone] were the explanation," wrote Lenin, "it would not be so bad; young people are preordained to talk such nonsense for a period."[75] But leftist or neoleftist immaturity could afflict the young at heart of all ages. At best, he wrote elsewhere, one might tolerate leftism like a parent tolerated a child's growing pains.[76] Nearly every subsequent critique of new lefts by both socialists and nonsocialists would take that same condescending tone.

The international debate over revolutionary forms turned deadly. The Bolsheviks under Lenin expressed growing discomfort with spontaneous popular actions. In March 1921, sailors at the naval base of Kronstadt rose up in revolt against the Bolshevik government. Among other things, they demanded new elections to the soviets, freedom of speech for anarchists and other leftists, and the release of political prisoners who belonged to non-Bolshevik factions. The workers of nearby Petrograd declared solidarity with the sailors. Given the ongoing civil war, it is perhaps not surprising that the Bolshevik reaction was ruthless. The Red Army invaded Kronstadt, killed more than a thousand rebels in combat, executed thousands more afterward, and sent the rest to prison camps. For many critics, the Kronstadt tragedy proved that the Bolsheviks had betrayed the revolution by setting up an authoritarian party dictatorship.[77]

75. Lenin, 70.

76. Lenin, *Collected Works*, 31: 185. His criticism of the journal *Kommunismus* explicitly diagnosed Lukács's circle with the infantile disorder. See *Collected Works*, 31: 165–67.

77. For example, see Emma Goldman, *The Crushing of the Russian Revolution* (London: Freedom Press, 1922); Volin, *The Unknown Revolution, 1917–1921* (New York: Free Life, 1947); and Serge, *Memoirs of a Revolutionary*, 146–54. Mensheviks, Social-Revolutionaries, and the Workers' Opposition were suppressed after the Kronstadt uprising, which occurred during the Tenth Party Congress. There Lenin succeeded in passing a ban on factions, thus ending any pretense to "democratic centralism" as an organizational principle.

A Cursed Book: *History and Class Consciousness*

Lukács toed the Bolshevik line on Kronstadt. Linking the rebellion to the 1917 Kornilov affair, in which a renegade general had attempted a military putsch, he criticized the sailors' "counter-revolutionary attitude" as a "corrosive tendency in the service of the bourgeoisie."[78] While he did recognize Kronstadt's significance as a spontaneous workers' uprising, his strategic outlook had changed as a result of Lenin's antileftist critique.

At the end of 1922 Lukács finished writing a book that would forever cement his place in the intellectual history of the left. The historian Paul Breines called *History and Class Consciousness* the cursed book of twentieth-century Marxism. "The revival of radical social movements in the 1960s," he explained, "had a great deal to do with the revival of interest in Lukács, particularly his controversial book."[79] A member of the Lukácsian Budapest School agreed: "Lukács was already a classic in the twenties: friends and foes alike admit that *History and Class Consciousness* was the single major contribution to the history of Marxism as philosophy since Marx's death."[80] According to Breines, the philosopher Lucien Goldmann, who popularized Lukács's ideas in postwar France, speculated that Martin Heidegger's monumental work *Being and Time* (1927) "was in important respects a response to Lukács's [book], seeking to transpose the latter's historical concepts of reification, false consciousness, and class consciousness back into transhistorical attributes of a human essence (Dasein, authenticity, and so forth)."[81]

For such an influential book, *History and Class Consciousness* was unusual. It consisted of a hodgepodge of essays: some old, some revised, and a few new. This inconsistent and unsystematic work also marked a watershed in Lukács's biography. In between the lines, one witnesses his difficult transition from the leftist heterodoxy that had guided him since 1918 into a defense of Communist orthodoxy. He concluded that only the Communist "party of a new type" could control the creative-destructive force unleashed by the new era of revolutions. But the book's transitional nature meant that it contained enough radical remnants to inspire neoleftist and even anti-Communist readings. In this way it resembles the philosopher G.W.F. Hegel's *Phenomenology of Spirit*, a pivotal work of the early nineteenth century whose emancipatory potential

---

78. Lukács, *History and Class Consciousness*, 293.

79. Breines, "Young Lukács, Old Lukács," 533.

80. Ferenc Fehér, "Lukács in Weimar," *Telos*, no. 39 (Spring 1979): 113–36 (at 113).

81. Breines, "Young Lukács, Old Lukács," 536n7. See Lucien Goldmann, *Lukács and Heidegger: Towards a New Philosophy* [posth. 1973], trans. William Q. Boelhower (London: Routledge and Kegan Paul, 1977).

exceeded the intentions of its author.[82] Not coincidentally, Lukács's cursed book made the most compelling case to date for the centrality of Hegelian concepts in Marx's method.

The premise of the book, which appeared in early 1923, was that humans unconsciously behave as if according to natural laws. In reality, this "natural" behavior evolved historically through objective social determinations. But it seems natural because nobody has any control over it. In the modern era, for example, people automatically obey economic self-interest and the profit motive. Those are observable facts from which economists can deduce laws of supply and demand, rational choice theories, statistical probabilities, and so forth. Lukács generalized the phenomenon by claiming that the history of existing society has in fact progressed naturally—that is, without conscious human intervention. All history effectively has been natural history, not because humans were fated by evolution to conform to their animal natures, but precisely because they have not yet transcended those natures and achieved their full humanity. Hegel had distinguished between the realm of necessity and the realm of freedom. Lukács further historicized that distinction, drawing out all its political, cultural, and social consequences. The moment when the working class becomes conscious of itself as a historical agent would represent a radical "turning in the direction of something qualitatively new," a leap into the realm of freedom.[83]

Lukács argued that capitalism exerts so much force over people's lives because it too obeys seemingly natural laws. Its continued dominance depends on everyone remaining unconscious and passive with respect to supply and demand, profit rates, investment strategies, and so on. Seen from this historico-philosophical perspective, *Homo economicus* emerges as an animal species fated to dominate and be dominated. By contrast, conscious action, or praxis, opens up the realm of freedom. As Lukács defined it, world revolution would defy the very laws of nature. It could never happen gradually or inevitably, as some evolutionary socialists such as Bernstein believed. Here Lukács abandoned his earlier leftism. Spontaneous mass action, he now argued, provides just as little guarantee of revolutionary success as waiting for capitalism to collapse on its own. Between the voluntarist utopia of mass spontaneity and the crude empiricism of Social Democracy there hovered a third option: the conscious action of a revolutionary vanguard.[84]

---

82. Lichtheim hinted at such a resemblance in *George Lukács* (75), and Lukács himself devoted an entire book to the subject: *Young Hegel*.

83. Lukács, *History and Class Consciousness*, 250. On Lukács's concept of newness in that book, see Kavoulakos, *Georg Lukács's Philosophy of Praxis*, 185–97 and 221–22.

84. Lukács, *History and Class Consciousness*, 77.

One of the most controversial parts of the book concerned the origin of class consciousness. True consciousness of the social totality, Lukács argued, can never develop automatically in the most oppressed sectors of the population. The proletariat certainly is aware of everyday exploitation—poor working conditions, low wages, unfair laws—but that awareness functions merely as a partial, empirically given consciousness. It even can become false consciousness if coupled with the dominant ideology of the ruling class (e.g., anti-union attitudes among workers today who believe in everyone's "right to work"). Only Marxist method, Lukács insisted, can reveal the systemic injustice of capitalism and the historical necessity of its overthrow. Essentially, the proletariat needs the guidance of Marxist intellectuals and advanced workers organized in a party elite. Revolutionary and therefore true consciousness is ascribed or imputed (*zugerechnet*) to the working class through culture and education. Ideology thus played a more active role in Lukács's book than was typical for orthodox Marxist analyses of the superstructure. Culture, interpreted as conscious action or praxis, would provide the tool for breaking through the second nature of existing social relations.

The problem of organization continued to dominate his thinking about the leftist dilemma. The book's first essay—"What Is Orthodox Marxism?"—featured heavily revised passages from a 1919 article of the same name. This essay explored the relationship between class consciousness and correct action. The failure of the Central European revolutions indicated to Lukács that a serious disjuncture had arisen between theory and practice. He distinguished between the demystifying effect of Marxist method and the leftist commitment to revolutionary purity. "Every attempt to rescue the 'ultimate goal' or the 'essence' of the proletariat from every impure contact with—capitalist—existence," he wrote, "leads ultimately to the same remoteness from reality, from 'practical, critical activity' and to the same relapse into the utopian dualism of subject and object, of theory and practice to which [Social Democracy] has succumbed."[85] In their insistence on pure forms, leftists had given up on the task of reconciling theory and practice.

His most direct reckoning with leftism came in his critique of Luxemburg, the Polish-German theorist and revolutionary martyr. In *The Mass Strike* (1906) and her various essays on Bolshevism, Luxemburg interpreted revolutions as the most radical links in a historical chain of mass actions that included labor strikes, protests, and also voting in elections. In most respects, the mass movement was more important to her than any revolutionary party. Against anarcho-syndicalists like Sorel who believed in an eternal myth of the

---

85. Lukács, *History and Class Consciousness*, 13 and 22. In a footnote to this passage he cited Lenin's *"Left-Wing" Communism* (26n38).

general strike, and against Bolsheviks like Lenin who favored the imposition of a vanguardist cadre party, she defended the concrete history of grassroots democracy. She excoriated the Bolshevik tendency toward authoritarian control. Proletarian democracy required multiparty rule by all sectors of the working class, she believed, including Mensheviks, Social-Revolutionaries, anarchists, and other lefts.[86]

Despite his praise for her sophisticated theory of imperialism, Lukács took issue with Luxemburg's views on the Russian Revolution. Because she had overestimated the maturity of the Russian industrial proletariat at the time of the revolution (and underestimated the peasants and other nonproletarian strata), her analysis supposedly ignored "*the role of the party* in the revolution and of its conscious political action, as opposed to the necessity of being driven along by the elemental forces of economic development."[87] According to Lukács, in other words, she had put too much faith in the spontaneity of the workers. The Bolsheviks knew better, and that explained why they erected a tutelary party dictatorship. In portraying Luxemburg as an advocate of pure forms, Lukács might have projected his past leftist identity onto her in order to distance himself from it. He was now the revolutionary adult in the room.[88]

Lukács wrestled with Luxemburg's ideas perhaps because he still felt ambivalent about the leftist dilemma of sustaining new forms. The Communist Party was a bitter pill to swallow. *History and Class Consciousness* was a cursed book because its author expressed potentially anti-Communist (or anti-Stalinist) arguments in Leninist terms. Out from behind certain passages shone the youthful élan of Lukács's leftism from previous years. But "the continuous regrouping of revolutionary energies," he now specified, had to occur within the framework of the Communist Party. The new era of world revolution had thrown everything into flux, so the party had to embody, so to speak, two physical states at once: fluid and fixed. Had Luxemburg lived longer, he concluded, she too would have recognized "her mistaken view . . . of the structure and function of the revolutionary party itself."[89] One can only speculate.

Lukács's essay "Reification and the Consciousness of the Proletariat" was the book's longest, and it consisted of all new material. Its payoff was the idea that a restoration of objects and human beings to their authentic status as

86. Rosa Luxemburg, "The Russian Revolution" [1918], in *Rosa Luxemburg Reader*, 281–310.

87. Lukács, "Critical Observations on Rosa Luxemburg's 'Critique of the Russian Revolution'" [1922], in *History and Class Consciousness*, 272–94 (at 274–75).

88. Lukács, 276–77.

89. Lukács, 292–93.

living processes within a social totality must involve permanent revolution and self-reflection. Only through a constant reworking of revolutionary forms can we resist the reification (thingification) that results from modern bureaucracy and the commodity market.[90] Reification threatens all forms of organization. The uniquely flexible form of the Communist Party arose in response to capitalist reification. The party constantly alters its theory and tactics, Lukács claimed, seeking to counteract processes of reification within its own ranks. But even so, given the tragedy of culture, "these tendencies will necessarily persist." Did he foresee the future of Communist degeneration under Stalin? He did observe that "the requirements of purposeful action . . . compel the Party to introduce the division of labour to a considerable degree and this inevitably invokes the dangers of ossification, bureaucratization and corruption." If the danger of internal ossification were ignored, then the party would devolve into "a hierarchy of officials isolated from the mass or ordinary members who are normally given the role of passive onlookers." Alienated members would then develop "a certain indifference composed equally of blind trust and apathy with regard to the day-to-day actions of the leadership."[91] Precisely that feeling of alienation from bureaucratic leadership would catalyze future new lefts.

The anti-Communist potential of such passages put Lukács in hot water. In 1924 he tried to prove his Communist bona fides by publishing a laudatory book on Lenin. Its central concept was the actuality of revolution, or Lenin's interpretation of all events from the perspective of the coming world revolution. The revolution will never develop organically, Lukács explained, so an awareness of its actuality means recognizing the need for a disciplined party that can incubate the still immature proletariat.[92] On its own, the fragmented working class can neither perceive the actuality of the revolution nor sustain spontaneous action. The revolution will always be premature. "If events had to be delayed until the proletariat entered the decisive struggle united and clear in its aims," he argued, "there would never be a revolutionary situation." The independent organization of the party both prepared for the revolution and accelerated the proletariat's maturation.[93] More clearly than in *History and Class Consciousness*, Lukács in this book came out in favor of Lenin over Luxemburg. He even defended what he called revolutionary realpolitik, or a pragmatism guided by the actuality of revolution rather than existing power

90. Lukács, "Reification and the Consciousness of the Proletariat," in *History and Class Consciousness*, 83–222 (at 197).

91. Lukács, "Towards a Methodology of the Problem of Organisation," in *History and Class Consciousness*, 295–342 (at 335–37).

92. Lukács, *Lenin*, 26–27.

93. Lukács, 29–32.

relations. His defense of Lenin boiled down to the need for extending Soviet power by any means necessary, even if that meant making peace with a leader like Stalin.[94]

Despite his newfound loyalty to the Soviet Union, Lukács would always retain a leftist appreciation of form. He went on to write multiple books about classical realism in literature, appropriating what later would be called the Western canon for the project of Soviet civilization. In terms of politics, his inner leftist went underground in the mid-1920s. The scholar Michael Löwy has interpreted Lukács's revolutionary realpolitik as marking the end of his period of youthful rebellion, a middle-aged reckoning with reality.

The mid-1920s indeed gave European revolutionaries a strong dose of reality: a string of defeats followed by the apparent stabilization of global capitalism. "The ebbing of the revolutionary tide, and the internal changes in the USSR after 1924," Löwy wrote, "caused a profound and distressing disillusionment in Lukács, as in many intellectuals of that era." Löwy concluded that his writings from the mid-1920s onward, "despite their intelligence, their undeniable interest, and their theoretical depth, are rather like the glowing embers of a dying furnace."[95] Aside from a few bold moments such as his 1925 essay on Ferdinand Lassalle, his 1926 essay on Moses Hess, his 1928 Blum Theses, and his unpublished manuscript "Tailism and the Dialectic," Lukács's mature literary criticism exuded the stale odor of convention and subservience to Moscow.[96] Under pressure from the party, he disowned *History and Class Consciousness* as a revisionist work. As one historian put it, such unending equivocations and dramatic recantations were "the price he paid for the privilege of continued participation in a movement whose controllers regarded him with unconcealed distrust."[97]

Flashes on the Horizon

Barely, Lukács managed to survive the Stalinist purges of the 1930s, World War II, the postwar purges, and the failed Hungarian Revolution of 1956. Only in 1968, not too long before his death, did he again stoke the furnace of leftism

---

94. Georg Lukács, "Revolutionary Realpolitik," in *Lenin*, 72–88. See Isaac Nakhimovsky, "Georg Lukács, Revolutionary Realpolitik, and the History of Political Thought," forthcoming in *Journal of the History of Ideas.*

95. Löwy, *Georg Lukács*, 205–6.

96. The first three are translated in *Tactics and Ethics*, 147–77, 181–223, and 227–53. A translation of the fourth appeared under the title *A Defence of "History and Class Consciousness": Tailism and the Dialectic.*

97. Lichtheim, *George Lukács*, 72. For an unsympathetic account of Lukács's relationship to Stalinism, see David Pike, *Lukács and Brecht* (Chapel Hill: University of North Carolina Press, 1985).

while observing the youth rebellions that swept across Europe. Debate over his legacy continues to this day. In 2017 the Budapest City Council decided to remove his statue from a park, and in 2018 the right-wing government of Viktor Orbán effectively shut down the Lukács Archive.[98]

Lukács was certainly not the only Western Marxist to face the leftist dilemma of sustaining new forms. Sorel, for example, had written about a socialist renaissance in his book *The Decomposition of Marxism* (1908), and he considered himself and his associates part of a new school of Marxist science. Antonio Gramsci and several other bright Italian socialists founded the journal *L'Ordine Nuovo* (The new order) in 1919, and for a while they advocated a leftist form of council communism. "I want every morning to be a New Year's Day for me," Gramsci memorably wrote. "Every day I want to reckon with myself, and every day I want to renew myself."[99]

The person whose confrontation with leftism and newness most resembled and challenged Lukács's own was Karl Korsch. In his book *Marxism and Philosophy* (1923), Korsch had independently come to many of the same conclusions as Lukács about the failings of Social Democracy as well as the Hegelian core of Marxist method. The new revolutionary era, Korsch argued, had redeemed Marxism by reuniting theory and practice. Like Lukács for a time, he was an avid leftist, participating in the Berlin factory council movement. Orthodox Communists condemned *Marxism and Philosophy* together with *History and Class Consciousness* as the work of revisionist professors.[100] But Korsch persisted longer in his leftism, eventually siding with the renegade Communist bloc around Bordiga and opposing the Stalinization of the German Communist Party (KPD). He was expelled from the KPD in 1926, not willing to swallow the bitter pill of recantation required for continued membership.

For my purposes, Lukács is paradigmatic for the type of engaged intellectual who gravitated toward new lefts. His synthesis of radical aesthetics and politics provides a framework for understanding why later neoleftists would

98. G. M. Tamás, "The Never-Ending Lukács Debate," *Los Angeles Review of Books*, March 6, 2017, https://lareviewofbooks.org/article/the-never-ending-lukacs-debate/, and Róbert Nárai, "Save the Lukács Archives!" petition on *change.org*, n.d., accessed June 2018, https://www.change.org/p/hungarian-academy-of-sciences-save-the-luk%C3%A1cs-archives-from-liquidation.

99. Antonio Gramsci, "I Hate New Year's Day" [1916], trans. Alberto Toscano, *Viewpoint Magazine*, January 1, 2015. See also the series of essays by Gramsci on the council system, "Soviets in Italy."

100. Fred Halliday, "Karl Korsch: An Introduction" [1970], in Korsch, *Marxism and Philosophy*, 7–26 (at 15–17).

obsess over the formal problem of organization. But Lukács and his generation, born roughly around 1890 and socialized in war and revolution, continued to act out scenes in the twilight drama of the old left: revolution or reform,
class contra class, and progress versus reaction. Leftism was the most radical
subplot to arise from that drama, but few members of that generation pursued
it for longer than a brief romance. In the mid-1920s, after several years of organizational loosening, official Communist and Social Democratic parties again
tightened their control over left politics. However, Lukács and his generation's
experiment with leftism, their attempt to politically realize and sustain a new
culture, and their actual experience of revolution provided a reference point
for a younger generation that would coalesce into the antifascist new left.

2

The Antifascist New Left

NEVER A MONOLITH, historical antifascism encompassed diverse individuals and groups. The prefix "anti" suggests that it denoted only a negative unity: against Italian Fascism, against German Nazism, and against the smaller fascist regimes and movements that cropped up everywhere in the 1920s and 1930s. "There was more than one antifascist trajectory," the historian Anson Rabinbach has noted, and indeed any history of antifascism must account for the great diversity of political currents that came under its banner.[1]

Roughly speaking, there were two main currents. The first and by far the largest was the Popular Front. That big-tent coalition brought together liberals, moderate Christians and conservatives, Social Democrats, and Communists. Popular Front governments formed in France and Spain, and despite its instrumental Communist origins, that current succeeded for a time in mobilizing the masses against the fascist threat. Besides politics, the Popular Front garnered widespread cultural appeal across the world.[2]

The second current one might call alternative antifascisms. Practitioners ranged from religious socialists to libertarian anarchists. Although divergent on social policy, alternative antifascists agreed on the chief flaw of the Popular Front—namely, its inclusion of Communists. They objected to the official Communist interpretation of fascism, which reduced that complex political and social phenomenon to a mere function of capitalist class interests. This chapter analyzes several alternative antifascist groups that fused into a new left. Whether by splintering or newly combining, small left groups proliferated on the margins of mainstream parties from the late 1920s through the mid-1930s.[3] Their members included workers, intellectuals, and worker-intellectuals. Their

---

1. Rabinbach, "Legacies of Antifascism," 10. See also Hobsbawm, "Era of Anti-fascism."

2. For example, see Michael Denning, *The Cultural Front: The Laboring of American Culture in the Twentieth Century* (London: Verso, 1998).

3. Rabinbach, "Paris, Capital of Antifascism," 184.

grassroots efforts to organize left unity and develop more sophisticated theories of fascism helped define a new left, perhaps even the first new left.[4]

Unlike the leftists described in the first chapter, these radical antifascists broke decisively with the organizational forms of Social Democracy and Communism: the democratic working-class party and the vanguardist cadre party, respectively. Radical antifascists were young rebels without a party. The revolution championed by this antifascist new left went beyond established politics and labor militancy to encompass sex, culture, and everyday life. Convinced that beating fascism required a total revolution of all spheres of life, it created a subculture of defiance that would persist even after World War II. Looking ahead, Rabinbach claimed that "the 'literary underground' of the student movement"—i.e., the pirated books that would inspire the sixties New Left—drew on an "antifascist culture that existed from the 1930s to the 1970s."[5] The radical tradition that made postwar new lefts possible originated in that crucial period between the rise of fascism and the onset of World War II.

While the antifascist new left experienced itself as a new left, it did not call itself by that name. The label refers to my own analytic concept of neoleftism. An affect and explicit rhetoric of "new beginning" nonetheless inspired the many small groups that germinated during the interwar years. The zigzag course of Soviet foreign policy bewildered many European Communists, and the Social Democratic parties that participated in government coalitions often failed to generate enthusiasm among rank-and-file members. Social Democracy's toleration of conservative and blatantly antidemocratic forces during that era disillusioned many of its followers. Space opened up in between the two major parties of the working class for experiments in sui generis anarchism and revolutionary socialism. After 1933, when fascism grew from an isolated Italian phenomenon into a general European threat, those experimental small groups such as New Beginning in and beyond Germany, Socialist Battle in France, Justice and Liberty (GL) in exile from Italy, and the Left Book Club in Britain coalesced into a loose neoleftist network. Their members forged transnational ties and exchanged ideas about strategy. These groups "sought to escape the sclerosis of the big political parties."[6] It was through their network that farsighted ideas entered the domain of left politics, such as

4. For a different chronology, cf. Kenny, *First New Left*. I care less about establishing the priority of one new left or another than about defining midcentury neoleftism as a general phenomenon.

5. Rabinbach, "Legacies of Antifascism," 14. On the return of antifascist rhetoric in the 1960s, see Mercer, "Specters of Fascism."

6. Droz, *Histoire de l'antifascisme en Europe*, 10. All translations are mine unless otherwise noted.

psychoanalysis and sexual liberation. Against the backdrop of rising fascism and global economic meltdown, the years around 1930 witnessed an astounding collapse of the European workers' movement. Unexpectedly, that dire moment expanded the creative frontiers of left theory and practice. Crisis provoked innovation as the major parties loosened their hold over organization on the left.

There are many detailed studies of each country's native antifascist movements. Moreover, the variation between antifascisms in Germany, France, Italy, Spain, Britain, Eastern Europe, and so on might undermine the usefulness of the concept. Like fascism itself, antifascism appears as "a phenomenon simultaneously one and many."[7] Analyzing even a specific tendency like the antifascist new left faces the same difficulty. Rather than provide a comprehensive account, I will illustrate this brand of radical antifascism by focusing on one salient case.

A German group emerged around 1930 that embodied the ethos and style of the antifascist new left. Its particular history was both representative and generative of European new lefts. In the wake of the global economic collapse and the precipitous rise of the Nazi Party, a faction of Marxist intellectuals began meeting in Berlin. Called the Org, this faction emerged out of a discussion circle of ex-Communists who had either resigned or been expelled from the party for opposing Stalinism. These mavericks considered themselves more revolutionary than the Social Democrats but more realistic than the Communists. They claimed to conspire for socialist unity, but their aims would require the German and international left to move in a decidedly new direction. An underground pamphlet titled *Neu beginnen!* appeared in the fall of 1933, which described a process of socialist renewal that would replace the defunct ideas and leaders of the old workers' movement. The pamphlet propagated the group's vision of a grassroots antifascist revolution in Europe led by the young generation.

Quality, Not Quantity

On a summer day two years later, Berlin police responded to a call about two large suitcases that had washed up on the shore of the Müggelsee, a lake in the city's eastern suburbs. When they pried them open, they found reams of paper: personnel files, situation reports, meeting minutes, subversive Marxist literature. Some of it was encrypted in arcane numerical code. A few stones

---

7. Droz, *Histoire de l'antifascisme*, 7–9. On the problem of defining antifascism's positive content, see Copsey, "New Anti-fascist 'Minimum'?"

inside suggested that someone had tried to sink the suitcases. After analyzing the soaked documents, Nazi authorities concluded that they must be the records of an apparently vast underground resistance network called New Beginning.

The secret police overestimated New Beginning's size, but not its disproportionate influence at the time. Its origins as the Org only make sense in the context of the German left's fraught history since the end of World War I. Revolution had broken out in November 1918 and yielded Germany's first democracy, the Weimar Republic. But the price paid for democracy was dear. On the far left of the workers' movement, the Spartacus League had tried to steer the revolution toward communism, emulating the Bolsheviks in Russia. Its former comrades in the German Social Democratic Party (SPD) joined with the liberal, Catholic Center, and moderate conservative parties to stop the revolution before it went too far. The League, which laid the foundation for the KPD, called a general strike in January 1919 but suffered a mortal blow when right-wing soldiers of the paramilitary Free Corps assassinated its leaders Rosa Luxemburg and Karl Liebknecht. Gustav Noske, the SPD minister of defense, had unleashed the Free Corps to crush the revolution. In the years that followed, German Communists would never forgive their siblings in the SPD for that betrayal. Combined with the loss of the war, the resulting economic breakdown, and the traditional advancement of German socialism relative to movements in other countries, the intensity of this fratricidal conflict made Germany a cradle of European new lefts.

After his discharge from the army, the twenty-two-year-old Berlin native Walter Loewenheim joined the Spartacus League and acquired a leading post in its affiliated Free Socialist Youth. The failed general strike in January 1919 only intensified his commitment to communism, so he joined the League's successor, the KPD, and became active in its youth organization. In the early 1920s, Loewenheim visited Moscow as a delegate to the youth division of the Communist International (Comintern). But the relationship between German Communists and their Russian comrades was unstable. The Bolsheviks exercised ever-greater control over the Comintern's member parties. Most German Communists complied enthusiastically, but a minority within the KPD grew restless with Moscow's overbearing attitude.[8] Among the leaders of that disaffected minority was Paul Levi, whom the party expelled in 1921 for opposing its ill-considered putsch attempt, the March Action. Loewenheim considered Levi his mentor. He followed Levi's example and quit the party in

---

8. On the tense relationship between the early KPD and the Comintern, see Epstein, *Last Revolutionaries*, ch. 1, and Weitz, *Creating German Communism*, ch. 2.

1927 out of frustration at its strategy of splitting off left-wing elements from the SPD. The two men agreed that this splitting policy further divided the workers' movement at a historical moment that demanded unity.[9]

Over the next few years, Loewenheim conceived of a clandestine organization that might heal the divisions in the workers' movement. That organization crystallized in late 1929 following the Wall Street Crash and the rapid global fallout. Revolutionary hope again fired up the formerly disillusioned ex-Communists in Loewenheim's milieu—what one scholar has called a "subculture on the left" inhabiting a new political landscape.[10] Capitalism seemed to have entered a new crisis period of unforeseeable duration. Now was the time to deploy a group of professional revolutionaries who could unite the working class without asking for the party leaders' permission. A unified workers' movement had to act while the Western democracies faltered. If revolutionary socialists did not seize power, Loewenheim feared, then fascists surely would. Across the capitalist countries of Europe and North America, the winter months of 1929–30 were marked by a profound sense of crisis.[11] For radicals like Loewenheim, that took the form of an urgent decision between two mutually exclusive options: socialism or fascism. Belief in that critical choice provided a major impetus behind the antifascist new left across Europe.

Loewenheim, his younger brother Ernst, and Ernst's first wife Traute Kahn gathered together a few like-minded militants in Berlin. All were born roughly between 1895 and 1905 and most had once belonged to the KPD. A few had also belonged to the Communist Party–Opposition (KPO) led by the renegades Heinrich Brandler and August Thalheimer.[12] They called themselves the Leninist Organization, or the Org for short. Over the next three years before the Nazi takeover, the Org recruited intensively from left youth groups and disgruntled factions of both major workers' parties. It was small, hardly exceeding one hundred core members, a few hundred peripheral members, and perhaps one thousand sympathizers. (By comparison, the KPO had three to four thousand members.) One-third of the core were proletarian workers, another third salaried employees, and the rest intellectuals: students,

---

9. See Charlotte Beradt, *Paul Levi. Ein demokratischer Sozialist in der Weimarer Republik* (Frankfurt am Main: Europäische Verlagsanstalt, 1969).

10. Cox, *Circles of Resistance*, 34.

11. R. Graf and Föllmer, "Culture of 'Crisis.'" Cf. Tobias Straumann, who has argued that the real crisis for the German economy started in 1931 with the collapse of the Austrian bank Creditanstalt. Straumann, *1931: Debt, Crisis, and the Rise of Hitler* (Oxford: Oxford University Press, 2019).

12. The KPO represented the right wing of the Communist Party because it advocated compromises with Social Democrats and bourgeois parties during the Comintern's uncompromising Third Period (1928–34). See Bergmann, *"Gegen den Strom."*

academics, and journalists. About 80 percent were male and 35 percent Jewish, and in 1933 they averaged twenty-eight years old. The demographic profile of the Org basically matched the composition of the antifascist new left emerging across Europe: mostly male, disproportionately Jewish, and young.

For guidance, the Org turned to Lenin's pamphlet *What Is to Be Done?* (1902). The choice of that particular work meant that, at least initially, Org members identified more with the conspiratorial Lenin of the prerevolutionary period than the insurgent Lenin of *The State and Revolution* (1917) or the ruling Lenin of *"Left-Wing" Communism* (1920).[13] Spontaneous action by the masses, Lenin had written in 1902, always resulted in populist demagoguery or bourgeois democracy, not socialism. Reading this around 1930, the Org convinced itself that German workers would never rise up automatically in revolution against a reactionary conservative regime. Bourgeois ideology's hold over them was too strong. A perception of tightening authoritarian control, even within working-class organizations, explains why the nascent Org compared its own situation in late Weimar Germany to that of socialists in late tsarist Russia.

Only professional revolutionaries, or those who made revolution their full-time occupation, could accomplish the grand historical task confronting the proletariat. For Lenin, everyday oppression under tsarist autocracy had meant that professional revolutionaries had to work underground. He recognized that an illegal socialist organization had to be small and recruit its members carefully, quipping that "it is far more difficult to catch a dozen wise men than it is to catch a hundred fools."[14] Quality therefore took precedence over quantity—a distinctive marker of new lefts to come.

An important difference between Lenin's situation in 1902 and the German situation in 1930 was that a Communist Party already existed that claimed to operate according to Lenin's principles. Loewenheim responded by creating a new Leninist organization for the fascist era. The earliest theories of the Org claimed that Communists had lost sight of both Marx's method of historical materialism and Lenin's principles of organization. Loewenheim thought that the Comintern parties had succumbed to bourgeois ideology just as much as the Social Democrats. The Org thus turned Lenin's 1902 critique back against existing Communists.[15] Now they were the fools who believed in the spontaneity of the masses and the voluntarist power of a cadre party to force

13. See chapter 1 and also Kliem, "Der sozialistische Widerstand gegen das Dritte Reich," endnote 34.

14. V. I. Lenin, "What Is to Be Done?" in *Essential Works of Lenin*, 147.

15. Kurt Menz [Walter Loewenheim], "Die proletarische Revolution: Allgemeine Grundzüge ihrer Theorie und ihrer Besonderheiten in Deutschland" [ca. 1930], in Loewenheim, *Geschichte der Org*, 35–67.

historical change regardless of objective conditions. The Russian Revolution was a great success for the international left, the Org freely admitted, but it was only the first step. Echoing Georg Lukács's leftist interpretation of the Hungarian Soviet Republic and drawing on Karl Mannheim's ideology critique, Loewenheim claimed that a new revolution in Germany would supersede the Russian original.

The left reorganization that Loewenheim had in mind excluded any tactic that might further divide or politically isolate the workers' movement. In fact, the early Org tried to convince members of other factions to rejoin either the Communists or the Social Democrats. Conceiving of itself as an antiparty that sought only to create conditions for its own dissolution, the Org formulated a long-term solution to the leftist dilemma. Slowly, over many years, Org infiltrators would occupy key positions within the two major parties of the left and convert their functionaries to the cause of left unity. Theoretically, this process would achieve unity neither from the top down nor the bottom up, but the middle out. It involved nothing less than co-opting the existing parties. Divergent goals and ideology aside, this approach resembled the Trotskyist tactic of entryism. Thus, at first, the Org did not propose anything like a horizontalist, decentralized, or grassroots solution to the problem of party bureaucracy. It wanted to capture the existing party bureaucracies and redirect them toward its desired end of left unity. The Org's original plan was elitist and top secret.

Even when the Org shifted its priority to antifascist resistance in 1932–33, it continued to conceal its existence from Communists, Social Democrats, and Nazis alike. Conspiracy, Loewenheim emphasized, must precede all other considerations, or else the Org would end up exposed and stigmatized as just another splinter group with a particular agenda. The first phase of the Org's history involved a structural transformation of the old left from within. Org members did not yet desire a new left outside of the old parties. Midcentury neoleftism often started as a frustrated effort at internal reform.

Following Lenin's principles of organization, the Org consisted of multiple five-person cadres that carried out practical tasks and served as miniforums for critical debate. The rules of conspiracy allowed only the leader of each group of five access to the central Org circle. Outside the cadres an assortment of loosely organized peripheral members would provide the Org with intelligence, meeting space, and respectable cover stories. But the peripheral members themselves possessed only partial knowledge of the Org's master plan. The periphery functioned as a buffer zone between the fully initiated core and the uninitiated public.[16]

16. See Simmel, "Sociology of Secrecy," 489.

Internally, the Org applied the Leninist principle of democratic centralism. Loewenheim explained that "before our comrades' own creative activity should be posed . . . as few organizational and bureaucratic barriers as possible." Inside the Org should reign the "freest intellectual democracy," but externally it should act as one disciplined unit.[17] Already this basic principle contained a contradiction between the organization's need for stability and the danger of bureaucratic sclerosis. Org cadres frequently debated whether the core and periphery should expand or contract. Tension between the Org leaders' authoritarian desire to control members' creativity and the members' internally democratic desire for consensus would soon reach a breaking point.

Educating the Org/New Beginning

In 1930, Loewenheim and friends met in a summer cottage near the S-Bahn train station Berlin-Karlshorst for the first meeting of what would become the Org's primary training mechanism: the Advanced Course (*Fortgeschrittener Kursus*), also known as the F-Course. Besides Loewenheim (alias Kurt Menz), this first meeting, known as F1, consisted of Otto Sperling (alias Funk), Walter Dupré (alias Hans Pohl), Erich Busse (alias Starke), Kurt Ziebart (alias Rechlin), and Paul Klapper (alias Lange).[18] All were former members of the KPO who, following the Org conception, had rejoined one of the major workers' parties. In this case, it was the SPD. They averaged a few years younger than the original cohort that Loewenheim had assembled in late 1929.[19] Subsequent F-Courses drew in members from the SPD, KPD, trade unions, and splinter groups. Nonproletarian or unaffiliated intellectuals could participate too, so long as they met the Org's strict standards of recruitment. All core members of the Org had to enroll in an F-Course, which provided them a modern revolutionary catechism.

The F-Course lasted sixteen to eighteen evening sessions, which could take anywhere from three to four months to complete (the average length of a college semester). Having developed from a more elementary course called "A Gallop through History," the F-Course curriculum covered Marx's method of historical materialism; the history of bourgeois revolutions in Europe; the history of Social Democracy and the Second International; the development of Lenin's ideas and their realization by the Bolsheviks; the limitations of Soviet Communism; the history of the SPD and the KPD since World War I; an

17. Menz [Loewenheim], "Die proletarische Revolution," 63.
18. Recollection of Otto Sperling in Sandvoß, *Die "andere" Reichshauptstadt*, 227–28.
19. Sandvoß, 227n182.

analysis of electoral democracy in the Weimar Republic; and, finally, an over-view of the Org conception and the most pressing political tasks.[20]

Archival copies of agendas for each class session offer some insight into how the F-Course was structured. Each evening the teacher or discussion leader (often Loewenheim incognito) would present the material in question-and-answer format. For example, one discussion prompt read, "Why did people in bourgeois revolutions pose very similar demands independently of one an-other, and why did they fight without agreeing on a common direction?" The teacher would field answers from students and steer them toward the one cor-rect answer: "Because all individual wills were compelled in the same direction by the same causes (feudal-absolutist lawlessness, etc. . . .)."[21] None of the questions were open-ended. Their prescribed answers followed logically from the total Org conception. Loewenheim wanted to train professional revolu-tionaries who could independently apply the Marxist method, but not think outside the box. To think freely, in the colloquial sense, meant to fall back into bourgeois habits. Revolution required disciplined thought.

If agendas in the archive represent the teacher's perspective, then memoirs offer something like retrospective course evaluations from the students' per-spective. Erich Schmidt (alias Richter, alias Kirchner), a young printer who joined the Org in the summer of 1931, recalled what he learned:

> Complicated processes of ideology formation dependent on bourgeois soci-ety were considered chief factors for the failure of the workers' movement—of both the reformist SPD as well as the subjectivist KPD. . . . Salvation can only occur through the (at first necessary) conspiratorial activity in both workers' parties, which have been fatally paralyzed by their division.[22]

Schmidt appreciated the course's use of ideology critique against currents on the left, not only against social classes that upheld capitalism. Loewenheim wanted to turn militant workers and intellectuals into revolutionaries. He chipped away at their "anti-Leninist reservations" by subjecting them to au-thoritarian discipline and a self-contained doctrine. Schmidt's generally posi-tive evaluation indicates that he was willing to subject himself to that disci-pline. But here we see a paradox within the Org: By adhering to Marxist method as prescribed by Loewenheim, members of the group were "forced to be free" of their bourgeois preconceptions. Through theoretical rigor and ra-tional discipline, the Org believed that it could build cadres that would

20. F-Course materials are located in IISG, NB Archives, 62–79.

21. "Alter F., A[bend] I," IISG, NB Archives, 63/1.

22. Erich Schmidt, *Meine Jugend in Groß-Berlin*, 142.

eventually unify the German workers' movement. Only a united movement would produce the new ideas and leaders necessary to beat fascism.

During her initiation in 1933, Julia Rahmer (alias Lilly) heard that the F-Course was "something rather special—an intellectual experience and a kind of promotion into the inner ranks" of the Org.[23] Another initiate, Gerhard Bry (alias Paul Kemp, alias Bauman), was twenty years old when he joined. He recalled the effect of the course: "in the depth of the Great Depression and in the face of the helplessness of the democratic system and its labor components, the message was electrifying. Here was new thought, new organization, new hope, a new beginning."[24] For Schmidt, Rahmer, Bry, and others, voluntary discipline within the Org in accordance with its guiding conception provided a sense of rational control over a chaotic situation.

Sometimes the older or more experienced students did not play by the classroom rules. Bry remembered his amazement at discovering that one of his classmates was none other than Karl Frank (alias Fred, alias Willi Müller), whom he recognized as "a living legend in parts of the radical labor movement."[25] Frank had taken part in numerous exploits over the years, starting with the antiwar protest letter he sent to Emperor Franz Joseph while serving as an artillery lieutenant in the Austro-Hungarian Army. He was discharged for "health" reasons. During the 1920s he wrote for various Communist journals, including the Austrian edition of *Die Rote Fahne*. In 1928, after having moved to Berlin, he orchestrated the kidnapping of an SPD official scheduled to deliver a radio address about world peace so that a KPD functionary could deliver a counteraddress denouncing German naval rearmament instead. Following the incident he went to jail and staged a hunger strike until his release, this time truly for health reasons. Handsome, intelligent, and courageous, Frank was said to possess more charisma than the entire Org leadership combined. In Bry's recollection he was "the only member in the F-Course who questioned some of the basic tenets of the new organization."[26] Frank would soon prove more than Loewenheim could handle.

Understandably, the F-Course impressed younger initiates the most. But they too sometimes questioned the dogmatic tenor of the curriculum. Rahmer had an unpleasant experience. She recalled that her teacher Loewenheim spoke "in a very authoritative manner and at breathtaking speed. It soon became clear that he did not like to be interrupted." While Richard Löwenthal

---

23. Julia Rahmer, "Some Reminiscences and Reflections about Neu Beginnen," IISG, NB Archives, 83/1. Her husband Bernd Rahmer was also a member of the Org.

24. Bry, *Resistance*, 38.

25. Bry, 39.

26. Bry, 43, and Erich Schmidt, *Meine Emigrantenjahre*, 35. See also Renaud, "German Resistance in New York."

(alias Gleich, alias Paul Sering), who had a reputation as a brilliant youth leader, sat there playing "the humble role of student," Rahmer dared to openly disagree with Loewenheim's conclusions. He kicked her out of class. "I was appalled," she remembered. "This was thought-control! One accepted restrictions in one's personal freedom of speech for the sake of our security . . . [b]ut this was a blatant attempt to silence a divergent view! I felt outraged."[27] Even if he did not speak up, the humble student Löwenthal also objected to some of Loewenheim's arguments. Both he and Frank would play central roles in the leadership change that occurred later in 1935. This antifascist new left, like its sixties scion, would start as a student revolt.

In June 1931, the German Communist Youth Association invited the Socialist Worker Youth (SAJ) to an assembly in a music hall near Bülowplatz (today's Rosa-Luxemburg-Platz). This was one of the most densely Communist areas of Berlin. The SAJ leaders accepted the invitation without informing the Berlin SPD executive board, which surely would have forbidden it. The hall was packed with some five hundred Socialist youth, four hundred Communist youth, and numerous KPD stewards who stood along the walls for security. For the SAJ, Erich Schmidt delivered an unexpected speech. The Communists had expected him to defend the Social Democrats' policy of toleration toward the conservative government of Heinrich Brüning. Instead, Schmidt used Marxist arguments to criticize both the SPD and the KPD. Social Democrats were guilty of compromise with the conservative forces of order, he argued. But he faulted Communists for a series of un-Marxist errors since the November Revolution and for alienating Social Democrats, whose mass support they needed for any effective politics. Jeers and shouts of disapproval by the young Communists interrupted the speech, and the crowd averted a brawl only by joining together in a chorus of "The Internationale." Loewenheim and the Org had orchestrated the whole thing, from Schmidt's speech to various interjections by Org claqueurs.

In the SAJ rank and file, the speech's effect was immense. Never before had they heard a critique of Communist politics from a revolutionary Marxist point of view. Social Democrats had only ever offered them reformist platitudes. "Very soon," recalled Schmidt, "our organization became immune to Communist agitation." Almost the entire Berlin SAJ leadership joined the Org, and thereafter thousands of SAJ members unknowingly served the Org's interests. Something like a revolutionary socialist alternative, or indeed a new left, began to take shape in the twilight years of the Weimar Republic.[28]

27. Rahmer, "Some Reminiscences," 13 and 18.

28. Schmidt, *Meine Jugend in Groß-Berlin*, 143–46, and Soell, *Fritz Erler*, 1: 23. See also Walter, *"Republik, das ist nicht viel."* On the variety of currents within the SPD at the end of the Weimar Republic, see Smaldone, *Confronting Hitler*, and Harsch, *German Social Democracy*.

The Org's conspiratorial methods contrasted with the open militancy of, say, Antifascist Action, a Communist-sponsored initiative that began in July 1932. The earliest ancestor of today's Antifa, Antifascist Action promoted the creation of local self-defense committees in working-class neighborhoods. While it did follow the Comintern line of "united fronts from below," which aimed to undermine the "social fascist" leadership of the SPD, Antifascist Action also represented a genuine response to paramilitary violence by fascist gangs.[29] Before 1933, the Org had little interest in mass campaigns or public action of any sort. Its members refrained from violence and open militancy less out of principle than out of loyalty to the Org conception.

By the time the Nazis seized power in January 1933, the Org had built clandestine cells all over Germany, infiltrating the major workers' parties, trade unions, and industrial concerns such as Siemens, Deutsche Reichsbahn, Telefunken, and Bergmann Electrical Works. Later on, Org members managed to infiltrate Nazi organizations such as the Hitler Youth, the brownshirt Storm Detachment, and the Nazi Factory Cell Organization. Besides Loewenheim's brother Ernst (alias Fritz Brill), the leadership circle included the brothers Eberhard and Wolfgang Wiskow, Heinrich Jakubowicz (alias Neumann, alias Henry Hellmann), Walter Dupré (alias Pforten, alias Hans Pohl), and Franz Schleiter (alias Richard). Eberhard Wiskow (alias Heinrich Zahn), a former officer in the German army, oversaw the Org rules of conspiracy.

The Org's multiplication of aliases, which drew on a long conspiratorial tradition, broke the normal chain of connections that the police might use to establish a person's identity. It might also have contributed to the assumption among Org members and Nazi investigators alike that the group comprised many more people than it actually did. Walter Loewenheim multiplied himself a half dozen times: Kurt Menz, Rita, Kurt Berger, Miles, Scipio, and so on. Dissociation, division, and dissemblance constituted the fundamentals of conspiracy.

Conspiracy extended to the management of documents and the arrangement of meetings. According to Bry, Org members:

> learned how to use concealed code in writing and in telephone conversations, shift meeting times and places by pre-arranged rotations that made them different from those agreed upon by phone, arrange for

---

29. See Rosenhaft, *Beating the Fascists?* On the connection between Antifascist Action and the later Antifa movement, see Mark Bray, *Antifa: The Anti-fascist Handbook* (New York: Melville House, 2017).

danger signals, avoid being followed, discover trails, shred carbon and other papers, develop individual codes for telephone numbers or addresses, prepare hiding places, arrange for alibis, and many other tricks of the trade.[30]

The technology of conspiracy ranged from writing messages with lemon juice visible only when ironed hot to the sophisticated, quick-burning, no-residue paper developed for the Org by the chemist and future East German dissident Robert Havemann. Other means included microphotography and "capsules in which undeveloped microfilm could be carried in the mouth and quickly destroyed." But the human element mattered most. Before every meeting, members would perform a five- to ten-minute "Con": a precautionary chat to get the meeting's cover story straight.[31]

Conspiracy meant undertaking a tedious set of preparations for the most mundane tasks. Every contact, every meeting place, every step had to be painstakingly vetted. In keeping with the Org's conception, each move turned into a consciously theorized and deliberate action. Nothing could happen naturally, but to the outside world everything had to seem natural. Members paid attention to the minutiae of everyday life, and especially to how the ruling ideology conditioned unconscious behaviors.

The culture of the Org revolved around constant analysis of and adjustment to changing circumstances. Given the flow of reports, frequency of cadre meetings, and continuous revision of the guiding theory, one wonders when Org members managed to eat, sleep, or relax. All members had to be inconspicuous by holding down regular jobs, going shopping, chatting with neighbors, socializing with friends, and so forth. The leadership monitored every aspect of members' personal lives, adding periodic reports to their personnel files in the Org Archive.

Loewenheim thought of the Org as a grand social experiment. After fifteen years of bitter enmity since the unfinished revolution of 1918–19, Social Democrats and Communists were usually at each other's throats. Within the Org, the two political types learned the advantages of engaging in common discourse and cooperative action. The feeling of camaraderie was like holding a skeleton key to the whole workers' movement. Similarly to the Freemasons, the Org functioned as a place where doors separating people of different class backgrounds were unlocked. There the impressionable youth in particular might experience the coming unity of the socialist revolution, the telos of the

30. Bry, *Resistance*, 53–54.
31. Bry, 54; Bry, 53–54.

Org conception in practice.[32] Neoleftism then and later fostered a solidarity that transcended traditional Social Democratic and Communist identities.

The Org's attention to private lives reached unusual extremes. Loewenheim declared that "a true revolutionary has no private life." Treating the personal as the political, the leadership kept tabs on all members' friendships and sexual relations.[33] Perhaps not surprisingly, a number of marriages resulted between men and women who met in the Org. But the high ratio of men to women (approximately four to one) meant that many Org members had uninitiated partners. The leadership sought to minimize that potential liability through surveillance.

As a consequence of the Org's hierarchical structure and conspiratorial rules, nobody except for those at the top had any real idea about how many people belonged to the organization. Most rank-and-file members tended to exaggerate the Org's size, making estimates in the tens of thousands. This waxing consciousness of size and strength contrasted sharply with Loewenheim's own anxiety about degeneration. Ironically using the same rhetoric as the far right, he described the age of fascist dictatorships as an "era of the spiritual and cultural decline of society, of the growing physical distress of the masses and the moral decay of the ruling classes." Decadence characterized not only society at large but also the organizations of the working class, which according to him would soon be fully exhausted.[34]

This psychology of degeneration and expectation of loss led Loewenheim to abandon all hope for revolution in Germany. The Org required both its members and its founder to put forth a lot of effort for minimal results. One could easily lose one's nerve. Understandably, then, the Org retained its own lawyers as well as an in-house psychoanalyst.[35]

Sex and Fascism

In early 1932, the group experienced a breach of security when it discovered that some of its theories had been leaked to the public. Org member Sergei Feitelberg (alias Werber) had shared his own synthesis of Freudian psychoanalysis and the Org conception with his colleagues outside the Org. This infuriated

---

32. Loewenheim, *Geschichte der Org*, 109–11. Cf. Georg Simmel on the "king's peace" [*Burgfrieden*] that typically reigns within secret societies. "Sociology of Secrecy," 492.

33. Loewenheim, *Geschichte der Org*, 111.

34. Miles [Loewenheim], *Socialism's New Beginning*, 87 and 129. His rhetoric mimicked conservative critiques of modernity by the likes of Oswald Spengler, whose book *The Decline of the West* (1918–22) was enormously popular at the time. Max Nordau's book *Degeneration* (1892) helped found the genre.

35. Bry, *Resistance*, 104–5.

Loewenheim. Besides the fact that Feitelberg had broken the rules of conspiracy, Loewenheim believed that the Freudian drama of human emancipation from within the individual psyche was antithetical to a Marxist conception of social emancipation.

But the Org conception did overlap with psychoanalysis, both in its emphasis on self-criticism and in the type of person that it attracted. The raffish Org member Karl Frank, for example, had studied psychology at the University of Vienna. In 1918, after his discharge from the army, he completed his dissertation "Contributions to the Psychology of Lying" under the supervision of Adolf Stöhr and Alois Höfler. The young Doctor Frank delivered a lecture in 1919 to the Austrian Association for Individual Psychology on "The Partisanship of the Nationally and Racially Superstitious Person."[36] Over subsequent years, he abandoned the study of psychology for journalism and political activism. But later in life, he established a psychoanalytic practice in New York and rekindled his desire to write a book about the irrationality of mass politics. During his years in the Berlin Org, Frank shared an apartment with Siegfried Bernfeld, whom he knew already from his days in the Vienna youth movement. Bernfeld was a leading representative of the Freudian left and a collaborator with Feitelberg.[37]

While Loewenheim resisted any intrusion of psychoanalysis into the Org, it was bound to happen: By the early 1930s, Berlin rivaled Vienna as the capital of experimental psychoanalysis.[38] The Org's own analyst, Edith Jacobson, had explored the new theories then proliferating in Berlin. She attended a seminar at Magnus Hirschfeld's Institute for Sexual Science and received her analytic training from Otto Fenichel at the Berlin Psychoanalytic Institute (BPI). The legacy of Melanie Klein and a private seminar taught there by Anna Freud prompted her to specialize in child psychology. After the Nazi takeover, she remained in Berlin and joined the BPI faculty. She eventually entered the administration despite her Jewish heritage. Jacobson's patients included social workers and kindergarten teachers, and in secret she treated members of the Org.[39]

36. Karl Frank, "Beiträge zur Psychologie der Lüge" (PhD thesis, University of Vienna, 1918). The manuscript was never published and appears to have been lost. However, reader reports by Stöhr and Höfler survive in the archive of the University of Vienna, PH RA 4540 Frank, Karl, 1918.05.16–1918.06.30.

37. Paul Hagen [Karl Frank] to Calvin Hoover (Office of Strategic Services, Washington, DC), July 31, 1942, Hoover, Karl B. Frank Papers, 7/7. On the intersection of Marxism and Freudian psychoanalysis, see Jacoby, *Repression of Psychoanalysis*, and Robinson, *Freudian Left*.

38. See Fuechtner, *Berlin Psychoanalytic*.

39. Schröter, Mühlleitner, and May, "Edith Jacobson." Her name was originally spelled "Jacobssohn."

According to one scholar, the BPI was "a center for progressive psychoanalytic thought that attracted in particular the younger generation of psychoanalysts." For the younger analysts, Fenichel ran the so-called Kids Seminar, which included Jacobson, Bernfeld, the later Frankfurt School luminary Erich Fromm, Annie Pink, and her husband Wilhelm Reich.[40] Its purpose was to elaborate a synthesis of Marxism and Freudian psychoanalysis.

The most creative version of that synthesis emanated from the mind of Reich. His basic concern was to show that erotic, life-affirming impulses are fundamental to human nature. Social structures developed historically to repress sexual desires, and out of that repression arose the aggressive or destructive tendencies characteristic of the authoritarian personality. If Freud had argued that sexual repression was always necessary for culture and social order, then Reich countered that only certain kinds of societies require it: those based on class domination. Sexual misery, like economic misery, had a history.[41] Citing Friedrich Engels's book on the origins of the family and Bronisław Malinowski's studies of matriarchy, Reich historicized the Oedipus complex and claimed that socialism would abolish it along with the patriarchal family. His theory amounted to "a sweeping indictment of the sexual life of civilized man."[42] Sexual freedom is our natural condition, he claimed, so any successful therapy must liberate the libido. He considered the uninhibited orgasm a revolutionary experience that both recalls our original human condition and anticipates the new society to come. Modern alienation, he thought, has as much to do with puritanical morality as it does with class rule. The capitalist economy has its corresponding sexual economy, and a crisis of capitalism would surely occasion a sexual crisis. The only way to overthrow the patriarchy together with capitalism, he claimed in *The Sexual Struggle of the Youth* (1932) and *The Sexual Revolution* (1936), was what later countercultural rebels would call free love.[43] The socialist movement should therefore encourage sexual

40. Fuechtner, *Berlin Psychoanalytic*, 10. Supposedly Frank was romantically involved with Annie Pink just before she married Reich. The Reichs would separate in 1933. Christopher Turner, *Adventures in the Orgasmatron: How the Sexual Revolution Came to America* (New York: Farrar, Straus, and Giroux, 2011), 121–22.

41. Wilhelm Reich, "The Imposition of Sexual Morality" [1932/35], in *Sex-Pol*, 89–249 (at 230–31).

42. Rycroft, *Wilhelm Reich*, 27. Herbert Marcuse later criticized Reich for failing to see the connection between sex instincts and the death drive. Reich's theory of sexual liberation struck him as "a sweeping primitivism" and an undifferentiated "panacea for individual and social ills." Marcuse, *Eros and Civilization*, 239.

43. One biographer claimed that "the contemporary slogan Make Love Not War . . . contains Reich in a nutshell." Rycroft, *Wilhelm Reich*, 30. Dagmar Herzog wrote something similar: "No

rebellion among the working-class youth. Reich believed that the young generation would always "represent the next step of civilization."[44]

Loewenheim considered psychoanalysis a bad moral influence on the Org probably because of this Reichian association with sexual freedom.[45] Yet he and Reich shared many characteristics. Both focused on "seemingly irrelevant everyday habits" and insisted that for revolutionary socialists, the personal is political.[46] And both believed in the real possibility of a world without domination, while at the same time displaying a domineering impulse in their own personalities.[47] Such an ironic link between anti-authoritarian goals and authoritarian leadership would often become visible over time, as neoleftist movements hardened into dogmatic sects.

Jacobson was a close friend of the Reichs. She worked with Wilhelm at his sex counseling clinic in Berlin-Charlottenburg, where she offered advice to working-class clients. The idea behind Reich's German Association for Proletarian Sexual Politics (Sex-Pol) was "to unite several sexual-reform movements into a sex-political organization under the aegis" of the Communist Party. Reich believed that a sex-affirmative ideology might even convert Christian and Nazi youth to the Communist cause, because young people everywhere wanted to have sex and talk about it. That desire lent itself to pathological rebellion, he admitted. But through healthy discussion, left organizations could steer young people away from mere rebellion toward a rational sexual revolution. According to Reich, "the core of revolutionary cultural politics must . . . be the sexual question."[48] He lectured throughout Germany, and between 1930 and 1932 Sex-Pol had tens of thousands of participants. Already in Vienna before his move to Berlin, he had opened sex clinics for blue- and

---

other intellectual so inspired the [sixties] student movement in its early days." Herzog, *Sex after Fascism*, 159. Later in life, a more-conservative Reich worried that his ideas might unleash "a free-for-all fucking epidemic." Quoted in Robinson, *Freudian Left*, 72.

44. Quoted in Palmier, *Wilhelm Reich*, 85. Emphasis removed.

45. Loewenheim, *Geschichte der Org*, 116–17. Reich's theories from the late 1930s onward grew increasingly bizarre: bioenergy, orgones, vegetotherapy, and so on. "If Reich's political ideas were utopian," concluded Robinson, "his biological and cosmological speculations can only be called insane." *Freudian Left*, 59. For an attempt to redeem Reich's work as a lab scientist during his period of Norwegian exile (1934–39), see James E. Strick, *Wilhelm Reich, Biologist* (Cambridge, MA: Harvard University Press, 2015).

46. "Sex life is not a private affair if it preoccupies you . . . [and] interferes with the political struggle." Reich, "Politicizing the Sexual Problem of Youth," in *Sex-Pol*, 251–74 (at 254). Cf. Hanisch, "Personal Is Political."

47. Rycroft, *Wilhelm Reich*, 52.

48. Reich, *Mass Psychology of Fascism*, 114 and 142.

white-collar workers that "dispensed information on birth control, abortion, [and] sex education." Staff at the Berlin Sex-Pol project put Marxist psychoanalysis into practice. Instead of overtly commenting on politics, Jacobson and others used "clinical work to demonstrate the scientific validity of the leftist position."[49] Their focus on the silent suffering of everyday life drew on a long tradition of social work and also anticipated the postwar theories of Henri Lefebvre and Raoul Vaneigem. And Reich's conviction that sexual liberation must entail women's liberation inspired second-wave feminists.[50]

Reich's ideas did not sit well with mainstream Social Democrats, Communists, and Freudians. Like other neoleftist pioneers, he was marginalized by existing political and scientific institutions. The Communist Party expelled him in 1933, and the International Psychoanalytic Association did the same in 1934. The old left had a sexual blind spot just as orthodox Freudians had a political blind spot. Even progressive Marxist thinkers such as Lukács had failed to engage with psychology.[51]

The Org's treatment of fascism as a genuine mass phenomenon, rather than a coup by a reactionary elite, resonated with Reich's analysis in *The Mass Psychology of Fascism* (1933). In that remarkable book, he identified bourgeois sexual morality, the authoritarian family, racism, and the church as core components of the fascist consensus. Those components may have middle-class

49. Bertell Ollman, introduction to Reich, *Sex-Pol*, xi–xxvii (at xiii); Anson Rabinbach, "The Politicization of Wilhelm Reich," *New German Critique*, no. 1 (Winter 1973): 90–97 (at 92); and Schröter, Mühlleitner, and May, "Edith Jacobson," 206. See also Andreas Peglau, *Unpolitische Wissenschaft? Wilhelm Reich und die Psychoanalyse im Nationalsozialismus* (Giessen, Germany: Psychosozial-Verlag, 2015), and Ulrike May, "Das Verhältnis von politischer Überzeugung und analytischer Arbeit, erörtert anhand der Berliner Aufsätze von Edith Jacobson (1930–1937)," *Luzifer-Amor* 18, no. 35 (2005): 7–45. On the general context of Weimar-era sex reform, see Atina Grossmann, *Reforming Sex: The German Movement for Birth Control and Abortion Reform, 1920–50* (New York: Oxford University Press, 1995).

50. See Lefebvre, *Critique of Everyday Life*, vol. 1, and Vaneigem, *Revolution of Everyday Life*. Shulamith Firestone, Germaine Greer, Juliet Mitchell, and Kate Millett were among Reich's later feminist interpreters. Turner, *Adventures in the Orgasmatron*, 14. Just as for the 1960s sexual revolution, however, free love for Reich meant phallocentric, heterosexual love. Although an ardent feminist, he considered homosexuality masochistic and refused to treat gay patients. Still, the historian Eli Zaretsky considers him "exemplary of the political Freudian tradition," which was far more progressive than Freud himself. Zaretsky, *Political Freud: A History* (New York: Columbia University Press, 2015), 9–10.

51. While its affiliates disagreed with Reich's own conclusions, the Frankfurt School did engage seriously with psychoanalysis, which helps explain why postwar new lefts were attracted to its ideas. Jay, *Dialectical Imagination*, ch. 3.

associations, he claimed, but the working class was by no means immune. As the Italian theorist Antonio Gramsci might have said, fascist culture achieves hegemony over all social strata.

Fascism, wrote Reich, "is only the organized political expression of the structure of the average man's character, a structure that is confined neither to certain races or nations nor to certain parties, but is general and international." It was a modern phenomenon, possible only in the age of mass politics and advanced capitalism. The Nazis in particular "made conscious use of revolutionary melodies, to which they sang reactionary lyrics." Fascism was not actually revolutionary: its basic irrationality and failure to get to the roots of social problems corresponded to a deluded form of rebellion. Reich viewed fascism as a secular religion that repackaged male domination and sexual violence for the modern age. It preached directly to the irrational mass man and inculcated in him "conservatism, fear of freedom, [and] reactionary thinking."[52] Showing how the fascist private and public spheres were intimately related, Reich linked for example the lower middle-class family's anxiety about providing for its children to the Nazis' expansionist foreign policy of living space (Lebensraum): "familial imperialism is ideologically reproduced in national imperialism."[53] This was exactly the kind of analogy that would make Reich's antifascism so popular with sixties anti-authoritarians.

Marxian psychoanalysis helped explain why something did not happen that objectively should have, like an antifascist uprising. Reich's approach "resolved the discrepancy in Marxist theory created by the fact . . . that the masses do not pursue the real economic interests of their own class but are instead only too willing to follow authoritarian leaders."[54] Emotions and irrational drives must be taken into account alongside economic interests. He argued that "sexual inhibition changes the structure of economically suppressed man in such a way that he acts, feels, and thinks contrary to his own material interests." In analyzing the fascist phenomenon, Reich leveled a serious critique at orthodox Marxism and the major workers' parties. "The Marxist parties in Europe failed and came to naught," he wrote, "because they tried to comprehend twentieth-century fascism—something completely new—with concepts belonging to the nineteenth century." Marxism had degenerated into hollow formulas in the mouths of party bureaucrats.

52. Reich, *Mass Psychology of Fascism*, xiv, 31, and 99. Cf. Historikus [Rosenberg], *Der Faschismus als Massenbewegung*.

53. Reich, 59. Erich Fromm would make similar arguments in *Escape from Freedom*.

54. Rycroft, *Wilhelm Reich*, 43, and Wilhelm Reich, "Dialectical Materialism and Psychoanalysis" [1929/34], in *Sex-Pol*, 1–74 (at 72–73).

In order "to seek out the seed of the new cultural form and to assist its germination," the left needed a conceptual vocabulary that integrated psychoanalysis.[55] In *Mass Psychology*'s original preface, which was removed from later editions, Reich criticized the empty phrases and bureaucratic maneuvers used by the workers' parties against fascism. Instead, one needed true knowledge, enthusiasm, and internally democratic organizations.[56] For an antifascist revolution to succeed, the rank and file must seize control of the existing workers' organizations and use them to win over fascism's mass base. Reich's book was published outside Germany in late 1933, but a clandestine edition was smuggled into the Nazi regime. During its underground circulation, it crossed paths with another antifascist book released that fall: the Org's own manifesto, *Neu beginnen!*

While Communists labored under the illusion that a proletarian uprising lay just around the corner and Social Democrats treated fascism as a passing episode, the Org dug in for a long battle. Toward the end of 1933, it started to expand its operations and conceive of illegal work more explicitly as a struggle against the fascist state. Org members collected information about every aspect of German society, from the attitude of factory workers at Siemens to rumors circulating in working-class pubs and hostels. They smuggled those reports abroad, where Western observers and German socialists in exile read them with rapt attention.[57]

The group's biggest success came in September 1933 with the publication of the pamphlet *Neu beginnen!* Writing under the pseudonym Miles (Latin for "soldier"), Loewenheim reworked his earlier theses and portions of the F-Course into a concise manifesto of left renewal. According to one historian, Loewenheim and his brother's partner Traute Kahn traveled in June with a copy of the manuscript to Switzerland, where they apparently handed it over to Robert Grimm, a leading Social Democrat there.[58] But Erich Schmidt claimed, perhaps more reliably, that he and Walter Dupré first smuggled the manuscript to friends in Mannheim. It had been typed on silk paper so that it would tuck easily into their clothing. Once in Mannheim, their Org comrades hid the manuscript in the spare tire of an Opel sports car and drove it across the Swiss border.[59] Grimm shared the manuscript with the executive board of the German Social Democratic Party in exile—known as the

55. Reich, *Mass Psychology of Fascism*, xxi, 7, 32, and 86.
56. Reich, *Massenpsychologie des Faschismus*, 5–6.
57. See chapter 3 and also Stöver, *Berichte über die Lage in Deutschland*.
58. Reichhardt, "Neu Beginnen," 161.
59. Erich Schmidt, *Meine Emigrantenjahre*, 14–15.

Sopade—which authorized its publication by the Sopade's press Graphia in Carlsbad (Karlovy Vary). The *Neu beginnen!* pamphlet appeared in standard format for German readers in exile, but the Sopade created a smaller format for smuggling back into Germany. Its false title page read: "Arthur Schopenhauer, On Religion: A Dialogue."[60]

Although difficult to measure, the impact of both formats was substantial. French, British, and American editions appeared over the winter of 1933–34.[61] People began referring to the hitherto nameless Org by both the title of the pamphlet (New Beginning) and the author's name (Miles Group). The pamphlet "created a considerable stir," according to the scholar Lewis J. Edinger. For the left across Europe and North America, the spectacular failure of the German workers to prevent a fascist takeover unsettled long-held assumptions about the viability of working-class parties. The pamphlet "spoke for the members of small conspiratorial underground groups, for men and women who were too young to wield any influence in the parties that allowed themselves to be destroyed without a blow, who were now trying to live down the suicidal quarrel that separated [Social Democrats] from Communists by drawing their 'soldiers' from both camps."[62] Writing in the mid-1950s, Edinger interpreted the arrival of New Beginning on the international scene as the intervention of a "New Left" against representatives of the major workers' parties (i.e., the Sopade and the central committee of the KPD). This New Left, he claimed, also distinguished itself from the "Old Left" of Trotskyist sects and splinter groups like the Socialist Workers' Party (SAP).[63] Amid the twin crises of capitalism and democracy, when both the Communist and the Social Democratic parties had fallen to fascism, New Beginning rallied the young rebels without a party.

60. Miles [Loewenheim], *Neu beginnen!* It was later republished in Klotzbach, *Drei Schriften aus dem Exil*.

61. Alexandre Bracke, cofounder of the French Section of the Workers' International (SFIO), wrote the introduction to the French edition (*Nouveau départ*); H. N. Brailsford, a prominent left-wing journalist, introduced the British edition (*Socialism's New Start*); and Norman Thomas, the Socialist Party of America's perennial candidate for president, introduced the US edition (*Socialism's New Beginning*). All of those translations nominalized the German title, which technically was the imperative verb *neu beginnen*, meaning "begin anew." Also, in German the group was referred to by the gerunds *Neubeginnen* and *Neues Beginnen*—i.e., "new beginning." The name Neu Beginnen (or New Beginning) eventually stuck.

62. Edinger, *German Exile Politics*, 83.

63. Edinger, 83–90. Edinger's definitions of "new left" and "old left" were narrower than my own. It is unclear whether he knew about the French *Nouvelle gauche* and British New Left, which formed around the time he published his book. See chapter 7.

In the pamphlet, Loewenheim summarized the Org conception for a general audience. The major workers' parties had become creatures of bourgeois democracy, he claimed, and therefore they lacked credibility in Germany's changed situation. Both parties placed a naïve faith in some "revolutionary spontaneity inherent in the proletariat": the Sopade simply waited for the masses to make the first move, while the Communists continued to underestimate fascism's power over the country. The workers' parties needed new leaders, he insisted, and those would emerge only from the underground struggle itself. Composed primarily of the young generation, this new revolutionary elite banged on the door of the dilapidated party hierarchies. The time had come for the old leaders to step aside.[64]

The political crisis that accompanied the global economic collapse around 1930 was a delayed manifestation of capitalism's heightened contradictions since the imperialist world war. Loewenheim interpreted the crisis as "the fatal turning-point in the capitalist system which has so long been predicted by socialists, and which will lead to a catastrophe for western civilization unless it succeeds in breaking its way through to a socialist society."[65] If this crisis of capitalism were allowed to develop naturally, then fascism would consummate the destruction of civilization in a second world war, unleashing industrial forces on a scarcely imaginable scale. Fascism arose out of the capitalist owner class's willingness to sacrifice its political freedom to a populist demagogue in exchange for economic security. By contrast, socialism would restore political freedom and transfer economic power to the people. Loewenheim claimed that only socialism, as a structural response to the world economic crisis, could guarantee the survival of political democracy. Class-conscious workers along with bourgeois intellectuals sympathetic to socialism could initiate a progressive cultural process. In Loewenheim's apocalyptic telling, antifascist resistance functioned as the direct intervention of a revolutionary elite against the current of history, which, if not diverted, would surely lead to barbarism.[66]

The Org's theory of fascism was more sophisticated than the standard Marxist account propagated by the Comintern, which defined fascism as "the open terrorist dictatorship of the most reactionary, most chauvinist and most

---

64. Miles [Loewenheim], *Socialism's New Beginning*, 20–23 and 98–99.

65. Miles [Loewenheim], 33.

66. Miles [Loewenheim], 81–82. The metaphor "against the current" was popular at the time especially in the KPO. See Bergmann, *"Gegen den Strom."* Lenin and Zinoviev had earlier published a collection of essays called *Gegen den Strom* (Hamburg, 1921).

imperialist elements of finance capital."[67] According to the Org/New Beginning, fascism depends on a truly mass movement. Members of every class gravitate toward a charismatic dictator who claims he can solve all social problems by decree. The Org based its theory on Marx's *Eighteenth Brumaire of Louis Napoleon* (1852), which treated such a populist dictator as the logical consequence of a failed bourgeois revolution. Marx had argued that owners of capital wanted to free the market from the feudal constraints of the old regime. But they did not actually want to assume political responsibility. When an economic crisis raised the specter of social revolution like in France in 1848, the bourgeoisie would welcome a coup d'état by an authoritarian poser like Louis Napoleon Bonaparte—so long as capitalist ownership was secured. While economically conservative, the populist dictator would sideline the bourgeoisie politically, neutralize the working class, and empower two hitherto powerless social strata: the peasantry and the *Lumpenproletariat*. The latter group comprised all sorts of dropouts, professional criminals, déclassé aristocrats, and urban riffraff: the abject nonclass of people into which anyone can sink when times are hard. Loewenheim applied Marx's model to Germany's abortive revolution of 1918–19 and the ensuing democratic republic, which ended with Hitler's seizure of power in 1933. The German bourgeoisie chose political disenfranchisement in exchange for material security: Nazi plans for military rearmament and imperial expansion promised an economic boom. Hitler's revanchist nationalism also appealed to the protectionist desires of the German peasantry, *Lumpenproletariat*, and lower middle class.[68]

The New Beginning pamphlet played on the profound frustration of workers who could not understand why Social Democrats and Communists continued to quarrel despite facing a common foe. That frustration sapped their political will and made the working class amenable to Hitler's promises. According to the pamphlet, only a militant antifascist organization could reactivate the revolutionary consciousness of depressed and atomized workers.[69] A

67. Georgi Dimitrov, "The Fascist Offensive and the Tasks of the Communist International in the Struggle of the Working Class against Fascism" (August 2, 1935), Main Report delivered at the Seventh World Congress of the Comintern, Marxists Internet Archive, accessed December 2017, https://www.marxists.org/reference/archive/dimitrov/works/1935/08_02.htm.

68. This became known as the Bonapartism theory of fascism. Its most notable advocate was August Thalheimer of the KPO. See Thalheimer, "On Fascism." See also Frank Adler, "Thalheimer, Bonapartism and Fascism," *Telos*, no. 40 (1979), 95–108; Düffler, "Bonapartism"; and Martin Kitchen, "August Thalheimer's Theory of Fascism," *Journal of the History of Ideas* 34, no. 1 (January–March 1973): 67–78. That racism and antisemitism played little role in the Bonapartism theory indicated an important blind spot in interwar Marxism.

69. Miles [Loewenheim], *Socialism's New Beginning*, 40 and 49.

left united front just might turn that sack of potatoes, as Marx had described atomized smallholding peasants, back into a revolutionary class.

After defeating the Nazis, Loewenheim concluded, the antifascist new left would temporarily concentrate state power into its hands. A transition to socialism could only approximate the democratic norms championed by moderates. Only a dictatorship of the proletariat, rightly understood, could yield a "true democracy of the workers."[70] At the same time, he noted, the antifascist new left must resist all bureaucratic tendencies. Here Loewenheim faced the leftist dilemma. A revolutionary organization must remain flexible, he claimed, which meant allowing members free rein to discuss and criticize the organization's direction. But how could you preserve freedom within a group that was engaged in a desperate underground struggle against fascism?

Internal Democracy and External Arrests

Loewenheim's own authoritarian conduct demonstrated just how difficult it would be to sustain the dynamism of this new left. The F-Courses had explicitly limited freedom of discussion so that new recruits could unlearn their bourgeois habits of thought. Working under conditions of illegality furthered the need for control over members' behavior. Now that the New Beginning pamphlet had publicized the Org's message, this new left faced the additional problem of controlling how nonmembers reacted to it.

According to internal Org analyses and émigré reports, discussion of the pamphlet lit up resistance cells throughout Germany. It was read in the factories, pubs, and apartments of Berlin's working-class neighborhoods; in large shipping centers like Hamburg and Bremen; in the industrial heartland of the Ruhr; and even in Nazi strongholds like Munich.[71] Although perhaps only a few thousand copies of the pamphlet's illegal format made it into Germany, one can speculate that each copy reached an underground cell of half a dozen or more members. Its call for unity on the left resonated widely, despite the circumstances of state surveillance and heavy censorship. Wilhelm Reich explicitly referenced the New Beginning pamphlet in his discussion of the need for a new cadre of revolutionary leaders.[72] Loewenheim's pragmatic

---

70. Miles [Loewenheim], 60–62. On the ambiguous concept of the dictatorship of the proletariat, see Asad Haider, "Dictatorship Dies in Darkness," *Viewpoint Magazine*, November 7, 2017.

71. The reading radius of the pamphlet is difficult to determine with any kind of precision. Indirect sources like Gestapo reports in BArch-Berlin, R58/2, do corroborate the Org's own claim that the pamphlet proliferated widely.

72. Wilhelm Reich, "What Is Class Consciousness?" [1934], in *Sex-Pol*, 275–358 (at 285).

prose likely appealed to workers and intellectuals who were dissatisfied with the unrealistic proposals made by their former leaders in exile, such as the Sopade. In the Org's encryption system that used "Harmsdorf" for Berlin and "Pollyville" for Paris, the codename for the Org itself was usually "The Realists." As Reich put it: "To see to it that reality is not glossed over is . . . the first commandment of anti-fascist education."[73]

In a generational appeal, Loewenheim declared that "the younger, energetic elements" should take charge of the antifascist new left. Young militants who managed to get their hands on the pamphlet must have been inspired by this call for "renewal of the socialist core" and "the freest and most critical discussion among all those elements who regard the revival of the socialist movement in a militant spirit, based on Marxist theory, as necessary."[74] The psychological appeal of beginning anew was strong for young socialists like Schmidt and Bry, who had known only times of hardship.[75]

According to one historian, small discussion groups across Germany identified so closely with the pamphlet that they felt as though they actually belonged to the organization: "'New Beginning' soon became a concept and comprised many people who had no connection whatsoever with the actual 'Org' and about whose existence and development the [Org] leaders possessed no knowledge."[76] As with future new lefts, an exciting new rhetoric displaced older identities and political assumptions. The reception of the pamphlet inside Germany during the winter of 1933–34 thus marked the birth of New Beginning, a public name for the secret organization and a symbol for the antifascist new left. For many workers and intellectuals inside Nazi Germany and abroad, New Beginning became legend.

As the pamphlet circulated, however, Loewenheim cast doubt on the prospects of resistance inside Germany. Ironically, the pamphlet's call to action proved to be the Org founders' final act. In late June 1934, Hitler purged the Nazi Party of most actual and perceived rivals during the so-called Night of the Long Knives. Six months later, the Saar plebiscite resulted in 90 percent of that German-speaking region, which had been occupied since the war, voting

---

73. Reich, *Mass Psychology of Fascism*, 196.

74. Miles [Loewenheim], *Socialism's New Beginning*, 132–33.

75. Soell, *Fritz Erler*, 1: 518n103. The rhetoric of renewal was not confined to the left. Hermann Göring, for example, published a short book for English readers in 1934 called *Germany Reborn* (London: E. Mathews and Marrot), in which he praised the "German freedom revolution" carried out by the Nazis. The interwar cult of youth was also pervasive. For example, see Ruth Ben-Ghiat, *Fascist Modernities: Italy, 1922–1945* (Berkeley: University of California Press, 2001), ch. 4, and Whitney, *Mobilizing Youth*.

76. Reichhardt, "Neu Beginnen," 162.

to rejoin the German Reich. Such factors seemed to strengthen the Nazi regime, so Loewenheim and company determined that a mass uprising was not likely. The continuation of illegal work no longer made sense to them.[77] A maximum of twenty Org/New Beginning members should remain in Berlin and other key cities, but the rest should emigrate. Loewenheim framed his new conception just as ambitiously as the original: New Beginning in exile would now infiltrate the left parties of Europe in order to steer them toward antifascist unity. "There was a megalomaniacal trait in him," according to Frank's diagnosis, "but that is probably unavoidable when one plans to do so much; he had always seen himself as the German Lenin."[78] Most New Beginning members would not accept this change of course. They accused Loewenheim of defeatism and of putting too much faith in the antifascist work that could be done in exile.[79]

One year earlier, as part of an effort to strengthen its domestic and international positions, the Org had established a foreign bureau in Prague under the directorship of Frank. Some speculated that Loewenheim found this a convenient way to get rid of him. Frank's Austrian accent, independent cast of mind, and proclivity for daring exploits supposedly made him unsuitable for underground work. The Org leadership always "held him at arm's length."[80] Abroad, his reputation grew so great that the Secret State Police (Gestapo) for a while mistook him for Miles, author of the nefarious *Neu beginnen!* pamphlet.[81] Schmidt described this remarkable personality as "a full-blooded politician, clever, brave, a man for his time, . . . [and] a debater with considerable diplomatic talent." Even Loewenheim grudgingly had to admit that Frank "was the most suitable person for democratic representation" abroad.[82]

Frank gathered around him the younger, more radical members of the Org who wanted to expand the group's activities. Forgetting that he too once entertained a similar idea, Loewenheim dismissed their ambition in retrospect

77. "Rücktritterklärung der alten Leitung," IISG, NB Archives, 10/1.

78. Quoted in Erich Schmidt, *Meine Emigrantenjahre*, 39.

79. "Zum Leitungswechsel in der Organisation," July 16, 1935, IISG, NB Archives, 10/2.

80. Reichhardt, "Neu Beginnen," 160; Bry, *Resistance*, 93; Rahmer, "Some Reminiscences," 28–29; and Erich Schmidt, *Meine Emigrantenjahre*, 34–35.

81. Report by Josef Kluske (Staatspolizeistelle für den Regierungsbezirk Breslau) to Reinhard Heydrich (Gestapa Berlin), July 17, 1935; report by Gestapa Berlin Abt. II 1A 2, re. "Miles-Gruppe," September 1935; and "Lagebericht über die kommunistische Bewegung für die Monate (Juni), Juli, August u. September 1935" (Gestapa Berlin Abt. II 1A), October 3, 1935, all BArch-Berlin, R58/2. By 1936 the Gestapo had determined that Frank was not Miles, but only in 1939 did they identify Loewenheim—by then safely out of the country—as the right man.

82. Erich Schmidt, *Meine Emigrantenjahre*, 35, and Loewenheim, *Geschichte der Org*, 183.

as a foolish attempt to create "a kind of European New Beginning organization."[83] Frank's faction abroad combined with another faction inside Germany around Löwenthal and Werner Peuke (alias Wilke, alias Konrad). Löwenthal had made a name for himself as a Communist student leader. Under the influence of his friend and mentor Franz Borkenau, he had revised Loewenheim's theory of fascism into a precursor of the totalitarianism theory that would prevail in the 1940s and 1950s.[84] Peuke was a heterodox Communist worker who provided the Org with important contacts in the railways and factory unions. With Frank and the foreign bureau's help, Löwenthal and Peuke devised a plan to depose Loewenheim and his leadership circle.

Within weeks, they succeeded in convincing three-quarters of Org/New Beginning members that Loewenheim's "liquidationist" course could no longer be tolerated. Antifascist resistance inside Germany had become a psychological necessity for the group's expanding rank and file. The grass roots demanded a radicalism that the original leaders could no longer deliver. On June 25, 1935, the Frank-Löwenthal-Peuke faction held several meetings in Berlin and other cities that finally decided the issue.[85] Loewenheim and his associates were presented with a fait accompli: a majority resolution expelling them from the organization that they had founded. As in many revolutions, this antifascist new left devoured its children.[86]

The new leaders surprised even themselves with how quickly they pulled off the coup, going so far as to consider that validation of "the correctness of the orientation of the oppositional forces who have now taken over the Org."[87] The redeployment of the old Org's resources would involve a significant democratization and decentralization of New Beginning's decision-making process. Authority would devolve to the lower-level cadres so that the group could better respond to local circumstances. The old leaders allegedly suffered from "reality-adverse dogmatism" and "sectarian passivity" in the face of real developments that proved the defiant spirit of the German proletariat. According to the new leaders, Loewenheim's circle had hermetically sealed itself off from the lower cadres, and as a result the Org showed signs of

83. Loewenheim, *Geschichte der Org*, 183.

84. See W. Jones, *Lost Debate*, 78. For a short time Borkenau considered himself a fellow traveler of the Org. Under the pseudonym Ludwig Neureither he defended Loewenheim against his critics in the pages of the *Zeitschrift für Sozialismus*, the Sopade's theoretical journal. See Keßler, *Kommunismuskritik im westlichen Nachkriegsdeutschland*.

85. Erich Schmidt, *Meine Emigrantenjahre*, 39.

86. The phrase "like Saturn, the Revolution devours its children" was coined by Jacques Mallet du Pan, a royalist critic of the French Revolution.

87. "Zum Leitungswechsel in der Organisation."

bureaucratic sclerosis: "mutual spying instead of discussion among comrades" had become the chief mode of operation.[88]

The new leaders wanted to reverse that process of bureaucratization and revive the grassroots activism they had experienced in the Org's early days. This effort to democratize the group would condition much of its activity over the coming years. Besides continuing the fight inside Germany, the new leaders had one main goal: to preserve a revolutionary elite for the moment when the fascist regime would fall, following either a homegrown uprising or Germany's military defeat in a world war (they viewed both as equally probable). The new leaders set out to harness the energy unleashed by Loewenheim's pamphlet two years earlier. But they took the pamphlet's ideas one step further: New Beginning members now declared themselves ready to undertake illegal work by means of an internally democratic organization. This indicated the group's newfound commitment to prefigurative politics: the movement's organizational form had to align with its radically democratic goal.

Was the network of sympathizers still out there? Could the new organization connect with the innumerable New Beginning members in spirit? While the group liberated itself from the authoritarian Leninism of the old left, this antifascist new left never had a chance to tap into its imagined reservoir of resisters.[89] Because the Gestapo acted first.

Four members of the Org cell in Mannheim had already been arrested in 1934.[90] But the first arrests to affect the Berlin core occurred in early September 1935, right around the time when the deposed Loewenheim and company fled the country. The journalist and Quaker pacifist Alfons Paquet, who sometimes acted as courier between the Berlin core and cadres in other cities, was detained briefly by the Gestapo and might have given up information. Following his arrest, in any case, the Gestapo rounded up Edith Schumann, Georg Eliasberg, Gerhard Hein, the psychoanalyst Jacobson, and several others. Schumann, who had once worked as secretary for the Communist theorist and politician Clara Zetkin, attempted suicide while in custody by slitting her

88. "Absetzungserklärung" by the provisional leaders of the Org, June 1935, IISG, NB Archives, 48/1.

89. The question of how many German workers actually opposed the Nazi regime has remained controversial. See T. Mason, *Nazism, Fascism and the Working Class*, and *Social Policy in the Third Reich*.

90. Indictment against Karl [Carl Maria] Kiesel, Wilhelm Pabst, Josef Karl Wilhelm, and Hans Bruno Egger, by the Oberreichsanwalt (Zweigstelle Berlin), December 22, 1934, IISG, NB Archives 59/1.

throat with the broken lens of her glasses.[91] The Gestapo continued following leads and building its case over the winter months until late March 1936, when it rounded up more New Beginning members in Berlin, including Bry's younger brother Ernst, Eberhard Hesse, Fritz Tinz, Rudolf Heuseler, Theo Thiele, and Hedwig Leibetseder. Also an ex-Communist, Leibetseder tried to evade capture by jumping out of her sixth-floor apartment window. Miraculously she survived without serious injuries, but she was arrested.[92]

The official indictments show that Nazi authorities knew they had discovered the group behind the 1933 pamphlet. Regarding the actual size and scope of New Beginning and its prehistory as the Org, however, they knew relatively little. The Gestapo had surveilled a number of cadre meetings and took note of some of the group's conspiratorial tactics. The indictments also corroborated rumors about the two improperly sunk suitcases that had washed up on the banks of the Müggelsee. Interrogators presented Hein with the suitcases and their dried-out contents. They comprised a significant portion of the Org Archive, albeit still encrypted.[93] While the Gestapo managed to gather basic information about the group through investigation and a bit of luck, they lacked any comprehensive notion about New Beginning's structure. They still knew enough to convict about three dozen members for treason at the People's Court between March 1936 and January 1937. Sentences ranged from eight months in prison to four years in the concentration camps at Dachau, Sachsenhausen, and Buchenwald.[94] Most of the New Beginning inmates were released before the war broke out, and they either emigrated or tried to reestablish contacts with the underground. About thirty members remained undetected in Berlin, including Fritz Erler, Kurt Schmidt, Ernst Jegelka, and Hans Braun.[95] Limited illegal work continued there and in other cities, but it would take years before remnants of New Beginning rebuilt anything like the underground network that existed before.

Did the arrests prove Loewenheim right? Had work inside Germany become too dangerous? Or might the group have avoided arrests altogether had Loewenheim never embarked on his defeatist course and prompted the

91. Sandvoß, Die "andere" Reichshauptstadt, 237. Jacobson's time in prison prompted her to analyze the psychological effects of incarceration on female prisoners. She later wrote several papers on the subject. Schröter, Mühlleitner, and May, "Edith Jacobson," 210.

92. Sandvoß, Die "andere" Reichshauptstadt, 232–38.

93. Sandvoß, 233. It is unclear whether the Gestapo actually decoded any of the suitcase documents. Agents may well have used them only as props during interrogation.

94. "Sitzung des 4. Strafsenates des Kammergerichtes vom 7. und 9. Januar 1937," IISG, NB Archives, 59/5.

95. Kliem, "Der sozialistische Widerstand gegen das Dritte Reich," ch. 3, § 7.

leadership coup in the first place? That only one death resulted from the Gestapo raids suggests that both the old and the new leaders took precautions to protect their comrades from the worst of fates. The one exception was Liesel Paxmann (alias Ellen), who had worked for Max Horkheimer at the Institute for Social Research in Frankfurt before joining the Org and becoming Loewenheim's secretary. She was arrested by the Gestapo at the Czechoslovak border in September 1935. Rather than risk giving up information under torture, she committed suicide in a Dresden jail.[96]

"Everything Is Possible!"

Across Western Europe the antifascist new left faced daunting odds. Not only did its adherents oppose capitalist states often backed by reactionary mass movements, but they also rebelled against the old left's existing parties and unions. New Beginning was one example of a larger phenomenon. Several other German groups called for the renewal of left theory and practice at the same time. The International Socialist Militant League (ISK), for example, combined radical activism with a deep commitment to Kantian ethics. The group's mentor Leonard Nelson was a philosopher who advocated ethical socialism and animal rights. Vegetarianism and abstinence from alcohol formed part of the alternative lifestyle practiced by members of ISK. Because they did not subscribe to Marxism, they stood well outside official Social Democracy and Communism. Such nonconformism suited their elitist concept of politics. Like Loewenheim's Org, the group thought of itself as a vanguard of the coming revolution. The discipline, camaraderie, and moral fortitude cultivated in ISK prepared its members such as Minna Specht, Willi Eichler, Fritz Eberhard, and Hilde Meisel for the antifascist struggle.

The neoleftist phenomenon extended beyond Germany. The Italian group Justice and Liberty (GL) attempted a new synthesis of socialism and liberalism. Its leaders Carlo Rosselli and Carlo Levi campaigned in exile for an antifascist alliance to overthrow Mussolini. Rosselli's book *Liberal Socialism* (1930) took aim at all existing organizations and theories of the left, including

---

96. Kliem, 169. "Protokoll von den Kindermädchen (Fanny und Gertrud) aufgenommen am 1.11.35 in der Wohnung von Hartmann," IISG, NB Archives, 12/12. See also Max Horkheimer to Moshe Schwabe, March 24, 1952, in Horkheimer, *Life in Letters*, 290–92. Some New Beginning members suspected that Paxmann was in fact murdered by the Gestapo. Evelyn Anderson (née Eleonore "Lore" Seligmann, alias Evelyn Lend) dedicated her history of the German workers' movement, *Hammer or Anvil* (1945), to Paxmann's memory. Paxmann was one of the Org members psychoanalyzed by Jacobson. Schröter, Mühlleitner, and May, "Edith Jacobson," 208.

Marxism. He was labeled a heretic by Italian Socialists and Communists alike. Despite GL's support for electoral democracy, the group agreed with other European new lefts that overthrowing fascism required extraparliamentary action: nothing short of an antifascist revolution.[97]

A sense of boundless possibility was unmistakable in France's new left, which had two main currents. On the left wing of the Socialist party, the French Section of the Workers' International (SFIO), there arose fresh dynamism in the late 1920s. Marceau Pivert was a radical schoolteacher and syndicalist whose charisma attracted young socialists who were equally dissatisfied with the parliamentarist SFIO, the Moscow-dependent Communist Party (PCF), and the conservative trade unions. Within the SFIO's Paris section, Federation of the Seine, Pivert joined Jean Zyromski's Marxist faction Socialist Battle in 1926. This faction sought to reunify the French workers' movement on the basis of revolutionary socialism.

Pivert and Zyromski belonged to the same generation as Loewenheim and the German founders of the Org. Their gradual break from the French old left took place on a similar timeline, with the world economic crisis around 1930 serving as catalyst. At that point Pivert intensified his criticism of the SFIO leadership, especially on the issue of national defense. He spoke out against Socialists' tacit support for the "military apparatus of the bourgeoisie," articulating a radical antiwar sentiment based on international working-class solidarity. He opposed what he perceived as the militarization of French society, and he extolled the "rising young generations" whose decisions would soon reconstitute socialism. According to Pivert, the SFIO's focus on electoral campaigns prevented it from engaging in class struggle.[98]

As French fascist leagues proliferated in 1934–35, Pivert took an increasingly determined stance. While he supported united fronts with Communists and the Popular Front with bourgeois democrats, he insisted on less idealistic

---

97. See Stanislao G. Pugliese, *Carlo Rosselli: Socialist Heretic and Antifascist Exile* (Cambridge, MA: Harvard University Press, 1999); Wilkinson, *Intellectual Resistance in Europe*, pt. 3; and Droz, *Histoire de l'antifascisme en Europe*, ch. 2. Rosselli and Levi's ideas were influenced by Piero Gobetti's journal from the early 1920s, *La Rivoluzione liberale*.

98. Marceau Pivert, intervention at the 28th Congress of the SFIO at Tours (May 1931), "PS-SFIO-28 Tours 1931. XXVIIIe Congrès national . . . ," Gallica bibliothèque numérique, accessed December 2017, https://bataillesocialiste.files.wordpress.com/2007/07/pivert1931.pdf; intervention at the 29th Congress of the SFIO at Paris (May–June 1932), "PS-SFIO-29 Paris 1932. XXIXe Congrès national . . . ," Gallica bibliothèque numérique, accessed December 2017, https://bataillesocialiste.files.wordpress.com/2007/07/pivert1932.pdf; and "Contre le fascisme! Contre la guerre!: L'unité révolutionnaire," *Le Populaire*, March 14, 1933.

posturing and more militant action.[99] Speaking as a tribune of the people, he placed his hope in grassroots unity from below—often contrary to the wishes of party bureaucrats. In 1935 he gathered together a number of young socialists, including Michel Collinet, Daniel Guérin, and Colette Audry, to form the faction Revolutionary Left. This group tried to steer the SFIO toward a more radical antifascist and antiwar line.

The general strike of May–June 1936, which followed the electoral victory of the Popular Front under Léon Blum, seemed to open up space for a new left in France. While the SFIO and PCF gained power through the government coalition, the parties lost their hegemony over left political organization. In that context, Pivert published his best-known article, "Everything Is Possible!" Capturing the heady mood of the strike, he declared that in this new atmosphere "everything is possible for the daring." The French people demanded "an immediate and radical change in the political and economic situation," he claimed, and the Popular Front coalition of Socialists, Communists, and Radicals might actually deliver. After outlining what the major workers' parties had to learn from one another, Pivert broke from party orthodoxy and called for the creation of popular antifascist committees.[100] His faction Revolutionary Left eventually broke with the SFIO and founded a new group in 1938, the Workers and Peasants' Socialist Party. The new party recruited between eight and ten thousand members. Until its dissolution in 1940, this neoleftist group promoted antifascist committees from below as the organizational means for a "renaissance of revolutionary socialism."[101]

Pivert was fiercely anticlerical in his pursuit of a new left. The second main current of neoleftism in France, by contrast, brought together socialism and heterodox Catholicism. Emmanuel Mounier possessed the same degree of charisma as Pivert and Frank. In 1932, he founded the magazine *Esprit* as a forum for literary, philosophical, and political protest against all existing institutions: its first special issue was devoted to the theme of a "break between the Christian order and the established disorder." Contributors to *Esprit* were young intellectuals who felt disillusioned with both the Church and modern bourgeois society. Scholars sometimes bracket them with other nonconformist

---

99. Marceau Pivert, "Du Front populaire de parade au Front populaire de combat," *Le Populaire*, September 25, 1935.

100. Pivert, "Everything Is Possible."

101. Marceau Pivert, "Excellent départ," *Juin 36*, July 22, 1938. See Jacques Kergoat, *Marceau Pivert, "socialiste de gauche"* (Paris: Éditions de l'Atelier, 1994); Jean-Paul Joubert, *Révolutionnaires de la S.F.I.O.: Marceau Pivert et le pivertisme* (Paris: Presses de la Fondation nationale des sciences politiques, 1977); Donald N. Baker, *Two Paths to Socialism: Marcel Déat and Marceau Pivert* (London: Sage, 1976); and Rabaut, *Tout est possible!*

intellectuals in the 1930s who combined ideas from the right and the left.[102] When juxtaposed with people like Pivert and Frank, however, Mounier's neoleftist qualities come to the fore.

He outlined his general philosophy in the books *Personalist and Communitarian Revolution* (1935) and *A Personalist Manifesto* (1936). Personalism derived from a theological understanding of the human being as a whole person, recognized by God and living in community with fellow humans. Politically, it represented a middle way between liberal individualism and socialist collectivism. The communitarian anti-capitalism of *Esprit* derived from a critique of estranged man very similar to the Marxist critique of alienation. For the angry young men of Mounier's milieu, personalism entailed a "rethinking of the foundations of modern life and . . . a rebuilding of communitarian sensibilities in modern society." The anarchist subtext of this ideology turned it into a weapon against Marxism. The French personalists rejected the authoritarian state that they believed Marxism required in favor of "decentralization, federation of enterprises, and cooperative movements" on the syndicalist model. The historian John Hellman has correctly labeled Mounier's experiment a New Catholic Left.[103]

Groups like these across Western Europe aimed to mobilize the youth for the antifascist cause. New lefts also took advantage of the crisis situation circa 1930, when the control exercised by the major workers' parties over left politics loosened. Similar to what Kristin Ross argues about the Paris Commune, I interpret the organizational splintering of the left in the 1930s not as a symptom of defeat but rather as a creative sign of renewal in response to fascism, Stalinism, and the crisis of global capitalism.[104] This radical regrouping of the left even had a carnivalesque quality. The antifascist new left condensed within what one scholar has described in another context as an "atmosphere of limitless possibility and colorful aspiration." Neoleftists emerged out of "a relatively sudden rupture in the normal or familiar practices of politics and society."[105] Given the existential struggle against fascism, however, the carnivalesque often played out as a danse macabre. Under constant threat of death, torture, and

102. Loubet del Bayle, *Les non-conformistes*.

103. B. Jaye Miller, "Anarchism and French Catholicism in *Esprit*," *Journal of the History of Ideas* 37, no. 1 (January–March 1976): 163–74 (at 163 and 166), and Hellman, *Emmanuel Mounier*. On the Stalinist direction taken by some advocates of Mounier's personalism, see Piotr H. Kosicki, *Catholics on the Barricades: Poland, France, and "Revolution," 1891–1956* (New Haven, CT: Yale University Press, 2018).

104. Ross, *Communal Luxury*.

105. Padraic Kenney, *A Carnival of Revolution: Central Europe 1989* (Princeton, NJ: Princeton University Press, 2002), 3 and 305.

imprisonment, the left's political values and institutions slipped out of place. Into that gap of indeterminacy stepped the small groups that had been marginalized by the major parties. Electoral results no longer provided a sure measure of importance during the midcentury left's greatest historical crisis. In the fascist emergency, often it was the neoleftist small groups that exhibited the most creativity and intellectual force.

While the antifascist new left in France could pursue domestic political goals for several more years, the Italian and German new lefts had to emigrate to Prague, Paris, London, and New York. In this radical diaspora, organizational and theoretical experiments continued, but under changed circumstances. Especially in the context of the Spanish Civil War, as the next chapter will show, the transnational network required for exile politics opened up new horizons for neoleftism.

3

Exile and the Spanish Experiment

ANTIFASCISM HAS BEEN described as a culture of exile, and one might say the same about neoleftism.[1] After Mussolini's march on Rome in 1922 and especially after Hitler's seizure of power in 1933, antifascists emigrated in droves, desperately seeking safety and alliances abroad. Prague, Paris, London, and New York were hubs of exile politics during the interwar years. There antifascists confronted the classic problems of all refugees: economic hardship, visa troubles, discrimination, and despair. Worse still, exile intensified the narcissism of small differences that already afflicted the left. Every nuance of political opinion contained the seed of a bitter personal feud. Like the initial defeat by fascism, however, the left diaspora provided an opportunity for renewal. Exile involved confronting new lands, new people, and new ideas. In historical hindsight, I apply an analytic of optimism to that empirically dire situation in order to answer the question: Which modes of left organization did the fascist crisis make possible?

As the exiled rumps of Social Democratic and Communist parties competed for foreign aid, neoleftist small groups like New Beginning jockeyed for influence. Now they were on an even playing field with the parties of the old left, which had lost their mass base and/or cadre infrastructure. Whichever group could win the greatest amount of international support, whether through fundraising or lobbying, might determine the shape of socialism to come. Petty infighting and cynicism paralyzed many émigré leaders of the old left. According to the heterodox leftist Victor Serge, "only in the minority parties . . . and among isolated individuals did conscience still burn."[2] Exile extinguished the left's power in Europe, but it also forced a revision of theory and strategy. Defeat gave small nonparty groups the chance they had been waiting for.

1. Traverso, *Fire and Blood*, 262.
2. Serge, *Memoirs of a Revolutionary*, 395.

The year 1935 marked a turning point for New Beginning. A few months after the organization's leadership change that summer, the Gestapo made its first series of arrests. As a result, most of the remaining core members of the group had emigrated by year's end. Many peripheral members and sympathizers lost all contact with the group. Underground work continued inside Germany, but the group's scope of activity there narrowed. Police surveillance became oppressive as the Nazi regime tightened its grip over the populace and implemented an aggressive foreign policy. Having established a foreign bureau in 1933 and engaged in exile politics in Prague, Paris, Brussels, and elsewhere for several years, New Beginning was no stranger to work beyond German borders. But with the sudden rush of emigration in late 1935, the group's center of gravity shifted abroad.

There was an indirect relationship between the intensity of New Beginning's engagement in exile politics and its connection with the underground struggle. In exile, New Beginning and the antifascist new left in general transformed from resistance cells into lobbyists. No longer a concrete task carried out among the masses, renewing the left now became an idea that neoleftists pitched to patrons abroad. The idea of socialist renewal was the calling card of the antifascist new left in exile. Not only Germans, but also Italian and Spanish neoleftist émigrés claimed to offer an alternative to the failed politics of Social Democracy and Communism. Cautiously they did support efforts to form either a left united front or a broadly democratic Popular Front against fascism. But for the small nonparty groups, overcoming the left's disunity required breaking with shibboleths. Those included the old left's treatment of culture as a byproduct of economics, its narrow understanding of revolution as political violence, and its focus on Europe at the expense of the underdeveloped colonial periphery. Most importantly, small groups grappled with how to prevent their fluid organizations from bureaucratically hardening. The neoleftist dilemma followed them into exile.

New Beginning in exile both symbolized and stimulated the phenomenon of new lefts. Despite the group's small size, it managed to win disproportionate influence within the Zürich- then Brussels-based Labour and Socialist International (LSI). It counted among its backers Léon Blum's Popular Front government in France, the foreign ministry of the Spanish Republic, the left wing of the British Labour Party, and the progressive wing of the American labor movement. New Beginning stood for the young generation of socialists who had grown up after World War I and whose lives were defined by fascism and the global economic crisis.

In addition to rival ideologies, exile politics involved a clash of age cohorts. The older generation that participated in the democratic struggles of the late nineteenth century had vied with the front generation, which was defined by its experience of World War I and the aftermath of the Russian Revolution. The front generation in turn faced a challenge by a younger interwar generation that knew only times of crisis. Those experiences conditioned how antifascists used the rhetoric of renewal. From a generational perspective, antifascist politics cannot be plotted simply on a spectrum that spans from left to center to right. The 1930s witnessed a temporalization of those political coordinates, or what the sociologist Gøsta Esping-Andersen in another context has called chronopolitics.[3] Now it made sense to distinguish between new lefts and old lefts, new centers and old centers, new rights and old rights. It was a moment of flux when the size of a political current alone no longer determined whether people would listen to it.

Antifascists without Borders

In addition to targeting certain age groups, antifascists depended on international networks of solidarity. Not since the peak years of the Second International had the European left cultivated such a robust international consciousness.[4] After the antifascist era, the next great transnational moment for the left came during the Global Sixties. Accordingly, the historian Dan Stone has called for the internationalization of research on antifascism, and scholars like David Featherstone have already started analyzing antifascism's "spatial politics."[5] Such a spatial turn will certainly improve our understanding of historical antifascism. But in dealing with the antifascist new left, the spatial turn might leave something out: the continuity of new lefts over time. An analysis of New Beginning's exile network reveals the crucial link between the spatiality and the temporality of left politics during the 1930s.

3. Gøsta Esping-Andersen defined chronopolitics as the reorientation of political preferences in the late twentieth century around the issue of welfare benefits such as childcare and unemployment relief, with younger people in support of expanding benefits and entrenched older people generally opposed. Esping-Andersen, *Social Foundations*, 147–48.

4. See Horn, *European Socialists Respond to Fascism*. For an account that downplays antifascist internationalism in the 1930s, see Imlay, *Practice of Socialist Internationalism*, Entr'acte (251–60).

5. Stone, *Goodbye to All That?*, and David Featherstone, "Black Internationalism, Subaltern Cosmopolitanism, and the Spatial Politics of Antifascism," *Annals of the Association of American Geographers* 103, no. 6 (November 2013): 1406–20. Cf. the parallel internationalism of the far right in Federico Finchelstein, *Transatlantic Fascism: Ideology, Violence, and the Sacred in Argentina and Italy, 1919–1945* (Durham, NC: Duke University Press, 2009), and Arnd Bauerkämper and Grzegorz Rossolinski, eds., *Fascism without Borders: Transnational Connections and Cooperation between Movements and Regimes in Europe from 1918 to 1945* (New York: Berghahn, 2017).

It is impossible to say for sure how many people fled Nazi Germany, whether for political, economic, or ethnic reasons. In individual cases it was sometimes a combination of all three. Official state records do not help much. German authorities quickly revoked the citizenship of famous refugees, while the denaturalization and expropriation of ordinary refugees proceeded intermittently. Many who left Germany declared at the border that they were going on vacation, so they never applied at foreign consuls for long-term visas. Refugee relief agencies in Czechoslovakia, France, Belgium, and elsewhere registered thousands of people, but it can be assumed that just as many either did not register or registered multiple times at different agencies. Moreover, a significant portion of those agencies' records were destroyed or lost during the advance of German armies after 1938. The total number of emigrants by 1935 was probably less than one hundred thousand, the majority of whom were ethnic (i.e., Jewish) refugees rather than political ones.[6] The higher public profile of the political émigrés owed in part to the preferential treatment they received under most countries' asylum policies. Then as now, those classified merely as victims of ethnic or racial persecution were deemed undesirable.

Estimating the number of New Beginning members who went into exile also presents problems. Of the 171 core members of the group that I have been able to identify, 72 found themselves outside Germany at the end of 1935. Between then and the spring of 1936, about 35 members were arrested inside Germany and roughly an equal number fled into exile to avoid arrest. Most of the group in exile had already been working in some capacity for the foreign bureau before the Gestapo made its move. The transience of New Beginning and other neoleftist small groups—their frequently changing headquarters and meeting places, their use of couriers to communicate with the outside, the routine with which they crossed borders—suggests that the distinction between domestic politics and exile politics never applied as strictly to them as to the major parties of the old left. Also, the small groups typically did not engage in electoral politics (or at least not primarily), so their activities were never limited to the national frame.

The historian Jan Foitzik thus mapped antifascist small groups like New Beginning as transnational networks that combined exilic and nonexilic nodes.[7] New Beginning originated in Berlin and established nodes in other urban centers throughout Germany, such as Mannheim, Frankfurt am Main, and Düsseldorf. By 1935 it had cultivated a web of contacts across German borders. Following the German annexation of the Sudetenland in October 1938, the foreign

6. See Grossmann, *Emigration*, 43, 52, and 151, and Palmier, *Weimar in Exile*, 104.
7. Foitzik, *Zwischen den Fronten*.

bureau moved from Prague to Paris. The purely exilic nodes in New Beginning's network then grew in importance relative to its border stations at Neuern (Nýrsko), Carlsbad (Karlovy Vary), and St. Gallen, which previously had served to maintain contacts with the German underground.

Walter Loewenheim remarked that New Beginning's "political fate . . . was not decided inside Germany, but outside."[8] Convinced by the 1933 Miles pamphlet, the group's international supporters included Friedrich Adler of the LSI, Robert Grimm and Ernst Reinhard of the Swiss Social Democratic Party, Otto Bauer and Joseph Buttinger of the Austrian Revolutionary Socialists, and Edo Fimmen of the International Transport Workers' Federation. Aside from the Nazis, the group's enemies included several important representatives of the old left: the central committee-in-exile of the KPD, the banished but still influential theorist Leon Trotsky, and Jacob Walcher of the German Socialist Workers' Party (SAP). The Communists even commissioned a counterpamphlet that attacked New Beginning's theories of fascism and socialist renewal.[9]

The reaction by German Social Democrats in exile was ambivalent. They certainly did not approve when New Beginning undermined the émigrés' claim to represent Social Democrats inside Germany. And Loewenheim's principles of organization probably struck them as Communism by another name. But the SPD executive board-in-exile, known as the Sopade, underwent a crisis of legitimacy in the winter of 1933–34 that made it amenable to radical change. One member of the board, Paul Hertz, favored a leftward turn that would align the Sopade with young militants in the underground. A few older Social Democrats viewed an alliance with New Beginning as a way to bolster the party's left wing. These sympathizers succeeded in convincing the Sopade to publish the Miles pamphlet. But opposition to New Beginning grew among the moderate and right-wing members of the board. Conservative Social Democrats like Otto Wels, Hans Vogel, Erich Ollenhauer, and Siegmund Crummenerl demanded an official response.

The response came in January 1934 with the Prague Manifesto, published on the front page of the Sopade newspaper *Neuer Vorwärts* and smuggled into Germany disguised as a promotional booklet for razor blades. The Sopade sought to wrap its reformist policies in more radical packaging. It did make a few statements that should have pleased militant readers. According to the manifesto, the fascist state had completely changed the conditions for political

---

8. Loewenheim, *Geschichte der Org*, 185.

9. See Rudolf Gerber, *Hitlerdeutschland, die Sozialdemokratie und die proletarische Revolution* (Reichenberg [Liberec], Czechoslovakia: Hadek, 1934). Walcher and his comrades in the SAP would later change their minds and collaborate with New Beginning.

work in Germany from those that had prevailed under the Weimar Republic. In the struggle against Nazi dictatorship, "there are no compromises; there is no place for reformism and legality." A new left organization led by a revolutionary elite should replace the defunct SPD and trade union apparatus inside Germany. This new course had been forced on the Sopade by the fascist takeover and the propaganda success of neoleftist small groups. But the Sopade clung to its faith in spontaneous action by the masses: the Nazis' exploitative economic policy, for example, would supposedly "compel the masses to fight for the security and improvement of their material existence."[10] Despite the revolutionary tone of the Prague Manifesto, the Sopade continued to fall back on tried-and-true formulas. For this old left, antifascism meant substituting political democracy for Nazi dictatorship, not abolishing fascism's economic basis in capitalism. Only by recapturing rights of free speech and assembly, the Sopade believed, might the German workers overthrow Hitler.

It was naïve to expect that the Nazis would ever liberalize German politics or that differences within the workers' movement would automatically disappear in the common fight against fascism.[11] But the Sopade made three proclamations that opened the door to cooperation with the antifascist new left. The first permitted Social Democrats to form local alliances with non–Social Democrat resistance cells. More concretely, the second proclamation committed the Sopade to funding any underground group "whose revolutionary spirit ensures that it subordinates its activity to the overthrow of the National Socialist dictatorship within the framework of the unity of the working class." Finally, the Sopade opened up the columns of its newspaper and other publications for discussion of revolutionary socialism. With this last pledge, the Sopade might have tried putting the genie back in the bottle: By converting its publications into open discussion forums, it could potentially control the discourse and legitimize its claim to represent all German socialists. Pressure from neoleftist groups such as New Beginning thus prompted a leftward turn in German Social Democracy, if only for a brief period.

In October 1933 the Sopade's publishing house in Carlsbad began issuing the *Zeitschrift für Sozialismus* (Journal for socialism). This journal testified to the rich intellectual life of the antifascist emigration. Edited by Rudolf Hilferding (alias Richard Kern), the thirty-six issues of the *Zeitschrift* included contributions by the Austrian writer Franz Borkenau (alias Ludwig Neureither), the

---

10. Sopade, "Kampf und Ziel," 1.

11. "Whether Social Democrat or Communist or supporter of the many splinter groups, the enemy of dictatorship becomes in the struggle—through the requirements of the struggle itself—the same socialist revolutionary." Sopade, 2.

German journalist and naziologist Konrad Heiden, the SPD elder theorist Karl Kautsky, the British political scientist Harold J. Laski, the German theorist and Frankfurt School affiliate Franz L. Neumann (alias Leopold Franz), the German historian Arthur Rosenberg (alias Historicus), and several New Beginning members.[12] In his programmatic introduction to the first issue, Hilferding declared that "the struggle against the total state can only be a total revolution" and that the journal's task was "the intellectual preparation for waging the struggle and exercising power [afterward]." To that end, he continued, the journal "will be a revolutionary organ, revolutionary not only in combatting the adversary, but also in its ruthlessness toward its own movement [i.e., Social Democracy], its flaws, and its backwardness." The task for left intellectuals abroad was to discuss, clarify, and solve the problems that an antifascist movement would face when it took power.[13] Articles combined partisan commitment with sober analysis. Every word published in the *Zeitschrift für Sozialismus* from October 1933 to September 1936 represented a victory wrenched from the powers of darkness.[14]

The journal gave voice to all left-wing except Communist tendencies of the antifascist emigration, including opponents of the Sopade. One faction formed around Karl Böchel and Siegfried Aufhäuser that called itself the German Revolutionary Socialists (RSD). The RSD built a following inside Germany among left-wing Social Democrats in the states of Saxony and Thuringia, and with the help of a sympathetic Sopade border secretary, the faction maintained a network of underground contacts. In its official platform, the RSD called for "the reconstruction of the revolutionary socialist unity party" based on the Gotha and Erfurt programs of pre-1914 Social Democracy.[15] Social Democrats and Communists could not be reconciled by any new party, the RSD claimed, but only by restoring the original unity of the workers' movement.

In contrast to restorationist old lefts like the RSD, neoleftist small groups such as New Beginning and ISK stressed the historical novelty of fascism and the need for new theories, new personnel, and new forms of organization.

---

12. New Beginning contributors included Richard Löwenthal (alias Paul Sering), Karl B. Frank (Willi Müller, Paul Hagen), Henry W. Ehrmann (Fritz Alsen), Peter M. Bergmann (Kurt Marso), and Moses Blatt (J. Landau).

13. [Rudolf Hilferding], "Die Zeit und die Aufgabe," *Zeitschrift für Sozialismus* 1, no. 1 (October 1933): 1–11 (at 10).

14. I borrow this phrase from a letter that Walter Benjamin wrote to Gershom Scholem on January 11, 1940. Scholem, ed., *The Correspondence of Walter Benjamin and Gershom Scholem, 1932–1940*, trans. Gary Smith and André Lefevere (New York: Schocken, 1989), 262–64 (at 262).

15. Arbeitskreis revolutionärer Sozialisten [RSD], "Der Weg zum sozialistischen Deutschland," 406. See Freyberg, *Sozialdemokraten und Kommunisten*.

With a few exceptions like Karl Frank, their leaders were in their mid-twenties and represented a younger generation than Böchel and Aufhäuser, the Sopade, and the Communist central committee-in-exile. Age surely did not determine one's political stance in the antifascist emigration, but people tended to associate youth with the most avant-garde positions. New Beginning envisioned a reorganization of the left carried out by young underground resisters who would abolish the oligarchical structure of the major workers' parties. This new left broke from left tradition in a way that simultaneously preserved that tradition's best elements. In the Marxist jargon of the time, such a negation of the past was understood as "dialectical" rather than mechanical or abstract.

New Beginning's foreign bureau capitalized on the energy, training, and expertise of its young members. Henry W. Ehrmann for example was born in 1908 in Berlin, where he joined the Socialist Worker Youth (SAJ) and then the SPD. He studied law at the universities of Berlin and Freiburg until 1932, when he earned his doctorate in jurisprudence. His career as a jurist in Berlin was cut short by the Nazi seizure of power, but it was long enough for him to get recruited by the Org/New Beginning. One of the only members to get arrested during the early days of the regime, Ehrmann spent almost a year in the Oranienburg concentration camp before his release in 1934. He emigrated immediately, settling in Paris and running New Beginning's operations there under the pseudonym Paul Bernhard. Ehrmann also wrote for the *Zeitschrift für Sozialismus* under the name Fritz Alsen. Fluent in French and well connected in French Popular Front circles, Ehrmann proved one of the most useful assets in New Beginning's antifascist network.

The group's man in Bern, Switzerland, where stricter refugee policies made it harder to practice exile politics, was Erich Schmidt. Born in Berlin's working-class district Prenzlauer Berg in 1910, Schmidt learned the printer's trade and joined the SAJ in 1926. He was one of the first leaders of the SAJ to secretly join the Org in 1932, and Loewenheim considered him a protégé. After his arrest in 1933 and accidental release as the wrong "Erich Schmidt," he made his way to Bern, where he won the support of Swiss Social Democrats and ran a New Beginning station under the name Kirchner. He published journal articles there under the pseudonym Erwin Sander, a prudent move given the Swiss law that forbade refugees from working in any capacity. Not least because of his precarious employment, Schmidt identified with the general plight of European refugees, who were "people without civil rights, without the means of making a living, without a future."[16]

---

16. Erich Schmidt, *Meine Emigrantenjahre*, 45. See also Wichers, *Im Kampf gegen Hitler*, 256–71.

In addition to its core membership, New Beginning's periphery remained active. Ossip K. Flechtheim was a good example of someone who originally belonged to an Org cadre (in his case Düsseldorf) but drifted onto the group's periphery in exile. He was the nephew of Alfred Flechtheim, a well-known dealer of modernist art. After his arrest and brief detainment, Ossip left Germany for Switzerland, where he enrolled at the Graduate Institute for International Advanced Studies in Geneva. Faculty at the Institute included the émigré jurist Hans Kelsen and the economists Ludwig von Mises and Wilhelm Röpke. There Flechtheim fell in with young socialists like the literary critic Hans Mayer, the historian Ernst Engelberg, and the political scientist John H. Herz. All of these friends had undergone roughly the same political training in Germany's oppositional Communist milieu of the late 1920s, but only Flechtheim had direct ties to New Beginning.[17] Letters between him and Richard Löwenthal, New Beginning's chief theorist after 1935, indicated that Flechtheim provided financial support to the group and served as a conduit for news and intelligence.[18] He corresponded regularly with Schmidt, Frank, and his own ex-girlfriend in the group, Vera Franke (later Eliasberg). Those core members used aliases, but like most people on New Beginning's periphery Flechtheim always used his real name.

In addition to Paris (Ehrmann), Bern (Schmidt), and Geneva (Flechtheim), the New Beginning foreign bureau established stations in cities such as Vienna, Amsterdam, and Brussels. Members who ran those stations focused on cultivating local contacts, winning the support of workers' parties there, and, whenever appropriate, appealing directly to foreign publics. Members without a station assignment traveled as couriers, coordinators, and mobile discussion leaders. Those included Löwenthal, Francis L. Carsten, Lucy Ackerknecht, Lotte Abrahamsohn, Evelyn Anderson, Horst Mendershausen, Jerry Jeremias, Georg Eliasberg, and Else Gronenberg. All were in their mid-twenties. Coded letters and reports circulated among the group's rank and file. Meetings were run democratically, although agendas were usually set in advance. All decisions required a consensus.

While New Beginning liberated itself from the authoritarian strictures of Loewenheim's Org, its young members now deferred to a new charismatic leader in the person of Karl Frank. Despite being in his forties, Frank's

17. Keßler, *Ossip K. Flechtheim*, 45–60. The Geneva Graduate Institute was the forerunner of today's Graduate Institute of International and Development Studies.

18. Various letters from Richard Löwenthal to Ossip K. Flechtheim (Geneva), November 1935–October 1937, DNB, NL Flechtheim, EB 98/179. The central committee of the KPD, which intercepted some messages to New Beginning's foreign bureau, identified Flechtheim as the "Miles representative in Geneva." See "Schlüssel" (ca. summer 1937), BArch-Berlin, RY1/I 2/3/405.

youthful demeanor, radical politics, and countless adventures endeared him to the antifascist new left. Going under the name Willi Müller, he combined a reputation as "cool, calculating professional revolutionary" with a dashing appearance that brought to mind "the heartthrob pop stars in French avant-garde films of those years." Schmidt claimed that "no other politician in the emigration . . . attracted so much trust and admiration."[19] Frank also attracted plenty of mistrust. His enemies in the Sopade were suspicious of his "amazing, unimpeded trips into the German interior, whose success could not be explained by intelligence and courage alone nor simply by luck."[20] They wondered, was he a Nazi double agent? Or, just as bad, a Soviet spy? Those suspicions were baseless. It was indeed Frank's intelligence, courage, and luck that enabled him to cross borders and administer New Beginning's antifascist network.

Sometimes luck wore thin. Police nearly captured Frank twice: once in Berlin when the Gestapo raided the apartment of a political contact he was visiting, and again while crossing over the Giant Mountains from Czechoslovakia into German Silesia. He apparently skied into a snowstorm, fell unconscious, and was picked up by Czechoslovak border guards who planned to turn him over to the Germans. After waking up, he escaped the guards' hut and skied cross-country to Breslau and then Berlin, where he arrived with frostbitten limbs.[21] "It was the established principle of our organization," he later wrote, "that members abroad should be ready to take as great [a risk] as the members inside."[22] This spirit of solidarity and self-sacrifice he imparted to admirers such as the revolutionary socialist Buttinger and the Sopade border secretaries Erwin Schoettle, Waldemar von Knoeringen, and Franz Bögler. Friends described him as a true comrade who would stay up late at night drinking wine and telling tales. Karl Frank stood larger than life, and his charisma was probably the main reason why New Beginning could sustain its influence in exile politics long after the excitement over the Miles pamphlet died down.

His charisma failed to sway the Sopade in Prague, however. At first the émigré Social Democrats grudgingly agreed to finance the work of New Beginning. Here was a group of young socialists who had an actual underground

---

19. Erich Schmidt, *Meine Emigrantenjahre*, 35. Schmidt might have had in mind Jean Gabin, star of Jean Renoir's films *La Grande Illusion* (1937) and *La Bête humaine* (1938), who bore a rugged resemblance to Frank.

20. Erich Schmidt, *Meine Emigrantenjahre*, 35.

21. James A. Wechsler, "An Early Anti-Nazi," *PM*, n.d. (ca. 1944), Hoover, Frank Papers, 3.

22. Paul Hagen [Karl Frank] to Calvin Hoover (Office of Strategic Services, Washington, DC), July 31, 1942, Hoover, Frank Papers, 7/7.

apparatus in Germany and prestige abroad. In the fall of 1933, the embattled Sopade decided to sponsor this neoleftist small group, publish its pamphlet, and use it to bolster the Sopade's own reputation in the émigré public sphere. Shortly after the Miles pamphlet appeared, Frank wrote diplomatically to the Sopade that reviews of the English edition had portrayed the Sopade "just as honorably" as New Beginning. The proliferation of new lefts, implied Frank, benefitted the antifascist movement as a whole.[23] For a while at least, the Sopade found it convenient to agree with him.

Social Democrats in exile were anxious to establish themselves as the legitimate representatives of the German working class. While the Sopade did publish an impressive series of reports on German domestic affairs,[24] its ties to the underground were severed by the wave of Gestapo arrests in 1935–36. Half the Sopade border secretaries in the Sudetenland, Switzerland, France, Belgium, and Poland whose job it was to cultivate those ties had fallen under the influence of New Beginning anyway. For a while, New Beginning's *Reports on the Situation in Germany* enjoyed a better reputation than the Sopade's own.[25] A rivalry simmered between the old Social Democratic left and this antifascist new left.

In December 1934, the Sopade cut off funding to New Beginning. The executive board reached its decision at a meeting in Prague while Frank was absent. One of his deputies sat in for him until the board withdrew behind closed doors. The Sopade had obtained confidential letters from Böchel's files that allegedly proved that the RSD and New Beginning had conspired against the Sopade. What exactly the letters said and how the Sopade obtained them remain a mystery, but they were used as a pretext for purging revolutionary socialists old and new from the émigré ranks of Social Democracy. Since that summer, the Sopade had been backpedaling from the radicalism of the Prague Manifesto into a more moderate stance. When Frank complained about

23. Willi Müller [Karl Frank] (London) to Siegmund Crummenerl (Prague), November 22, 1933, IISG, NB Archives, 1/44.

24. These were known informally as the Green Reports owing to the color of their covers. Starting in 1937, the British Labour Party commissioned an English translation called *Germany Reports*. When the Graphia publishing house relocated to Paris after the German annexation of the Sudetenland, a French edition appeared under the title *Rapports d'Allemagne*. See the reprint of the original German edition, Sopade, *Deutschland-Berichte*.

25. Stöver, *Berichte über die Lage in Deutschland*. Out of the thirteen Sopade border secretaries, at least six worked directly for or in sympathy with New Beginning: Knoeringen in Neuern (Nýrsko); Schoettle in St. Gallen; Bögler in Trautenau (Trutnov); Willy Lange in Carlsbad (Karlovy Vary); Emil Kirschmann in Saarbrücken, Forbach, and Mulhouse; and Georg Reinbold in Strasbourg and Luxemburg.

undemocratic procedures, the board tabled the matter until after the winter holidays.

Frank immediately appealed to the secretary-general of the LSI, Friedrich Adler. He also informed the Sopade that, because it now withheld "an already agreed-upon sum, an immediate danger has arisen for our comrades in the Reich."[26] Together with leaders of the RSD, he penned a protest letter in late January 1935 that demanded the reinstatement of New Beginning's funding and an investigation into how the Sopade had obtained the confidential letters. The protest denounced the Sopade's "arbitrary acts" that served only to injure those "comrades in Germany who confront fascism under the most awful conditions of terror." Reminding the Sopade that its Prague Manifesto had declared "the old [party] apparatus dead and attempts to revive it denied," Frank and his RSD allies warned that "the worst habits of the old apparatus are celebrating a resurrection."[27] This feud was about more than money. It expressed the hostility between old lefts and new lefts that brewed in the German antifascist emigration.

Regardless of whether the protest letter was correct on the details, the Sopade had fallen back into old habits by the end of 1934. The leftward turn announced by the Prague Manifesto lasted about six months before the Sopade reverted to its default skepticism of revolution. Between 1935 and 1939, its relationship with groups like New Beginning soured. The Sopade went so far as to expel Aufhäuser and Böchel from the board, cut off funding to New Beginning, and distance itself from Hertz, who had started to work closely with Frank and the New Beginning foreign bureau.[28]

A theorist who tried to justify the Sopade's moderate stance was Curt Geyer (alias Max Klinger), whose 1939 pamphlet *The Party of Freedom* defended liberal democracy against the "dictatorial" ideas of New Beginning and its recently deceased Austromarxist ally, Otto Bauer. Although some of Geyer's ideas went beyond what Sopade leaders were willing to endorse, his rejection of class struggle and embrace of a democratic welfare state anticipated the

---

26. Willi Müller [Karl Frank] to Siegmund Crummenerl (Prague), December 27, 1934, IISG, NB Archives, 1/26.

27. Karl Böchel, Willy Lange, Willi Müller [Karl Frank], and Siegfried Aufhäuser (Prague) to the office of the Sopade (Prague), January 22, 1935, IISG, NB Archives, 7/1.

28. Hertz edited the Sopade journal *Sozialistische Aktion*, a miniature version of *Neuer Vorwärts* that was smuggled into Germany. Through this journal, he advocated on behalf of New Beginning and other new lefts, thus sustaining the radicalism announced by the Prague Manifesto long after the Sopade board changed its position. By 1938, Hertz was excluded from board meetings. Edinger, *German Exile Politics*, 216.

direction taken by the SPD in the two decades after World War II.[29] One historian described this moderate socialist tendency of the 1930s as "political humanism of a Western European character." It aligned well with the rational and liberal norms promoted by mainstream antifascists under the banner of the Popular Front.[30] Like the Italian group Justice and Liberty, Geyer and the Sopade's right wing imagined a postfascist order based on universal suffrage, multiparty democracy, and the pursuit of working-class goals through legislation and limited factory codetermination. They wanted to transform Social Democracy from a democratic working-class party into a catch-all popular party (*Volkspartei*). This variant of socialism in exile valued freedom and democracy as ethical ideals, rather than material realities. Marxism and class struggle took a back seat.

Another very different innovation in exile was a Central European tendency called folk socialism (*Volkssozialismus*). Perhaps best understood as a brand of populism, folk socialism was an ideology that aimed to siphon off fascism's mass appeal by extolling national unity alongside a critique of capitalism. If New Beginning and other small groups constituted the antifascist new left, then folk socialists laid the conceptual groundwork for a new right. The Sudeten Social Democrat Wenzel Jaksch's 1936 book *Folk and Workers* exemplified this tendency. While not subscribing to the biological race theories that animated fascist propaganda, Jaksch did reframe the interwar crisis as an essentially national problem that required stronger bonds between each country's workers, farmers, and middle classes. His call for a national factory community echoed the Nazi concept of folk community (*Volksgemeinschaft*), an echo that left-wing critics as well as Sudeten nationalists pointed out.[31] Another folk socialist was Emil Franzel, whose 1936 book *Occidental Revolution* recalled European conservatives' worry about the decline of the West. Likewise, the Social Democrat Wilhelm Sollmann wrote paeans to the German worker and peasant soul. Folk socialism had an elective affinity with both National Bolshevism—a strange brew concocted by Ernst Niekisch and Karl Otto Paetel, among others—and the left wing of the Nazi Party around Otto

---

29. Curt Geyer, *Die Partei der Freiheit* (Paris: Graphia, 1939), reprinted in Klotzbach, *Drei Schriften aus dem Exil*, along with the primary objects of his critique: Miles [Loewenheim], *Neu beginnen!* (1933) and Otto Bauer, *Die illegale Partei* (posth. 1939). See Matthias, *Sozialdemokratie und Nation*, 219–22 and 331–32n178. After emigrating to London, Geyer joined a British circle of anti-Germans known as the Vansittartists. He was expelled from the SPD in 1942.

30. Matthias, *Sozialdemokratie und Nation*, 47. See Hobsbawm, "Era of Anti-fascism."

31. Wenzel Jaksch, *Volk und Arbeiter. Deutschlands europäische Sendung* (Bratislava: Eugen Prager Verlag, 1936). See Matthias, *Sozialdemokratie und Nation*, 216–34.

Strasser.[32] Unlike the antifascist new left, this populist new right did not care much about organizational problems. Folk socialists never faced the leftist dilemma of sustaining democratic forms or prefiguring the new society within their ranks. Instead they propagated a nostalgic vision of restored organic communities, and racism lay just beneath the surface.

The political spectrum of the antifascist emigration defied the traditional logic of left versus right that had long characterized European politics. This circumstance owed in part to the dizzying multiplication of parties during the interwar years. In the Weimar Republic, for example, nine large parties had at various times contended with one another and more than thirty smaller parties. According to the traditional logic, New Beginning would have occupied a position on the political spectrum somewhere in between Social Democracy and Communism. As fascism decimated the political landscape, however, a temporalized logic emerged that distinguished between old lefts and new lefts. Neoleftist small groups symbolized an alternative to the old politics. Only by embracing alternatives, argued Löwenthal, could "socialist workers' parties *modernize* themselves."[33]

Left innovations occurred mainly in the émigré capitals of Prague, Paris, London, and New York. Not all were initiated by neoleftist small groups. Among Communists, for example, the publicist Willi Münzenberg launched elaborate propaganda campaigns to discredit fascism. His media savvy had already served him well during the Weimar Republic, when he collaborated with avant-garde artists like John Heartfield and writers like Anna Seghers to produce the influential photo magazine *Arbeiter–Illustrierte–Zeitung* (Workers' illustrated paper). Outside Germany the magazine stayed in print until 1938.

Münzenberg organized all manner of humanitarian campaigns during the 1920s and 1930s, such as the International Workers' Aid and the League Against Imperialism. In 1933, he and his colleague Otto Katz published the *Brown Book on the Reichstag Fire and Hitler Terror*, a scathing commentary on the trial of four Communists and one council communist accused of burning the Reichstag building. The historian Anson Rabinbach has argued that, more than a book, "it was a staged event and the center of an international campaign that convinced much of the world that the Nazis had conspired to burn the Reichstag as the pretext to establishing a dictatorship."[34] The four Communist

---

32. Sering [Löwenthal], "Was ist der Volkssozialismus?" An English version of this essay appeared as the pamphlet *What Is Folksocialism? A Critical Analysis*, trans. Harriet Young and Mary Fox (New York: League for Industrial Democracy, 1937).

33. Sering [Löwenthal], "Was ist der Volkssozialismus?" 1120–21. Emphasis in original.

34. Rabinbach, "Staging Antifascism," 97. The current scholarly consensus holds that the Dutch council communist Marinus van der Lubbe was the sole person responsible for the

defendants were actually acquitted. Although Münzenberg belonged to a party of the old left, his intellectual and operational independence pushed him into a marginal position not unlike that of neoleftists. He was forced out of the Communist Party in 1938–39, and in Paris he formed an autonomous group of antifascist émigrés called Friends of Socialist Unity. Münzenberg also launched a new journal called *Die Zukunft* (The future), which worked toward a "rapprochement of the various groups in exile" and developed a program for postfascist Germany. Its editorial board included the newly ex-Communist writers Arthur Koestler and Manès Sperber as well as the New Beginning theorist Löwenthal.[35] Sadly, Münzenberg himself would never experience a postfascist future: he died under mysterious circumstances in October 1940, most likely at the hands of Soviet agents.

Another media-savvy innovator was Victor Gollancz. Although not an émigré, Gollancz built an energetic publishing house in London that featured émigré writers alongside leading lights of the British left. His best invention was the Left Book Club (LBC), which he founded in 1936 along with Stafford Cripps, John Strachey, and Harold Laski. Each month the club picked a book that fit with its general project of revitalizing the British left through a united antifascist front. Tens of thousands of people subscribed, and across Britain hundreds of reading groups met to discuss the latest book of the month. Examples included Gaetano Salvemini's pioneering Italian study *Under the Axe of Fascism* (1936); George Orwell's chronicle of British working-class life *The Road to Wigan Pier* (1937); Ellen Wilkinson's book about the Jarrow march of the unemployed, *The Town that Was Murdered* (1939); and Franz Neumann's landmark analysis of the Nazi regime, *Behemoth* (1942). All books had distinctive orange and later red covers. Their low cost appealed to "the taste and pocketbook of a previously untapped left-wing audience." A New Beginning circle in London collaborated with the club, ensuring that a cheap edition of Frank's 1942 book *Will Germany Crack?* appeared there as well as a history of the German workers' movement written by New Beginning member Evelyn Anderson, *Hammer or Anvil?* (1945). Like the Org/New Beginning, the LBC underwent a leadership crisis: in 1937, its local chapters tried to break Gollancz's control over book selection. Unlike Loewenheim and company, Gollancz withstood this grassroots revolt and maintained his position.[36]

Reichstag arson. On Münzenberg, see Kasper Braskén, *The International Workers' Relief, Communism, and Transnational Solidarity: Willi Münzenberg in Weimar Germany* (London: Palgrave Macmillan, 2015), and Gross, *Willi Münzenberg*.

35. Koestler, *Invisible Writing*, 406–7.

36. Samuels, "Left Book Club."

The club's politics derived from an internal critique of Labour Party reformism and a cautious embrace of the Communist Party's Popular Front strategy. But that changed after the Nazi-Soviet Pact in 1939. Membership in the LBC plummeted as people despaired of ever achieving antifascist unity. Gollancz himself turned fiercely anti-Communist. For several years, however, the LBC breathed new life into left culture in Britain. Its peak membership of fifty-seven thousand included "disgruntled liberals, professional communists, disillusioned labourites, and a large number of newcomers to the political arena."[37] Club members read and debated politics, culture, empire, race, sex, and everyday life. The LBC was a neoleftist trendsetter. In organizing a diverse cross section of British society beyond traditional party politics, it functioned as an extraparliamentary opposition. The club held rallies, showed films, and launched a popular newsletter, *Left News*, that prefigured the *New Left Review* of the postwar era.[38]

Mobilizing for Spain

One reason for the success of ventures like the LBC was mounting public interest in the Spanish Civil War. In July 1936, Francisco Franco and other Nationalist generals rebelled against the Spanish Republic, launching a military coup on the peninsula and in the protectorate of Morocco. Their goal was to overthrow the democratically elected Popular Front government and replace it with a fascist dictatorship. Observers widely assumed that militarization of the antifascist struggle in Europe would benefit reactionary forces, so they were surprised by the vitality of Republican resistance. Republicans beat back the first Nationalist offensive and retained control over the country's most populous regions, including the major cities of Madrid, Barcelona, and Valencia. Across Europe, antifascists at home and in exile declared solidarity with their Spanish comrades.

The LBC published Koestler's *Spanish Testament* (1937) and several other tracts concerned with events in Spain. But more importantly, its local chapters took the initiative in making clothes for the International Brigades, building motorcycle ambulances, adopting Basque refugee children, and organizing food drives on behalf of the Spanish people.[39] Contemporary scholars may interpret such grassroots initiatives as part of a trend toward global humanitarian

---

37. Samuels, 76.

38. Pluto Press relaunched the Left Book Club in 2015, this time as a conventional series rather than a subscription club.

39. Samuels, "Left Book Club," 68.

activism. The Hands Off Ethiopia campaign against Italy's imperialist adventure operated that way, too, anticipating later campaigns by Oxfam, Save the Children, and Amnesty International. More than humanitarian aid as such, however, mobilization around the Spanish Civil War gave rise to a global antifascist culture in which new lefts played a key role.[40]

Spain functioned as antifascism's foreign front, a sort of proxy for the global south. Because the country was economically underdeveloped yet provided a site for armed conflict with capitalist forces, I interpret the participation of Northern European new lefts in the Spanish Civil War as functionally similar to European radicals' solidarity with Third World anticolonial struggles in the 1950s and 1960s. Nationalist forces in Spain looked like imperialist invaders—Franco had in fact invaded from Morocco—while Republican forces in a Popular Front coalition appeared as scrappy underdogs, desperately hanging on to their independence. The Spanish debate over agrarian reform and land collectivization resembled debates that would take place decades later about projects in Africa and Asia. Just as Third World politics would inspire student rebels in the 1960s to adopt new strategies and tactics, the Spanish Civil War prompted antifascists in the 1930s to experiment with new organizational forms.[41] The historian Stéfanie Prezioso argues that neoleftist groups like the Italian Justice and Liberty (GL) viewed the civil war as "a step towards the reworking of political tendencies and the reconstruction of militant antifascism." In Spain, antifascist émigrés and volunteers from around the world invented forms of militancy that they might bring back home. As the GL leader Carlo Rosselli declared, "Today in Spain, tomorrow in Italy."[42]

Of course, not only new lefts rallied to the Spanish Republican cause. The Comintern's commitment to fighting Franco by providing material aid, organizing the International Brigades, and propping up the Republican government raised the prestige of Communism everywhere. However, events in Spain helped crystallize the distinction between old lefts and new lefts in the 1930s.

---

40. See Hugo García et al., introduction to *Rethinking Antifascism*, 1–19, and Joseph Fronczak, "Local People's Global Politics: A Transnational History of the Hands Off Ethiopia Movement of 1935," *Diplomatic History* 39, no. 2 (April 2015): 245–74. See also Maria Framke, "Political Humanitarianism in the 1930s: Indian Aid for Republican Spain," *European Review of History* 23, no. 1/2 (2016): 63–81; Emily Mason, *Democracy, Deeds and Dilemmas: Support for the Spanish Republic within British Civil Society, 1936–1939* (Brighton, UK: Sussex Academic Press, 2017); and Jim Fyrth, *The Signal Was Spain: The Spanish Aid Movement in Britain, 1936–39* (London: Lawrence and Wishart, 1986).

41. See Tom Buchanan, "'The Dark Millions in the Colonies Are Unavenged': Anti-fascism and Anti-Imperialism in the 1930s," *Contemporary European History* 25, no. 4 (2016): 645–65.

42. Prezioso, "'Aujourd'hui en Espagne,'" 91.

Communist actions during the civil war pushed many leftists out of Moscow's orbit, embittering them against the vanguardist cadre party as an organizational form. Spain gave them a chance to experiment with neoleftist alternatives: committees, councils, and militias.

Some people on the left relished the opportunity to take up arms against their fascist foes. In that era, social activists did not categorically abstain from physical violence as they would during the postwar decades. Western European antifascists in the 1930s grew impatient with their governments' refusal to come to Spain's aid, especially when Italy and Germany agreed to back the Nationalists. In particular, France's refusal to intervene on behalf of its fellow Popular Front was baffling and signaled the end of both governments.[43]

New Beginning cultivated useful contacts among the Spanish Republicans, including Julio Álvarez del Vayo of the Socialist Workers' Party (PSOE) and representatives of the more radical Workers' Party of Marxist Unification (POUM).[44] A number of Germans had emigrated already to Spain for political and economic reasons, so groups like New Beginning did not start from scratch. Prominent anarchists such as Augustin Souchy naturally gravitated there, where anarcho-syndicalism had deep roots. After the electoral victory of the Popular Front in 1936, the flow of émigrés to Spain increased. Foreign-language newspapers were sold widely in Madrid and Barcelona, including the émigré paper *Die neue Weltbühne* (The new world stage). One could hang out at German clubs, restaurants, and bookstores. In July 1936, scores of émigrés traveled to Barcelona to attend the People's Olympiad, an event organized in protest against the Summer Olympics held in Berlin the following month.[45]

43. See Jackson, *Popular Front in France*, 201–9.

44. Report by Gestapo informant "Bernhard" (Munich) to Gestapa Berlin II.1.A., February 18, 1937, BArch-Berlin, R58/2, and Jean-François Berdah, "Un réseau de renseignement antinazi au service de la République espagnole (1936–1939): Le mouvement Neu Beginnen et le Servicio de Información Diplomático Especial (SIDE)," in *Naissance et évolution du renseignement dans l'espace européen, 1870–1940: Entre démocratie et totalitarisme*, ed. Frédéric Guelton and Abdil Bicer (Paris: Service historique de la defense, 2006), 295–322.

45. Zur Mühlen, *Spanien war ihre Hoffnung*, 36–37, and Xavier Pujadas and Carles Santacana, "The Popular Olympic Games, Barcelona 1936: Olympians and Antifascists," *International Review for the Sociology of Sport* 27, no. 2 (1992): 139–48. New Beginning members in the underground subverted the Berlin Olympics by offering illicit city tours to foreign visitors. By driving through depressed working-class neighborhoods such as Wedding, these New Beginning resisters shattered the Nazi spectacle and "showed a few hundred people from abroad the reality of the Third Reich." Fritz Erler (Bonn) to Henry Hellmann (London), October 6, 1951, FES, NL Löwenthal, 4. According to reports by the Nazi Propaganda Ministry, the Olympics were not the international propaganda success that Hitler had expected. See Arndt Krüger, *Die*

Revolutionary spirits rode high. But the émigrés still lay within reach of Nazi authorities, who acted through the German consulates, as well as Spanish police, who feared foreign subversion. Relief groups such as the International Red Aid helped whenever possible.

For New Beginning and other neoleftist small groups, the Spanish Socialist Party seemed at first to offer the best hope for a left revival. The PSOE had endured seven years of dictatorship under Miguel Primo de Rivera, often making painful concessions in order preserve its mass organization. The proclamation of the Second Spanish Republic in 1931 had finally given the party a chance to exercise real power in a coalition government.[46] But not all Socialists wanted to participate in what they considered a bourgeois state in service of capital.

Over the next few years, the left wing of the PSOE radicalized. An important faction coalesced behind the trade union firebrand Francisco Largo Caballero, who would become prime minister of the Republic in 1936. Nicknamed "the Spanish Lenin," Largo called for revolutionary unity between workers and peasants. He pointed out the limits of electoral politics in Spain, stressing the need for a dictatorship of the proletariat. The PSOE under Largo did distinguish itself from Republican middle-class parties. According to the scholar Paul Heywood, "once Largo began to mouth Marxist maximalism, rather like the sorcerer's apprentice he released forces which quickly moved beyond his control." His moving speeches and symbolic appeal bolstered a left socialist current within an otherwise reformist PSOE. However, by personal inclination, Largo himself remained "a union bureaucrat."[47]

The PSOE left wing published a journal called *Leviatán*. Scholars now recognize it as "the most important Marxist journal ever to have been published in Spain," even if its theoretical debates went over the heads of most Socialists at the time.[48] *Leviatán* functioned analogously to the Sopade's *Zeitschrift für Sozialismus* in its mixture of intellectual currents from the major parties and

Olympischen Spiele 1936 und die Weltmeinung (West Berlin: Bartels and Wernitz, 1972), and Soell, *Fritz Erler*, 1: 523n155.

46. Leftist critics frequently pointed out the PSOE's collaboration with Primo's dictatorship. For example, see Joaquín Maurín, *Los hombres de la dictadura: Sánchez Guerra, Cambó, Iglesias, Largo Caballero, Lerroux, Melquíades Álvarez* (Madrid: Editorial Cenit, 1930).

47. Heywood, *Marxism*, 124–25 and 133. See also Payne, *Spanish Revolution*, 107–9 and 173, and Thomas, *Spanish Civil War*, 98–99.

48. Heywood suggests that the journal "has enjoyed a rather inflated reputation . . . largely on account of the lack of any alternative forum in [Franco's] Spain devoted to developing Marxist theory." *Marxism*, 162. See Preston, *Leviatán*, and Marta Bizcarrondo, *Araquistáin y la crisis socialista en la II República: "Leviatán" (1934–1936)* (Madrid: Siglo XXI, 1975).

diverse leftists. It was edited by Largo's supporter Luis Araquistáin, whose articles defended a revolutionary socialist line. "Let us not trust in parliamentary democracy," he wrote in the first issue, "even if sometimes socialism wins a majority; if violence is not used, capitalism will defeat socialism on other fronts with its formidable economic weapons."[49] Araquistáin argued that the only way to intellectually renew socialism was by revisiting the theory and practice of Marx and Engels. Contributors to the journal included the Catalan dissident Joaquín Maurín, the reformist socialist Julián Besteiro, the philosopher José Ortega y Gasset, and the Austromarxist Otto Bauer. The journal's title (Leviathan) alluded to the political theory of Thomas Hobbes, joining a chorus of neoleftist inquiries during the 1930s and 1940s into the nature of sovereignty, civil war, and differences between bourgeois, socialist, and fascist states.[50]

Spanish intellectuals fiercely debated the character of the Republican state that had formed in 1931. Was it fundamentally bourgeois and thus a tool of the capitalist class? Should socialists support it as a necessary transition stage in Spain's modernization process? The first major crisis of the Republic occurred in October 1934, when coalminers in the northwestern region of Asturias rebelled against a national government they thought had drifted too far to the right. Plans for an armed revolt had been in place since the elections of November 1933, which brought defeat to the Socialists and victory to a far-right party, the Spanish Confederation of Autonomous Rights. In an impressive act of workers' resistance, the predominantly young Asturian miners (60 percent of them were under thirty) seized control of their workplaces and regional administration. The left wing of the PSOE and its affiliated trade union, the General Union of Workers, called a general strike in solidarity. One historian has called the two-week-long Asturian commune "the most intensive, destructive proletarian insurrection in the history of western Europe to that date."[51] The strikers relented only after a concerted attack by government troops under the command of Franco, among others. More than a thousand miners died, tens of thousands were imprisoned, and widespread repression of leftist dissent followed.[52] To many observers on the left, the Republican government's reaction to the strike was equivalent to the Bolshevik suppression of the 1921

49. Quoted in Payne, *Spanish Revolution*, 137.

50. Franz L. Neumann's book *Behemoth* (1942, rev. ed. 1944), borrowed its title from another book Hobbes wrote, in 1668, the sequel to *Leviathan* (1651). Leviathan and Behemoth are a pair of monsters mentioned in the Old Testament.

51. Payne, *Spanish Revolution*, 153–55. Presumably Payne did not consider the Paris Commune a proletarian insurrection.

52. See Shubert, *Road to Revolution*.

sailor's rebellion at Kronstadt: both acts delegitimized supposedly progressive governments and emboldened leftists to seek antisystemic alternatives.

The Spanish Federation of Socialist Youth took a more militant course than its parent organization, the PSOE. The publisher of its journal *Renovación* released a pamphlet in 1935 called *October: The Second Stage*. Authored by Santiago Carrillo and two other young radicals, this manifesto explained why the general strike failed and how a future revolution might succeed. The pamphlet made several demands: bolshevize the PSOE, unify the Spanish proletariat, align it with the interests of the international workers' movement, and recognize the legitimacy of the Spanish Communist Party (PCE).[53] Heywood has described the pamphlet's conclusion as "a series of unrealistic demands which reflected, above all else, youthful radicalism."[54] In other words, it used a neoleftist style even if its call to bolshevize the PSOE clashed with neoleftist critiques of the vanguardist cadre party.

The general strike of October 1934 did fail, but it profoundly impacted the future of the Spanish left. The revolutionary socialists around Largo Caballero concluded that the uprising suffered from a lack of centralized party organization. They agreed with the young authors of the *October* pamphlet that the PSOE must transform from a democratic class party oriented toward legislative reforms into a vanguardist cadre party oriented toward revolution. Moderate socialists around Indalecio Prieto, on the other hand, thought that the failed uprising proved the inefficacy of revolutionary means and the need for pragmatic alliances with middle-class Republicans. The feud between Caballeristas and Prietistas, as the two camps came to be known, sowed division within the PSOE and greatly weakened the power of organized socialism in Spain in the run-up to the civil war.

Despite or even because of this division, the years 1934–36 were fruitful for Marxist theory. Heywood has argued that the older PSOE leaders held "a distinctively narrow vision of Marxist theory" that limited their political options. The fragmentation of the party between 1931 and 1936 represented "the logical culmination of theoretical ambiguities which had marked the party since its inception." Moreover, Heywood claims that "the establishment of the Popular Front coalition at the start of 1936 not only represented the final triumph of the reformists over the revolutionists, but also the effective abandonment of

53. Ricard Viñas, *La formación de las Juventudes Socialistas Unificadas (1934–1936)* (Madrid: Siglo XXI, 1978), 30. The pamphlet *October* was signed only by Carlos Hernández Zancajo, but Carrillo and Amaro del Rosal were the unnamed coauthors. The journal *Renovación* continued publication in exile. Carrillo joined the PCE in 1936 after unifying the Socialist and Communist youth leagues. In 1960, he would become the PCE general secretary.

54. Heywood, *Marxism*, 159. See also see Preston, *Coming of the Spanish Civil War*, 220–21.

Marxism as the party's guiding ideological principle." Not only the PSOE, but also a few neoleftist small groups were forced "to abandon their Marxist principles in face of the harsh realities of Realpolitik and join the expressly reformist Popular Front coalition."[55]

Observing a "basic ideological and organizational incoherence" within the left socialist camp, the historian Helen Graham likewise argues that Largo's downfall was long in the making. Already during the 1934 strike, Largo's left socialists faced criticism for their allegedly deficient revolutionary credentials. Graham also notes the contradiction between left socialists' "hollow revolutionary rhetoric" and their "inveterate reformism" in practice.[56] Despite the fact that left socialists claimed to offer a more radical alternative to parliamentary socialism, they remained beholden to trade union bureaucracy and centralized forms of organization. One critic targeted such organizational conservatism in a 1935 book titled *Reformist Bureaucracy in the Workers' Movement*. The book likened the psychology and tactics of labor bureaucrats to those of bourgeois members of parliament. This leftist critique revived arguments made by council communists in the early 1920s. The revolution in Spain, the book concluded, must be seen as a struggle against bureaucratic forms in all sectors of society.[57]

Largo and allies such as Araquistáin commanded a lot of media attention, but their revolutionary rhetoric meant little to their syndicalist base. The unions valued organizational continuity above all else. Eventually PSOE moderates and Prieto's right wing won control over the party, sidelining the left socialists. Within the framework of the Popular Front, the PSOE would abandon Marxism and class struggle altogether.

The Socialist decision to participate in the Popular Front that formed in early 1936 owed as much to pragmatic calculation as it did to Prieto's commitment to electoral democracy. The Popular Front bargain required an indefinite postponement of revolutionary goals. That worried some left intellectuals, who debated whether the PSOE now stood in the way of a radical transformation of Spanish society. Intellectually and organizationally, the Spanish left entered what one historian dubbed "a perpetual state of revolutionary effervescence."[58] Factions, splinter groups, and small nonparty groups proliferated in the period just before the civil war. Would they band together against

55. Heywood, *Marxism*, ix, xii–xiii, and 147.

56. Graham, "Eclipse of the Socialist Left," 127 and 128–29. See also Preston, *Coming of the Spanish Civil War*, 2 and 231–32.

57. Juan Andrade, *La burocracia reformista en el movimiento obrero* (Madrid: Ed. Gleba, 1935).

58. Thomas, *Spanish Civil War*, 6.

the fascist threat? Despite his plan to centralize the PSOE on a Bolshevik model, Largo Caballero opposed any united front with the Communists and was skeptical of the neoleftist small groups. It was actually the moderate Socialists around Prieto who offered to collaborate with Communists and Manuel Azaña's Republican Left. That coalition laid the groundwork for Spain's Popular Front under the presidency of Azaña.

German émigrés applauded this antifascist coalition. New Beginning explicitly modeled its plan for a German Popular Front on what happened in Spain in early 1936 and would recur in France that May. Karl Frank admired Largo in particular and accused the Sopade of "criminal indifference, lack of sympathy, and even sabotage" for its reserved attitude toward Spanish antifascists.[59] Left socialists may have grumbled about the PSOE under the control of Prieto, but to outside observers the party's participation in the Popular Front looked like a step forward in the global antifascist struggle.

The civil war that broke out in July 1936 caused Socialists and Communists to cooperate in an unprecedented way. Bred of necessity, that unity of action was the finest accomplishment of mainstream antifascism. From a wide-angle view, it looked as though the Spanish left had found the magic formula of unity. On closer inspection, that unity actually excluded diverse lefts such as the anarchists. The Spanish Popular Front represented the ideological convergence of PSOE moderates and the now socially conservative PCE. This bipartisan old left pushed anarchists and neoleftists out onto the periphery. Occasionally these marginalized lefts would unite in opposition to the center-left establishment, but usually they were fragmented. Representing organizational fragmentation, new lefts might be seen as a distraction from the military campaign against fascism: the civil war would rage for the next three years. The military emergency only worsened political sectarianism, which became so fierce that the German observer and onetime New Beginning ally Franz Borkenau wrote of the Spanish cockpit.[60] The negative aspects of this fragmentation have so far dominated scholarship on the civil war. It is also worth examining the cockpit's positive experimentation in left theory and organization.

POUM, Militias, and Free Women

By 1935, an alternative antifascist coalition had formed between Largo's left socialists and two neoleftist small groups, the Catalan Workers and Peasants' Bloc (BOC) and the Spanish Communist Left. Those two would merge into

59. Quoted in Zur Mühlen, *Spanien war ihre Hoffnung*, 109. Translation mine.

60. Borkenau, *Spanish Cockpit*.

the celebrated Workers' Party of Marxist Unification (POUM). As Heywood puts it, this alternative coalition's "shared aim was the revolutionary overthrow of the Republic and the establishment of a Socialist regime."[61] Already before the Popular Front, it pitted itself against the government.

The brief ascendancy of Largo Caballero and the PSOE's left wing would give revolutionary Marxist groups like POUM a bigger stage. After watching the German workers' movement collapse in 1933 when the fascists seized power, the Catalan intellectual and politician Joaquín Maurín sketched out a plan for a big-tent unity coalition called the Worker Alliance. "What the soviet was for the Russian revolution," he wrote, "the Worker Alliance is for the Spanish revolution."[62] Unlike representatives of the old left, Maurín recognized the need to mobilize the most revolutionary social forces in Spain, no matter which class they belonged to. That required flexibility in Marxist theory. The landless peasantry must join industrial workers on the revolutionary vanguard: "Agrarian revolution and industrial revolution are two faces of the same coin," he wrote in his 1932 book *The Spanish Revolution*: "The one cannot exist without the other. We are entering full-scale social revolution."[63] Maurín's original group, the BOC, published a journal called *La nueva era* (The new era), which featured articles on "Marxism and art, literature and the Mexican revolution, Gandhi, the tragedy of Mark Twain, and the theatre." According to Heywood, his general thesis was that "Spain must carry through a democratic-Socialist revolution or fall into the grip of counter-revolution and fascism."[64] Half measures would not suffice, and the Republican center could not hold. Indeed, like the Miles pamphlet, the final chapter of Maurín's 1935 book *Toward the Second Revolution* insisted that action by the left would decide whether the crisis ended in socialism or fascism.[65]

Heywood calls Catalonia "the centre of probably the most advanced indigenous Marxism ever known in Spain."[66] There the workers' revolution went the furthest. In Barcelona, according to another scholar, "Expropriation was the rule—hotels, stores, banks, factories were either requisitioned or closed." Antifascist committees and militias held most levers of power. In addition to controlling the means of production and civil administration, they sought to stamp out bourgeois culture from everyday life. To wear a tie was to risk arrest.[67]

61. Heywood, *Marxism*, 112. See also Sennett, *Revolutionary Marxism in Spain*.
62. Quoted in Payne, *Spanish Revolution*, 139.
63. Quoted in Heywood, *Marxism*, 143.
64. Heywood, 136 and 143.
65. Maurín, *Hacia la segunda revolución*.
66. Heywood, *Marxism*, 135.
67. Thomas, *Spanish Civil War*, 187–88.

It was no accident that Catalonia and its neighboring region Aragon also hosted the largest number of anarcho-syndicalists, grouped in the National Confederation of Labor and its political arm, the Iberian Anarchist Federation. With their distaste for hierarchy and centralized organization, new lefts have often exhibited an anarchist streak. In the mid-1930s, neoleftists, anarchists, and Trotskyists converged in a shared critique of old left bureaucracy, whether Stalinist or Social Democratic. Those three currents combined in POUM, which represented a new left similar to the kind that New Beginning wanted to be for Germany. Standard histories present POUM as the main party of autonomous Marxism in Spain. For my purposes, the group serves as that country's best example of the antifascist new left. Known as Poumistas, its members wished to carry out an independent socialist revolution that aligned with neither the Comintern nor the Labour and Socialist International.[68] Foreign revolutionary socialists were therefore attracted to POUM. In the words of one unsympathetic historian, antifascist émigrés sided with the Spanish party "in the romantic supposition that it indeed embodied a magnificent Utopian aspiration."[69]

Aside from Maurín, another Catalan Marxist leader to emerge in the early 1930s was Andrés (or Andreu) Nin, a former Communist and former Trotskyist. Although he had broken with Trotsky over tactical disagreements, Nin retained the latter's concept of permanent revolution. Both he and Maurín were former schoolteachers, like their French neoleftist counterpart Marceau Pivert. They gathered around them a host of likeminded Spanish intellectuals and heterodox leftists such as Julián Gorkin, who would later help organize the anti-Stalinist left in Mexico, and Alberto Véga, who emigrated to France in 1939 and after World War II would cofound the influential group Socialism or Barbarism: another link in the neoleftist chain.[70]

In 1934, even before the Asturian uprising, Maurín and Nin proposed a new national organization to prepare for a general strike. Largo Caballero declined their proposal. His primary interest was to maintain the existing Socialist Party and the General Union of Workers "as the organisational fulcrum of the working class." Despite his fiery rhetoric, Largo supported policies that favored the PSOE's "national bureaucratic imperialism over the workers' movement."[71] So, even when Poumistas like Maurín and Nin agreed with the Caballeristas

68. Payne, *Spanish Revolution*, 170 and 288.

69. Thomas, *Spanish Civil War*, 191.

70. See Solano, *POUM*, and Alba and Schwartz, *Spanish Marxism versus Soviet Communism*.

71. Heywood, *Marxism*, 138.

on the need for a revolutionary offensive, they disagreed on the manner of organization. For POUM, the paradigmatic form of organization was the antifascist committees, or Spanish soviets, that cropped up throughout Catalonia in the latter half of 1936.[72] These committees carried out a grassroots revolution parallel and often contrary to the Popular Front government, all while opposing the Nationalists in armed struggle.

POUM has achieved legendary status in histories of the Spanish Civil War largely owing to the reportage by the British writer George Orwell. Surfing the wave of antifascist volunteers, the thirty-three-year-old Orwell arrived in Barcelona in late December 1936 with the intention of taking up arms in defense of the Republic. According to his famous account in *Homage to Catalonia* (1938), he happened to join a POUM militia unit without knowing anything about the group's politics except that it was antifascist. Immediately, what he experienced in the militia diverged from his expectations for a military outfit engaged in civil war. The POUM *milicianos* resembled a "mob of eager children" who disregarded traditional discipline and decorum. Instead they practiced a "democratic 'revolutionary' type of discipline" based on class solidarity, persuasion, and consent. Unlike a regular army, Orwell observed, the militia operated nearly without defined ranks, bullying, or abuse. Troops elected their own officers, and those derelict in their duty were tried by soldiers' courts. Everyone was addressed as "comrade," and militia discipline depended entirely on political consciousness, or "an understanding of *why* orders must be obeyed."[73]

The militia system was a neoleftist experiment in anti-authoritarian organization. POUM and the anarchists resisted attempts to "bourgeoisify" the workers' militias, police forces, and other units. Not blind obedience but rational adherence would keep units together on the front lines. Eventually, however, the course of the war and political developments behind the front led to the imposition of a more centralized army system. This process was known as militarization, and it occurred largely because of Spain's growing dependence on Soviet aid. Aside from external pressures, the militias also faced an internal dilemma much as council communists and other leftists had before them. Out of necessity, the introduction of centralized leadership, formal officer ranks, and traditional discipline turned fluid militias into fixed military units.

Orwell recalled that hundreds of German and Italian émigrés served in the POUM militias, many of whom belonged to a special force called the Shock

---

72. Payne, *Spanish Revolution*, 248–49 and 296.

73. Orwell, *Homage to Catalonia*, 10 and 28.

Battalion. Other neoleftist groups, such as GL, formed autonomous columns of their own. Together with their Spanish comrades, émigré militiamen formed "the only community of any size in Western Europe where political consciousness and disbelief in capitalism were more normal than their opposites." Orwell detected in the militias' organization a sort of prefigurative politics. Their nearly perfect equality gave him "a foretaste of Socialism." The militia created a new culture and microcosm of classless society. He realized that although the feeling of equality could not last for long, it nevertheless actualized his desire for a postcapitalist society.[74] Newness appeared in concrete form as a community of hope engaged in a common antifascist struggle. Orwell's remembrance of having been "in contact with something strange and valuable" resembled what Hannah Arendt would later call the lost treasure of revolutionary community.[75] Importantly, for Orwell it represented real socialism and not the "humbug" preached by the Communist Party.

His focus on militia*men* obscured another radical dimension. The historian Enzo Traverso interprets the Spanish Civil War as a great moment for women's liberation. The figure of the antifascist *miliciana* "took over such traditional attributes of masculinity as military uniform and weapons, courage and participation in battle." The revolutionary atmosphere in Madrid and elsewhere lent itself to sexual freedom and looser bonds of marriage. Divorce became easier and more common. While subverting the sexual order in a staunchly Catholic country, women during the civil war did however reinforce some traditional gender norms. Images of women in arms were juxtaposed with "weeping mothers and suffering victims." One POUM banner read, "Better the widow of a hero than the wife of a coward!"[76]

The most famous female icon of the war was the Communist writer and politician Dolores Ibárruri, better known as La Pasionaria. One historian described her as "a kind of revolutionary saint . . . celebrated for her appeals to Spanish womanhood to bear sons without the encumbrance of husbands." In her rousing speeches against fascism, La Pasionaria invoked a tradition of guerrilla resistance dating back to the Spanish War of Independence against Napoleon. Famously, she proclaimed that "It is better to die on your feet than to live on your knees! They shall not pass!" The phrase ¡No pasarán! became a rallying cry of the Republic.[77] While her rhetoric inspired people across the

74. Orwell, *Homage to Catalonia*, 60 and 103–5.

75. Orwell, 104, and Arendt, *On Revolution*, ch. 6.

76. Traverso, *Fire and Blood*, 217–18. See also Thomas, *Spanish Civil War*, 184.

77. Thomas, *Spanish Civil War*, 8 and 140. As evidence of an emerging global antifascist culture, the chant "They shall not pass!" was immediately adopted by British antifascists at the infamous Battle of Cable Street in October 1936. Nigel Copsey, "'Every Time They Made

world to take a stand against fascism, her portrait of the defiant Spanish mother fell short of radical feminist ideals—just as her ardent Stalinism fell short of neoleftist ideals.

Still, the historian Mercedes Yusta Rodrigo claims that a distinctly feminine political culture developed through Spanish antifascism. Yusta emphasizes the organizational skill, administrative experience, and ethos of care practiced by antifascist women prior to the start of the war. Once the war began, a bellicose style overtook antifascism and turned it into a more masculine affair. The feminine political culture did survive, but less conspicuously. During and well after the war, Spanish women sustained antifascist organizations underground and in exile.[78]

The Comintern wanted to recruit militant women for the Popular Front in order to connect antifascism to older traditions of bourgeois pacifism. Feminist antifascism was closely associated with pacifism in the 1930s.[79] But antifascist women broke with older feminist leagues, which they thought had succumbed to the same sort of bureaucratic sclerosis that afflicted the parties and unions of the old left. According to the historian Christine Bard, the antifascist era witnessed a crisis of feminism in which the older generation of the women's movement failed to transmit its values to a younger, more militant generation.[80] Militant women across Europe came to view fascism as an ideology of male domination, so many decided to subsume feminist goals under the general struggle against fascism.[81] Writing about France, another scholar calls such antifascist women the lost generation between the founders of the

---

a Communist, They Made a Fascist': The Labour Party and Popular Anti-fascism in the 1930s," in *Varieties of Anti-fascism: Britain in the Inter-War Period*, ed. Copsey and Andrzej Olechnowicz (Basingstoke, UK: Palgrave Macmillan, 2010), 52–72 (at 64). The phrase "better to die on your feet" seems to have originated with the Mexican revolutionary Emiliano Zapata.

78. Yusta Rodrigo, "Cultura política femenina." She builds on the pioneering scholarship of Mary Nash, *Defying Male Civilization: Women in the Spanish Civil War* (Denver: Arden, 1995). Yusta's account revises feminist critiques that viewed antifascism in Southern Europe as an exclusively male phenomenon. Cf. Patrizia Gabrielli, *Tempio di virilità: L'antifascismo, il genere, la storia* (Milan: F. Angeli, 2008).

79. For example, see Emmanuelle Carle, "Women, Anti-fascism and Peace in Interwar France: Gabrielle Duchêne's Itinerary," *French History* 18, no. 3 (September 2004): 291–314.

80. Christine Bard, "La crise du féminisme en France dans les années trente: L'impossible transmission," *Les cahiers du CEDREF*, no. 4–5 (1995): 13–27.

81. Yusta Rodrigo, "Cultura política femenina," 259.

international women's movement and the second-wave feminists.[82] In its re-volt against established feminist organizations and its subversion of gender roles, this lost generation at least found a home in the antifascist new left.

POUM had all-women volunteer battalions, and some leftists went further in advancing women's liberation as part of the Spanish revolution. The Free Women (Mujeres Libres) were an anarchist group founded by the lesbian ac-tivist Lucía Sánchez Saornil and others who refused to accept the sexist poli-tics of mainstream antifascism. For them, women's liberation could occur only together with social revolution. Like Wilhelm Reich's Sex-Pol experiment in Austria and Germany, the Free Women engaged in clinical work that included education in sexual and reproductive health. To their tens of thousands of members they provided their own journal, libraries, job training facilities, and day cares. In building such parallel institutons, the Free Women aimed for radical autonomy.[83]

These most radical currents of the Spanish left encountered staunch resis-tance from within the Republican camp. In particular, POUM's sharp analyses of Soviet foreign policy made it a target for Communist intrigue. In Novem-ber 1936, the POUM journal *La batalla* (The battle) published an article claim-ing that "Stalin's concern is not really the fate of the Spanish and international proletariat, but the protection of the Soviet government."[84] The Stalinist bu-reaucracy had become alienated from the original goals of the Bolshevik Party, POUM writers argued, and its control over the Comintern posed a real danger to the international working class. This critique aligned with Trotsky's inter-pretation of the Soviet Union as a degenerated workers' state,[85] which was why Communists associated POUM with a Trotskyite plot to undermine the So-viet Union. From their perspective, the Spanish new left functioned objec-tively as an ally of fascism. In early 1937, Spanish Communists managed to cut off pay and supplies to the POUM militia on the Madrid front, forcing that unit to disband.

The rivalry between POUM and the Communist-Socialist old left came to a head during the May 1937 uprising in Barcelona. These May Days resulted from a backlash against the expropriations and other revolutionary measures taken by the neoleftist regional government. When the Communists and

82. Siân Reynolds, "The Lost Generation of French Feminists? Anti-fascist Women in the 1930s," *Women's Studies International Forum* 23, no. 6 (November–December 2000): 679–88.

83. Martha A. Ackelsberg, *Free Women of Spain: Anarchism and the Struggle for the Emancipa-tion of Women* (Bloomington: Indiana University Press, 1991).

84. Quoted in Anthony Beevor, *The Spanish Civil War* [1982] (London: Cassell, 1999), 140.

85. See Trotsky, *Revolution Betrayed*.

Catalan nationalists moved to cripple that government (with the blessing of Republican leaders in Madrid), anarchists in Barcelona rebelled and called on POUM for support. Street battles ensued, in which antifascist factions tragically shot at one another. The Communists blamed Poumistas for the uprising, even though they had entered the fray only in support of their anarchist allies. Both groups were decried as Trotskyites, or "Franco's Fifth Column." The divide between Communists and Republicans on one side and anarchists and POUM on the other became unbridgeable.

After the fighting ended, Poumistas and anarchists were subjected to systematic repression. The prime minister Largo Caballero resigned after refusing a Communist demand for harsh penalties against POUM. Furthermore, he opposed Communist proposals for "centralization, state control, police terror, reduction of [anarchist] membership in the cabinet, or Russian dictation of military affairs."[86] After taking over for Largo, the moderate socialist Juan Negrín agreed to shut down the POUM newspaper *La batalla*. This was part of his pragmatic deal "to sacrifice the POUM to Stalin in order to maintain arms supplies."[87] On June 16, POUM was outlawed. Its organization and leaders were soon liquidated by the Communist-controlled secret police. Nin disappeared after his arrest. An international campaign asked "Where is Nin?" but received no answer from Republican officials and Comintern agents. According to later reports, Communist interrogators tried to force Nin to confess to absurd crimes in a similar fashion to defendants in the ongoing Moscow show trials. When he refused, they tortured him in a secret prison and then murdered him. Many other Poumistas were rounded up. Maurín had actually been captured by Franco's Nationalists at the beginning of the war, which ironically may have saved his life.[88]

After the purge of POUM and other new lefts, and especially while the Republic collapsed in the winter of 1938–39, countless Spanish antifascists became refugees. Waves of the destitute and disillusioned crossed over the Pyrenees mountains into France. Refugees found themselves stuck on ships in the Mediterranean Sea with nowhere to dock. The war's endgame was a humanitarian catastrophe that foreshadowed the horrors of World War II. It also foreshadowed the European migrant crisis that began in 2015 as a result of, among other things, the Syrian Civil War.[89]

86. Payne, *Spanish Revolution*, 298–99.

87. Beevor, *Spanish Civil War*, 193.

88. Payne, *Spanish Revolution*, 313, and Thomas, *Spanish Civil War*, 454–55.

89. Thomas, *Spanish Civil War*, 574–77 and 604–5. See also Scott Soo, *The Routes to Exile: France and the Spanish Civil War Refugees, 1939–2009* (New York: Manchester University Press,

Despite resulting in Nationalist victory, which represented a triumph for European fascism, the Spanish Civil War nonetheless functioned as "the great moment of hope for an entire [young] generation angry at the apparent cynicism, indolence and hypocrisy of an older generation with whom they were out of sympathy." Even conservative historians such as Hugh Thomas have correctly interpreted the left's defeat as generative, unleashing "a burst of creative energy."[90] Amid crisis, a new left briefly flashed on an otherwise dark horizon.

2013), and Robert Mackey, "In a Fight over Syria, Echoes of Spain's Civil War and the Battle for Truth in Guernica," *Intercept*, May 2, 2018.

90. Thomas, *Spanish Civil War*, 616–17.

4

Revolutionary Hope and Despair

THE SPANISH CIVIL WAR was a focal point of hope and despair on the left in the latter half of the 1930s. Even before the purge of POUM that followed the May 1937 uprising in Barcelona, Spanish Communists and their Soviet handlers targeted foreign émigrés who collaborated with the neoleftist party. For that reason, suspicion immediately fell on Communists when the young New Beginning member Mark Rein disappeared near Barcelona in April 1937. As the historian Patrik von zur Mühlen has explained, Rein "was indeed neither a prominent personality, nor did his disappearance trigger any special political developments. But his affair was fiercely debated in the emigration, and as a result of comprehensive inquiries it was the most thoroughly investigated case of its kind."[1] For New Beginning and its allies, the Rein affair permanently soured relations with German Communists. Plans for a united front ground to a halt. Just as importantly, neoleftist small groups became conscious of offering an antisystemic alternative: neither Communist nor Social Democratic nor bourgeois democratic, but something new.

Born in Russia in 1909, Rein was twice a refugee. His father Raphael Abramovitch, a leading Menshevik, emigrated with his family to Germany in 1920. For years Abramovitch ran afoul of the Comintern, which undoubtedly played a role in his son's disappearance.[2] Mark Rein spent his teenage years in Berlin, trained as a radio engineer, and joined the Socialist Worker Youth (SAJ) as had so many recruits to the Org/New Beginning. After the Nazi takeover in 1933, he emigrated to Paris, where he proved invaluable to New Beginning in gaining the support of the wider socialist emigration.

1. Zur Mühlen, *Spanien war ihre Hoffnung*, 167. See also Broué, *Staline et la révolution*.

2. On the activities of Russian Menshevik émigrés in the 1920s and 1930s, see André Liebich, *From the Other Shore: Russian Social Democracy after 1921* (Cambridge, MA: Harvard University Press, 1997).

Rein volunteered for the Republican cause and left for Spain in early 1937. His sole political acts there were to travel to Valencia in March to attend a meeting with Karl Frank and other New Beginning members and, in early April, to sign a declaration in favor of a German Popular Front (*Volksfront*). Sometime during the night of April 9–10, Rein walked out of his Barcelona hotel with two unknown individuals. The scattered belongings he left behind indicated that he departed in haste. A week later, a friend received a brief letter in Russian apparently handwritten by Rein that claimed he had traveled to Madrid to take care of urgent business. The friend was immediately suspicious, however, because the date on the postage stamp did not match Rein's alleged travel dates.[3] It smelled like a cover-up. Rein had in fact vanished.

Investigations from afar produced unsatisfying results. With the approval of the Spanish Republican government, a New Beginning delegation traveled to Barcelona in July to make direct inquiries. A young agent of the German Socialist Workers' Party (SAP), Willy Brandt, aided the investigation.[4] Frank, his new American wife Anna Caples (alias Nelly), their ally in the Sopade Paul Hertz, and Rein's father Abramovitch narrowed down all possible explanations to one: a Communist assassination. Catalan officials and German Communist agents in Spain provided evasive answers to New Beginning's questions. Frank and Hertz cowrote a letter of protest to the German Communist Party (KPD) central committee in Prague, and it took the Communist leader Walter Ulbricht two months to reply. He dismissed the investigation into Rein's likely death as a distraction from more urgent matters. As for the specific allegations, Ulbricht blamed the "Trotskyites" in POUM for devising a plot to discredit the Communist Party.[5]

The German Communists may or may not have had information about Rein's disappearance. Either way, they referred the matter to the Comintern

3. Zur Mühlen, *Spanien war ihre Hoffnung*, 168. New Beginning suspected that the letter and a second one just like it were either forged or forcibly extracted from Rein. BArch-Berlin, RY1/I 2/3/405.

4. After World War II, Brandt would become a leader of the SPD and chancellor of West Germany. On his youth activities in Spain, see Brandt, *In Exile*, ch. 4.

5. Report by Willi Müller [Karl Frank] to Friedrich Adler, "Bericht über Nachforschungen im Falle des Genossen Mark Rein in Spanien vom 1.–10. Juli 1937," July 13, 1937, IISG, NB Archives, 17/7; "Zusammenfassung der Tatsachen und Hypothesen zum Fall Mark Rein in Barcelona," late 1937, IISG, NB Archives, 15/5; Willi Müller and Paul Hertz to the ZK der KPD (Prague), July 28, 1937, BArch-Berlin, RY1/I 2/3/405; and ZK der KPD to Paul Hertz and Willi Müller, September 24, 1937, IISG, NB Archives, 15/2.

and Soviet secret police (NKVD).[6] Although New Beginning's investigation was inconclusive, the group did submit a report to Friedrich Adler of the Labour and Socialist International (LSI) that essentially blamed the NKVD for Rein's death. As it turns out, that theory was correct. Later scholarship has proven that Rein disappeared as part of an NKVD operation directed by Alexander Orlov. Various elements of the affair—for example, "sending letters signed and sometimes even written by people who were dead by the time the letter was dispatched"—were trademarks of Orlov's purge techniques against POUM and its émigré allies.[7]

During the investigation, Frank did uncover a Soviet spy in New Beginning who might have supplied intelligence on Rein to the NKVD. The Austrian socialist Leopold Kulcsar (alias Paul Maresch) worked for the Spanish consulate in Prague in cooperation with the New Beginning foreign bureau. Aside from fundraising, he helped the group gather military intelligence and recruit German volunteers for the Republican cause. Kulcsar and his wife Ilse were a militant couple whose ambition "was to become the Austrian counterpart of the founders of the German New Beginners."[8] Their Spark Group, named for Lenin's old journal *Iskra* (Spark), never amounted to anything, but Leopold did become a shady operator in the underworld of exile politics. He aroused suspicion when he stonewalled Frank and the other investigators of Rein's disappearance. Although he had resigned from the Austrian Communist Party years before, New Beginning leaders suspected that he still maintained contacts with the Comintern and carried out its orders in Spain. In October 1937, the group placed Kulcsar "on ice" for three months, a practice of ostracism meant to neutralize leakers and infiltrators.[9] The next year, as the Spanish Civil War neared its end, Kulcsar himself died in Paris under mysterious circumstances. Ironically, like Rein he probably met his fate at the hands of the NKVD.

6. Report by "Br." to ZK der KPD, "Verschwinden von Mark Rein (Abramowicz, jun) in Spanien (Barcelona)," July 27, 1937, BArch-Berlin, RY1/I 2/3/405.

7. Boris Volodarsky, *Stalin's Agent: The Life and Death of Alexander Orlov* (Oxford: Oxford University Press, 2015), 245–49. The Communist agents responsible for kidnapping and killing Rein were Alfred Herz, Mariano Gómez Emperador, and an unknown secret informer. Herz worked as part of the KPD intelligence service in Paris.

8. Buttinger, *Twilight of Socialism*, 23. See also Ilse Barea-Kulcsar's memoir *Vienna: Legend and Reality* (London: Secker and Warburg, 1966), and Volodarsky, *Stalin's Agent*, 247.

9. Memo from the New Beginning foreign bureau, "Mitteilung zur Angelegenheit Maresch an die St. Leiter," October 22, 1937, IISG, NB Archives, 16/9. See also Paul Maresch [Leopold Kulcsar] to New Beginning foreign bureau, September 10, 1937, IISG, NB Archives, 16/15, and Mehringer, *Waldemar von Knoeringen*, 148.

Set against the backdrop of Stalinist purges, the Rein affair worsened New Beginning's relationship with Communists and eroded the group's faith in the progressive role of the Soviet Union. As revolutionary socialists, members of New Beginning had long treated the rivalry between Social Democrats and Communists as a false alternative. A new left, the group thought, required a united workers' movement that would supersede the bureaucratic apparatuses of the old left. But in its pursuit of unity, the group had made overtures to Communists. New Beginning members rejected the dogmatic anti-Communism of Social Democrats just as they did the dogmatic Stalinism of Communist apparatchiks. Many of them had acquired their earliest political education in the Communist youth movement. The fire of Red October still burned bright for leftists of all stripes. But antifascists in exile became steadily disillusioned with the Soviet Union.

A German Popular Front?

After 1933, rank-and-file Communists in the anti-Nazi underground sometimes ignored the directives of party leaders in exile and entered into tactical alliances with Social Democrats and other non-Communist resisters. In 1934–35, the KPD central committee dialed back its accusations of "social fascism" against Social Democrats and made a concerted effort to build a left united front. But the Sopade greeted this change of policy with skepticism.[10] Although pleased with the new Communist line, New Beginning also remained cautious. In July 1934, Walter Loewenheim arranged a meeting with the Czech Communist leader Klement Gottwald, but to little effect: Gottwald, he noted derisively, made a "very bigwig-like impression [sehr verbonzten Eindruck]."[11]

The KPD tried repeatedly to split off the left wing of the Social Democratic emigration and use it for its own united front plans. Karl Böchel and Siegfried Aufhäuser seemed like easy targets for this splitting policy, especially because their own faction, the German Revolutionary Socialists (RSD), had propagandized loudly in favor of a united front. Suspicion that Böchel and Aufhäuser actually entertained a Communist offer (which they did not) provided the Sopade an excuse to cut off funding to their group and their New Beginning allies in December 1934.[12] In any case, the Communists' splitting policy

---

10. For a thorough analysis of the KPD during this period, see Duhnke, *Die KPD von 1933 bis 1945*.

11. Log-book entry "Aufsuchen von Gottwald," IISG, NB Archives, 5/11. See also Foitzik, *Zwischen den Fronten*, 106.

12. Karl Böchel, Willy Lange, Willi Müller [Karl Frank], and Siegfried Aufhäuser (Prague) to the office of the Sopade (Prague), January 22, 1935, IISG, NB Archives, 7/1. See chapter 3.

made New Beginning wary of becoming a pawn in their game. The KPD central committee itself expressed concern in 1935 that New Beginning might try to split off and co-opt Communists inside Germany. That concern was partly justified.[13]

In July and August of that year, the Comintern held its seventh and final World Congress in Moscow. With Stalin's blessing, Georgi Dimitrov announced the new policy of the Popular Front, which officially ended the infamous Third Period of noncooperation with Social Democrats and other socialists. The Popular Front would remain the party line for the next four years. Across Europe, the new line enabled pragmatic cooperation between Communists, Social Democrats, and progressive liberals against the common fascist threat. Such cooperation occurred in different combinations according to the circumstances of each country.

Talks about building a German Popular Front in exile occurred at the Hotel Lutetia in Paris between September 1935 and April 1937. The impresario Willi Münzenberg organized these meetings of the SPD's French regional committee, the KPD, the SAP, the RSD, and the International Socialist Militant League (ISK), along with celebrity writers in the German emigration such as Heinrich Mann and Lion Feuchtwanger.[14]

Neither New Beginning nor the Sopade attended officially, but the former group did cultivate ties with Léon Blum's Popular Front government in France. Through his aptly named chief of staff André Blumel, the prime minister Blum secretly provided New Beginning a monthly stipend of between eight and ten thousand francs. The group's ally in the Sopade, Hertz, also convinced the French propaganda ministry to put its Strasbourg radio station at New Beginning's disposal for broadcasting messages into Germany.[15]

---

13. Report "Zur hiesigen Lage/St. Gallen," 1935, BArch-Berlin, RY1/I 2/3/312. After meeting with "Miles" (maybe Loewenheim, but the report suggests that it might actually have been Frank) in February 1935, a KPD operative had the impression that "Miles himself does not know how strong the position of the Left [i.e., New Beginning and the RSD] is in the Social Democratic organizations inside [Germany]." Report by Franz, "Aussprache mit Miles Mitte Februar," received on April 1, 1935, BArch-Berlin, RY1/I 2/3/402.

14. For the definitive history with documents, see Langkau-Alex, *Deutsche Volksfront*.

15. See report by Gestapo informant "Bernhard" (Munich) to Gestapa Berlin II. 1. A., February 18, 1937, BArch-Berlin, R58/2. According to Henry W. Ehrmann (coincidentally also called "Bernhard"), the monthly stipend continued after the fall of the Popular Front while Blum was still vice-president. It ceased only with the Munich Agreement at the end of September 1938. Hurwitz, *Demokratie und Antikommunismus*, 4 (1), 51. Kurt Kliem, who received the same information from Ehrmann, added that New Beginning could cultivate such high connections in France only because of the French Socialists' antipathy toward the Sopade. Kliem, "Der

At a group conference in June 1936, the New Beginning theorist Richard Löwenthal outlined a strategy for a Popular Front inside Germany, not just in exile. Conditions of illegality as well as fascism's hold over the economy, he thought, meant that an underground Popular Front had to prioritize radical social transformation rather than democratic elections to a national assembly, which currently was the focus of talks at the Hotel Lutetia. Löwenthal called for the "destruction of the fascist power apparatus [and] nationalization of heavy industry" by a popular movement led by a revolutionary elite. New Beginning's own underground apparatus provided a template for such a movement. Social revolution would have to precede any bourgeois electoral schemes, he thought. But another member, the future historian Francis L. Carsten, urged caution:

> There cannot be any popular front under stable fascism. The émigrés' popular front shenanigans [Volksfrontspielerei] could have fatal consequences inside Germany, especially if they have positive results. . . . We should warn groups in the Reich against any direct cooperation with the individual parties [e.g., the KPD]. All these forms of operation are dangerous inside Germany. . . . We must emphasize the practical demands of illegal work; that is the most important condition for participation [in popular front efforts].

Evelyn Anderson agreed. She believed that inside Nazi Germany only conspiratorial cells could survive, not a mass movement. In its debate over a German Popular Front, New Beginning began to distinguish more starkly between the conditions of work inside Germany versus in exile. Despite her reservations about any broad-based organization under the fascist dictatorship, however, Anderson noted that "the Popular Front, United Front, etc. on the outside [i.e., in exile] need not be rejected out of consideration for the inside."[16] Such waffling reflected the uncertainty about antifascist strategy among New Beginning's leaders as the decade wore on.

New Beginning's stance on a potential German Popular Front remained ambivalent. Fear of being swallowed along with more gullible groups "into the great KP stomach," as Lucy Ackerknecht put it, prevented the group from joining Communist-led unity initiatives. Even though antifascist unity aligned with New Beginning's long-term goals, the danger of becoming Moscow's

---

sozialistische Widerstand gegen das Dritte Reich," endnote 49. See Kliem's letter of inquiry to Ehrmann (Boulder, CO), November 19, 1956, IISG, NL Abendroth, 1041, and also Henry W. Ehrmann, "The Blum Experiment and the Fall of France," *Foreign Affairs* 20, no. 1 (October 1941): 152–64.

16. "Protokoll Westkonferenz vom 14. und 15.6.36," IISG, NB Archives, 55/1.

pawn in the short term never diminished. At the same time, the group did not want to follow the Sopade in its categorical rejection of all Communist offers for cooperation. From the summer of 1936 into 1937, New Beginning kept the Popular Front at arm's length but still within reach, as opposed to the Sopade's total withdrawal. Henry W. Ehrmann indeed put the group on guard against becoming "social-democratized" (*versozialdemokratet*).[17] The two magnetic poles of the emigration, Social Democracy and Communism, pulled hard in opposite directions. That made it difficult for neoleftist small groups to hold any kind of middle ground. New Beginning's commitment to a *new* left, at least, signaled a temporal detour around the spatial left–right impasse of interwar antifascism. The group appealed to radical youth as a generational cohort that could possibly transcend old sectarian ties.

One successful collaboration between New Beginning and young German Communists did occur. Before his departure for Spain, Rein teamed up with Ackerknecht to organize the handful of former SAJ members in Paris. Born Lucie Krüger in 1913, the talented and beautiful Ackerknecht entered the leadership of the Berlin SAJ shortly before the Nazi takeover. She then went into exile. In a jealous recollection, her first husband described her as a real asset for New Beginning because the general secretary of the International Transport Workers' Federation, Edo Fimmen, was enamored of her: "That brought in a lot of money for them."[18] The émigré group in Paris that she built together with Rein drew many young, gifted militants into New Beginning's orbit. At the end of 1935, they decided to join with the youth wing of the SAP and the German Communist Youth Association to create the Action Group of Proletarian Youth Organizations. It soon renamed itself the Free German Youth (FDJ). This new coalition published the bimonthly journal *Freie Deutsche Jugend*, which was no small feat for a bunch of refugees on a shoestring budget. Communists outnumbered New Beginning members and other lefts in the FDJ, but an observer later quipped that the non-Communist youth dominated the journal's editorial staff because only they knew how to write.[19]

Inside Germany, New Beginning formed a new leadership circle around the former SAJ leaders Kurt Schmidt and Fritz Erler, the religious socialist Erich Kürschner, and the young Social Democrat economist Oskar Umrath. They

---

17. "Protokoll Westkonferenz vom 14. und 15.6.36."

18. Interview of Erwin H. Ackerknecht by Werner Röder (Zürich), March 29, 1971, IfZ-Munich, ZS-2077. She later married the New Beginning member Ehrmann.

19. Erich Schmidt, *Meine Emigrantenjahre*, 55. After the war the FDJ transformed into an official appendage of the East German Socialist Unity Party. See McDougall, *Youth Politics in East Germany*.

worked with a group of older Social Democrats and Communists that called itself—with no relation to the Lutetia Circle in Paris—the German Popular Front. Led by Hermann L. Brill and Otto Brass, this underground Popular Front wrote a ten-point program calling for the overthrow of the Nazi dictatorship and the socialization of the economy.[20] New Beginning provided the group with funding, access to its technical apparatus, and contacts abroad. Against New Beginning's advice, however, the older group decided to publish its program illegally inside Germany. Eventually in 1938, that false step led to all of their arrests.[21]

Schmidt, Erler, Kürschner, and Umrath received heavy sentences. The four were split up into different penal and concentration camps. Compared with Communist cells and other more brazen resistance groups, New Beginning suffered few casualties as a result of its antifascist activity. For that reason, Umrath's subsequent death in 1943 hit the group hard. According to the official report, he died from illness in prison. The unofficial story was that his guards assigned him to a penal detail tasked with removing unexploded bombs from the streets of Berlin, and one went off.[22]

The New Beginning foreign bureau continued to experiment with schemes for antifascist unity. Löwenthal welcomed the Popular Fronts in France and Spain as signs of progress in the fight against fascism. But he criticized the way that Communists, in their push for practical cooperation between diverse partners, had reduced antifascism to an ideological minimum. The minimal goal of safeguarding democracy might attract the masses to the antifascist movement, he argued, but it would not keep that movement in power. Instead antifascists needed a robust socialist program that went beyond a rearguard defense of electoral democracy. Such a program could only be realized through a revolutionary grassroots uprising against fascist regimes everywhere.[23] Löwenthal wanted to transition from the defensive to the offensive in the

20. Because of this program, it was also known as the Ten Points Group. See Moraw, *Die Parole der "Einheit,"* 47–53; Kliem, "Der sozialistische Widerstand gegen das Dritte Reich," 219–20; and Brill, *Gegen den Strom,* 15–17.

21. Fritz Erler (Tuttlingen) to Hermann Brill (Wiesbaden), November 11, 1947, FES, NL Löwenthal, 4.

22. Erich Schmidt, *Meine Emigrantenjahre,* 42. See the entry for Umrath in Annedore Leber, *Conscience in Revolt: Sixty-Four Stories of Resistance in Germany, 1933–45,* trans. R. O'Neill (London: Vallentine and Mitchell, 1957). Erler remembered an ironic moment at their trial when the vice-president of the People's Court, Karl Engert, told Umrath, "We know that you are intelligent, Defendant. That speaks not for you, but against you." Erler to Eugen Umrath (Berlin-Dahlem), December 20, 1954, FES, NL Erler, 224C.

23. "Protokoll Westkonferenz vom 14. und 15.6.36."

antifascist struggle. Downplaying Soviet leadership, he insisted that the real strength behind the Popular Front was the European working class.

For new lefts, the news coming from Russia was bad. Beginning in August 1936 and lasting into 1938, the Moscow show trials of veteran Bolsheviks such as Grigory Zinoviev and Nicolai Bukharin unsettled New Beginning's faith in the possibility of ever working productively with the Communist Party. If Stalinists continued to devour their own children, then how could the European left ever trust them to help build socialism? Erich Schmidt later described feeling as though the much-hoped-for unity of the working class was a "shimmering mirage."[24] Together with the Rein affair in Spain, the Moscow trials prepared New Beginning members psychologically for a break with the Soviet Union. But the nonaggression pact between Nazi Germany and the Soviet Union, signed in late August 1939, came as a shock.

Along with people on the left everywhere, New Beginning's foreign bureau struggled to understand the Soviet rationale for allying with the great fascist enemy. All the Communist rhetoric about fighting capitalism, racism, and imperialism fell to pieces. New Beginning could not help but conclude that this Molotov-Ribbentrop Pact "has the character not only of reckless interest-driven politics, but also of a no-limit, dangerous game of all-or-nothing [Va-Banque-Spiel]." For the group, it was now crystal clear that "the immediate interests of the Russian state need not coincide with the interests of the socialist movement as a whole—that those interests can indeed be opposed."[25] Löwenthal claimed that Soviet motives made sense only when judged from the standpoint of raw geopolitics. The concrete goals of socialism or antifascism were irrelevant. "The Stalin regime," he declared, "has ceased to be a factor in the socialist movement and has become a fetter on the international level." The struggle against fascism and, through it, the left's quest for power in Europe must proceed without the Soviet Union. Löwenthal foresaw that in a world divided between two geopolitical blocs, one fascist-capitalist and the other totalitarian-communist, "there will be no real possibility for a socialist movement aiming to transition into a planned economy without private property . . . and with the support of the working masses."[26] The European left, old and new, must reject that bipolar world.

24. Erich Schmidt, *Meine Emigrantenjahre*, 44. See also "Der Moskauer Kommunistenprozess und die internationale Arbeiterbewegung," late 1936, IISG, NB Archives, 34/10.

25. "Die Sozialisten und der deutsch-russische Pakt," autumn 1939, IISG, NB Archives, 34/24.

26. Paul Sering [Richard Löwenthal], "Zur Einschätzung der deutsch-russischen Zusammenarbeit," October 1, 1939, IISG, NB Archives, 41/2.

Löwenthal developed a critique of what he called Russian-German Bonapartism. He drew on the theory of fascism that August Thalheimer and others had formulated around 1930, which had also influenced Loewenheim in the Miles pamphlet.[27] By historical analogy to France under Napoleon Bonaparte and again under his nephew Louis Napoleon, Germany under Hitler and Russia under Stalin both appeared to Löwenthal as dictatorships that suppressed social revolution at home and enabled imperialist expansion abroad. Bonapartism was related to the concept of totalitarianism, which originated as a description of Mussolini's novel dictatorship in Italy. But totalitarianism did not feature as prominently in New Beginning's thinking on the eve of World War II as did the specter of worldwide counterrevolution, or a Bonapartist revolution from above in reaction to the crisis of capitalism.[28] No matter how national alliances played out, Löwenthal and his comrades feared, the coming world war might forever disable the working class and destroy any possibility of progressive social change.

New Beginning moved its foreign bureau to Paris in 1938. After that, the border-crossing internet that the group had used for antifascist work inside Germany and in exile broke into two separate *intra*nets, one for inside and another for outside. Minimal communication occurred between these two networks even before all ties were severed by the outbreak of war in September 1939. Debates continued within the remaining New Beginning cells over how exactly to coordinate underground work and exile politics, and whether the tactical differences of working in one sector versus the other required a new overall strategy.

Wartime Europe and America

By the end of the 1930s, the scope of antifascist action had narrowed. Away from the broad Popular Front initiatives of 1935–36, neoleftist small groups had already shifted to a workers' united front plan that excluded bourgeois democrats. Now they settled on a strategy of "socialist concentration," which excluded Communists. Although the fate of antifascist new lefts never depended on raw numbers, this more limited cooperation with other progressive forces demoralized their ranks.

27. "Nochmals zur Frage der Revolution von oben und des russisch-deutschen Bonapartismus," n.d., IISG, NB Archives, 41/4. See chapter 2.

28. On Löwenthal and especially Franz Borkenau's theories, see W. Jones, *Lost Debate*. See also Chappel, *Catholic Modern*, and Greenberg, *Weimar Century*, ch. 3.

Was failure a foregone conclusion for antifascists in exile? Being refugees did impose objective constraints on political action of any sort. Host countries such as France, Britain, and the United States provided minimal to no support for refugees fleeing fascist regimes, and they sometimes banned exile politics altogether. Aside from overt discrimination, émigrés coped with hunger, stress, isolation, poverty, inadequate housing, and the dissolution of personal identity. In Parisian exile, dark clouds of the coming world war overshadowed everything. Schmidt recalled that "our 'group life' was carried on by just a few activists. I was overcome by contemplating the apocalyptic historical circumstances, and the problems and small joys of everyday life receded into the background."[29] Such an apocalyptic mood crippled most political projects.

In July 1939, New Beginning contributed to its last major publication in exile, a pamphlet called *The Coming World War*. A product of the socialist concentration strategy, the pamphlet was coauthored by Löwenthal and Frank of New Beginning and several theorists from the SAP and the Austrian Revolutionary Socialists. The pamphlet explained the aims of neoleftist small groups and criticized the unrealistic expectations of the old workers' parties. Blame for the success of fascism and the inevitability of world war, the authors argued, lay squarely with the capitalist class, "which in the crucial beginning stages of fascist expansion feared strengthening the international workers' movement for the purpose of overthrowing fascism more than it did strengthening fascism through further concessions." Thus the Western powers' policy of appeasement toward Hitler seemed less like a desperate attempt to avoid war than a deliberate strategy of confounding international socialism. Appeasement together with divisions in the workers' movement itself prevented the left from mounting any effective resistance to the fascist counterrevolution. Not knowing what would happen just one month later, the pamphlet's authors treated the Soviet Union as a last bastion of hope, despite its Stalinist deformations.[30]

The Molotov-Ribbentrop Pact was signed on August 23 and war broke out on September 1. Of course, armed conflict had raged in various places across the world for most of that decade. But now the full force of European, North American, and Asian militaries would decide the struggle. Immediately after the outbreak of war, the French government ordered the internment of most

29. Erich Schmidt, *Meine Emigrantenjahre*, 45.

30. Neu Beginnen, Sozialistische Arbeiterpartei Deutschlands, and Revolutionäre Sozialisten Österreichs, *Der kommende Weltkrieg*.

German refugees in that country.[31] Dozens of New Beginning members were detained and sent to internment camps at Meslay-du-Maine, Le Vernet, and elsewhere.[32] Schmidt's wife Hilde (née Paul) ended up in the camp at Gurs in southwestern France. There she was quartered with political refugees in a special barracks, whose inmates generally received worse treatment than the main camp population. Nearly ten months later, on the day that France surrendered to Germany, Hilde's New Beginning friends finally forged the paperwork necessary to transfer her out of the barracks.[33] This bureaucratic subterfuge for a small victory inside an internment camp symbolized the wartime limits of antifascist work in exile.

As a precaution, New Beginning's foreign bureau had already relocated again from Paris to London in the fall of 1939. Meanwhile Frank had set up a base of operations in New York City. On both sides of the Atlantic the group prepared for the transition to wartime. That hard transition would involve unexpected compromises. Despite their opposition to capitalism, bourgeois democracy, and militarism, many antifascist new lefts would transform into cooperative partners in the Allied war effort.

To be sure, New Beginning was able to theoretically justify helping the Allies with propaganda, research and analysis, and even physical manpower. Only a military defeat of fascism, the group ultimately decided, could create the conditions necessary for a democratic revolution in Germany and a renewal of socialism across Europe. "Socialism or fascism" remained the existential choice that shaped the group's world view. For that reason, New Beginning entered into a temporary alliance with Western capitalist democracies, expecting better opportunities for socialism in the future. But the group insisted on preserving its organizational and ideological autonomy. Thus it chose the Scylla of partial compromise over the Charybdis of total isolation.

Like France, Britain interned German refugees after the outbreak of war. Both New Beginning's current leaders and the estranged Loewenheim circle, which had emigrated to London several years before, wound up at a camp on the Isle of Man. Because of its contacts on the left wing of the Labour Party, New Beginning arranged for the rapid release of its own people. But the group did not intervene on behalf of the half dozen members of the Loewenheim circle, because it either could not or would not do so. Loewenheim and

---

31. First it was men between the ages of 17 and 55 years old. Then, after German forces invaded France in May 1940, the round-up included all men under 65 and all childless women between 17 and 55. Erich Schmidt, *Meine Emigrantenjahre*, 64.

32. The French police found a list of interned members and friends of New Beginning when they arrested Franz Bögler. BArch-Berlin, R58/3292.

33. Hilde Paul, "Paris—Gurs," in Erich Schmidt, *Meine Emigrantenjahre*, 66–70 (at 70).

company were stuck on the Isle of Man for many months longer. They never forgave New Beginning for that perceived slight, and it surely contributed to the acrimony between the two factions that lasted long afterward.[34]

The first thing that the New Beginning foreign bureau did upon arriving in London was publish an informational pamphlet in German called *New Beginning: What It Wants, What It Is, and How It Arose.*[35] The group wanted to reassure other factions in the German emigration about its intentions. Indicating the diminished funds available to the group, the mimeographed pamphlet featured a hand-drawn title page that looked something like the cover of a garage-band demo tape.

The pamphlet recounted the history of New Beginning from the perspective of the post-1935 leadership. Its narrative downplayed the importance of Loewenheim's Org, misrepresented the influx of young SAJ members in 1931 as the group's foundational moment, and selectively quoted the more democratic-sounding passages of the original Miles pamphlet. In British and American exile, New Beginning now identified as a democratic movement that had left behind its conspiratorial past. The year 1935, during which a devastating wave of arrests had occurred, was portrayed euphemistically in this London pamphlet as the start of the group's "Years of Growth."[36] New Beginning claimed to have traded its support for a revolutionary dictatorship of the proletariat for a more anodyne version of social democracy. It is hard to judge whether the pamphlet was propaganda designed to appease fellow émigrés or a true reflection of the group's new thinking after Spain, the Moscow trials, and the Nazi-Soviet pact. Probably a bit of both.

However, New Beginning continued to criticize the Sopade for blocking efforts at socialist concentration. Either Sopade leaders came to accept that criticism or, more likely, decided that the British public lacked patience for sectarian exile politics, because they agreed in March 1941 to cofound the Union of German Socialist Organizations in Great Britain (UDSO). New Beginning members such as Löwenthal, Anderson, Erwin Schoettle, and Waldemar von Knoeringen now sat alongside the Sopade representatives Hans Vogel and Erich Ollenhauer in a new union of the non-Communist German left. The small groups SAP and ISK got involved, too. Not only did the UDSO iron out

---

34. In 1940, while still in the camp, Loewenheim drafted a manifesto to herald his return to the political scene. In it, he argued even more strongly in favor of a mixed economy than he had in the original Miles pamphlet. A competitive market, he claimed, must be an essential part of socialist society. Loewenheim, "Am Scheideweg der Geschichte," FES, Sammlung Personalia, 6307.

35. Neu Beginnen, *Neu Beginnen.*

36. Neu Beginnen, 39.

policy disagreements between new lefts and old lefts, it also provided a forum for generational reconciliation. Contentious debates continued during the war, but this coalition of German socialists in Britain hung together. In 1945 the UDSO would issue a white paper called "Toward a Policy for German Socialists," which provided guidelines for the postwar Social Democratic Party.[37] Members of the UDSO including New Beginning underwent a process of ideological moderation. As a result, Marxism retreated from their rhetoric in favor of more liberal or ethical formulations of socialism. The wartime British exile of the German left, both old and new, foreshadowed the postwar modernization of Social Democracy.[38]

In addition to mending relations with German Social Democrats, New Beginning offered its services to the British war effort. From 1940 to 1942, its members worked for the BBC radio service to run the European Revolution Station, which broadcast German-language propaganda aimed at potential resisters inside Nazi Germany.[39] Projects like the European Revolution Station followed New Beginning's strategy of prioritizing an Allied military victory over fascism. Still, the émigrés constantly worried about losing their autonomy and deviating from their socialist goals. Before the war, the group had warned its fellow neoleftist small groups to avoid any "incorporation into the propaganda apparatus" of capitalist countries. The Allies might try to "transform émigré groups into recruitment offices for imperialism."[40] Such unease among socialist émigrés in the strongholds of global capitalism, Britain and the United States, did diminish over time. Regardless of whether the Allied propaganda apparatus co-opted them, groups like New Beginning changed their opinion of democratic capitalism and the welfare state. Thus new lefts in

37. UDSO, *Zur Politik deutscher Sozialisten*. See Tombs, "Identité européenne assiégée?"; Eiber, *Die Sozialdemokratie in der Emigration*; Ursula Adam, "'Wege zum neuen Deutschland'— Eine Debatte deutscher Emigranten in Großbritannien," in *Was aus Deutschland werden sollte. Konzepte des Widerstands, des Exils und der Alliierten*, ed. Reinhard Kühnl and Eckart Spoo (Heilbronn, Germany: Distel, 1995), 147–55; and Glees, *Exile Politics*. See also chapter 5.

38. These six years of British exile (1939–45) functioned analogously to the twelve years that German Social Democrat leaders spent there during the period of the Anti-Socialist Laws (1878–90), when theorists like Eduard Bernstein revised Marxism to align with British liberalism and Fabian socialist reformism. See Gay, *Dilemma of Democratic Socialism*.

39. Löwenthal, Knoeringen, Paul Anderson, Evelyn Anderson, and Karl Anders participated in this venture. Mehringer, *Waldemar von Knoeringen*, 213–28. Cf. Sheer Ganor, "Forbidden Words, Banished Voices: Jewish Refugees at the Service of BBC Propaganda to Wartime Germany," *Journal of Contemporary History* 55, no. 1 (2020): 97–119.

40. Neu Beginnen, Sozialistische Arbeiterpartei Deutschlands, and Revolutionäre Sozialisten Österreichs, *Der kommende Weltkrieg*, 38–39.

exile began to "mature." In an ironic turn that the second half of my book will explore, this wartime process of accommodation set many antifascists on a path to become antagonists of future new lefts.

In the United States, New Beginning had much less success in uniting the various factions of the antifascist emigration. When Erich and Hilde Schmidt arrived in New York Harbor in the fall of 1940, they were greeted by Frank and members of the organization that he had founded there to promote New Beginning's interests, the American Friends of German Freedom (AFGF). Five years earlier Frank had started fundraising in the United States under the alias Paul Hagen. He quickly won the support of B. Charney Vladeck of the Jewish Labor Committee, and he raised considerably more money than official representatives of the Sopade. The most tangible achievement of the AFGF was its formation in June 1940 of the Emergency Rescue Committee, which enabled the escape of refugee artists and intellectuals from Vichy France and, whenever possible, procured visas for entry into the United States. The committee's agent Varian Fry ran an operation out of Marseille that rescued more than one thousand refugees.[41]

Frank had a knack for making contacts beyond the typical socialist milieu. He recruited the left-leaning Protestant theologians Paul Tillich and Reinhold Niebuhr for a new venture that the AFGF helped launch in early 1944. The Council for a Democratic Germany (CDG) was conceived as an umbrella organization of German antifascists in the United States. It benefitted from the endorsement of American progressives like Niebuhr and respected German-American figures like Tillich. Broader based than the London UDSO, the CDG aimed for a Popular-Front-style coalition of liberals, Social Democrats, revolutionary socialists, and even Communists. Frank and the AFGF wagered correctly that such a big-tent approach would appeal more to American political sensibilities. But they underestimated the virulence of American anti-Communism.[42] Already, in various countries Communists had set up their own National Committee for a Free Germany, and in a way the CDG was designed as its democratic rival in the United States. The CDG announced that it would create a German government-in-exile to replace the Nazi government after the Allied victory. Frank even wrote to the novelist and Nobel laureate Thomas Mann to ask if he would consider serving as president-in-exile.

41. See Renaud, "German Resistance in New York," and "'This is our Dunkirk': Karl B. Frank and the Politics of the Emergency Rescue Committee," Terence Renaud's website, 2009, last modified December 2015, http://terencerenaud.com/The_Politics_of_the_ERC_FINAL .htm. See also Varian Fry's memoir *Surrender on Demand* (New York: Random House, 1945).

42. See Jennifer Luff, "Labor Anticommunism in the United States of America and the United Kingdom, 1920–49," *Journal of Contemporary History* 53, no. 1 (2018): 109–133.

Despite expressing enthusiasm for the CDG, Mann declined.[43] External pressure from anti-Communists along with internal disputes between the various factions halted the CDG's momentum. It would dissolve immediately after the war ended, exerting no influence on postwar reconstruction.[44]

The United States was far less hospitable to such an émigré congress than was Britain. Mann replied to Frank in August 1943 that "No one [here] asks us our opinion. On the one hand we are enemy-aliens, and on the other hand 'premature anti-fascists' and not at all popular."[45] But the US government did find a use for some refugees. Frank and other members of the neoleftist small groups had some success in volunteering for government intelligence and propaganda agencies. New Beginning members Georg Eliasberg and Bernhard Taurer went to work for the Office of War Information and Fred H. Sanderson for the Office of Strategic Services (OSS). Even the fabled Research and Analysis branch of the OSS, which employed the Frankfurt School affiliates Franz Neumann, Herbert Marcuse, and Otto Kirchheimer, looked very similar to an émigré intelligence plan that Frank had proposed to Allen Dulles in April 1942.[46]

Frank's memo to Dulles, "How to Prepare Collaboration with the Anti-Nazi Underground Movement," contained another more fantastic proposal. German agents trained by the United States could parachute behind enemy lines in order to make contact with underground resistance cells in occupied territories and Nazi Germany itself.[47] Remarkably, parachutes did drop down

43. Thomas Mann (Pacific Palisades, CA) to Paul Hagen [Karl Frank], August 6, 1943, Hoover, Frank Papers, 9/M.

44. See Heike Bungert, "Deutsche Emigranten im amerikanischen Kalkül: Die Regierung in Washington, Thomas Mann und die Gründung eines Emigrantenkomitees 1943," *Vierteljahrshefte für Zeitgeschichte* 46, no. 2 (April 1998): 253–68, and Friedrich Baerwald, "Zur politischen Tätigkeit deutscher Emigranten im Council for a Democratic Germany," *Vierteljahrshefte für Zeitgeschichte* 28, no. 3 (July 1980): 372–83.

45. Mann to Hagen, August 6, 1943.

46. "Memorandum by Paul Hagen: How to Collaborate with the Anti-Nazi Underground in Germany," document 1 (April 10, 1942), in Heideking and Mauch, *American Intelligence*, 17–19. See also Laudani, *Secret Reports on Nazi Germany*; Katz, *Foreign Intelligence*; and Alfons Söllner, *Archäologie der Demokratie in Deutschland*, vol. 1.

47. After an initial rebuff by Dulles, Frank turned to Lt. Col. Julius Klein and asked him to present his plan, the "Hagen formula," to the army intelligence section G-2. Klein did this in August 1942, recommending Frank as "one of the most suitable persons to be used for such activities." Confidential report to the War Department, General Staff, Army G-2, August 24, 1942, Hoover, Frank Papers, 7/7. This referral caught the attention of the OSS, and Robert D. Murphy, assistant to the director, William J. Donovan, took the matter in hand. Klein to Hagen, September 29, 1942, Hoover, Frank Papers, 7/7.

on German soil sometime in 1944. But the émigré agents dangling from their lines were not from New Beginning.[48] As far-fetched as the plan might have seemed, the OSS and US Army saw some value in stirring up trouble behind German lines. The British and Americans made similar arrangements with Charles de Gaulle and the Free French. But the lack of any recognized German government-in-exile made it difficult to find the right people for the job. Frank's plan was sound, but the US government trusted neither him nor his mysterious organization, New Beginning.[49] Instead, the OSS recruited from another neoleftist small group, ISK, whose non-Marxist brand of ethical socialism must have struck them as politically safer.[50] Operations such as this had little effect on the course of the war, but they did provide a psychological boost to their participants.[51]

Frank himself had better luck in publishing books. His first one, *Will Germany Crack?*, appeared in 1942 and his second, *Germany After Hitler*, in 1944.[52] After reading the manuscript of the second, the novelist Mann called it "the clearest, most rational, and most realistic preview of things in store for Germany that I have come across." One can only hope, he continued, "that [the victors] are familiar with the thoughts that your work offers."[53] Frank's plan

48. One New Beginning member, the former Sopade border secretary Franz Bögler, was approached by an OSS agent in Zürich (possibly Dulles himself) who asked whether he would be willing to parachute into Germany. Interview of Bögler by Wolfgang Jean Stock (Speyer), December 20, 1972, IfZ-Munich, ZS-3113.

49. Frank provided the OSS with a detailed explanation of his political activities since 1933 in order to prove his credibility and "destroy the atmosphere of doubt, which is not only disagreeable for me but which is hindering my work." Hagen to Calvin Hoover (Office of Strategic Services, Washington, DC), July 31, 1942, Hoover, Frank Papers, 7/7.

50. From the end of 1943 through 1945, ISK parachutists were trained in England by the Labor Branch of the OSS and the British Special Operations Executive for an operation called the Faust Project. Participants included Josef Kappius, Anna Beyer, and Hilde Meisel. Meisel was shot and killed while attempting to cross the Austria-Switzerland border. People continued to talk about Kappius's exploits as parachute jumper well after the war. Kaden, *Einheit oder Freiheit*, 152.

51. They also supplied material for popular histories of the covert war against Hitler. For example, see Joseph E. Persico, *Piercing the Reich: The Penetration of Nazi Germany by American Secret Agents during World War II* (New York: Viking, 1979). For a more scholarly account, see Christof Mauch, *The Shadow War against Hitler: The Covert Operations of America's Wartime Secret Intelligence Service* (New York: Columbia University Press, 2003).

52. Hagen [Frank], *Will Germany Crack?* and *Germany after Hitler*. For an analysis, see Renaud "German Resistance in New York," ch. 4.

53. Thomas Mann (Pacific Palisades, CA) to Paul Hagen, July 13, 1943, Hoover, Frank Papers, 9/M.

for postwar Germany involved a thoroughgoing denazification of civil society and the state. But he also insisted on expanding political liberties for the defeated population, based on his assumption that democratic forces lay ready in wait. He argued that the fascist regime had so much power over ordinary Germans because it had atomized them, co-opted their civic associations and labor organizations, and suppressed their capacity for collective deliberation. All that remained was blind devotion to the leader. The Allied military occupation must certainly impose restrictions, he allowed, but it should also help the German people regain their ability to practice democracy. To that end, he vehemently opposed any division of the country or major territorial losses relative to Germany's pre-1938 borders. Doing that would only stoke the same nationalist resentment that fueled Hitler's rise to power, he thought. Most importantly, Frank argued that the Allies must destroy fascism's economic basis by socializing all privately owned heavy industries and banks.

In the mainstream American press, reviewers greeted *Germany after Hitler* favorably. But the most frequent criticism was that the book's author showed too much optimism about Germany's and Europe's future. Antifascist émigrés had always oscillated between revolutionary hope and despair. It must have been hard for Frank and his New York allies to sustain their optimism, especially while the New Beginning network disintegrated. Even members who made it safely out of Europe drifted out of the group's orbit. For example, Ossip K. Flechtheim arrived in New York in 1939 and immediately organized a discussion circle similar to the one he had created in Geneva while serving as New Beginning's contact there. This New York circle included the leftist theorist Karl Korsch, the economist Fritz Sternberg, the New Beginning confidant Sanderson, and several affiliates of the Institute for Social Research (i.e., the Frankfurt School).[54] But Flechtheim's ties to New Beginning were severed after he accepted academic posts at Clark College in Atlanta and later at Bates

54. Karl Korsch (Boston) to Ossip Flechtheim (New York), November 7, 1939, and January 12, 1940, DNB, NL Flechtheim, EB 98/179. The Frankfurt School affiliate Friedrich Pollock's name appears in Korsch's second letter, although it is uncertain whether he actually participated in the circle. Flechtheim was good friends at the time with another Frankfurt School affiliate in New York, A.R.L. Gurland. Franz L. Neumann had sympathized with New Beginning in the mid-1930s when he contributed to the *Zeitschrift für Sozialismus* under the pseudonym Leopold Franz. He very well might have collaborated with the group while in London and New York exile, especially given the similarities between New Beginning's plans for postwar reconstruction and the arguments of Neumann's 1942 book *Behemoth*. Frank listed Neumann as a character witness in a report to the OSS. See Hagen to Hoover, July 31, 1942. Admittedly, this is circumstantial evidence. Gerhard Bry recalled that Neumann "was a strong sympathizer, but not a declared member of our group. . . . Some [affiliates of the Frankfurt School] expressed broad

College in Lewiston, Maine. Another member of the group who drifted away
in exile, Georg Eliasberg, had been arrested by the Gestapo in 1935, detained
in a number of German prisons, deported to Italy, and finally allowed to emigrate to the Dominican Republic in 1940. In a letter, he chided Flechtheim for
his pessimistic retreat from politics into "professorial dignity."[55]

Some New Beginning members in American and British exile never abandoned hope for a democratic revolution in Germany. By osmosis as much as
by choice, however, their concept of socialism and plan for a postwar new left
took on increasingly liberal hues. Party pluralism and intellectual freedom
replaced some of the hardline tenets of revolutionary Marxism that they had
espoused during the interwar period. Even back then, Schmidt recalled, the
Org/New Beginning had metamorphosed "from its strictly elitist, centralized
existence as a secret society into a more relaxed, democratic organizational
form that allowed more room for [individual] initiative."[56] This change in
organizational form corresponded to the group's change in ideology. Since at
least 1939, New Beginning theorists had warned about the danger of political
dictatorship. The mark of a truly revolutionary organization, they wrote, is "*not
needing* a totalitarian special status in order to accomplish its tasks and, due to
its recognition of the importance of freedom as a vital principle of socialism,
by *not wanting* such a status."[57] The Communist betrayal during the Spanish
Civil War, the spectacle of the Moscow trials, and the abomination of the Nazi-
Soviet pact ended New Beginning's admiration for the Soviet Union. "From
our oft-expressed critical affinity for the Soviet Union, while maintaining our
independence from it," wrote Schmidt, "we now had to pass very sharply into
a fundamental critique and rejection of this system."[58] After spending several
years in wartime Britain and America, the group subjected itself to criticism
and discarded whichever ideas and organizational forms seemed obsolete.

Along with other neoleftist small groups like ISK, New Beginning did try
to preserve its independence. It fought for a brand of democratic socialism
that was distinct from and opposed to the world's largest purportedly socialist

----

sympathy with our organization which they knew from pre-Nazi times, but Neumann was the
only political activist—at least as far as I knew." Bry, *Resistance*, 175 and 188–89.

55. Stefan Weyl [Georg Eliasberg] (Sosua/Puerto Plata, DR) to Flechtheim (New York),
November 19, 1940, DNB, NL Flechtheim, EB 98/179.

56. Erich Schmidt, *Meine Emigrantenjahre*, 13.

57. Neu Beginnen, Sozialistische Arbeiterpartei Deutschlands, and Revolutionäre Sozialisten Österreichs, *Der kommende Weltkrieg*, 25. Emphasis in original. For a different assessment
of democratic organization written around the same time, cf. the philosopher Simone Weil's
essay *Abolition of All Political Parties*.

58. Erich Schmidt, *Meine Emigrantenjahre*, 49.

power, the Soviet Union. The liberal institutions of the West, despite their capitalist character, at least in theory allowed for that sort of independence—not only in the public sphere but also within left organizations themselves. Regarding the Frankfurt School, Gerhard Bry once remarked that "Perhaps they were not undogmatic, but at least everybody had his own dogma."[59] He might have said the same about the antifascist new left.

The deradicalization of New Beginning owed as much to the objective conditions of exile and external political pressure as it did to a genuine, internal conversion. As a result of this deradicalization and members' own refugee experiences, the group broadened its concept of the proletariat. Now it included persecuted strata of all kinds alongside the industrial working class. This new concept provided a template for the postwar transformation of Social Democracy from a class party into a popular party, a transformation that occurred unevenly across Western Europe. It was through their support for the Allied war effort and assimilation of liberal democratic norms that antifascists in exile regained a measure of hope during a time of apocalyptic despair.

The German philosopher Ernst Bloch wrote *The Principle of Hope* while in American exile. In that magnum opus, he charted the psychological and historical bases of utopian thinking since the beginnings of civilization. Modern, future-oriented utopias were grounded in their anticipation of the "not yet" and their imagination of the "as if." Bloch thought that such utopian hope represented the true progressive force of history. But hope in exile was a fragile thing. "How does man live with doom, with the continuous crumbling away before his eyes of everything that makes life worth living?" asked Schmidt as if in response to Bloch. "With the principle of hope for another last straw? For us émigrés, this straw was always yet another country where we could continue our fight, a place where we refugees still had a chance to start again from the beginning." Changing countries more often than their shoes, as the poet Bertolt Brecht put it, antifascists in exile clutched at the thinnest hope for a new beginning.[60] Some despaired. Others prepared for an uncertain return to Europe and a chance to shape its postfascist future. The next chapter surveys new lefts that emerged from the rubble in Germany and elsewhere in Europe during the first years after the war.

59. Bry, *Resistance*, 188–89.

60. Erich Schmidt, *Meine Emigrantenjahre*, 59; Bertolt Brecht, "An die Nachgeborenen" [1939], Lyrik-line, accessed February 2019, https://www.lyrikline.org/de/gedichte/die -nachgeborenen-740; and Bloch, *Principle of Hope*.

5

Postwar New Beginning

THE END OF WAR in Europe on May 8, 1945, caused uneasiness among New Beginning members. Whereas during the previous twelve years German neoleftist groups like it had one clear enemy in fascism and, in wartime, one clear purpose in survival, the prospect of Europe's postfascist future now opened up before them. In France, this had happened already with the Liberation one year before. Now at Germany's so-called zero hour, the first thing New Beginning members did was seek out survivors and count the fallen. Above all, they wanted to rebuild the close-knit community of action that they remembered from the prewar years.

For émigrés, contacting survivors inside Germany went hand in hand with resuming their role as lobbyists for a renewed European left. For survivors, communicating with comrades abroad meant ending years of isolation and accessing moral and material resources that would prove crucial in the hard times ahead. As Karl Frank observed, "the illegal anti-Nazi groups in Germany were atomized. . . . It was necessary to search them out, to learn something about their activity, to break through the double ring of isolation that had been placed around Germany by the Nazi regime and the state of war." By gathering intelligence through direct and indirect channels, he hoped to reassemble the broken pieces of the antifascist new left.[1]

And Frank saw a third ring of isolation around Germany: Allied occupation policy. At the Yalta Conference in February 1945, Allied political and military leaders had reaffirmed their commitment to the unconditional surrender of Nazi Germany and the eventual division of the country into multiple occupation zones. They doubted that "the German people has the inclination, the energy, or the organization to break the Nazi grip and to take active steps to end the war." The failed attempt to assassinate Hitler on July 20, 1944, had nullified any military and conservative resistance, and the "underground

---

1. American Association for a Democratic Germany, *Der neue Kampf um Freiheit*, 7.

opposition of German workers is not strong enough to constitute an effective political force prior to German collapse."[2] So, in the spring of 1945, as British and American armies approached from the west and the Soviet Red Army from the east, the official plan for reconstruction demanded Germany's total subjugation.

The US Joint Chiefs of Staff directive JCS 1067, adopted in secret for the American occupation zone, stipulated that "no political activities of any kind shall be countenanced unless authorized" by the military government. Similar orders applied in the other zones, and on June 5 the Allies collectively declared their sovereignty over German territory.[3] In addition to dismantling the German military, government, and heavy industries, the occupation authorities closed all schools and universities, shut down radio stations and newspapers, censored correspondence, banned uniforms, grounded aircraft, and forbade organized politics. Not surprisingly, then, the first contact that New Beginning émigrés had with survivors was mediated by Allied occupation personnel.

Fred H. Sanderson, an agronomist working for the US Office of Strategic Services, arrived in Berlin on September 11, 1945.[4] Originally from Kassel, he had entered the New Beginning periphery in Geneva exile around 1935. There he participated in a discussion circle with Ossip K. Flechtheim, among others.[5] After emigrating further to New York, he teamed up with the AFGF, where he continued his friendship with Flechtheim and grew close to Frank and the latter's most regular collaborator Vera Eliasberg (née Franke).[6] Before Sanderson returned to Europe in 1945 as an agent of the OSS, Frank gave

2. Report by the Combined Intelligence Committee, "Estimate of the Enemy Situation— Europe (as of 23 January 1945)," in *Argonaut* [Yalta] *Conference, January–February 1945: Papers and Minutes of Meetings* (Washington, DC: Joint History Office, 2002), 29–43 (at 32–33).

3. Wikisource contributors, "JCS 1067: Directive to Commander-in-Chief of United States Forces of Occupation Regarding the Military Government of Germany," Section 9a, *Wikisource*, accessed July 2014, http://en.wikisource.org/wiki/JCS_1067, in effect already in May 1945 but not publicized until October 17, 1945, and "Declaration Regarding the Defeat of Germany and the Assumption of Supreme Authority by Allied Powers," Berlin, June 5, 1945, Avalon Project, Yale Law School, Lillian Goldman Law Library, accessed July 2014, http://avalon.law.yale.edu/wwii/ger01.asp.

4. Hurwitz, *Demokratie und Antikommunismus*, 4 (1): 47.

5. Sanderson (OSS Mission to Germany, Wiesbaden) to Flechtheim (Lewiston, ME), August 19, 1945, DNB, NL Flechtheim, EB 98/179; Hurwitz, *Demokratie und Antikommunismus*, 4 (1): 59–60; and an interview of Flechtheim by Wolfgang Jean Stock (Berlin), June 26, 1972, IfZ-Munich, ZS-3016.

6. Karl Korsch (Boston, MA) to Flechtheim, January 12, 1940, DNB, NL Flechtheim, EB 98/179.

him a list of New Beginning members to locate. On his tour of Berlin that fall, he managed to find most people on the list: Kurt Schmidt, Georg Müller, Theo Thiele, Kurt Mattick, Erich Kürschner, Werner Peuke, Ernst Jegelka, and others.[7] Not merely alive, these survivors had already found one another and formed a socialist working group.

Sanderson sent a report back to New York and to Richard Löwenthal in London. He praised the survivors' efforts, but noted that their discussions were "still characterized by a certain lack of specificity and a long-windedness which has been so characteristic of German left-wing thought."[8] Their intellectual development had been stunted by years of persecution and isolation. Sanderson's ambivalent report nonetheless delighted the émigrés. Hans Braun wrote from San Francisco that "never has a piece of news brought me so much joy as your message that most of our old friends were able to survive those difficult years."[9] Proof of New Beginning's survival meant that the group had at least partially achieved its original goal: to preserve a left leadership elite for postfascist Germany.

Neoleftists inside Germany had suffered intimidation, arrest, interrogation, beatings, and imprisonment in concentration camps. Some had served in penal battalions or the regular army, witnessing firsthand the destruction wrought by Hitler's war machine. A few had survived undetected in German society, conforming outwardly to the demands of the Nazi state. Those in exile had endured the common fate of all refugees and displaced persons: poverty, legal uncertainty, psychological stress, and political impotence. But the first few years after the war provided neoleftists everywhere a chance to begin anew. "This short period," writes the historian Dan Stone, "was one of experimentation and openness to new ideas across Europe. Or rather, of a kind of continuity of old ones, as an antifascism reminiscent of the Popular Front days of the mid-1930s reappeared."[10] Thus the postwar new beginning was suspended between lefts old and new.

As part of their long-term occupation strategy, the Western Allies aimed to democratize German politics by reintroducing party pluralism, open

7. Hurwitz, *Demokratie und Antikommunismus*, 4 (1): 61.

8. Sanderson to Karl Frank, October 7, 1945, quoted in Hurwitz, *Demokratie und Antikommunismus*, 4 (1): 62. See also the nearly verbatim letter from Sanderson to Löwenthal (London), October 9, 1945, IISG, NB Archives, 25/1.

9. Braun (San Francisco) to Vera Eliasberg, November 1945, RHG, NL Hurwitz, 103. For a similarly joyous letter sent directly to the New Beginning survivors, see Stefan Neuberg [Georg Eliasberg] to Kurt Schmidt et al. (Berlin), January 7, 1946, U of O, Goldbloom Papers, 4/15.

10. Stone, *Goodbye to All That?* 65.

elections, liberal education, and a free press. But in the short term, political reconstruction in the Western zones took a back seat to military security and infrastructural repair. Only the Soviets put a premium on restarting political life and, in particular, rebuilding socialist organizations. In the crucial ten months from June 1945 to April 1946, all currents of the German left in the Eastern zone would be swept up in the Soviet plan to create a Socialist Unity Party (SED). Debates raged between Social Democrats, Communists, and neoleftists over the desirability of this fusion of the SPD and KPD. Not only Communists supported the plan. This chance at left unity also attracted many Social Democrats who wanted to overcome the division of the workers' movement and atone for past sins.

Opponents of the plan worried that any fusion of the left in the Soviet zone would take place entirely on Communist terms. New Beginning survivors in Berlin and their comrades in exile remembered the agony of Communist betrayal in Spain and the disgrace of the Nazi-Soviet pact. To them the SED represented a false messiah, promising a socialist future but in fact delivering the German left into Stalin's hands. Amid the ruins of Berlin and the surrounding provinces, the fusion struggle of 1945–46 caused a major realignment of German left politics.[11] New Beginning and other remnants of the antifascist new left split into two camps: those who joined East-oriented fusionists in the old SPD and KPD, and those who joined West-oriented Social Democrats in the antifusionist opposition. At that moment politically, there was no third way. And organizationally, the traditional party and union forms ended up ruling the day. Whereas in other countries, like France, prospects for a postwar new left remained bright for several years, the German new left would again go on hiatus by the spring of 1946.

Restarting the Left in Occupied Germany

In the late summer and fall of 1945, Social Democrats and Communists across the four occupied sectors of the city of Berlin began serious discussions about unifying the two workers' parties. But there were stumbling blocks: the domineering attitude of Communists who returned from Russian exile, the military and political pressure exerted by the Soviet occupiers, and the traditionalism

11. At the time, there were rival names for the debate on the creation of the SED: "forced fusion" (favored by anti-Communists) versus "voluntary merger" or "push for unity" (favored by Communists and their allies). The name that I use, fusion struggle, was less common but lacks the bias of those historical alternatives.

of many Social Democrats and trade unionists. In that fraught situation, neoleftists struggled to define theoretical and organizational alternatives.

The immediate postwar months did witness experiments in neoleftist organization that occurred outside the control of the traditional workers' parties. Most visible were the numerous Antifascist Committees (Antifa), which hearkened back to the Antifascist Action initiative of 1932. The emergence of these local, spontaneous united fronts of Social Democrats and Communists ready to practice self-administration disproves the common assumption that postwar Germans were politically apathetic. Historians have described how the Antifa created a police force to purge and expropriate Nazis; organized work squads to clear away rubble, repair houses and factories, and protect supply depots from looting; managed the distribution of food and fuel; and built a network between neighborhood committees, factory councils, and the many willing participants in democratic reconstruction. Although they lacked overall coordination between localities or regions, the Antifa popped up like mushrooms in a consistent pattern across unoccupied areas during the spring of 1945. These practical new lefts relied on decentralized forms of organization geared toward mutual aid. In the words of the historian Lutz Niethammer and colleagues, the Antifa enabled the populace "to mobilize for collective self-help."[12]

The Antifa lost their authority as Allied occupation forces imposed bureaucratic systems of administration from above. But there were other examples of neoleftist organization. Inmates of the concentration camp at Buchenwald in Thuringia clandestinely built a united front during the final months of the Nazi regime. Two days after the US Army liberated the camp, on April 13, this coalition of Social Democrats, Communists, and left-wing Catholics issued the Buchenwald Manifesto. It was addressed mainly to Communists elsewhere in Germany who, as the camp inmates had heard, wanted to rebuild the old KPD. The now-liberated inmates declared that they had no intention of refounding either of the old parties, the SPD or the KPD. Instead they announced a new organization based on the model of the Popular Front. They called it the League of Democratic Socialists (BdS). Their manifesto envisioned a German People's Republic based on participatory democracy and not limited to "empty, formal parliamentarism." Governed by the antifascist BdS, this republic would ensure both democratic freedoms and worker-friendly welfare

---

12. Niethammer, Borsdorf, and Brandt, *Arbeiterinitiative 1945*, 11–12. See also Agocs, *Antifascist Humanism*, ch. 3, which connects the Antifa to antifascist exile politics in the 1930s and interprets them as the "'other Germany' from below" (54). For a study that downplays the importance of the Antifa, cf. Pritchard, *Niemandsland*.

policies. Heavy industries, banks, and consumer goods production would be socialized and planned. In addition to favoring the peaceful reintegration of Germany into the international community, the Buchenwald Manifesto called for cooperation with the Soviet Union and other socialist states in order to build a socialist Europe. Accomplishing left unity on the basis of "revolutionary democratic socialism" was the prerequisite of all of these tasks. Neither Social Democrats, nor Communists, nor neoleftists should maintain a separate existence.[13]

One of the leading BdS members was Hermann Brill, the Social Democrat jurist and politician whose underground resistance cell German Popular Front had formed an alliance with New Beginning back in 1937. He continued to identify as a member and even a leader of New Beginning well into the postwar years, which strictly speaking was untrue.[14] Brill and the BdS repeatedly ran afoul of the Soviet occupation authorities in Thuringia. They also annoyed representatives of the old workers' parties, who could not countenance such an autonomous left.[15]

Despite their august traditions, the old workers' parties also had to reinvent themselves at Germany's zero hour. The most proactive were Communists in the Soviet zone. This was largely because the Red Army had complete control over the city of Berlin for two whole months before American, British, and French troops arrived to occupy their respective sectors. The Soviet Military Administration in Germany (SMAD) was the first occupying power to permit the formation of parties and unions.[16] For the time being, Soviet policy across Eastern and Central Europe resembled its Popular Front line of the mid-1930s: secure bourgeois democracy, draft national constitutions, build antifascist blocs, and support at least the appearance of party pluralism.[17] Unlike the Thuringian BdS, however, the Soviets opposed the immediate unification of the German workers' movement.

13. "Buchenwalder Manifest," in Brill, *Gegen den Strom*, 96–102. For a related document, cf. the Action Program of the Hamburg SPD and KPD (July 24, 1945), analyzed somewhat uncharitably by Albrecht Kaden in *Einheit oder Freiheit*, 53–54.

14. See Manfred Overesch, *Hermann Brill in Thüringen, 1895–1946: Ein Kämpfer gegen Hitler und Ulbricht* (Bonn: Dietz, 1992).

15. For example, see the critique of the BdS by Otto Grotewohl, "Interne Rede vor SPD-Funktionären in Leipzig am 6. September 1945," in Grotewohl, *Otto Grotewohl*, 1: 105–22 (at 117).

16. "Befehl des Obersten Chefs der Sowjetischen Militärverwaltung in Deutschland, Nr. 2," June 10, 1945, in Reichhardt, Treutler, and Lampe, *Berlin*, 748–49.

17. See Zbigniew K. Brzezinski, *The Soviet Bloc: Unity and Conflict*, rev. ed. (Cambridge, MA: Harvard University Press, 1967), pt. 1.

Why? This question is perhaps the most confusing part of how left politics restarted in postwar Germany. A fusion of the left into a new Socialist Unity Party was certainly the strategic goal of German Communists and their Soviet handlers. But given the preponderance of Social Democrats in every area, the Communists chose a delaying tactic. Fusion had to wait until they could either infiltrate Social Democratic organizations or otherwise establish Communist hegemony.

The central committee of the KPD, always ready with finished documents in hand, published its founding proclamation the day after SMAD permitted the formation of parties. Referring to the historic defeat of the workers' movement in 1932–33, the proclamation stated that unity could have prevented the Nazi seizure of power—not working-class unity, but "the will of a unified *people* ready to fight." It admitted that Communists shared blame for that defeat insofar as they were "unable to forge the antifascist unity of workers, peasants, and intellectuals in spite of the blood sacrifice of our best fighters and because of a series of our errors." While gesturing at the party's divisive "social fascism" theory of the early 1930s, the proclamation nevertheless presented the KPD as the only group that had tried to unify the German people against Hitler. Likewise, in referring to the stunted German Revolution of 1918–19, the proclamation highlighted the failures of the SPD, which had allegedly betrayed the cause of democracy and opened the door to far-right reaction. Needless to say, this founding declaration of the postwar KPD whitewashed the past in order to legitimize its present claim to lead the masses. This tactical offensive against Social Democrats was part of the Communists' strategy to improve their position in the coming fusion struggle.[18]

Unlike the refounded KPD, Social Democrats in the Soviet zone had no trained cadres flown in from Moscow with ready-made plans. Former SPD functionaries in Berlin were slower to issue their own proclamation, mostly because of their uncertain status vis-à-vis SMAD and the comparatively ad hoc nature of their party apparatus. No one knew who should lead the refounded SPD. Besides the old Berlin functionaries, Social Democrat cells had formed again in the Western zones, too, especially around Kurt Schumacher in Hannover. In exile, the Sopade had subsumed its prior leadership claim under the broader Union of German Socialist Organizations in Great

18. "Aufruf der Kommunistischen Partei Deutschlands," in Reichhardt, Treutler, and Lampe, *Berlin*, pt. 1, 755–61. Emphasis mine. Among the signatories of the proclamation were Wilhelm Pieck, Walter Ulbricht, and Anton Ackermann—all middle-aged returnees from Russian exile. They represented the last elected central committee of the illegal KPD in 1939. See Leonhard, *Child of the Revolution*.

Britain (UDSO). And then of course there were the neoleftist small groups like New Beginning, whose émigré members might have made peace with the Sopade but whose survivors in Germany still believed in their own mandate for leadership. Some Social Democrats wondered whether the party should be refounded at all. Organizationally, German Social Democracy had ceased to exist in any unified form.

The influence of party tradition and the awareness of Communists' rapid redeployment across the occupation zones convinced most Social Democrats of the need to reconstruct the SPD. According to the democratic statutes of the old organization, however, only a national congress could elect a new leadership. That was unlikely to happen anytime soon, given Allied restrictions on movement across the zones and on political activity in general.

That was why the fusion struggle in the Soviet zone and especially Berlin assumed such great importance. Social Democrat functionaries there emerged from the crowds of liberated camp inmates and the masses of older party members who had kept their heads down under the Nazi regime. Members of the earliest Social Democrat cells in postwar Berlin averaged fifty years old.[19] Most younger males in their twenties or thirties would have served in the military and, if they survived, likely ended up in prisoner of war camps abroad. The civilian young women and men may have proven their worth in the antifascist underground, but they were not well known and had never held party office. Thus, initially, the Berlin SPD reunited as a gerontocracy. The refounded party embodied older reformist values, such as trust in the party's parliamentary faction and faith in gradual progress. For their whole lives prior to the Nazi dictatorship, such Social Democrats had participated in proletarian mass organizations like choirs and sports clubs. They lived and breathed working-class culture. Now, after fascism, many yearned for that lost world of labor. Recreating that world meant accepting the bureaucratic management of party and union affairs, as they had been managed in the past. Theirs was decidedly an old left. Despite and even because of their fidelity to tradition, Berlin's older Social Democrats would mostly side with Communists in favor of a Socialist Unity Party.

The first central committee of the Berlin SPD formed in the office of Erich W. Gniffke and Otto Grotewohl near Nollendorfplatz in the district of

---

19. For a list of former trade union leaders and party functionaries assembled by Erich W. Gniffke and Otto Grotewohl, see Gniffke, *Jahre mit Ulbricht*, 19ff. At the same time as the Gniffke-Grotewohl meetings in Schöneberg, Max Fechner gathered Social Democrats at his grocery store in Neukölln. The age range of the Fechner circle was similar. Meyer, *Sozialdemokraten in der Entscheidung*, 42 and 207.

Schöneberg, located in the American sector. On June 15, several days after the KPD proclamation, this SPD group published its own founding declaration. Addressed to "Workers, Peasants, and Citizens," it followed the same rhetorical model used by the KPD. The Social Democrats declared themselves willing "to work together with all like-minded people and parties," including the KPD, whose proclamation they welcomed. Ignoring the latter's criticisms of Weimar Social Democracy, the Berlin SPD endorsed the Communists' call for "an antifascist democratic regime and a parliamentary-democratic republic with all democratic rights and freedoms."[20] This new republic would eliminate all vestiges of fascist militarism and reinvigorate the German youth. It would also compensate the many victims of Nazism at home and abroad. The economy had to be restructured from the ground up, redistributing large property holdings and socializing banks, insurance companies, mines, power companies, and most other heavy industries. These socialization and capital-steering measures actually went further than the KPD's proposal, which mentioned only land reform, limited self-management of factories, and compromise with private owners.

Postwar calls for left unity and renewal merged into a combined expectation of renewal through unity. Most Social Democrats and Communists wanted to find common ground, especially the rank and file who had occasionally worked together in the antifascist underground. Wilhelm Leuschner was a Social Democrat and antifascist martyr. His last words before being executed at Plötzensee Prison in late September 1944 were supposedly "Make unity happen! [Schafft die Einheit!]."[21] The slogan of unity, as the historian Frank Moraw argued, functioned as panacea and embodiment of all deferred socialist hopes. It was the solution favored by most ordinary Social Democrats and Communists who had remained in Germany, whether free or in prison. Moraw traced the slogan back to left discourse in the 1930s and concluded that, despite its variable meanings, unity "became a hope for the future beyond any rational analysis of the political force field."[22] This desire for unity, even among Social

20. "Aufruf der Sozialdemokratischen Partei Deutschlands," Berlin, June 15, 1945, in Reichhardt, Treutler, and Lampe, *Berlin*, pt. 1, 761–64 (at 762).

21. For an interpretation of Leuschner's last words as a "binding legacy of the dead," see Gustav Dahrendorf, "Vermächtnis der Toten" [September 9, 1945], in *Mensch, das Maß aller Dinge*, 61–64.

22. Moraw, *Die Parole der "Einheit,"* 53. Drafters of the Berlin SPD proclamation acknowledged that they looked backward for inspiration to the Sopade's revolutionary Prague Manifesto of 1934. Gniffke, *Jahre mit Ulbricht*, 30. See also Gerd-Rainer Horn, "The Social Origins of Unity Sentiments in the German Socialist Underground, 1933 to 1936," in Barclay and Weitz, *Between Reform and Revolution*, 341–55.

Democrats ideologically opposed to Communism, helps explain the near in-evitability of the SED in the Eastern zone. The only question that remained was: On whose terms would the party fusion occur?[23]

The Social Democrats wanted fusion as soon as possible. In the summer of 1945 they made repeated proposals for unity to SMAD and the KPD central committee, all of which were turned down. While Social Democrats and Com-munists did establish "unity of action" between June and September, which involved joint meetings and administrative coordination between the two central committees, Gniffke recalled that his Communist counterparts and especially Walter Ulbricht made it clear that they considered organizational unity premature.[24]

Despite its preferential treatment by the Soviets, the KPD knew that it lacked hegemony in the Eastern zone. It had still not even centralized its own party apparatus. Rumors circulated about "considerable differences . . . be-tween the rapidly emerging groups of former [Communist] functionaries and the emigrants who suddenly showed up in large numbers from the So-viet Union, differences whose reconciliation had required a lot of effort." It was said that the Soviet secret police (NKVD) "brainwashed" old Commu-nists who expressed a desire for greater independence from Moscow.[25] Moreover, the undisciplined Red Army terrorized the civilian population through rape and pillage.[26] Combined with a strong anti-Bolshevik preju-dice held over from the Nazi years, those circumstances tended to discour-age popular sympathy for the Communists. In that respect as in others, oc-cupied Germany differed markedly from liberated France and Italy, where Communists enjoyed great popularity owing to their role in the antifascist

23. Andreas Agocs argues that, since the mid-1930s, antifascists of diverse backgrounds viewed German culture as a better ground for unity than any particular national or interna-tional politics. Such a view reached fruition in the Cultural League for the Democratic Re-newal of Germany (Kulturbund), which was founded in the Soviet occupation zone in June 1945. For the Kulturbund, whose members included the New Beginning veteran Robert Havemann, democratic renewal could occur by reclaiming the great German art, music, lit-erature, and science that the Nazis had erased or corrupted. Agocs, *Antifascist Humanism*. Similarly, Sean Forner has analyzed the activity of "engaged democrats" in the American zone, such as Alexander Mitscherlich, Alfred Weber, and Dolf Sternberger, who pursued another version of democratic renewal based on progressive elements of German culture. Forner, *German Intellectuals*.

24. Gniffke, *Jahre mit Ulbricht*, 32.

25. Gniffke, 35.

26. See the harrowing account by Anonymous [Marta Hillers], *A Woman in Berlin* [1954], trans. Philip Boehm (London: Virago, 2005).

resistance. The refounded KPD, by contrast, fought an uphill battle. If it agreed to left unity and carried out organizational fusion too soon, then Social Democrats would constitute the majority in the new party and likely deviate from the Soviet line.

After several months of reorganizing at the local level, reeducating old functionaries, and monopolizing administrative posts, Communist leaders decided that the time had come. In a speech at a mass rally on September 19, 1945, Wilhelm Pieck called for "a unification of both parties as soon as possible."[27] He claimed that a unified workers' party would serve as the vanguard of "the whole antifascist democratic movement" in Germany. Social Democrats by and large welcomed this Communist turnaround. But the delaying tactic had not gone unnoticed. Suspicion of the fusion plan grew in some circles. The hottest political debate was no longer about whether the SPD and KPD should fuse, but whether a fusion on the Communists' timeline, only in the Soviet zone, would result in a permanent division of Germany and its working class.[28]

The New Beginning Working Group

One of the New Beginning survivors, Kurt Schmidt, managed to get a job in the office of Gustav Klingelhöfer, who soon became the Berlin SPD's economic-political secretary. After returning to Berlin following the Nazi collapse, Schmidt's first order of business was to secure "a politically influential post in the SPD."[29] He fully intended to continue New Beginning's mission of working covertly within the existing organizations of the left. Klingelhöfer's office gave him a foothold, and in August 1945 the thirty-two-year-old Schmidt also joined the Social Democratic youth committee. Sanderson reported that

27. Wilhelm Pieck, "Die demokratische Bodenreform. Deutschlands Aufbauproblem. Die Kraft der demokratischen Einheit," in *Reden und Aufsätze*, 2: 11–27 (at 21).

28. Thus the historian Mike Schmeitzner interprets the fusion struggle in the spring of 1946 as "the first great caesura of division" in postwar German history. Schmeitzner, "Auf dem Weg zur Diktatur des Proletariats: Die KPD/SED als Instrument der Diktaturdurchsetzung," in *Die Geschichte der SED: Eine Bestandsaufnahme*, ed. Jens Gieseke and Hermann Wentker (Berlin: Metropol, 2011), 61–83 (at 75).

29. Schmidt to Karl Frank, December 1945, quoted in Hurwitz, *Demokratie und Antikommunismus*, 4 (1): 44. Bernhard Meyer described Klingelhöfer's position as "economic-political secretary," whereas Klaus-Peter Schulz referred to his "political bureau." Meyer, *Sozialdemokraten in der Entscheidung*, 85, and Schulz, *Auftakt zum Kalten Krieg*, 43. See also Gniffke, *Jahre mit Ulbricht*, 47–48.

"Klingelhöfer, Schmidt, and other members of the economic committee of the SPD function as a sort of brains trust" for the SPD central committee.[30]

Schmidt was part of the trio that had assumed leadership of New Beginning inside Germany from 1936 until his arrest in the fall of 1938. He suffered physically during seven years in prison and concentration camps, and he was still in poor health when he first contacted Karl Frank in December 1945.[31] Schmidt wrote an emotional letter to his erstwhile comrade, whom he had idolized in the past. The thing that sustained him through all those years under fascism, he claimed, was "the knowledge that our friends abroad would do everything personally and politically to ease our fate."[32] Such psychological dependence on friends abroad preserved the morale of New Beginning survivors well into the postwar months, when many other Germans experienced profound isolation. The spirit of the antifascist new left thus persisted, even after its actual organization in Germany had collapsed.

But spirit alone was not enough for Schmidt. Immediately after liberation, he began organizing fellow New Beginning survivors in Berlin. By July, twenty to thirty members of the prewar organization reconstituted themselves as the Socialist Working Group and started holding regular discussions and lectures. Like its antifascist predecessor, this group operated with a degree of conspiratorial caution. It formed before the Allied occupiers officially permitted political activity, and it wanted to avoid the attention of Communists, who surely would remember the conflicts with New Beginning in the 1930s. The Working Group also had to avoid appearing as a rival to the Berlin SPD. The divisions within the old left as well as an authoritarian "state" in the form of SMAD created conditions for neoleftist action that were not unlike those of the interwar years. New Beginning survivors fell back into clandestine habits. But now they resisted the dogmatism, cadre structure, and bureaucratic rules of the old Org.[33]

For example, the Working Group did not withhold information from younger members. Fritz Benke, who entered New Beginning's periphery in

---

30. Hurwitz, *Demokratie und Antikommunismus,* 4 (1): 44, and Sanderson to Richard Löwenthal (London), October 9, 1945, IISG, NB Archives, 25/1.

31. Brill met him once in prison and remembered him looking terrible, even for a camp inmate. Otto Suhr and Hermann L. Brill, "Kurt Schmidt," *Das sozialistische Jahrhundert* 1, no. 17–18 (July 1947): 277.

32. Letter reprinted as "Brief von Kurt Schmidt an seine Freunde in New York. Berlin, im Dezember 1945," in American Association for a Democratic Germany, *Der neue Kampf um Freiheit,* 13–20 (at 13).

33. Meyer, *Sozialdemokraten in der Entscheidung,* 162, and Hurwitz, *Demokratie und Antikommunismus,* 4 (1): 34–35.

the 1930s, learned now for the first time that his cadre back then had belonged to a larger antifascist network. The Working Group featured some leading personalities such as Schmidt, the religious socialist Kürschner, and the union organizer Georg Müller. But its meetings were freer than before, more inclusive, and less sealed off from the outside world.

The meetings took place in the American sector of Berlin, often at the apartment of the chemist Robert Havemann near the Max Planck Institute in Dahlem or at the doctor's office of Willi Günther in Neukölln.[34] Thus, like the old New Beginning network, the Working Group relied on bourgeois professional covers. Its size fluctuated as the political situation changed in the fall and winter of 1945–46, never topping a few dozen participants. After returning from a British prisoner of war camp in September, another member of the prewar New Beginning leadership, Werner Peuke, joined Schmidt, Kürscher, and Müller at the group's head.

Their earliest discussions concerned Germany's dire economic situation and the challenges of political reconstruction. Schmidt admitted that Germans would have to suffer the fate of all conquered peoples: decreased production capacity, diminished territory, reparation payments. But he resented the fact that many Germans who opposed the Nazis should also suffer political repression by the occupation powers. The antifascist new left along with members of the old workers' parties had greeted the Allied armies as liberators, not as new oppressors. "At the moment," Schmidt complained, "we have no politics to practice, only orders to receive."[35]

He also worried about the reorganization of the Berlin SPD. The older functionaries shut out the younger militants just as they had during the Weimar Republic. One imagines the frustration coursing through the Working Group as it counted off Social Democrat leaders who never actively resisted the Nazis and now called for a return to how things used to be. The Communists, Schmidt added, remained prisoners of Marxist-Leninist dogma and the authoritarian party form. Still, in good New Beginning style, he hoped "to influence them positively and pedagogically, minimizing their backwards characteristics and supporting their positive-progressive ones until they predominate." This softer touch for the Communists reflected the Working Group's position on left unity at the end of 1945. Even though fusion did not meet neoleftist expectations, "it could be a crucial step forwards." A left unity party could function as "a bridge between the West and the East." Leaving aside the issue of organizational form, Schmidt argued that the biggest danger

34. Hurwitz, *Demokratie und Antikommunismus*, 4 (1): 45.
35. K. Schmidt, "Brief von Kurt Schmidt," 17.

for the German left was its loss of autonomy should it get sucked into the Allied superpower rivalry.[36]

Because it could not control the political situation, the Working Group aimed for intellectual independence as a way to avoid becoming pawns in the geopolitical game. A German-British observer noted that the survivors' isolation made them unaware "that there are Labour movements in existence in Western Europe, who are watching their decisions very closely and might even be prepared to give them some moral support in their struggle for democratic representation."[37] Such isolation pained Schmidt. Émigrés in the United States, he wrote to Frank, should help the Berlin group broaden its horizons by sending the latest books and material on "all progressive trains of thought." The Working Group wanted to "solve these problems [of German reconstruction] together with you and with all of our friends abroad, regardless of nationality."[38] In another letter to Georg Eliasberg in New York, Schmidt described how "after 12 years spent in an *intellectual concentration camp*, we are all famished [for knowledge] and would all be glad if you were able to close these gaps too as soon as possible." He asked first for the latest literature to satisfy his friends' spiritual needs before listing their material needs such as meat, fat, vitamins, medicine, shoes, and underwear, which so many Germans lacked.[39] The survivors also sought channels of communication between the four occupation zones. Eliasberg offered to send them clippings from the *Frankfurter Rundschau* and other newspapers in the Western zones. He remarked that "in these crazy times it is possible that the quickest way from Frankfurt to Berlin leads through New York."[40] Such material detours accounted for why members of the Working Group felt so adrift, and for the psychological necessity of their small community of action in Berlin.

Yet their theoretical and political abilities impressed anyone who encountered them. Jean Eisner, an economic analyst for the US Manpower Division, remembered Schmidt in particular as "a highly intelligent working-class socialist with an impeccable record of forceful political activity."[41] Another

36. K. Schmidt, 17–19.

37. Werner Klatt to Phil Neild (London), January 21, 1946, quoted in Hurwitz, *Demokratie und Antikommunismus*, 4 (1): 63.

38. K. Schmidt, "Brief von Kurt Schmidt," 19.

39. Fritz Brandt [Kurt Schmidt] to Eliasberg (Long Island, NY), end of December 1945, U of O, Goldbloom Papers, 4/13. Emphasis mine.

40. Stefan Neuberg [Georg Eliasberg] to Kurt Schmidt and friends (Berlin), January 7, 1946, U of O, Goldbloom Papers, 4/15.

41. Interview of Jean Eisner-Steinberg by Gerhard Bry, quoted in Bry, *Resistance*, 233. See also Jean Eisner to Harold Hurwitz, August 7, 1985, RHG, NL Hurwitz, 150.

American observer wrote that his "clear, logical thinking amazes us."[42] But others worried that Schmidt's conciliatory personality might be too soft for the demands of the fusion struggle. As the months went on, the driving force behind the Working Group turned out to be a harder personality, Georg Müller.

Born in the town of Brandenburg an der Havel in 1902, Müller moved to the Berlin neighborhood of Köpenick in his youth and followed in his father's footsteps by apprenticing as a plumber and pipefitter. From an early age, Müller was politically active. He joined the German Metalworkers Union and various left-wing organizations such as the Social Democratic Friends of Nature. Although he was too young to serve in World War I, the vicarious experience of it as well as the revolutionary wave that accompanied the war's end radicalized him for life. In the early 1920s he joined both the Communist Youth and the Communist organization for helping political prisoners, International Red Aid. But the vicissitudes of Comintern politics brought him into conflict with the KPD. He joined the German Communist Party–Opposition (KPO) in 1929 and then the SAP in 1931. After passing through these splinter groups, he found his way into Walter Loewenheim's Org.

Following the Org/New Beginning rule that members must operate from within one of the major workers' parties, Müller joined the SPD in 1932. For the next three years he worked in the Org underground organization. When the leadership change occurred in 1935, he stayed loyal to the Loewenheim faction. That fall he was arrested, along with several dozen other members. Released from prison in 1937, he made contact with what remained of the New Beginning organization. He avoided the next wave of arrests that hit the group in 1938.

During the war he kept his head down as a skilled worker, knowing that his movements were being watched. Immediately after the Nazi regime fell, he set about rebuilding trade unions in the Lichtenberg district of eastern Berlin. There he ran afoul of the KPD and the Soviet commandant's office. Far more staunchly than any of his comrades in the Socialist Working Group, Müller opposed the fusion plan. He interpreted every Communist action as a ploy. So naturally he criticized the Berlin SPD leaders and their cooperation with the Communists. Politically he occupied a no-man's land, seeing enemies on all sides.[43] Prone to abstract theory and conspiratorial intrigue, Müller's natural home was the Working Group. He became its most avid participant.

---

42. Bill Kemsley (Berlin) to Karl Frank, December 26, 1945, U of O, Goldbloom Papers, 4/13.

43. Meyer, *Sozialdemokraten in der Entscheidung*, 122. See also Tobias Kühne, "Das Netzwerk 'Neu Beginnen' und die Berliner SPD nach 1945," PhD thesis, TU-Berlin, 2014, 107–9, and Berliner Geschichtswerkstatt, "Müller, Georg (1902)," in *Widerstand in Berlin*, 5: 235.

It is understandable, then, that a rivalry developed between Müller and Schmidt. The two men had very different approaches to left politics. Müller still practiced the Org method of painstaking theoretical analysis, whereas Schmidt shared the more pragmatic approach of the New Beginning émigrés. Moreover, Müller had abandoned Marxism entirely in the late 1930s. He identified now as a socialist seeking "humane solutions for the workers based on the insights of 'social democratism.'"[44] The rivalry also made sense from a generational perspective: Müller (b. 1902) had more in common with Loewenheim and the ex-Communist renegades who founded the Org than he did with Schmidt (b. 1913), who had a background in the SAJ and thus identified more with New Beginning's post-1935 leadership.

Müller actually remade contact with Loewenheim, Henry Hellmann (Heinrich Jakubowicz), and Vicky Abrams (Hedwig Leibetseder, née Abranowicz), who had all emigrated to London before the war. Starting in the late summer of 1946, his correspondence with the Loewenheim faction displayed a familiar Org style of discourse, stressing the need for a "new conception."[45] In Frank's estimate, Müller was "certainly an outstanding functionary and he has acquired completely correct insights into essential questions[;] but when he tries to express them, the danger exists of confused theories that would be difficult for older party comrades to understand."[46] The rivalry between Müller and Schmidt boiled down to their different ideas about which role the Working Group should play in future left politics. The former believed that the group should operate behind the scenes as a conspiratorial cell, while the latter envisioned a looser network of like-minded friends that would gradually dissolve into the ranks of a new socialist party.

Left Fusion in the Soviet Zone

Already in the spring of 1945, the veteran Social Democrat and concentration camp survivor Kurt Schumacher had begun reorganizing the SPD in the area around Hannover, which had been liberated by American troops but became part of the British occupation zone. There he delivered a long speech on May 6 at the first postwar gathering of Social Democrat functionaries. Members of

44. Meyer, *Sozialdemokraten in der Entscheidung*, 122.

45. Georg [Müller] (Berlin) to Vicky Abrams (London), August 7, 194[6], Wiener Library, Vicky Abrams Papers, 1031/1/158–196, and Georg Müller to Heinrich Jakubowicz, September 13, 1946, RHG, NL Hurwitz, 46.

46. Frank recounted how Müller even tried to school the former SAP functionary and New Beginning confidant Werner Klatt in the manner of an Org F-Course. Frank to Erwin Schoettle and Richard Löwenthal (London), February 26, 1946, FES, NL Löwenthal, 4.

the old SPD welcomed the Allies' demand for democracy, Schumacher declared, because democracy was "the fundamental idea of our past and of the future." Some "other parts of the population," however, would not find democracy so congenial.[47] Along with unrepentant Nazis, he surely had Communists in mind.

Schumacher acknowledged the need to end the bitter conflict between the two workers' parties. Ironically, like leaders of the refounded KPD, however, he warned against any rush into unity. He observed that in liberated countries across Europe, Social Democrats and Communists decided to reestablish separate organizations and develop their own policies. Why should Germans do otherwise? If no left unity party developed elsewhere, then it seemed unlikely to succeed in occupied Germany. Moreover, Communists were bound to the interests of one occupation power, the Soviets. "We cannot and will not be the autocratically wielded instrument of any foreign imperial interest," he asserted. Social Democrats would have much greater success in making peace with the neoleftist small groups. A unified and renewed Social Democratic Party might function as "a magnet for all splinters." No faction would have preeminence in this refounded SPD. In Schumacher's vision, the old-guard functionaries who had remained in Germany and the émigrés who had left would set aside their differences for the sake of rebuilding Social Democracy.[48]

In Hannover and throughout the Western zones, Schumacher worked on bringing the old-guard functionaries together. He also entered into regular correspondence with Sopade leaders in London such as Erich Ollenhauer, Fritz Heine, and Hans Vogel. "Despite formal restrictions on political activities and poor communications," wrote one scholar, Schumacher quickly "gained acceptance for Hannover as a rival center to Berlin in the reorganization of a national party organization."[49] His pamphlet *Political Guidelines* (August 1945) further established his position as Social Democracy's leader in the West.[50] His charisma and commanding leadership style made him a formidable figure on the postwar German left. He both symbolized in his person and expressed in his speeches "the social democratic succession myth" that linked the refounded SPD to the anti-Nazi underground movement and back

47. Kurt Schumacher, "Wir verzweifeln nicht!" (May 6, 1945), in *Reden—Schriften—Korrespondenzen*, 203–36 (at 219).

48. Schumacher, 230.

49. Edinger, *Kurt Schumacher*, 101.

50. Kurt Schumacher, "Politische Richtlinien für die SPD in ihrem Verhältnis zu den anderen politischen Faktoren" (August 25, 1945), in *Reden—Schriften—Korrespondenzen*, 256–86.

to Weimar Social Democracy. He insisted that the party must never repeat its past mistakes when faced with right-wing reaction. Last, but not least, he was a stalwart anti-Communist like most Social Democrats outside of Berlin.[51]

A rivalry grew between Schumacher and the Berlin SPD, for which Grotewohl now claimed to speak. On September 15, Schumacher circulated a letter to the regional executive boards of the SPD in the Western zones in which he warned that "the Berliners assert a central claim to validity for the whole Reich." While the Western SPD should recognize the Berlin central committee's jurisdiction in the Soviet zone, "we must ward off" its claim to national leadership.[52]

Several weeks later, Schumacher organized a so-called national congress of the SPD in the three Western zones. It would take place in Wennigsen outside Hannover. The exclusion of delegates from the Soviet zone owed officially to restrictions placed on the meeting by the British authorities, but unofficially such exclusion suited Schumacher's purposes. The Berlin central committee was allowed to send only observers, not voting delegates. When they arrived, however, they were denied entry to the plenary session and had to meet separately in a nearby building.[53] The Berlin observers were furious. Nevertheless, on the last day of the congress Schumacher and Grotewohl met personally to discuss the future of the party. They agreed that so long as the German nation was divided into occupation zones, organizational unity of the SPD was impossible. The Berliners should lead Social Democrats in the Soviet zone, while the Schumacher bureau would assume leadership in the Western zones. It was a fateful agreement.[54]

In October the Berliners accepted an offer by the KPD to create a joint committee in the Soviet zone. The committee would prepare for the first major event of the fusion struggle, a meeting of thirty representatives each from the KPD and the SPD on December 20–21. This "Conference of Sixty" marked a turning point in the uneasy relationship between the two central committees. Grotewohl set aside his suspicions about the Communist delaying tactic and came out strongly in favor of fusion. The conference generally affirmed his

51. Edinger, *Kurt Schumacher*, 138.

52. Quoted in Kaden, *Einheit oder Freiheit*, 130.

53. See Matthias Loeding, *Otto Grotewohl kontra Kurt Schumacher: Die Wennigsener Konferenz im Oktober 1945* (Hamburg: Kovac, 2004); Albrecht Kaden, "Entscheidung in Wennigsen," *Die Neue Gesellschaft* 7, no. 6 (November–December 1960); and Sopade, *Die Wiedergeburt der deutschen Sozialdemokratie: Bericht über Vorgeschichte und Verlauf der sozialdemokratischen Parteikonferenz von Hannover vom 5. bis 7. Oktober 1945* (London, 1945).

54. Kaden, *Einheit oder Freiheit*, 149–53.

stance.[55] The majority decided to carry out the fusion of the German left within the next three months.

Not everyone was happy. Klingelhöfer attended the conference and delivered the concluding remarks. He drew attention to the pressure on Social Democrats in the Soviet zone and the unequal treatment of the SPD and KPD by the Soviet authorities. Fusion in the Soviet zone alone, he warned, might result in a permanent division of the German nation.[56] But in the end, he too voted in favor of fusion.

Most of the New Beginning Working Group shared Klingelhöfer's reservations, and over time they grew even more uncomfortable with the push toward unity. In a manuscript written toward the end of December 1945, Schmidt emphasized the need for new ideas to fit the changed situation. The old Marxist prediction of an imminent collapse of capitalism, the need to expropriate the expropriators, and so on, he argued, no longer applied to Germany, given the wholesale destruction of its means of production in the war. That did not disprove Marxism. On the contrary, he insisted that Marx himself would arrive at the same conclusion. Schmidt pointed out the peculiarity of Germany's new beginning: the old workers' movement was decimated by fascism, and because of the lack of intellectual freedom under the Nazi regime, the working class never developed new insights. Therefore, "old ideas have today become shackles on [both] parties."[57]

Those old ideas made the German left prone to manipulation by outside forces. Schmidt suggested that the reality of the Allied occupation and the rivalry between the Western powers and the Soviet Union would undermine any attempt at left unity. Only the SPD seemed able to seize the initiative in reorganizing German political life independently from the great powers. In theory if not always in practice, the SPD valued internal democracy and freedom of opinion. Schmidt recommended neoleftist action within the ranks of Social Democracy, which should not be allowed to backslide into oligarchical or bureaucratic tendencies. The SPD must keep space open for discussion and delegate authority to younger members in order to

55. "Rede Otto Grotewohls auf der gemeinsamen Konferenz von Vertretern der SPD und KPD, 20. Dezember 1945," in Reichhardt, Treutler, and Lampe, *Berlin*, pt. 1, 794–805. See also Josef Gabert, Hans-Joachim Krusch, and Andreas Malycha, eds., *Einheitsdrang oder Zwangsvereinigung? Die Sechziger-Konferenzen von KPD und SPD, 1945 und 1946* (Berlin: Dietz, 1990).

56. Meyer, *Sozialdemokraten in der Entscheidung*, 86.

57. Kurt Schmidt, "Ueber die Aufgaben der Sozialdemokratie" (end of December 1945), in American Association for a Democratic Germany, *Der neue Kampf um Freiheit*, 21–25 (at 23).

overcome the party's reputation of being "overly old [überaltert]." Just as in the interwar years, Schmidt called on the young generation to take control over left politics.[58]

He also noted that ordinary Social Democrats in Berlin were disgruntled with the top-down manner in which the SPD central committee carried out the fusion negotiations.[59] Once again, New Beginning focused on the widening gap between the party's leaders and its alienated rank and file. Schmidt and the Working Group managed to win Klingelhöfer over to their side. On January 3, 1946, the latter wrote to Grotewohl informing him of his misgivings about how the central committee was handling the situation. The decision for fusion, he claimed, marked "the opening of the strategic struggle for leadership of the German working class." Klingelhöfer had in fact just met with an emissary from the British Labour Party recently arrived in Germany, a certain German-Englishman named Holt. This person was in fact the New Beginning émigré Waldemar von Knoeringen. That meeting convinced Klingelhöfer that Western parties such as Labour might not back the fusion plan, in which case the German left in the Soviet zone would become totally disconnected from the international workers' movement (such as it was). Klingelhöfer pleaded with Grotewohl to defend the autonomy of the SPD and ensure that Social Democrats retained control over "the tempo of unity." After all, he estimated that they had more than a two to one electoral advantage over the Communists. Everything depended on the unification of the German left at the correct pace and on a national scale.[60]

In the first two months of 1946, Schmidt emerged as the leading opponent of rapid fusion in the SPD's Neukölln district. He knew that "the mistrust with which the leaderships of the SPD and the KPD always viewed the New Beginning Group would be rekindled, and thus the debut of its former members in these parties would be endangered."[61] German Communists and Soviet authorities began harassing the Working Group and other opponents of rapid fusion, a diverse camp that I call the antifusionists.[62] Sanderson heard that a Communist-run office of the Berlin Magistrate had interrogated former New

---

58. K. Schmidt, 25.

59. Soldt [Kurt Schmidt] to Richard Löwenthal, January 10, 1946, IISG, NB Archives, 25/3.

60. Klingelhöfer to Grotewohl, January 3, 1946, U of O, Goldbloom Papers, 4/15.

61. Soell, *Fritz Erler*, 1: 66.

62. Theo Thiele, for example, had lain in a sickbed throughout much of 1945, but he still was politically exposed enough that Schmidt wanted to find him an "escape route into the West." Hurwitz, *Demokratie und Antikommunismus*, 4 (1): 44.

Beginning members and even pressured some to sign a declaration of the group's liquidation.[63]

In some circles, Schmidt's "foreign connections" to the New Beginning émigrés in London and New York gave him credibility. The Working Group still needed these connections in order to get up to speed on the latest theoretical and political developments. Löwenthal informed the Berliners about the many shifts in the Soviet line since the 1930s, and Schmidt asked him to write a concise history of the KPD for the group. Given the mounting pressure on antifusionists, he also wanted Löwenthal's help in obtaining the official backing of the British government for the SPD. With that kind of support, he thought, the Berlin central committee might show some backbone and slow down the fusion process. The situation was critical. Without support from the outside, "we will not be able to hold out much longer as the bridgehead of democracy in Berlin." Notably, Schmidt's metaphor for Berlin had changed from a conciliatory bridge between East and West to a contested bridgehead against the Communist threat.[64]

At the first assembly of young Social Democrats in Neukölln on February 10, Schmidt delivered his most important speech of the fusion struggle. Following staid remarks by the central committee delegate Max Fechner, Schmidt spoke on behalf of all the young women and men who had spent the best years of their lives under fascist rule. He meant his own New Beginning generation, now in its thirties. These veterans of the antifascist underground knew the weaknesses of both parties of the working class. While Social Democrats advocated individual freedom and a democratic state, Schmidt claimed, Communists openly embraced authoritarianism and in the past had promoted the destructive social fascism theory, which did so much to divide workers. Communists today, he continued, still persecuted internal dissidents as faultfinders [*Kritikaster*], heretics, opportunists, and renegades. Speaking implicitly on behalf of New Beginning, he said that in the 1930s "we were clear about the fact that a renewal of socialist thought is necessary, and the practical experience of fascism has corroborated this insight."[65] Now was the time to make good on that insight and develop a program for the postwar left.

---

63. Hurwitz, *Demokratie und Antikommunismus*, 4 (1): 47. He might have referred to Fritz Erler's attempt to publicly disband New Beginning in August 1945. See chapter 6.

64. Fritz Brandt [Kurt Schmidt] to Richard Löwenthal, February 2, 1946, IISG, NB Archives, 25/4. The history of the KPD that Schmidt requested would be written not by Löwenthal, but by Ossip K. Flechtheim: *Die Kommunistische Partei Deutschlands in der Weimarer Republik*. On Berlin's role as a bridgehead of democracy, see Krause, *Cold War Democracy*.

65. Kurt Schmidt, "Rede von Kurt Schmidt auf der ersten Versammlung der jungen Sozialdemokraten in Berlin am 10. Februar 1946," in American Association for a Democratic Germany, *Der neue Kampf um Freiheit*, 26–32 (at 28).

As with many renewal campaigns, Schmidt moved forward by looking back. He drew on Marx's book *The Eighteenth Brumaire of Louis Napoleon* (1852) to link socialist renewal to the traditions of the workers' movement. One should not confuse tradition, Schmidt argued, with a literal repetition of the achievements of dead generations, which weigh like a nightmare on the brains of the living. Marxist tradition entailed an "affinity for a living idea." For him, that meant staying true to Marx's *method* of historical materialism, rather than any specific conclusions by Marx about his own nineteenth-century moment. It involved recognizing general forms of action and critique, rather than repeating particular actions. And it meant "making the effort to do what the great minds of the workers' movement would have done if they stood in our place." Similar to Erich Schmidt's speech in June 1931 before a joint meeting of Socialist and Communist youth, Kurt Schmidt here characterized himself and his generation as undogmatic revolutionary socialists. A new left required moving socialism forward beyond the immobile doctrines of reformist Social Democracy and authoritarian Communism. Whether a renewed SPD or a Socialist Unity Party, a new left organization must enable fresh ideas and a healthy turnover of leaders. Schmidt hoped to break Michels's iron law of oligarchy by forever cultivating internal democracy.[66]

He built his closing remarks around a quote from the Italian socialist and antifascist martyr Giacomo Matteotti: "Freedom is like the sun. One has to have lost it in order to know that one cannot live without it." The experience of both fascism and Communist betrayal had made Schmidt and his New Beginning comrades allergic to dictatorial parties, which represented "the foundation of this epoch of modern spiritual and material barbarism."[67] Right after the Neukölln assembly, he wrote to Löwenthal in London about how his speech "raised a great storm." He considered it a prelude to a campaign that would rally the antifusionists in Berlin. Having received alarming reports about unification congresses being rushed through in Thuringia, Saxony, and Mecklenburg, he and his comrades in the Working Group agreed "that the pressure in the provinces is so strong that the sole possibility of still rising up against it exists only in Berlin." They had no illusions about the personal danger they faced in going against the current of Soviet-sponsored fusion. His letter to Löwenthal spoke of "a political state of war" and "battles of encirclement which aim to eliminate SP[D] members." He sounded more and more like his rival Müller when he described preparations for "Con-style

66. K. Schmidt, 28.
67. K. Schmidt, 30–31.

continuation of work [konmäßige Weiterarbeit]" in the event of a total Soviet crackdown: that was shorthand for reviving the Org rules of conspiracy.[68] Neoleftists like Schmidt openly compared the fusion struggle of 1945–46 to the fascist crisis of 1932–33.

By mid-February, Schmidt's boss Klingelhöfer had broken with Grotewohl and the SPD central committee, throwing his support behind the antifusionists. Differences of opinion about the tempo of unity or its regional versus national scale receded into the background as two antagonistic camps took shape: fusionists versus antifusionists. The Communist minority in Berlin obviously joined the former camp, while Social Democrats split between the two. Antifusionist Social Democrats and neoleftists alike began using the same rhetoric of resistance that animated the anti-Nazi underground. Now they resisted Communist "forced unification."[69] Schmidt even despaired of continuing resistance in Berlin, suggesting that the only option "for the active comrades of the O. [the old abbreviation for Loewenheim's Org]" might be to emigrate and carry on the struggle from the West. Whether consciously or not, his words echoed the discourse surrounding New Beginning's leadership change back in 1935.[70]

As the fusion struggle progressed, the geopolitical orientation of the two camps soon aligned with the "democratic" West versus the "dictatorial" East. This West–East alignment caused debate on the left to deteriorate, including the discussions in the New Beginning Working Group. Defending democracy against dictatorship, however vital, had a limiting and ideologically reductive effect. Problems of social or economic structure were pushed aside by an obsession over political forms, which admittedly was a hazard of neoleftist thought.

On February 14, the district chairman of the SPD in Tempelhof, Curt Swolinzky, hosted the first combined meeting of antifusionists at his fabric store. They met again three days later at the district and section leader conference held at the party headquarters in Mitte. Swolinzky summed up the determined attitude of all involved: "Better to go hungry under a democracy than

---

68. Fritz Brandt [Kurt Schmidt] to Löwenthal, February 10, 1946, IISG, NB Archives, 25/4.

69. Schmidt to Karl Frank and Vera Eliasberg (New York), February 16, 1946, quoted in American Association for a Democratic Germany, *Der neue Kampf um Freiheit*, 53–55 (at 54). Frank and the New York émigrés started referring to "the new struggle for freedom" against "the new 'Gleichschaltung.'" They argued for the need "to counteract the semi-totalitarian pressure" faced by Social Democrats. "Important Political Developments in Berlin," manuscript (New York), February 19, 1946, IISG, NB Archives, 25/2.

70. Fritz Brandt [Kurt Schmidt] to Paul [likely Karl Frank], February 16, 1946, RHG, NL Hurwitz, 108. Cf. chapter 2.

be full under a dictatorship." Two days later, the fusionist SPD central committee announced a party conference for April 19–20 that would decide the
question of unity once and for all.[71]

On February 21, Swolinzky invited Klingelhöfer and several members of
the New Beginning Working Group to an emergency meeting at a pub in
Tempelhof.[72] Most outspoken were the ringleaders Swolinzky and the young
firebrand Klaus-Peter Schulz. Perhaps already observing the rules of conspiracy, New Beginning members kept a low profile. The discussion revolved
around how to make contact with Schumacher, who was visiting Berlin at the
time. Grotewohl and the party central committee wanted to keep him away
from the antifusionists. Nevertheless, the Swolinzky-Schulz circle used covert
means to arrange a meeting with the "guest from Hannover" two days later.
Schulz remembered how an "involuntary emotion took hold of those present"
when Schumacher entered the room accompanied by his British officer chap-
erone.[73] While this retrospective account was melodramatic, it did indicate a
shift in mentality on the German left. Until that day, Schumacher represented
to Berliners only the intransigence of the Western SPD. Now he appeared as
a messiah, an embodiment of socialist militancy, and a champion of what now
had transformed into an utterly anti-Communist struggle.

Klingelhöfer, Schulz, and others still favored a cartel model of relations
between the SPD and the KPD, which would allow the two parties to develop
a common program but maintain separate lists of candidates for elections.[74]
Schumacher apparently rejected this model as too conciliatory toward the
Communists. Besides, the quickening pace of events rendered a cartel model
obsolete. The central committees of both parties announced on February 26
that they had set the date of the Unification Congress for April 20–21; that is,
immediately after the SPD party conference that was supposed to decide
whether to unify.[75] This announcement indicated that the official party leaders considered unification an accomplished fact.

Meanwhile, antifusionists were on the move. On a snowy Friday, March 1,
they took their most decisive step to date at the SPD functionaries' conference held at the Admiral Palace theater on Friedrichstraße. The central

71. Meyer, *Sozialdemokraten in der Entscheidung*, 132, 165, 171, and 179, and "Beschluß des
Zentralausschusses der SPD über die Einberufung eines Parteitages, 19. Februar 1946," in Reichhardt, Treutler, and Lampe, *Berlin*, pt. 1, 827.

72. Meyer, *Sozialdemokraten in der Entscheidung*, 87, 115, 121, 163, and 185.

73. Schulz, *Auftakt zum Kalten Krieg*, 127.

74. Meyer, *Sozialdemokraten in der Entscheidung*, 87 and 171.

75. "Organisationsbeschluß des ZA der SPD und des ZK der KPD, 26. Februar 1946," in
Reichhardt, Treutler, and Lampe, *Berlin*, pt. 1, 827–28.

committee had scheduled the conference on a weekday morning with the expectation that it would draw in a small but respectable quorum for ratifying its handling of the unity question. The plan was to create the impression of rank-and-file support.[76] But the central committee had not reckoned with the growing strength of the antifusionist opposition, now emboldened by Schumacher's visit and the moral support of the Western SPD. Around two thousand functionaries showed up, filling the theater "to the ceiling" and dumbfounding the event planners. Many of these section and district functionaries were young and had been in office only since the end of 1945. As Schulz later put it, they demonstrated the Berlin SPD's "biological rejuvenation process."[77] Grotewohl could hardly get a word in without interruptions from the angry crowd.

Backstage, Schulz conspired to line up several antifusionists to speak right after Grotewohl. He then reentered the audience and acted as claqueur, demonstratively clapping for the opposition and heckling the central committee. Schmidt and other members of the New Beginning Working Group apparently joined in. Franz Neumann, the Reinickendorf district chief, was the man of the hour.[78] Several days before, his district had recommended that the SPD in the Soviet zone hold a party plebiscite on the fusion question. Hardly anyone took notice of that recommendation until he repeated it at the Admiral Palace. The audience roared in approval, which caught the central committee off guard.[79] A motion carried, and the date for a party plebiscite was set for March 31. This was a revolt of the middle ranks against the bureaucratic party leadership.

With this triumph at the functionaries' conference, antifusionists for the first time received media attention in Germany and abroad.[80] Even if the battle in the provinces was lost, as Schmidt had admitted two weeks earlier, antifusionists in Berlin would continue to fight for a democratic decision of

76. Schulz, *Auftakt zum Kalten Krieg*, 140.

77. Schulz, 143.

78. Meyer, *Sozialdemokraten in der Entscheidung*, 150, 163, and 171, and Schulz, *Auftakt zum Kalten Krieg*, 141. This Franz Neumann (b. 1904) should not be confused with the Frankfurt School affiliate Franz L. Neumann (b. 1900), although both did have loose ties to New Beginning in the 1930s and 1940s.

79. Schulz, *Auftakt zum Kalten Krieg*, 143 and 148n45.

80. For example, see "Germans Hold Up Communists' Bid—Berlin Socialists Demonstrate against Merger and then Call for Secret Vote," *New York Times*, March 2, 1946, 3; "Berlin Social Democrats—Opposition to Fusion," *The Times* (London), March 2, 1946, 4; and "German Party Plebiscite—Fusion Campaign in Berlin," *The Times* (London) March 13, 1946, 3.

the unity question.[81] The struggle climaxed in mid-March. The SPD central committee member Gustav Dahrendorf abruptly resigned and fled to the West, and on March 9, Klingelhöfer resigned as well. The latter immediately joined the antifusionists, whom he told about the central committee's plan to block the plebiscite. The next day, antifusionists formed an action committee to run its campaign.[82] Over the next few weeks, the gulf between fusionists and antifusionists became unbridgeable.

Many members of the Working Group agitated against fusion. They worked at the local level, trying to get new antifusionist leaders elected to neighborhood councils and, if possible, to co-opt the SPD regional committee. They also tried to found an independent newspaper in order to break what Schmidt called the fusionist monopoly on public opinion (he referred to central committee control over the paper *Das Volk*). The technical difficulties of organizing a resistance movement in occupied Berlin included such mundane things as paper shortages and lack of automobiles. But a personnel shortage loomed larger: Schmidt complained about the "lack of qualified people" and asked New Beginning émigrés for help in vetting staff for what he now called the SPD–Opposition.[83]

Agitation involved attending local party meetings and making sure that the antifusionist position won out. At the Britz section assembly of the SPD in Neukölln on March 10, Schmidt teamed up with Maria Hannemann to bring forward an antifusionist motion. It passed, 720 votes to 60.[84] As the first discussant at the Berlin conference of the SPD factory groups two days later, Hannemann raised another motion against fusion. "I belong not to the Opposition," she declared, "but to the majority of the Berlin party."[85] While her motion failed, it set up Müller, who later at the conference raised a similar motion, which passed.[86]

81. Schmidt to Frank and Eliasberg, February 16, 1946, quoted in American Association for a Democratic Germany, *Der neue Kampf um Freiheit*, 53–55 (at 55).

82. Meyer, *Sozialdemokraten in der Entscheidung*, 87 and 132–33. Shortly after arriving in the British zone, Dahrendorf published a scathing critique of the central committee's fusion campaign, *Zwangsvereinigung der Kommunistischen und der Sozialdemokratischen Partei in der russischen Zone* (Hannover, 1946), reprinted in Dahrendorf, *Der Mensch, das Maß aller Dinge*, 89–124.

83. Excerpt of letter from Sold [Kurt Schmidt] to Paul [Karl Frank], March 3, 1946, IISG, NB Archives, 25/15.

84. Meyer, *Sozialdemokraten in der Entscheidung*, 63 and 163.

85. Quoted in Reichhardt, Treutler, and Lampe, *Berlin*, 856–57n126.

86. Meyer, *Sozialdemokraten in der Entscheidung*, 63, and Reichhardt, Treutler, and Lampe, *Berlin*, 856–57n126.

Seeing which way the wind was blowing, Soviet authorities ramped up their intimidation campaign against antifusionists working in the Soviet sector. Ernst Moewes, the district chairman of the SPD in Mitte and friend of the New Beginning Working Group, and Werner Rüdiger, an outspoken leader of the SPD in Prenzlauer Berg, were arrested by the secret police on March 17 and spent three days in custody.[87] On the day of their arrests, Schmidt delivered a stirring speech at the Neukölln delegates' assembly in which he contrasted the divergent political cultures of Social Democracy and Communism. To make a point, he exaggerated the extent to which the SPD had historically practiced internal democracy. Party members, in his telling, settled differences of opinion "through objective discussion and panel debate." This portrait of the democratic class party was a fantasy that blurred real bureaucratic elements that had alienated neoleftists in the past. By contrast, Schmidt portrayed the KPD as "a centralistic party with absolute party discipline, in which each member has the duty to carry out unconditionally the decisions of the central committee even when they are not in accord with his opinions and conscience." A vanguardist cadre party required the repression of individual responsibility. Schmidt defined internal democracy as a constant struggle against dogmatism and oligarchical degeneration. While that definition arose out of the neoleftist dilemma, his idealization of the SPD as an internally democratic party diverged from typical neoleftist arguments in favor of nonparty forms.[88]

Regardless, Schmidt's speech succeeded in portraying the official leaders of the Berlin SPD as tools of Communist manipulation. Schulz thought that "it was primarily thanks to [his] initiative that the majority of the Neukölln district took the side of the fusion opponents in the spring of 1946." The American observer George Silver reported that the Neukölln delegates' assembly seemed to him like "the first really democratic meeting in Germany."[89] Schmidt's speech combined revolutionary socialism and radical democracy in a way that was characteristic of the postwar new left across Western Europe, as I will demonstrate later. He pointed beyond the old left dichotomy of revolution versus reform. During the fusion struggle and against the wishes of party leaders, Berlin's young Social Democrats imagined a new dichotomy: bureaucratic pseudorevolution versus dynamic socialist renewal.

87. Meyer, *Sozialdemokraten in der Entscheidung*, 121 and 151.
88. "Rede von Kurt Schmidt . . . auf Kreisdelegiertenversammlung, Neukölln, 17. März 1946," RHG, NL Hurwitz, 119.
89. Schulz, *Auftakt zum Kalten Krieg*, 379, and excerpt of a letter from George Silver to an unspecified recipient (probably the American Association for a Democratic Germany, New York), March 19, 1946, IISG, NB Archives, 25/15.

The SPD central committee reacted with administrative measures against the antifusionists. The party expelled Swolinzky, Schulz, and another Opposition ringleader.[90] And the Communists, finally noticing that one of their apostates, Müller, was now an antifusionist, persuaded SPD leaders to dismiss him from his post. Fearing for his life, Müller fled to the American sector one month later.[91]

Despite such intimidation, almost twenty-four thousand Social Democrats in the Western sectors of Berlin showed up at the polls for the plebiscite on March 31, 1946. They made up 71 percent of eligible party members in West Berlin and 39 percent in Berlin overall. Predictably, Soviet authorities banned the plebiscite in the Eastern sector. Two questions appeared on the ballot in the West:

1. Are you for the immediate unification of both workers' parties? Yes or No.
2. Or are you for an alliance of both parties, which ensures cooperation and rules out fratricidal conflict? Yes or No.[92]

A huge, five-to-one majority voted "No" on question 1, while a three-to-two majority voted "Yes" on question 2. Most Social Democrats favored a cooperative alliance between the two parties, even if they opposed rapid fusion. The Opposition considered the plebiscite a victory, and the Western press agreed.[93]

On April 17, at the second party convention of the Berlin SPD held at the Zinnowwald School in Zehlendorf (American sector), antifusionists declared themselves the legitimate leaders of the party and denied the central

90. "Ausschluß von SPD-Mitglieder, die gegen eine sofortige Verschmelzung opponieren, 19. März 1946," in Reichhardt, Treutler, and Lampe, *Berlin*, 857–58.

91. Meyer, *Sozialdemokraten in der Entscheidung*, 123.

92. "Resolution der Funktionärkonferenz der Berliner SPD über eine Urabstimmung zur Frage der Vereinigung mit der KPD, 1. März 1946," in Reichhardt, Treutler, and Lampe, *Berlin*, 834–36 (at 835–36).

93. Schulz's chapter on the results was titled "David Prevails over Goliath," in *Auftakt zum Kalten Krieg*, 234–46. Even the fusionist newspapers struggled to give the result a positive spin. For example, see "Niederlage der Einheitsgegner in Berlin—selbst in den Westbezirken Berlins nur eine Minderheit der SPD-Mitglieder gegen die sofortige Vereinigung," *Deutsche Volkszeitung*, April 2, 1946. For reactions in the Western press, see Kathleen McLaughlin, "Berlin Socialists Reject Merger—Russians Bar Vote in Their Zone," *New York Times*, April 1, 1946, 1; "No Party Fusion in Berlin—Russians Prohibit Poll," *Manchester Guardian*, April 1, 1946, 5; and "Les social-démocrates berlinois se prononcent contre la fusion avec le parti communiste," *Le Monde*, April 2, 1946.

committee's mandate. They elected Neumann, Karl Germer Jr., and the expelled Swolinzky as cochairmen of a rival central committee. Schmidt assumed control of its Information Office, which was in charge of schooling functionaries, appointing experts to special committees, and the youth secretariat. Hannemann served as his deputy. She had already quit her job as speaker on women's issues for the Free German Youth (FDJ) after being expelled from the official SPD. The New Beginning member Theo Thiele joined the regional party secretariat and Müller the factory secretariat. Thus the New Beginning Working Group made its stand with the SPD–Opposition.[94]

On the weekend of April 20–21, both the KPD and the official SPD party conventions voted as planned in favor of immediate fusion. The Unification Congress took place that same Sunday, April 21, and stretched into the early hours of Monday. Grotewohl and Pieck were elected chairmen of the new SED. Their ceremonial handshake consummated the long-awaited reunification of the German workers' movement.[95] This ended the fusion struggle, but the antifusionist resistance did succeed in framing the result as a partial reunification only. Outside the Soviet zone, few people would treat the SED as a genuine organization of left unity.

Divisions within the Working Group deepened after the fusion struggle. A debate over the historical legacy of New Beginning and the viability of Marxism took place in the fall of 1946. Unlike Org veterans such as Müller and enthusiasts such as Havemann, Schmidt had no interest in developing a "new conception." He told the group that New Beginning "is dead and probably will not rise again. It belonged to an epoch associated with the defeat of the workers' movement. . . . Today we stand before entirely new conditions, and it would be an error in my opinion if at this stage we were to mobilize again out of inertia."[96] Werner Peuke disputed what may have seemed like Schmidt's cynical resignation to existing conditions. For Peuke, the Working Group was an ideal forum for hashing out a "more dialectical" form of Marxism. Havemann defended the Leninist stance of the old Org and wanted to talk about the seizure of state power. Müller downplayed the revolutionary elements of the old conception and focused instead on the basic goal of political democracy. Kurt Mattick chimed in with a plea to leave behind debates over Marxism,

94. Kühne, "Das Netzwerk 'Neu Beginnen,'" 273–80; Meyer, *Sozialdemokraten in der Entscheidung*, 63–64; and "Personalaufstellung," May 16, 1946, FES, NL Mattick, 87.

95. See the "Manifest der SED, 22. April 1946," in Reichhardt, Treutler, and Lampe, *Berlin*, 891–95.

96. "Protokoll der Sitzung am 20.XI.1946 in der Nassauischen Straße 49 in Berlin, mit einem Diskussionsbeitrag R. Havemanns über die marxistische Theorie von 'Neu Beginnen,'" RHG, NL Havemann, 4/11D.

which could only lead to deadlock. In short, members of the Working Group found it hard to agree on anything.[97]

Despite such fragmentation, the New Beginning Working Group continued to hold meetings in the Western sectors for several months. In the spring of 1947 the group made its headquarters at the historic Wannsee villa where the Nazis had planned the so-called Final Solution. Located in the American sector, the villa was now home to the August Bebel School for SPD functionaries, which Schmidt directed.[98] That summer, Müller and Ernst Jegelka proposed a return to conspiratorial tactics. They wanted to train secret cadres and thought that the August Bebel School might provide a steady stream of recruits. In their view, this was the only way to prepare the SPD–Opposition for continued struggle against the SED. From New York, Frank warned against the folly of their proposal, and Schmidt agreed with him.[99]

Some Working Group members like Havemann and Kürschner viewed the SED more favorably than Schmidt and certainly more so than the diehard anti-Communist Müller. While most members decided that left renewal could occur only within the ranks of Social Democracy, others including Jegelka, Peuke, and Karl Elgaß actually joined the SED with the intention of infiltrating the new party and transforming it from within. But Schmidt placed little hope in that strategy.[100]

Of the members who joined the SPD, many viewed their party membership as secondary to their abiding affiliation with New Beginning. Those two political identities, one Social Democratic and the other neoleftist, were now compatible in a way that interwar antifascists would have thought impossible. In a flattering light, Schmidt portrayed the refounded SPD as "the party of the youth, that is ready to go forward with new knowledge, that is ready to fight

97. Havemann (Berlin-Dahlem) to Gerhard Bry, December 5 and December 16, 1946, RHG, NL Hurwitz, 45. It later came to light that Havemann had been recruited by Soviet agents and was spying on the Working Group. This cloudy period in his life contrasted with his clear stance later as a leading East German dissident. See Harold Hurwitz, "Robert Havemann als Mitglied der Widerstandsgruppe 'Neu Beginnen,'" based on a lecture delivered at a meeting of the RHG in the Haus der Demokratie, Berlin, May 6, 1995, available as a printout at the RHG. See also Bernd Florath, *Annäherungen an Robert Havemann: Biografische Studien und Dokumente* (Göttingen: Vandenhoeck und Ruprecht, 2015).

98. Kühne, "Das Netzwerk 'Neu Beginnen,'" 294–311.

99. Paul Hagen [Karl Frank] to friends in Berlin, November 26, 1947, quoted in Hurwitz, *Demokratie und Antikommunismus*, 4 (1): 587n98.

100. Interview of Eisner-Steinberg in Bry, *Resistance*, 233, and Brandt to Löwenthal, February 10, 1946.

for the ideals of freedom, justice, personal and political integrity, critical thought, and reason."[101]

Rifts within the Working Group prevented coordinated action over the long term. It never again matched the political influence it wielded during the fusion struggle. Tragedy also struck. After complications from an appendectomy, Schmidt died suddenly on July 9, 1947, at the age of thirty-four.[102] He embodied his generation's hope for a new left. Just a few months earlier he had written to Frank that the current moment of "revolutionary loosening" offered the best chance for initiating a "cultural process" of left renewal.[103] The spirit and rhetoric of the Org/New Beginning had animated Kurt Schmidt, but it would not die with him.

Assembly or Bureaucracy?

The mounting stress of the Cold War caused or compounded local crises, such as the struggle for control over the Berlin trade unions in January–June 1948, the Berlin blockade from June 1948 to May 1949, and the railway workers' strike in June 1949.[104] Despite such labor militancy, the actual range of German left politics narrowed at the end of that decade. The neoleftist minority that emerged from the ruins after the war mostly dissolved into the ranks of Social Democracy, which itself slid into an overdetermined fight against Communism. The Eastern SED and the Western SPD were both instruments of the old left, playing variations on the centralized party theme.

The New Beginning Working Group was by no means the only postwar new left. In France, the situation after liberation favored a left renaissance. The political force with the most legitimacy was the variously organized Resistance. Although the antifascist struggle had woven together diverse ideological strands, the French Communist Party (PCF) in particular came out of the war with a great deal of popular support. And the Socialist French Section of the

101. Fritz Brandt [Kurt Schmidt] to Paul [Karl Frank], March 30, 1946, RHG, NL Hurwitz, 108, and Hurwitz, *Demokratie und Antikommunismus*, 4 (1): 35 and 45.

102. Jean Eisner described Schmidt's death as "one of the greatest losses of the SPD." Eisner to Harold Hurwitz, August 7, 1985, RHG, NL Hurwitz, 150.

103. Brandt to Paul, March 30, 1946.

104. Müller was instrumental in forming the Independent Trade Union Organization (UGO) in 1948 as a rival to the SED-affiliated Free German Federation of Trade Unions (FDGB). See Kühne, "Das Netzwerk 'Neu Beginnen,'" 265–73. On the railway workers' strike, see Paul Steege, "Finding the There, There: Local Space, Global Ritual, and Early Cold War Berlin," in *Earth Ways: Framing Geographical Meanings*, ed. Gary Backhaus and John Murungi (Lanham, MD: Lexington Books, 2004), 155–72.

Workers' International (SFIO) still had a good reputation as leader of the Popular Front. The earliest postfascist government was a coalition between the SFIO, the PCF, and a new Christian democratic alliance called the Popular Republican Movement. But many French militants also desired a united left that would transcend the old workers' parties. For its part, the nationalist right around Charles de Gaulle experimented with a novel multiparty formation, the Assembly of the French People (RPF). Essentially a populist movement, this rally or assembly (*rassemblement*) launched a campaign against parliament and for a stronger presidency. A moderate Assembly of Republican Lefts soon appeared as a rival electoral alliance. Those on the nonaligned left wished to create their own assembly, especially since this nonparty form seemed ideally suited for grassroots mobilization.

Amid a wave of industrial labor strikes in 1947 and a conflict between the SFIO and PCF over the expulsion of Communists from the governing coalition, the ex-Trotskyist David Rousset and the ex-Communist Georges Altman organized the Revolutionary Democratic Assembly (RDR). A flexible organization, this neoleftist group built a "community of struggle" that aimed to unite people on the left without requiring them to give up their party memberships. The philosopher Jean-Paul Sartre, who became its most famous spokesman, described the RDR as a collection of independent initiatives and "a network of 'neighborhood committees, village committees, [and] factory committees.'"[105] About two thousand intellectuals, Resistance veterans, camp survivors, workers, and factionalists of the interwar years would join the RDR during its brief existence from 1947 to 1949. Several thousands more attended its mass rallies. Ex-Trotskyists joined together with left-wing Socialists and heterodox Communists. They rejected the bureaucratic structures of the PCF and SFIO as well as the Cold War polarization of left politics across Europe. If De Gaulle had his own "totalitarian" assembly in the RPF, according to the RDR manifesto, its was a "democratic and revolutionary assembly from the world of labor." And unlike the Socialists and Communists, the RDR crusaded for a neutral and socialist Europe in defiance of the two global superpowers, the United States and Soviet Union.[106] This neoleftist assembly extended its nonaligned policy to France's colonies, promoting an anti-imperialist politics that anticipated new lefts to come.

Sartre declared his support for the working class in the book *What Is Literature?*, which first appeared as a series of essays in 1947. Writers in the present age must always side with the oppressed, he asserted. Not only did the

---

105. Quoted in Wilkinson, *Intellectual Resistance in Europe*, 102–3.
106. RDR founding manifesto, quoted in Birchall, "Neither Washington nor Moscow?" 368.

Resistance make that plain, but the creative act of writing itself required a commitment to absolute freedom. For art to keep its emancipatory potential, it must directly or indirectly promote emancipatory politics. Sartre defined authentic literature as an exercise in freedom that revitalized everyday life, overcame alienation, and enabled the "constant renewal of frameworks, and the continuous overthrowing of order once it tends to congeal. In short, literature is, in essence, the subjectivity of a society in permanent revolution."[107] Like the early Georg Lukács, Sartre imagined an analogy between aesthetic forms and political forms. The RDR would politically incarnate his aesthetic vision. He treated the neoleftist Assembly as a political space, a means of accessing the working class, and a vehicle for a new culture.

For his part, Rousset treated the Assembly as a nonparty way to mobilize two social groups at once: the industrial working class and the politically homeless middle class. Within the RDR, free discussion would reign. Major decisions would be made directly, without representation, by acclamation at mass meetings. In between meetings, members would communicate through the pages of a new journal, *La gauche*, and submit petitions to a steering committee with a rotating membership. But problems arose from the start. Expected allies such as Marceau Pivert strongly opposed the RDR as just another faction that eroded the Socialist base. Communist pundits portrayed RDR members as renegades who, like Tito in Yugoslavia, split international solidarity with the Soviet Union. Both the SFIO and the PCF took administrative measures that made it impossible for party members to belong to the RDR, undercutting the latter's operation as a pluralist umbrella group. Along with that external pressure, the Assembly itself lacked any coherent doctrine or program. One historian claimed that "if the RDR displayed a creditable activism and enthusiasm in pursuit of socialist aims, it nonetheless was based on a considerable political confusion, which eventually led to its downfall."[108] In the spring of 1949, Sartre and Jean-René Chauvin circulated a motion within the group that criticized both the breakdown of internal democracy and the steering committee's lack of accountability. The Sartre-Chauvin motion tried to prevent the RDR from hardening into a bureaucratic party. By then it was already too late. Rousset, who adopted a pro-American stance, along with Sartre, who began traveling abroad, basically abandoned the group.

Controversy in the Assembly ironically accelerated a process of disassembly on the French left. But the RDR did foreground the issue of organizational

---

107. Sartre, *What Is Literature?* 122.

108. Birchall, "Neither Washington nor Moscow?" 385. On Rousset, see Kuby, *Political Survivors*.

form. Another group made the critique of bureaucratic organization its main concern. The journal *Socialism or Barbarism* (*Socialisme ou barbarie*, SouB) and its circle of contributors were active from 1949 through the mid-1960s. Led by the Greek-French theorist Cornelius Castoriadis (alias Pierre Chaulieu, Paul Cardan, etc.) and the French enfant terrible philosopher Claude Lefort (alias Claude Montal)—both Trotskyists—the young intellectuals of SouB grappled with the neoleftist dilemma from the start. They studied the bureaucratization of social movements in general and Communist parties in particular. According to the historian Marcel van der Linden, their core questions were the following: "Is it an iron law that movements opposing the existing order either fall apart or change into rigid hierarchies? How can militants organize themselves without being absorbed or rigidified into a bureaucratic apparatus?"[109] Those questions troubled members of the SouB group throughout the 1950s, as they tried to figure out how to organize both themselves and the French working class.

The stakes were not just theoretical. Daniel Mothé launched a SouB campaign in the late 1950s to organize autoworkers in the Renault-Bilancourt factory outside Paris. Striking at the heart of the new left's organizational problem, this campaign prompted a debate over whether the group should work with or against the existing trade unions.[110] Just like within the RDR, ideological rifts within SouB led to its demise. The main disagreement arose between Castoriadis and Lefort. The former wanted to create a vanguard organization untainted by existing party and union bureaucracies, while the latter favored direct workers' control. Lefort's preference for spontaneity and "autonomous forms of organization" made his position more recognizably neoleftist. But Castoriadis had a sharper sense for the dilemma implied by that position. In an exchange of letters with the Dutch council communist Anton Pannekoek (by then in his eighties), Castoriadis argued that "the only 'guarantee' against bureaucratization is to be found in permanent action in the anti-bureaucratic sense, by fighting against the bureaucracy and by showing in practice, that a non-bureaucratic vanguard organization is possible."[111] He thought that any neoleftist organization must wage a permanent struggle against bureaucracy within its own ranks.

109. Van der Linden, "Socialisme ou Barbarie," 7.

110. See Stephen Hastings-King, *Looking for the Proletariat: "Socialisme ou Barbarie" and the Problem of Worker Writing* (Leiden: Brill, 2014).

111. Quoted in Van der Linden, "Socialisme ou Barbarie," 15. See the letters published and translated in *Viewpoint Magazine* (October 25, 2011, and August 6, 2013). See also Lefort, "Organisation et parti," and Cardan [Castoriadis], "Prolétariat et organisation."

SouB dissolved as the political terrain shifted in the early 1960s, a period covered later in this book. The group's legacies for the French left included its theory of workers' control and its grassroots challenge to bureaucratic capitalism and communism alike. The chief antagonist for its radical politics was the technocratic manager. Left socialists and future new lefts would continue developing critiques of technocracy, while the moderate socialist parties of Western Europe instead adapted to the new conditions of postwar capitalism. As the next chapter will show, social democratic modernization served as a popular but nonradical alternative to the old left.

6

Social Democratic Modernization

ECONOMIC RECOVERY OCCURRED unevenly across Western Europe, but with the help of the US Marshall Plan, postwar economies regained and often surpassed their prewar levels of production. The historian Eric Hobsbawm dubbed the period from 1947 to 1973 capitalism's golden age, and the 1950s in particular he called its golden years. Real wages rose, unemployment stayed low, and a mass consumer market developed on the American model. Soviet efforts at postcolonial development, too, acted "as a powerful accelerator of the modernization of backward agrarian countries." From a global perspective, the golden age brought more prosperity to more people than ever before in history: it constituted "the Great Leap Forward of the world economy."[1] The French economist Thomas Piketty has shown that, in advanced capitalist countries, this postwar era had the lowest degree of wealth inequality in modern history.[2]

Capitalism thrived, but it was capitalism of a different sort. Some amount of central planning and nationalization of heavy industries and infrastructures became standard. While not socialist, the mixed economies of Western Europe did regulate private capital, expand social services, and incorporate organized labor into decision-making about public investments. Even liberals agreed that capitalism "needed to be saved from itself to survive."[3] Drawing on Keynesian theories, social democratic economists proposed more deficit spending, progressive income taxes, and public ownership. Meanwhile, "ordoliberal" economists associated with Christian Democracy developed a theory

---

1. Hobsbawm, *Age of Extremes*, 9–10. See also Judt, *Postwar*, pt. 2.

2. Thomas Piketty, *Capital in the Twenty-First Century* [2013], trans. Arthur Goldhammer (Cambridge, MA: Harvard University Press, 2014).

3. Hobsbawm, *Age of Extremes*, 272–73. On the welfare state's role in stabilizing democratic capitalism, see Eberhard Schmidt, *Die verhinderte Neuordnung*, and Streeck, *Buying Time*.

of social market economy that preserved free trade while also building welfare institutions.[4] All in all, the postwar period was high tide for the welfare state.

Perceptions of class changed from those from before the war. According to the welfarist model, employers and employees no longer confronted each other in a life-or-death struggle. Instead they collaborated in a mutually beneficial social partnership. Unlike the disruptive strikes of the late 1940s, labor action in the 1950s was treated by policy makers as a normal part of the system. Popular consensus on welfarism prompted some commentators to imagine a post-ideological age, in which totalizing world views were "exhausted" and political decisions took the form of pragmatic compromise or technical calculation.[5] Faced with the unexpected success of democratic capitalism, Social Democrats across Europe reexamined their guiding ideology. As the historian George Lichtheim observed, the chief characteristic of Social Democracy had been its Marxist "insistence that the party of the working class must aim at the conquest of political power, within the context of democracy but not at the expense of socialism."[6] This gradualist approach had brought European workers real gains in the past, including public health insurance, social security, and unemployment benefits.[7] However, in the 1950s, Social Democratic parties were losing voters.

The British Labour Party lost its governing majority in 1951, and theorists in the party and beyond set about revising socialism to make it more practical.[8] The French SFIO participated in several governing coalitions in the 1950s, but controversy over its handling of the Algerian War led to a decline in popular support. The party split in 1958. As for the West German SPD, it never had entered government at the federal level and lost repeatedly to

4. See Ralf Ptak, *Vom Ordoliberalismus zur Sozialen Marktwirtschaft: Stationen des Neoliberalismus in Deutschland* (Wiesbaden: VS. Verlag für Sozialwissenschaften, 2004); Van Hook, *Rebuilding Germany*; and Nicholls, *Freedom with Responsibility*. On the history of a neoliberal current hostile to welfarism, see Quinn Slobodian, *Globalists: The End of Empire and the Birth of Neoliberalism* (Cambridge, MA: Harvard University Press, 2018). On the assimilation of ordo- and neoliberal economic policy by Social Democratic parties, see Mudge, *Leftism Reinvented*.

5. The most famous articulation of this view was Bell, *End of Ideology*. See also Iain Stewart, *Raymond Aron and Liberal Thought in the Twentieth Century* (Cambridge: Cambridge University Press, 2019), ch. 4.

6. Lichtheim, *Short History of Socialism*, 211.

7. See Eley, *Forging Democracy*. Sometimes those gains were achieved indirectly through concessions by authoritarian leaders such as Bismarck in Germany, not directly through democratic mobilization.

8. See the classic example by C.A.R. Crosland, *Future of Socialism*.

Christian Democrats in elections over the course of that decade. Only the Scandinavian Social Democrats enjoyed consistent electoral success during the 1950s and 1960s. In response to these mostly negative trends, Social Democrats across Europe called a retreat from Marxism in order to appeal to a larger public and adapt to the conditions of democratic capitalism. Party strategists presented this retreat from Marxist class politics as a retreat forwards, or *Flucht nach vorn* into modernization. With technocratic experts to fine-tune policy and an American-style campaign to target middle-class consumers, Social Democrats adopted what they imagined to be a modern identity. So it seemed that adaptation to liberal democratic norms and termination of class struggle represented a common destiny for European Social Democracy.[9]

The previous chapter showed how calls for working-class unity and left renewal merged then quickly diverged in postwar Germany. Allied occupation policy along with internal feuds drove a wedge between West-oriented Social Democrats and East-oriented Communists. In the process, the neoleftist ambitions of many young militants either disappeared or were diverted into revived party concepts. In East Germany, that could mean joining a "party of a new type" like the SED.[10] This chapter looks chiefly at former neoleftists in West Germany who subjected their own pasts to criticism and decided to throw in their lot with a modernized Social Democratic Party.

To its supporters, social democratic modernization seemed like a chance to build another, more pragmatic new left. The generation that had organized the antifascist new left now entered professional middle age. A group of New Beginning veterans were instrumental in reshaping the SPD. Among them, Fritz Erler evolved from an avid Communist just after the war into a local SPD official and eventually a leading anti-Marxist reformer on the party's executive committee. And Richard Löwenthal, once New Beginning's chief theorist, formulated a post-Marxist critique of capitalism after the war, worked as a journalist covering international Communism for British newspapers, then returned to Germany as a political scientist. These two figures and the generation they represented paved the way for the historic party conference at Bad Godesberg in 1959. While not a solution to the neoleftist dilemma, social democratic modernization seemed to them like the only responsible left politics. They traded radicalism for realism, but in so doing they risked alienating the militant youth. Once exemplars of the antifascist new left, Erler and Löwenthal turned into defenders of the democratic establishment.

---

9. Orlow, *Common Destiny.*
10. See Malycha and Winters, *Die SED.*

Fritz Erler: Socialism as a Task for the Present

In June 1945, the Office of Strategic Services agent and New Beginning confidant Fred Sanderson drove his jeep through the town of Biberach in Upper Swabia, which lay in the French occupation zone. There he found Fritz Erler, a member of the trio that had led New Beginning inside Germany between 1936 and 1938. He agreed to tell Sanderson his tale.

In the second wave of arrests to hit the group, Erler was rounded up by the Gestapo in the fall of 1938 along with Kurt Schmidt and Oscar Umrath. When Erler's trial finally took place in September 1939, just two weeks after war broke out, he was convicted of a *suspicion* of treason. The People's Court admitted that it could not prove its case. Such juridical proceedings under the Nazi regime were remarkable, with their demand for evidence and consideration of mitigating circumstances. The judge even allowed the defense attorney to lecture the court on the subtle differences between regular treason (*Landesverrat*) and high treason (*Hochverrat*).[11] Erler came away with a relatively light sentence of ten years' forced labor. Similar offences would receive far deadlier sentences as the war progressed.

Erler served most of his time as a "bog soldier" in the Aschendorf Bog penal camp, located in the low country along the Ems River in northwestern Germany. Working and living conditions were hard, reducing his six-foot frame to a skeleton weighing a mere 110 pounds. But he kept his spirits high and wrote to his wife Käthe in June 1942 that "you certainly know from Goethe: 'To be active is the ultimate determination of man,'" which likely signaled that he meant to carry on resistance activity.[12] Unlike Werner Peuke and Karl Elgaß, who set up a New Beginning cadre in the Sachsenhausen concentration camp, Erler at Aschendorf Bog fell under the spell of a Communist named Hans Glaser. The two had common acquaintants from underground work in Berlin and agreed that the antifascist struggle required a united left front. Glaser's charisma and humanistic knowledge helped him and Erler engage their exhausted fellow inmates in lively discussions. They even launched a "bog university," which included courses in English, French, Spanish, natural sciences, medicine, psychology, and history. It is possible that Glaser's heterodox Communist curriculum had a stronger influence on Erler at this vulnerable moment in his life than Walter Loewenheim's F-Course some years earlier.[13]

11. Soell, *Fritz Erler*, 1: 52.

12. Quoted in Soell, 1: 59.

13. On Glaser's influence, see Fritz Erler, "Der lange Hans—Bild eines Moorsoldaten," *Die Freie Gewerkschaft*, November 7–12, 1946.

As the war neared its end, the Germans transferred prisoners in the West away from the advancing British and American armies. During a brutal forced march in the spring of 1945, Erler and another inmate managed to escape. They hid near the town of Biberach. After the Allies conquered the town on April 30, Erler emerged from hiding and soon impressed the French occupation authorities with his organizing abilities. They appointed him district administrator (*Landrat*). Biberach's small population suffered from material shortages that were exasperated by an influx of thousands of German refugees expelled from the liberated countries of Eastern Europe. After meeting him that June, Sanderson recalled that Erler's efforts to alleviate the situation and restart left politics repeatedly ran afoul of the French occupiers.[14] Unlike the British and Americans who treated German civilians pretty well, and unlike the Soviets who at least permitted political activity in their zone, the French treated their vanquished enemies with contempt. One historian has referred to the "dismal French period" of 1945–49 and noted how Kurt Schumacher labeled the French "West Russians," comparing them to the rapacious Red Army. While that was hyperbole, the French did impose a military dictatorship and sealed off their zone from the outside. Occupation authorities took a hard line on postwar reconstruction, insisting that Germany should cease to exist as a unified state.[15] That said, the military chief of the French zone, Émile Laffon, did allow some grassroots initiative, local self-administration, and at first even the Antifa. The French occupiers also undertook a thorough denazification of society at least until 1947, when they adopted the weaker American model of the civilian court.

Erler was most frustrated with the French policy of intrazonal fragmentation, which made it impossible "to make contacts with like-minded political people across local borders and organize them into a party."[16] In August 1945, he abandoned his administrator post and embarked for his native city of Berlin. What he hoped to accomplish there remains shrouded in political controversy and autobiographical omission. Available evidence suggests that he had every intention of joining the Communist Party. Since his expulsion from the SPD in 1933 as a result of the so-called Berlin youth conflict, he had considered

14. Interview of Fred Sanderson by Harold Hurwitz (Washington, DC), November 1985, RHG, NL Hurwitz, 17. Erler in turn recalled his astonishment "when an American with flawless German greeted me in our house" and told him about the fate of New Beginning émigrés. Erler (Biberach) to Erich and Hilde Schmidt, May 16, 1946, RHG, NL Hurwitz, 136.

15. Edgar Wolfrum, "Französische Besatzungspolitik," in *Deutschland unter allierter Besatzung 1945–1949/55: Ein Handbuch*, ed. Wolfgang Benz (Berlin: Akademie Verlag, 1999), 60–72.

16. Soell, *Fritz Erler*, 1: 64–65.

himself without a party. And unlike the New Beginning émigrés, he had not dealt much with Western progressive democrats. His apprenticeship under Glaser in the Nazi penal camp likely converted him to Communism. Moreover, he wanted to return to his neighborhood of Prenzlauer Berg and assume some position of responsibility in the Soviet sector.

On the long journey from Biberach to Berlin, Erler came across a pamphlet published by the Union of German Socialist Organizations (UDSO) in Great Britain. The UDSO listed New Beginning among its members. In reading it, he detected "an emigrant spirit so foreign to the German reality" that in no way could it represent the interests of the New Beginning group inside Germany. As he explained in stilted language to Erich and Hilde Schmidt, the function of New Beginning was "so contingent on the demands of the underground period that I denied any further need for its official separate existence during the period of the democratic reconstruction of parties."[17] In other words, New Beginning had outlasted its usefulness. Erler decided that any cadres still in existence should be liquidated.

When he reached the Soviet zone, he made contact with the KPD in Halle and met directly with Walter Ulbricht. Erler asked the Communist leader for advice about his future but did not receive the enthusiastic response that he expected. Ulbricht told him "to campaign for a unity party [i.e., the SED] only if no appreciable [Social Democratic] residue was left over." Otherwise he should rejoin the SPD.[18] Ulbricht must have known about Erler's New Beginning past. He might have advised the thirty-two-year-old man to choose the SPD over the KPD or any future unity party because of the lingering distrust between Communist émigrés and the New Beginning foreign bureau. Somebody like Erler, who was intellectually independent and had a history in neoleftist small groups, might have seemed like more trouble than he was worth.

Erler's meeting with Ulbricht likely took place just before he made contact with Kurt Schmidt, Erich Kürschner, and the New Beginning Working Group in Berlin. This reunion of comrades did not go well. Erler later spoke of disagreements with Schmidt "that perhaps are attributable in part to abrupt treatment by me."[19] At the time he claimed that Schmidt was conspiring against

17. Erler to the Schmidts, May 16, 1946. The UDSO pamphlet that he read might have been *Die neue deutsche Republik*. In August 1945, the better known pamphlet *Zur Politik deutscher Sozialisten* had not yet appeared.

18. Fritz Erler (Tübingen) to Erich and Hilde Schmidt, September 6, 1946, RHG, NL Hurwitz, 136.

19. Erler to the Schmidts, May 16, 1946.

him. Schmidt probably did consider him another rival beside Georg Müller.[20] Whereas the Working Group viewed the prospect of a Socialist Unity Party with skepticism, owing in large part to their direct dealings with Soviet authorities, Erler supported a rapid fusion of the SPD and KPD. Moreover, he insisted that New Beginning publicly declare its own dissolution. He even drafted a declaration to that effect, a document that acknowledged the group's progressive function in the past but deemed it obsolete in the present: New Beginning members ought to rejoin a mainstream workers' party.[21] Müller and doubtless other Working Group members suspected that Erler was following Communist orders. The dissolution draft circulated widely enough in Berlin to cause mutual feelings of betrayal.[22]

Following Ulbricht's advice, Erler did actually rejoin the SPD. Berlin Social Democrats around Otto Ostrowski, the future governing mayor of the city, offered him a job as recruiter in the province of Brandenburg. He turned it down, perhaps because he would have preferred a position in the city of Berlin. After some storm and stress, Erler returned to Biberach. There he worked his way up the ladder of the local SPD and continued annoying the French. Tensions reached the point where, in January 1946, he was arrested under a pretext and sent to the internment camp at Balingen. Doing time alongside Nazi prisoners, he wrote his first political pamphlet, *Socialism as a Task for the Present* (*Sozialismus als Gegenwartsaufgabe*).

In this long essay, Erler criticized the political apathy that seemed to have taken hold of the German population. For many, the Nazi catastrophe delegitimized all forms of mass politics. Erler countered that the only antidote to catastrophic Nazi politics was a "rational politics conscious of its goal"— namely, socialism. He used dialectical reasoning to interpret Germans' rejection of politics in general as an abstract negation of Nazism, whereas democratic socialism was its determinate or concrete negation. In similar fashion, he called on antifascist resisters to overcome their "anti-attitude" and fight for something positive.[23]

Worse than apathy, Erler warned, would be "falling back into the traditions from before 1933." Socialists should look ahead to the future, renew their theory and practice based on present demands, and celebrate the militant youth: not only the youngest generation just coming of age, but also those who stayed

20. Interview of Erika Weidlich (Schmidt's girlfriend) and Gerda Eick (Erler's later assistant) by Soell, unspecified date, quoted in Soell, *Fritz Erler*, 1: 533n12. See chapter 5.

21. "An die Mitglieder der Organisation Neu Beginnen," FES, NL Erler, 906.

22. Georg Müller to Heinrich Jakubowicz (alias Henry Hellmann), September 13, 1946, RHG, NL Hurwitz, 46. Hurwitz, *Demokratie und Antikommunismus*, 4 (1): 47.

23. Erler, *Sozialismus als Gegenwartsaufgabe*, 5 and 8.

"young at heart through all the suffering of bitter persecution."[24] Erler turned thirty-three in 1946. His appeal to youth went hand in hand with his presentation of Marxism as a living body of thought that evolved continuously with changing social and economic circumstances.[25] Like Eduard Bernstein before him, he took seriously Marxism's claim to scientific objectivity. The only science worthy of the name must be one that moved beyond Marx's own nineteenth-century critique of political economy. Revising Marx meant working directly in Marx's own undogmatic spirit.[26] Erler's pamphlet did not go into detail about what that revision would entail, but already in 1946–47 he signaled that he was open to social democratic modernization.

This second stint in prison allowed Erler to reflect on postwar conditions and convinced him that the SPD must adapt. Frequently invoking Rosa Luxemburg, his subsequent articles in newspapers and journals criticized old Social Democrat and Communist beliefs in automatic progress beyond capitalism. Either socialism or barbarism could result from the crisis of capitalism: which one depended on the decisive actions of the workers' movement. He thought, however, that the postwar movement should no longer set its sights on revolution. Instead, it should win over the masses through democratic elections, which would channel revolutionary passions in a more pragmatic direction.[27] Erler recalibrated the revolutionary socialism of his youth into a plan to work through democratic institutions. The neoleftist had matured.

His new belief in the compatibility of socialism and electoral democracy—a Social Democratic article of faith—departed from earlier New Beginning theories of the bourgeois state. Witnessing the Berlin fusion struggle from afar also caused him to abandon his earlier enthusiasm for the SED. By the time Kurt Schmidt died in July 1947, Erler recognized that so long as German Communists served Soviet interests, left unity could never be achieved on a democratic basis. In a 1950 article on the legacy of antifascism, he wrote that "the struggle for freedom must be carried on in all directions, against every new servitude, no matter where it comes from." Staying true to the ideals of the antifascist resistance, he claimed, meant opposing Soviet tyranny in the East. In un-Marxist fashion, Erler alluded to a transhistorical contest between freedom and dictatorship. But in so doing he paraphrased his favorite Marxist, Luxemburg: "Nobody can fight for freedom if he only means his own freedom

24. Erler, 9 and 52.
25. Fritz Erler, "Lebendiger Marxismus" [1946], in *Politik für Deutschland*, 83–86.
26. See Bernstein, *Preconditions of Socialism*.
27. Erler, *Sozialismus als Gegenwartsaufgabe*, 26.

and not also that of people who think differently."[28] From the revolutionary Marxist tradition itself, then, Erler derived a democratic politics based on civil rights and social welfare. This politics aligned with the mainstream antifascism of the Popular Front, which had also subordinated class struggle to a primary struggle for democratic rights.

An essential part of Erler's conversion to social democratic modernization was his efforts in the early 1950s to promote research on and commemoration of left-wing antifascism. Since the disappointing results of the first West German federal elections in 1949, the SPD had played the role of loyal opposition to the Christian Democratic governing coalition.[29] Social Democrats believed that conservative hegemony in West Germany had a negative influence on the public's understanding of anti-Nazi resistance. Not only did people focus almost exclusively on examples of military or aristocratic resistance, such as Claus von Stauffenberg and the Kreisau Circle, but some conservative Germans even considered resistance during the war—even if it was a Nazi imperialist war—a betrayal of the Fatherland.

In 1954, on the tenth anniversary of the July 20 plot to assassinate Hitler, Erler wrote an article that promoted a broader definition of resistance to include nonviolent acts of defiance and nonconformism. The July 20 plot was not the only example of German resistance: "from the very first hours of the Hitler regime, [there was] a tough and courageous running battle waged by those who could not or would not reconcile themselves to the dictatorship. The first blows by those in power in 1933 were directed against the workers' political organizations and unions." Despite its inflated place in public memory, he admitted, the July 20 plot did symbolically show the world that "there were people in Germany who resisted the regime." It was the task of antifascist veterans like Erler to show further that most of those resisters were actually on the left.[30]

Erler started writing letters to former members of New Beginning in order to collect testimony about the group's activities. He received a number of responses from former members in West and East Germany as well as from émigrés who settled abroad. By gathering documentary material and building

---

28. Fritz Erler, "Kampf für die Freiheit" [1950], in *Politik für Deutschland*, 47–49. According to Luxemburg in her critique of Bolshevism, "freedom is always and exclusively freedom for the one who thinks differently." Luxemburg, "Russian Revolution," 305.

29. For his own take on the SPD's oppositional role, see Fritz Erler, "Konstruktive Opposition" [1949], in *Politik für Deutschland*, 316–19.

30. Fritz Erler, "Pflicht zum Widerstand" [1954], in *Politik für Deutschland*, 50–54 (at 51).

a research base for scholars, he aimed to set the record straight on the anti-Nazi resistance.[31]

As the 1950s progressed and he rose to prominence in the SPD, Erler's documentary efforts became increasingly political. Kurt Kliem, who was a doctoral student of Wolfgang Abendroth (another New Beginning affiliate) at the University of Marburg, finished a dissertation on New Beginning in 1957. Erler wrote to Kliem urging him to delay publishing his work until after the federal elections in September of that year. "It is surely to be feared," he explained, "that in the campaign atmosphere individual sentences would be torn completely out of context and exploited for use against the Social Democratic Party and some of its leading men."[32] In addition to New Beginning's frequent dealings with Communists in the 1930s, he alluded to the embarrassing rivalry between New Beginning and the SPD/Sopade. One episode in particular worried him: the Berlin youth conflict of 1932–33, when Erler along with several other young militants were expelled from the party for planning an underground organization to fight the Nazis (at the time, the bewildered SPD leadership insisted on legal democratic means). Erler's fears were unjustified: Kliem published his dissertation anyway, but few people bothered to read it.

Such minor episodes from the past would not have made much difference for the SPD's electoral prospects. After nearly matching the number of seats won by the Christian Democratic Union (CDU)/Christian Social Union (CSU) in the first federal election of 1949, Social Democrats' vote share dropped to 28.8 percent in 1953. It lost again in 1957, creeping up to 31.8 percent. By contrast, Christian Democrats under Konrad Adenauer strengthened their hold: 31 percent (1949), 45.2 percent (1953), and 50.2 percent (1957). Although he repeatedly lost to CDU candidates in his home districts of Tuttlingen and Pforzheim in Baden-Württemberg, Erler entered the Bundestag in 1949 by means of the SPD's provincial list of candidates (*Landesliste*). In his maiden speech in January 1950, he stressed the importance of parliamentary control over government and denounced the bureaucratic heavy-handedness of conservative ministers.[33]

Along with his role as political attack dog, Erler served on a number of committees. The most important one focused on West Germany's proposed military rearmament within a European Defense Community (EDC). In that

31. See letters in FES, NL Erler, 37.

32. Fritz Erler to Kurt Kliem (Marburg), July 2, 1957, FES, NL Erler, 3. See Kliem, "Der sozialistische Widerstand gegen das Dritte Reich."

33. Fritz Erler, "Parlament und Regierung" [January 23, 1950], in *Politik für Deutschland*, 320–27.

capacity, he quickly became the SPD's chief expert on foreign policy. He pushed for greater economic and political integration of West Germany into the European community. Following Schumacher and the SPD line, however, he opposed rearmament and accused Christian Democrats who supported the EDC of preventing a peaceful solution to the German national question.[34] The EDC plan eventually failed in the French parliament, but West Germany's military status along with the national question continued to preoccupy Erler in the Bundestag. In 1955, he warned of an intensifying East-West conflict and argued that the Federal Republic's proposed membership in the North Atlantic Treaty Organization (NATO) would endanger the peace process. Like the Revolutionary Democratic Assembly and nonaligned left in France, he favored a neutral West Germany that would work toward détente and nuclear disarmament.[35] From the fall of 1953 through the spring of 1957, he was actually the most frequent speaker of any party in the plenum of the Bundestag.[36]

As the daily demands of his political work mounted, Erler pulled back from discussions among party theorists about modernizing the SPD's guiding principles. His friend and New Beginning comrade Waldemar von Knoeringen carried on the dual life of politician-theorist and kept Erler informed. Both worked behind the scenes in the run-up to the special party convention at Bad Godesberg in 1959. Erler had become a Bonn political insider, but he stayed invested in the theoretical problems of postwar Social Democracy, including the fate of Marxism.

Richard Löwenthal: Beyond Capitalism

After more than a decade in exile, Richard Löwenthal's conversion from neoleftism to social democratic modernization began earlier than Erler's. He decided to maintain residency in London after the war's end, working as a reporter for Reuters and foreign correspondent for the *Observer*. The latter job involved assignments in Bonn, Berlin, Geneva, Paris, Strasbourg, the Nordic countries, and Yugoslavia. Löwenthal's beat was the Cold War. Urged on by his comrades, he published one last New Beginning manifesto in 1946, the

34. Fritz Erler, "Bundesstaat Europa" [August 24, 1949], and "Europäische Verteidigungsgemeinschaft" [July 10, 1952], in *Politik für Deutschland*, 427–31 and 432–47. See also Erler, "Zur Landesverteidigung" [speech at the Berlin SPD party convention on July 20–24, 1954], in *Politik für Deutschland*, 448–52.

35. Fritz Erler, "Sicherheit und Wiedervereinigung" [February 25, 1955], in *Politik für Deutschland*, 453–89. See Dietrich Orlow, "German Social Democracy and European Unification, 1945 to 1955," in Barclay and Weitz, *Between Reform and Revolution*, 467–88.

36. Soell, *Fritz Erler*, 1: 277–78.

book *Beyond Capitalism* (*Jenseits des Kapitalismus*). Through his journalistic work in the late 1940s and early 1950s, however, he cultivated a well-informed brand of anti-Communism and adopted the norms of Western liberal democracy.

From his international travels and London vantage point, Löwenthal kept abreast of political developments in occupied Germany. In October 1946, Knoeringen wrote to him after visiting Berlin and witnessing the fusion struggle: "the chance of Social Democracy lies above all in its liberal-political principles." Knoeringen wanted to recruit Löwenthal for a reconstituted New Beginning group with the purpose of influencing the postwar SPD. "Our great problem is that we have not yet overcome the rigidity in our own party and that we lack the inflow of new people," he wrote. "I orient myself mainly toward intellectual people especially from the younger generation." He admired the journal *Der Ruf* (The call), for example, which appeared in Munich that August as "the independent journal of the young generation" and served as a platform for the writers' collective Group 47: "In this circle of people one observes extremely interesting personalities who fit so well with the 'New Beginning type.'" He invited Löwenthal to move back to Germany and help him mentor the leftist youth: they needed that blend of realism and conviction that only veterans of the antifascist new left could provide.[37]

While he did not accept Knoeringen's invitation, Löwenthal did write a book that he hoped would bring the young generation up to speed on developments in left theory and international politics. He dedicated *Beyond Capitalism* to his "surviving friends in Germany"—that is, the New Beginning crew.[38] The book targeted two sets of readers. First, it addressed those neoleftist remnants who had survived twelve years of "material and spiritual isolation" and were hungry for modern ideas. Second, the book appealed to the youngest Germans, who had never been exposed to democratic socialism. To them

---

37. Waldemar von Knoeringen (Munich) to Richard Löwenthal (London), October 24, 1946, FES, NL Knoeringen, 84.

38. Sering [Löwenthal], *Jenseits des Kapitalismus*, 3. The book was published in late 1946, and there were two more printings in 1947 and 1948 by Nest-Verlag, a Vienna edition in 1948 by Verlag der Wiener Volksbuchhandlung, and a new edition in 1977 by J.H.W. Dietz Nachf. of West Berlin and Bonn-Bad Godesberg. The notion of going beyond capitalism was in the air: for example, see Pierre Dieterlen, *Au delà du capitalisme* (Paris: Presses universitaires de France, 1946). Already during the interwar years, the Italian revolutionary socialist Arturo Labriola had expressed this notion in his book *Al di là del capitalismo e del socialismo* (Paris: Casa editrice Respublica, 1931). On the US context, see Howard Brick, *Transcending Capitalism: Visions of a New Society in Modern American Thought* (Ithaca, NY: Cornell University Press, 2006).

Löwenthal offered a primer on "what socialists have to say about the historic tasks of our time."[39]

He began by describing the catastrophe that had befallen Germany under fascist rule. Fascism he defined as the extreme form of capitalist and imperialist exploitation, so its defeat opened the door to the great alternative—namely, socialism. Ironically, Löwenthal observed, socialism in practice had spread so widely across the political spectrum that the specific meaning of the word seemed to dissolve. This de facto hegemony of socialism in the postwar era confirmed Marx's vision of the future: after the collapse of capitalism (in this case, its extreme form of fascism), socialism would be accepted in practice by even its former enemies.[40]

Any modernization of left theory had to begin with a reassessment of Marxism. In February 1946, Löwenthal signed a letter to Karl Frank and the New York émigrés "with un-Marxist greetings."[41] But in the book *Beyond Capitalism*, he dealt more evenhandedly with this theoretical foundation of modern socialism. In good Western Marxist fashion, he emphasized the Hegelian roots of Marx's thought and grounded his own version of Marxism in "the tradition of European humanism."[42] Like Erler, he interpreted Marx through the lens of Luxemburg's political alternative of socialism or barbarism. Not only did that alternative highlight the fragility of socialist gains and unsettle the orthodox Marxist belief in the historical inevitability of socialism, it also presented socialism as the only means of safeguarding the achievements of Western civilization. This view might sound strange today, when outspoken defenders of civilization all seem to be on the right. But during the fascist and postfascist eras, the socialist left claimed with justification to offer Europe its only insurance against total destruction. Without democratic socialist intervention, capitalism would annihilate itself and everyone along with it.

According to Löwenthal, "living Marxism" provided the tools for navigating the myriad challenges of the modern world. One should guard against any stale application of nineteenth-century solutions to twentieth-century problems, he cautioned. Dogmatically citing Marx prevented serious analysis and led to "the opposite of scientific socialism."[43] He took as his main theme the phenomena of economic planning and state regulation of markets that began during the Depression and continued into the postwar years. Capitalist

---

39. Sering [Löwenthal], *Jenseits des Kapitalismus*, 5.

40. Sering [Löwenthal], 6.

41. Richard Löwenthal (London) to "Lieber Freund" [Karl Frank], February 24, 1946, IISG, NB Archives, 25/5.

42. Sering [Löwenthal], *Jenseits des Kapitalismus*, 14.

43. Sering [Löwenthal], 24.

planning, even when based on Keynesian economic theory, could in fact "reach its completion only as planned imperialism" and fascism. To achieve general welfare and full employment, he argued, capitalist planning had to give way to socialist planning. By that Löwenthal meant democratic control over the state's economic steering mechanisms. The failure of classical liberalism and its model of unregulated capitalism was itself a "product of the immanent economic and social dynamic of capitalism itself."[44] In the twentieth century, a new form of corporate capitalism had separated the owners of capital from the entrepreneurial function. Owners no longer made decisions on the factory floor nor maintained direct contact with their employees. Instead, a new class of managers, administrators, and chief executives—themselves holding shares in the corporation—took over day-to-day business. The capitalist class of majority shareholders turned into pure rentiers, living off their dividends. Echoing the American theorist James Burnham, Löwenthal noted the profound effect of this managerial revolution on the relations of production.[45]

Unlike entrepreneurial capitalism, the new corporate capitalism relied increasingly on the state to coordinate heavy industries and infrastructure. This corporate-state alliance meant that decisions of profound social importance were being made without democratic control. To ensure oversight as well as the durability of progressive reforms, the left needed to fight for democratic control over the state. The distribution of wealth and social power was not governed by immutable economic laws, but by economic policy. Here Löwenthal departed from his interwar concept of revolutionary socialism, which had involved direct ownership of the means of production. Socialists must focus instead on securing indirect ownership through state regulation. He acknowledged that periodic crises of capitalism might still damage the legitimacy of the state. The only way to avoid another crisis of democracy was for socialists to take the reins of economic planning and tame the volatility of the market. Democratic institutions could become "the real tool for the subordination of the production hierarchy to the collective will of the workers." Technological progress required new administrative and bureaucratic hierarchies, but socialists would subject them to a system of democratic control. Löwenthal criticized the "purely negative attitude toward the state" that prevailed among

44. Sering [Löwenthal], 28 and 108. His interpretation of the crisis of laissez-faire capitalism and the rise of economic planning resembled the approach of Karl Polanyi in *Great Transformation* (1944), a book that Löwenthal might have read in London exile. On planning in the two postwar Germanies, see Jarausch, *After Hitler*, 87–93.

45. Sering [Löwenthal], *Jenseits des Kapitalismus*, 44. See Burnham, *Managerial Revolution*.

leftists, who viewed it as an organ for oppressing workers. A state of a new type, the democratic welfare state, could actually emancipate workers.[46]

The welfare state constituted the national form of democratic socialism in Europe, Löwenthal believed. Internationally, he envisioned Europe as a third force situated "between the colossuses" of the corporate-capitalist USA and the totalitarian-communist USSR.[47] Rather than bourgeois internationalism and its abstract moral appeals, he called for a truly democratic internationalism to meet the concrete challenges of the postwar world.[48] An independent and democratic socialist Europe would encourage peaceful coexistence between nations, including the global superpowers. Löwenthal thus repackaged his interwar radicalism to fit the context of postwar modernization. No longer did he speak of revolutionary internationalism, only a "concrete" internationalism designed to avoid another world war.

In another departure from his neoleftist past, Löwenthal no longer spoke of bureaucratic hardening as a danger to political organizations such as the SPD. Now he criticized only the "ossification [Erstarrung] of socialist thought." One-dimensional and "dogmatically ossified ideas" accounted for the failure of the workers' parties against fascism in 1932–33, not their organizational structures. This marked an idealist turn in his writing about the left. The differences between Social Democrats and Communists, interwar lefts and postwar lefts, did not depend on which social bases they mobilized or whether they preserved internal democracy, he now believed, but rather on how they understood the concept of class struggle. Promoting the correct concept of class struggle—namely, the "struggle for leadership of the nation, for the democratic acquisition of state power in order to push through a concrete crisis program"—became the decisive factor for the middle-aged Löwenthal.[49]

Whatever organizational concerns he still had, he now applied to the state rather than political parties or social movements. His concept of democratic socialism involved converting the bourgeois state apparatus into a transparent decision-making body that incorporated public input at all levels. He no longer interpreted the state as the instrument of capitalist class rule. One reason for this shift in emphasis was Löwenthal's desire to refute theories of revolution predicated on a violent seizure of state power. No socialists today, he

46. Sering [Löwenthal], *Jenseits des Kapitalismus*, 50–51, 59–60, 70, and 82–83. See Sassoon, *One Hundred Years of Socialism*, pt. 2, and Steven Klein, *The Work of Politics: Making a Democratic Welfare State* (Cambridge: Cambridge University Press, 2020).

47. Sering [Löwenthal], *Jenseits des Kapitalismus*, 247. This should not be confused with the neoliberal "third way" of the 1990s and early 2000s. See Mudge, *Leftism Reinvented*, ch. 7.

48. Sering [Löwenthal], *Jenseits des Kapitalismus*, 256.

49. Sering [Löwenthal], 85–87.

wrote, should want to mount a violent uprising against the state in order to achieve their goals. Such a strategy could only result in a totalitarian suspension of the rule of law. Only by working within democratic institutions could socialists accomplish their goal of "rebuilding society as a whole." At the same time, socialists "must be ready to employ revolutionary force against fascist or reactionary dictatorships and to put down counter-revolutionary acts of violence against democracy by means of state coercion and mass mobilization." This idea of a militant democracy armed against internal threats was popular among German antifascists who witnessed the fall of the Weimar Republic.[50] Löwenthal did not explain how defensive state violence could be reconciled with mass mobilization, especially if the masses marched against the state. This theoretical contradiction was exposed during the controversy over West German emergency laws that started in 1958.[51] In any case, his vision in *Beyond Capitalism* depended on Social Democrats being in power and steering the economy toward general welfare. Things would not turn out quite as he imagined.

His prognosis for socialist planning in the Eastern bloc ended up truer to the mark. Regardless of any economic gains, he speculated, the Communist system would face its real challenge in the form of a political crisis. Here he applied the sort of neoleftist insights about organizational form that he omitted from his analysis of Western democracy. Anticipating the critique by the Yugoslav dissident Milovan Djilas and mirroring the arguments of the *Socialism or Barbarism* group in France, Löwenthal claimed that a dictatorial one-party state would create a new social hierarchy based on the prestige bestowed by one's place in the official bureaucracy. Even if Communism abolished the bourgeoisie, a new class of party apparatchiks would take its place. This party elite would enjoy social privileges not available to ordinary citizens. The process had already taken place in the Soviet Union, where the new class exercised a "monopoly of knowledge" that precluded any democratic control over economic planning. There was nothing inherently undemocratic or even uneconomical about the socialization of heavy industries, establishment of production quotas, and limitation of private enterprise. Only the decision-making process behind those policies determined whether people experienced the system as democratic, and in the Soviet bloc that process was undemocratic

---

50. Sering [Löwenthal], 199. Cf. Udi Greenberg's chapter on Karl Loewenstein in *Weimar Century*, ch. 4, and Jens Hacke's analysis of militant democracy, which downplays the role of Loewenstein, in *Existenzkrise der Demokratie: Zur politischen Theorie des Liberalismus in der Zwischenkriegszeit* (Berlin: Suhrkamp, 2018), ch. 4.

51. The Bundestag would actually pass the emergency laws in May 1968. See Schneider, *Demokratie in Gefahr?*

to the extreme. Löwenthal concluded that "the Soviet Union is economically free to pursue the goal of welfare planning. We now see that it is politically unfree to do this systematically."[52]

The tragic outcome of the Russian Revolution, he wrote, should teach the left that "between the socioeconomic goal of socialism and its political form there exists a necessary connection." Such a formal link between socialist ends and democratic means derived in part from Löwenthal's neoleftist past, but it aligned better with the project of social democratic modernization in the 1950s. In a kind of convergence theory, he wrote that Western capitalism and Eastern communism both operated in the context of a modern industrial society. They shared the same production hierarchies, administrative structures, and technologies. So the core question of the postwar period was: Does a state enable democratic control over that production hierarchy and thus prevent the formation of a new ruling class, or not?[53]

In a system of democratic socialist planning, Löwenthal claimed, economic efficiency (*Wirtschaftlichkeit*) would mean leveling the playing field by ensuring "equality of opportunities for advancement for all." Economic efficiency was never an end in itself. In a capitalist system, such efficiency maximized profits and opportunities for a wealthy minority. Unregulated capitalism thus limited democracy. Socialism enabled a fully expanded democracy. But he insisted that safeguarding democracy would involve a constant struggle. Resistance by capital would eventually grow weaker, but still capitalists would "ruthlessly take advantage of every socialist failure." Such capitalist backlash helps explain the temptation of totalitarian controls, he admitted. But any road other than democracy would lead to some form of bureaucratic domination.[54] In this book about the inconvenient truths of democratic socialism,

---

52. Sering [Löwenthal], *Jenseits des Kapitalismus*, 147 and 156–57. Cf. Djilas, *New Class*. In a review, Löwenthal praised Djilas's book as "a Marxist critique of Communism" that tracked the evolution of a new ruling class out of anti-capitalist and anti-imperialist vanguards operating in underdeveloped countries that lacked a native bourgeoisie. But he criticized Djilas's "rigid economic determinism" that downplayed "the importance of the centralist structure of the Leninist party in making it independent of any specific working-class basis and fit for totalitarian dictatorship." Löwenthal, "A Marxist Critic," *Observer*, September 8, 1957, 12.

53. Sering [Löwenthal], *Jenseits des Kapitalismus*, 157–58. The concept of industrial society was cemented in sociology and developmental economics by the early 1960s, for example in the work of Clark Kerr, Raymond Aron, Daniel Bell, Ralf Dahrendorf, and the former New Beginning member Reinhard Bendix. See David Sessions, "What Was 'Industrial Society'? Toward a Genealogy of a Concept, 1920–1965," paper presented to the Society for US Intellectual History, November 2019.

54. Sering [Löwenthal], *Jenseits des Kapitalismus*, 180, 182, 193, and 200.

Löwenthal sounded a lot like Max Weber, who famously remarked that in politics there are no easy solutions, only "a slow, powerful drilling through hard boards, with a mixture of passion and a sense of proportion."[55] So, Löwenthal had already started in late 1946 to use the rhetoric of hard choices that would turn him against the sixties New Left.

His book *Beyond Capitalism* combined New Beginning's insights from the 1930s with the immediate postwar consensus that capitalism in its old form had died. The new situation no longer required class struggle. In fact, Löwenthal claimed that the party of democratic socialism should appeal to as many people as possible, not only workers. As a catch-all popular party (*Volkspartei*), Social Democracy would overcome its traditional antagonistic class attitude.[56] This strategy would meet with resistance from young and old socialists alike, who had less faith than he did in the democratic state.

Löwenthal had shared the book manuscript with his New Beginning comrades Knoeringen and Abendroth.[57] Because they expected the book to have a big impact on the young generation, they tried to revise several of his arguments. The three debated the strengths and weaknesses of the manuscript from the fall of 1946 through January 1947. Despite their constructive intention, Löwenthal took offense at the tone of Knoeringen and Abendroth's criticisms. To him their revisions smelled "still too much like decades of sectarian discussions in Communist and left-socialist opposition groups." He even perceived a veiled threat in Knoeringen's claim that he "would not consider the book for use in an official party sense" if certain revisions were not made. Löwenthal defended his political independence and replied that the book should stand on its own as a work of theory, not mere propaganda.[58] As he wrote to Abendroth, any short-term instrumentalization of his book would come at the expense of "fundamental schooling" over the long term.[59]

The future of socialism in the Eastern bloc was a particular bone of contention. At this earliest stage of the Cold War, Knoeringen and Abendroth believed that the socialist states of Eastern Europe must join democratic socialists in Western Europe to form a neutral bloc in between the superpowers. Of

55. M. Weber, "Politics as a Vocation," 93.

56. On the concept of the catch-all party, see Kirchheimer, "Western European Party Systems."

57. Knoeringen to Löwenthal, October 24, 1946.

58. Richard Löwenthal to Waldemar von Knoeringen, December 30, 1946, FES, NL Knoeringen, 84.

59. Richard Löwenthal (London) to Wolf and Lisa Abendroth, December 30, 1946, IISG, NL Abendroth, 1177.

course, Löwenthal also believed in this prospect of a third force, but his book presented the degeneration of Soviet society into a new bureaucratic class system as inevitable. Knoeringen and Abendroth wanted the book to avoid giving that impression, because the logic of such an argument ruled out the possibility of détente. "Our whole struggle for peace and democratic social-ism," Knoeringen wrote, "only makes sense in the end if we can believe in this possibility of global rapprochement." In other words, Löwenthal drew too sharp a distinction between democratic planning in the West and totalitarian planning in the East. Knoeringen predicted that a one-sided critique of Soviet planning might also discredit the idea of welfarism in the West. Democratic socialism had to hold a middle ground between capitalism and communism. Löwenthal pushed back at first but eventually compromised. In response to Knoeringen and Abendroth's criticism, he added a section about the "loosen-ing" effect that democratic socialism in Western Europe was likely to have on the Eastern bloc.[60]

Reactions to the book were mostly positive. It fueled discussions among former members of New Beginning such as Erler and Kurt Schmidt, thus ac-complishing one of its goals. Erler even used the occasion to exchange letters with Löwenthal for the first time in a decade.[61] Reviews appeared in papers throughout occupied Germany, including the Soviet zone.[62] Despite the book's resonance, however, its author did not become Social Democracy's chief theorist as his comrades wanted. Löwenthal's journalism would some-times drift into reflections on the direction of German socialism. He would also contribute regularly to the SPD's theoretical journal *Die Neue Gesellschaft* and to US-sponsored periodicals in Germany such as *Der Monat*. But in the 1950s, he ground out article after article on world communism, fashioning

---

60. Waldemar von Knoeringen (Munich) to Richard Löwenthal (London), January 23, 1947, FES, NL Knoeringen, 84, and Löwenthal to the Abendroths, December 30, 1946. See Sering [Löwenthal], *Jenseits des Kapitalismus*, ch. 10.

61. Kurt Schmidt, "Europäische Planung," *Das Sozialistische Jahrhundert* 1, no. 3/4 (Decem-ber 1946): 54, and Grau [Fritz Erler] to Richard Löwenthal (London), April 14, 1948, FES, NL Löwenthal, 4.

62. The Communist economist Friedrich Behrens wrote a long and scathing review, "Jenseits des Kapitalismus?" *Einheit* 2, no. 8 (1947): 740–50. For reviews in the West, see "Jenseits des Kapitalismus," *Der Sozialdemokrat*, June 14, 1947, 5, and Marianne Pollak, "Jenseits des Kapital-ismus," *Arbeiter-Zeitung* (Vienna), November 1, 1947. In the anti-Communist journal *Der Monat*, Paul Kecskemeti speculated that Löwenthal's arguments about democratic planning actually took him beyond socialism as well as capitalism: "Jenseits des Sozialismus," *Der Monat*, no. 3 (1948): 103–6.

himself into one of Western Europe's leading Soviet experts.[63] He found his vocation as political commentator instead of party theorist.

To confirm that vocation, Löwenthal buried his New Beginning alter ego "Paul Sering." The book *Beyond Capitalism* appeared under that pseudonym, and some veterans of the antifascist new left still called him by it. His last piece published under the name Sering was an article in the short-lived periodical *Ernst Reuter Letters*. In this 1954 piece, "Socialist Renewal and the Case of Berlin," he surveyed the travails of Social Democrats in that city since the end of the war, highlighting the courageous leadership of Ernst Reuter during the blockade of 1948–49. Reversing claims that he made eight years earlier in *Beyond Capitalism*, Sering/Löwenthal now rejected the possibility of a democratic socialist Europe posing as a third force between the capitalist and communist blocs:

> So long as there is a global-political power bloc in which all democratic socialist attempts at struggle are pinned down by totalitarian means, socialists can only act as a progressive wing *within* the camp of freedom [i.e., the West], not as a "third force" *between* one allegedly capitalist and another "communist" camp.[64]

Gone was his critique of capitalism and far gone the revolutionary socialism that had given birth to Sering two decades before. Now spoke a pragmatic anti-Communist named Löwenthal, who crafted his mature identity to suit Europe's Cold War reality. As was the case with Erler, Löwenthal experienced this abandonment of his neoleftist identity as a retreat forward into the new identity of Social Democratic modernizer.

That same year he published an article in *Die Neue Gesellschaft* titled "Socialism without Utopia." The title was meant to sound liberating. Postwar socialists faced tasks that demanded real solutions, he claimed, not utopian ideas. The centralization of capitalist production and the advancement of monetary policy had "created the objective preconditions for a politics of full employment, just as the increase in productivity [created] the objective preconditions for a welfare state." Since material conditions already favored democratic socialism, all that remained was "a pure question of political power." Scandinavian Social Democrats and the British Labour Party had shown the way for

63. Cf. David C. Engerman, *Know Your Enemy: The Rise and Fall of America's Soviet Experts* (Oxford: Oxford University Press, 2009).

64. Paul Sering [Richard Löwenthal], "Sozialistische Erneuerung und der Fall Berlin," *Ernst-Reuter-Briefe*, no. 2 (January 1954), LArch Berlin, NL Klingelhöfer, 90, emphasis in original. Together with Willy Brandt, Löwenthal cowrote the first biography of Reuter, *Ernst Reuter—Ein Leben für die Freiheit: Eine politische Biographie* (Munich: Kindler, 1957).

the SPD, he thought. Socialism did not need utopia because the reality of its program was plain for all to see: full employment and the welfare state. "Not the belief in the imminent heaven on earth," Löwenthal declared, "but rather the prevention of hell on earth" defined the project of social democratic modernization. The left must reject any "nihilistic destruction of traditional values" and instead build stable and progressive institutions. He concluded his article with a quote about universal liberty from, of all people, Abraham Lincoln.[65] Löwenthal's liberal and pro-Western attitude matched the sentiments of a group of reformers within the SPD who prepared to reshape the party and the future of the German left.

The Road to Godesberg

German Social Democracy's abandonment of utopia would culminate at an actual topos: the Rhineland town of Bad Godesberg near Bonn. Cold War geopolitics, stalled talks on national reunification, and West Germany's economic boom under democratic capitalism coincided in the late 1950s with a generational turnover in the SPD leadership. Middle-aged and sensible, veterans of the antifascist new left now took the helm.

Historians' usual paradigm for the transformation of the SPD and West German society as a whole during the 1950s is the Westernization thesis, or more specifically the Americanization thesis.[66] The thesis cites as evidence the changes in culture during those years, the rise of consumerism, the borrowing of concepts from US political science, and the reliance on US military defense through NATO. Even the historian Konrad Jarausch, who prefers an East-West comparison to the one-directional Westernization view, uses Western liberal norms of human rights and civil society as his benchmarks for evaluation. He describes the 1959 Godesberg party convention as the final

---

65. Löwenthal, "Sozialismus ohne Utopie." Cf. Rabinbach, *Eclipse of the Utopias*.

66. See Axel Schildt, *Zwischen Abendland und Amerika: Studien zur westdeutschen Ideenlandschaft der 50er Jahre* (Munich: Oldenbourg, 1999); Doering-Manteuffel, *Wie westlich sind die Deutschen?*; Angster, *Konsenskapitalismus und Sozialdemokratie*; Stefan Paulus, *Vorbild USA? Amerikanisierung von Universität und Wissenschaft in Westdeutschland 1945–1976* (Munich: Oldenbourg, 2010); Volker R. Berghahn, *The Americanisation of West German Industry, 1945–1973* (Cambridge: Cambridge University Press, 1986). Even the widespread anti-Americanism among German intellectuals can be seen as a reaction to US dominance of mainstream culture. See Philipp Gassert, "The Anti-American as Americanizer: Revisiting the Anti-American Century in Germany," *German Politics and Society* 27, no. 1 (2009): 24–38.

"commitment to the West" made by the SPD, representing a broader shift in West German political culture.[67]

In the following account of social democratic modernization in Germany, I propose another explanation: the Godesberg convention represented the postwar SPD's final peace with the institutionalized party form, the geopolitical status quo, and democratic capitalism. Under the banner of renewal and modernization, the SPD ironically cemented its place in the old left. An examination of the internal debates before, during, and just after the convention show that veterans of New Beginning and other interwar new lefts played a leading role in this transformation. Organizationally, they accepted the electoral party form as the only vehicle for practicing left politics. Ideologically, they purged the last remnants of Marxism from the party program and, through disciplinary measures, from the party ranks.

As the last chapter showed in the case of the Berlin SPD in particular, the postwar reconstruction of the SPD in general tended to place older functionaries in positions of leadership. The 1952 Dortmund Action Program still bore the ideological stamp of Schumacher, who composed its foreword in the spirit of Weimar-era Social Democracy. Although he considered the SPD a popular party that represented the interests of all Germans, he nevertheless privileged the working class as the party's electoral base, cultural world, and ideological guide.[68]

After Schumacher's death in 1952 and the party's crushing electoral defeat in 1953, a new leadership around the former Sopade leader Erich Ollenhauer and the ex-Communist Herbert Wehner tasked a committee of party theorists to draft a new program. The committee included several people who were once radical antifascists: Willi Eichler, Fritz Borinski, and Josef Kappius of the International Socialist Militant League (ISK); Willy Brandt of the Socialist Workers' Party (SAP); Abendroth of the Communist Party–Opposition (KPO) and peripherally of New Beginning; and Erler and Knoeringen of New Beginning. Numbering thirty-four members in total, this program committee was formalized at the Berlin party convention in 1954. Subcommittees formed to tackle every area of German life: culture, education, foreign policy, social welfare, employer-employee relations, and so on.[69]

---

67. Jarausch, *After Hitler*, 13 and 117.

68. On the Dortmund Action Program, see Klotzbach, *Der Weg zur Staatspartei*, 255–64.

69. See the first committee circular from Willi Eichler (Bonn), March 15, 1955, IISG, NL Abendroth, 7.

Further defeat in the 1957 federal elections lent the work of the committee added urgency.[70] It presented a program draft to the Stuttgart party convention in May 1958. Over the next year and a half, every party district in the Federal Republic reviewed it and wrote motions for revision in advance of the special party convention at Bad Godesberg scheduled for November 1959. There Social Democrats would conclude the *Grundsatzdebatte*, or the debate on basic principles.

An analysis of the convention minutes shows that the twenty people who spoke most often (including the three rotating chairmen) belonged predominantly to the anti-Marxist reformer faction—that is, the modernizers. They included the former New Beginning members Erler and Knoeringen. Their average age was fifty-three years. Although not physically present, Löwenthal added his intellectual weight to this faction. Three frequent speakers who favored Marxist left socialism were Heinz-Joachim Heydorn, Peter von Oertzen, and Willi Birkelbach, whose average age was forty-one. While not a major generational difference, this age gap was enough to align the party's minority left wing with the militant youth. Of the 415 total attendees listed in the official minutes, a mere 12 percent were women. In the late 1950s, social democratic modernization was the enterprise of middle-aged men.[71]

Besides the confrontation between social democratic modernizers and Marxist left socialists, other ideological currents at the convention included right-wing traditionalists, who wanted to revive the agenda of the Weimar and Schumacher-era SPD, and left-wing traditionalists, who like the German Revolutionary Socialists of the mid-1930s wished to return to the unity programs of the pre-1914 SPD. A few smaller currents existed, too, such as the Protestant religious socialists around the ex-CDU convert Gustav Heinemann and the liberal humanists around Carlo Schmid.

---

70. See Erler's reflection on the 1957 defeat, "Gedanken zur Politik und inneren Ordnung der Sozialdemokratie," *Die Neue Gesellschaft* 5, no. 1 (1958), reprinted as "Konsequenzen aus der Bundestagswahl 1957," in *Politik für Deutschland*, 126–37.

71. These statistics are based on my analysis of the SPD (Vorstand)'s *Protokoll der Verhandlungen*. The SPD parliamentary faction for the period 1957–61 likewise consisted of only 12.2% women, which was at least higher than the CDU/CSU (7.9%) and the FDP (7.0%). From a peak of 9.2% in 1957, the total percentage of women in the Bundestag dropped steadily to a low of 5.8% in 1972. The real rise in female representation began only in 1983 with the entry of the Greens as the fourth major party. After the German federal election in 2017, the percentage of women representatives stood at 30.7%. By comparison, the percentage of women in the 116th US Congress (2019–21), even after a significant bump, was only 23.4%. As an indication of how the SPD itself has changed, the percentage of women in its Bundestag faction as of 2017 stood at 41.8%, and in 2018 it elected its first female leader, Andrea Nahles.

Critics of the program draft sensed already before the convention that they were faced with an accomplished fact.[72] It opened with a statement on the "core values of socialism," which included freedom, justice, and human solidarity. According to this ethical statement, democratic socialism was rooted primarily in Christian ethics, secular humanism, and Enlightenment reason, not scientific socialism. The modern SPD would present itself as "the party of intellectual freedom" and socialist volition. Its goal was to construct a humane society that coexisted peacefully with other nations, promoted democracy against dictatorship, and ensured the unfolding of "the multifaceted economic, social, and cultural" life of the individual.[73] In addition to pursuing social justice, individuals would share responsibility for upholding democratic institutions. The program in fact formalized older currents in Social Democratic thought that drew on the republican tradition and neo-Kantian idealism. While the concept of the unfolding (*Entfaltung*) of the human personality resembled what Marx had in mind for the future communist society, it read more like Leonard Nelson and the ethical socialism of interwar groups like ISK.[74]

The main sections of past SPD programs always began with an analysis of socioeconomic conditions in Germany, Europe, and the wider world. By contrast, the Godesberg program's first section focused on political order. It envisioned a democratic welfare state (*Sozialstaat*) whose purpose was to enable individual self-determination. At the same time, it described a lively political culture based on civic engagement and co-responsibility. Citizens would have the duty of maintaining public institutions, independent associations, and a free press. In terms of strategy, the modern SPD committed itself almost exclusively to electoral politics and legislative compromise within a parliamentary system.[75]

Social democratic modernization provided the rhetorical framework for this elevation of politics over economics. As the historian Axel Schildt has observed, many West Germans in the 1950s shared a sense of living in modern times.[76] A large panel on the wall of the convention hall proclaimed in modish lowercase print "get with the times—get with the SPD [geh mit der zeit—geh mit der SPD]." This modern identity prompted Social Democrats to rebrand

---

72. Abendroth, for example, had originally planned to attend the convention but canceled his hotel reservation at the last minute, possibly out of frustration with the program draft. Abendroth to Hotel Eden (Bad Godesberg), November 3, 1959, IISG, NL Abendroth, 62.

73. SPD (Vorstand), *Grundsatzprogramm der Sozialdemokratischen Partei*, 7–9.

74. For a left critique of ethical socialism, see Kofler, *Marxistischer oder ethischer Sozialismus?*

75. SPD (Vorstand), *Grundsatzprogramm der Sozialdemokratischen Partei*, 10–11.

76. Schildt, *Moderne Zeiten*.

their politics. Back in 1953, Erler had argued already that the renewal of Social Democracy required US-style campaigning: the SPD must learn from voter psychology and the "insights of modern advertising science in the evaluation of popular opinion polls."[77] He did warn about the manipulation of popular opinion by corporate mass media, but his support for social democratic modernization stayed firm.[78]

For the modernizers, rebranding chiefly meant eliminating all traces of Marxism from the party's program and public messaging. They pitched this change as an advance in socialist theory. True scientific socialism required a substantial revision of the analyses that Marx had pioneered a century earlier, the modernizers believed. The Godesberg program accordingly celebrated the party's progress beyond Marx. Still, residues of tradition remained. For example, a passage on the welfare state included the line: "The laws must be adapted in a timely fashion to social development so that they do not come into contradiction with the general sense of justice [Rechtsbewußtsein], but instead serve the realization of the idea of law [Rechtsidee]."[79] One could interpret that line as an expression of Marx's theory of contradiction under capitalism, in which forces of production ("social development") change faster than relations of production ("the laws"). Or one could interpret it simply as legal normativity in a non-Marxist sense. Regardless of possible Marxist residues, the modernizers understood crises solely in political terms. No longer did they speak of a general crisis of capitalism, or contradictions in the mode of production, or even economic crises as anything more serious than market fluctuations that could be solved by government policy.

The Godesberg program did warn of the growing accumulation and concentration of capital since the end of the war, along with the proliferation of lobbyists for big business. A Social Democratic government would therefore limit the power of cartels and monopolies. The modernizers' goal was not to create conditions for an alternative economic order, but rather to facilitate distributive justice within the existing capitalist system. The modern SPD committed itself to protecting private property, so long as that did not infringe on the public good. It would also support small and medium-sized businesses. Mixed public-private companies should predominate in heavy industries like fossil fuel extraction and transportation. While the SPD continued to support

77. Fritz Erler, "Nach der Bundestagswahl 1953" [October 17, 1953], in *Politik für Deutschland*, 91–94.

78. Fritz Erler, "Wird die öffentliche Meinung total manipulierbar?" [February 1958], in *Politik für Deutschland*, 328–31.

79. SPD (Vorstand), *Grundsatzprogramm der Sozialdemokratischen Partei*, 11.

a robust public sector, it now encouraged decentralization by means of local self-administration. The Godesberg program rejected any centralized accumulation of economic power by the state, even if that state were governed by Social Democrats.[80]

The Marxist holdouts in the party likely cringed at the program's call for free trade as a precondition for world peace: how could socialists ignore the systemic inequalities caused by capitalist imperialism? The program did mention aid for developing countries in order to ensure a fairer distribution of global wealth, but the modernizers seemed more concerned about "new forms oppression" (i.e., communism or military dictatorship) that might result if developing countries did not follow the path of democratic socialism.[81]

In recognition of Cold War geopolitics, the program reaffirmed the SPD's support for a West German military, an issue that had proven controversial since the early 1950s and roused considerable debate at the convention, too.[82] On the other hand, the program strongly opposed nuclear weapons: European countries should promote world peace, not a nuclear standoff. The program's section on national defense concluded with a call for general disarmament, which obviously contradicted its support for West German rearmament.[83] Its call for German national reunification exposed another contradiction. The program's aggressive rhetoric toward the German Democratic Republic clashed with its support for détente, economic cooperation, and normal diplomatic relations. It would take modernizers around Brandt several more years to develop a consistent policy toward East Germany and Eastern Europe (*Ostpolitik*).[84]

80. SPD (Vorstand), 15.

81. SPD (Vorstand), 25. On the inequalities of the capitalist world system, see Immanuel Wallerstein, *The Capitalist World-Economy: Essays* (Cambridge: Cambridge University Press, 1979); Giovanni Arrighi, *The Long Twentieth Century: Money, Power, and the Origins of Our Times* (London: Verso, 1994); and Michael Mann, *The Sources of Social Power*, vol. 4, *Globalizations, 1945–2011* (Cambridge: Cambridge University Press, 2012). On European socialist attitudes toward decolonization, see Imlay, *Practice of Socialist Internationalism*, ch. 9.

82. Motions 11 and 95 brought forward by the Marburg delegates (Abendroth's home district) aimed to secure West German neutrality by reversing the majority's decision in favor of a military draft. The motions failed. SPD (Vorstand), *Protokoll der Verhandlungen*, 156, 388–89, and 550–51.

83. SPD (Vorstand), *Grundsatzprogramm der Sozialdemokratischen Partei*, 11–12.

84. On the SPD's Germany Plan of 1959, see Fritz Erler, "Disengagement und Wiedervereinigung" [May 1959], in *Politik für Deutschland*, 537–51. See also Erler, "Bestandaufnahme," speech in the Bundestag [June 30, 1960], in *Politik für Deutschland*, 552–67. On the Ostpolitik negotiations under Brandt's chancellorship, see Julia von Dannenberg, *The Foundations of*

As for domestic affairs, the program placed most emphasis on economic growth as the means of sustaining welfare programs over the long term. Essentially repeating Bernstein's revisionist arguments from a half century before, the modernizers viewed the growth of the capitalist economy as beneficial for all, including the working class. In 1959, party leaders advocated a Keynesian approach to stabilizing the currency, maintaining full employment, increasing production, and expanding social services. Comprehensive health care, for example, would be a priority. State guidelines would ensure that the market economy conformed to the structural transformations of society. But such guidelines would not be mandates: according to the program, private businesses would retain "the right of free decision" whether to follow them. Reflecting the rise of professional economists within the party, the Godesberg program envisioned an organic mixture of state regulation and free-market dynamics. A market economy does not function efficiently on its own, the modernizers came to believe: state policy must build a framework for free competition, while correcting for extreme inequalities.[85]

Repeatedly, the program stressed the importance of free consumer choice, free choice of employment, free competition, and free enterprise. The historian Anthony J. Nicholls links the idea of "freedom with responsibility" to the model of social market economy in West Germany. Although one usually associates that model with Ludwig Erhard and the CDU, it influenced the SPD's economic policy, too.[86] The liberalization of social democratic economics across Western Europe in the 1950s and early 1960s reflected the primacy of politics in that era. Aside from Keynesian monetary policy, often that meant actively *limiting* political interference in private business. Economic freedom was understood as a political arrangement that maximized the decision-making power of both employers and employees, in contrast to the "totalitarian" command economy of the Soviet bloc. The Godesberg program's section on social order concluded with a new motto for the modern SPD: "Competition as much as possible—planning as much as necessary!"[87]

Ostpolitik: The Making of the Moscow Treaty between West Germany and the USSR (Oxford: Oxford University Press, 2008).

85. SPD (Vorstand), *Grundsatzprogramm der Sozialdemokratischen Partei*, 16–19. See Mudge, *Leftism Reinvented*, ch. 4.

86. Nicholls, *Freedom with Responsibility*. For example, the leading economist of the postwar SPD, Karl Schiller, subscribed to the social market economy model. See Matthias Hochstätter, "Karl Schiller—eine wirtschaftspolitische Biographie" (PhD thesis, University of Hannover, 2006).

87. SPD (Vorstand), *Grundsatzprogramm der Sozialdemokratischen Partei*, 14.

Social democratic modernizers rewrote the history of capitalism so that the protagonist was no longer workers, but citizen consumers: every person should have the opportunity to make money and accumulate savings, because every person aspires to become middle class.[88] Instead of the working class, which had been the target audience of past party programs, the Godesberg program addressed itself to the undifferentiated mass of salaried employees, civil servants, and working people that fit under the generic term "jobholders" (*Arbeitnehmer*). This term implied a looser application of class categories and downplayed real social antagonism between such diverse strata as skilled industrial workers, craftsmen, white-collar employees, unskilled laborers, and service workers. It even became convenient for Social Democrats to refer to economic citizens (*Wirtschaftsbürger*), which further divorced the party from the historical working class. At the same time, the Godesberg program reaffirmed the importance of trade unions. These would function as the "essential bearers of the constant democratization process."[89] The unions' fight for factory codetermination (*Mitbestimmung*), which had only partial success in the early 1950s, integrated West German workers into capitalist enterprise itself by giving union representatives seats on major industries' executive boards. If workers could not own the means of production, then they could at least help manage them. This followed the model of progressive American trade unions.[90]

In its appeal to the West German middle class, the Godesberg program transformed the party's traditional defense of the rights of the oppressed into a vision of just distribution for all. Exploitation or systemic injustice were not inherent to capitalism itself, the program implied, but owed rather to the unequal share of individuals in the benefits of capitalism. Income inequality, therefore, should be the target of progressive tax reform and redistributive efforts by a democratic welfare state. The program conspicuously lacked any substantive discussion, much less critique, of capitalism. The historian Hobsbawm noted that in general the word "capitalism" rarely appeared in

88. See Olsen, *Sovereign Consumer*.

89. SPD (Vorstand), *Grundsatzprogramm der Sozialdemokratischen Partei*, 15–18. See Walter, *Die SPD*.

90. See Angster, *Konsenskapitalismus und Sozialdemokratie*; Michael Schneider, *A Brief History of the German Trade Unions* [1989] (Bonn: J.H.W. Dietz, 1991); and Andrei S. Markovits, *The Politics of the West German Trade Unions: Strategies of Class and Interest Representation in Growth and Crisis* (Cambridge: Cambridge University Press, 1986).

public discourse during the 1950s, "since it had negative associations in the public mind." The preferred term was free enterprise.[91]

The program's final section surveyed the goals that the socialist movement had set for itself in the past: abolishing the privileges of the ruling class, emancipating the working class as a prelude to human emancipation, and so on. Once the object of exploitation by an inherently unjust capitalist system, however, "jobholders" now enjoyed full rights as citizens. Thus the modern SPD completed its evolution from a workers' party (*Arbeiterpartei*) into a popular party (*Volkspartei*). The new SPD also posed as a collective party (*Sammelpartei*) of (West) German socialism, absorbing all its various tendencies and splinter groups.[92]

In summary, two main features of the Godesberg program stand out. First, a rhetoric of "freedom" pervaded the document: the noun, its related adjectives and verbs, and its synonyms appeared far more frequently than the old language of "social," "socialism," or even "democracy." And second, the program's logic followed from the primacy of politics over economics: objective social forces could be mastered by democratic control. This was fully in line with Löwenthal's theory in *Beyond Capitalism*. Those two main features of the program—its rhetoric of freedom and primacy of politics—distinguished it from all prior programs adopted by the SPD over eighty years.[93]

In the back pages of the official program pamphlet, the publisher advertised a series of books that included the historian Werner Blumenberg's *Fighters for Freedom*, which collected short biographies of German socialist heroes as diverse as Reuter, Schumacher, Bernstein, Marx, and Wilhelm Weitling.[94] Even Social Democrat historians who did not participate in the convention, then, contributed to the modernization paradigm by creating a pantheon of socialist freedom fighters. Modernizers could claim people like Marx, Engels, and Luxemburg as their own, while ignoring their actual revolutionary politics. After twelve years of Nazi oppression and nearly fifteen years of defending its position against the Communist threat to the East, the modern SPD embraced

91. Hobsbawm, *Age of Extremes*, 273. Google Ngrams bear this out for "capitalism" in English, but the words in German, French, Italian, and Spanish all show a rise in usage from the early 1950s to a peak around 1975. See also Lawrence B. Glickman, *Free Enterprise: An American History* (New Haven, CT: Yale University Press, 2019).

92. SPD (Vorstand), *Grundsatzprogramm der Sozialdemokratischen Partei*, 26–27.

93. For a less historical defense of Social Democracy based on these features, cf. Berman, *Primacy of Politics*, and "Can Social Democrats Save the World (Again)?" *Foreign Policy*, January 15, 2020. See also Annelien de Dijn, *Freedom: An Unruly History* (Cambridge, MA: Harvard University Press, 2020).

94. Werner Blumenberg, *Kämpfer für die Freiheit* (West Berlin: J.H.W. Dietz Nachf., 1959).

freedom as its central tenet. The SPD's shift in focus away from economics and social forces to the realm of politics occurred both in an electoral sense and in terms of technocratic policy.

Evoking Bernstein, modernizers like Erler redefined socialism as an everyday task rather than a future goal. The difference between Bernstein's turn-of-the-century revisionism and social democratic modernization was that the postwar left was far less anchored in a mass social movement. Widespread apathy after the war had made mass politics suspect. Whereas before the war socialist parties and affiliated organizations had integrated their members into all-encompassing worlds of labor,[95] after the war the scope of the left narrowed to electoral campaigns and internal party affairs. The Western European socialist movement became more about going through the parliamentary motions. It would take a new left in the 1960s to resurrect the collective power of movement-based politics.

The day after the Godesberg convention, Erler gave an interview on Swiss radio. Observing that the party's adoption of this new program had proceeded more carefully and democratically than for any prior program, he considered the result a testament to the lessons learned by German antifascists and anti-Communists. Transforming the SPD into a "modern, liberal, and socialist" organization required a firm commitment to internal party democracy. Erler characterized the program's left socialist critics as dogmatic Marxists who, if they controlled the majority, would have the modernizers "burned as heretics." He made no secret that "some ideas of the socialist movement from the 19th century no longer fit into the present and consequently had to be dropped or modified. . . . [P]recisely that which does not fit with the present was swept away." Anticipating the charge of political opportunism, he insisted that the socialist triad of freedom, justice, and solidarity remained the party's North Star even while it competed for the most votes. But he admitted that not all Social Democrats were on board. Despite a clear majority in favor of the new program, it was not yet "the practical benchmark for behavior by the entire broad membership throughout the country."[96] He was right: over the next few years, a civil war broke out within the party over the meaning and effects of modernization. Once that civil war embroiled the youth, a radical new left took shape.

95. See Eric Hobsbawm, *Workers: Worlds of Labor* (New York: Pantheon, 1984).

96. Interview of Fritz Erler by Fritz René Allemann, Radio Beromünster, November 16, 1959, reprinted as "Zum Godesberg Programm," in *Politik für Deutschland*, 138–41.

Left Renewal, Ltd.

An analogous Godesberg moment occurred for socialists across Western Europe. In 1960, the Resistance veteran, journalist, and disgruntled former leader of the SFIO Édouard Depreux published the book *Renewal of Socialism* (*Renouvellement du socialisme*). A huge rift had opened within the SFIO over the Algerian War and the problem of French imperialism, subjects that the next two chapters will address. As a result Depreux and his allies quit the SFIO in 1958 to form the Autonomous Socialist Party. Unlike the West German modernizers who managed to co-opt an existing socialist party, the French modernizers split off to form their own. But their ideologies were similar. In his book, Depreux sought to bring socialism up to date without recourse to Marxism or any materialist critique of capitalism. Modern socialism, he claimed, ensured the survival of civilization by reconciling "respect for individual liberties with the democratic (and not bureaucratic) organization of the economy." Democratic socialism he understood as a humanistic third way between capitalism and communism. The goal should not be nationalization and state control over economic life, but rather the "liberation of man." Echoing Erler, he thought that a "modernized socialism adapted to present-day tasks" could harness economic growth for the "unfolding of the human personality." In terms of policy, he preferred the pragmatic approach of regulating private ownership rather than expanding public ownership.[97]

Depreux expressed frustration at the factional disputes on the left over who was or was not a genuine Marxist. All that mattered for him was what socialists did once in power. In order to draw the militant youth back into the socialist camp, he believed, a new party needed to revamp socialist language and principles. Without explicitly mentioning advertising, public relations, or American-style campaigning, this was Depreux's way of saying that French socialism needed to rebrand. Organizationally, he backed the democratic party form. That did not mean restricting politics to voting in elections, however. Having witnessed the appeal of both the postwar Revolutionary Democratic Assembly (RDR) and Gaullist authoritarian populism, he acknowledged the need for grassroots mobilization in the form of a democratic assembly (*rassemblement*). So, in effect Depreux proposed a hybrid party-assembly form. Transcending socialist left and right wings, Marxists and anti-Marxists, this nonsectarian catch-all party would be open to all. For success at the polls it required only unity of action.[98]

97. Depreux, *Renouvellement du socialisme*, 11, 33, and 45.
98. Depreux, 21, 186–87, and 190.

This new party of the left did in fact emerge that same year: the Unified Socialist Party (PSU), which resulted from a merger of Depreux's Autonomous Socialist Party and another group. From 1960 on, the PSU advocated modernization by means of a democratically regulated economy and market competition. The new party struck a chord with its call for left unity, recruiting thousands of members. In good faith, and unlike the post-Godesberg SPD, it never barred or purged Marxists from its ranks.[99] A historian once referred to the PSU as a "motley coalition of [left liberals] with technocratic leanings, and old-style left-wingers who had abandoned the two major parties because they were not radical enough, had dragged their feet during the Algerian war, and in general gave the impression of having accepted the status quo."[100] More charitably, one might say that the PSU represented the French version of social democratic modernization: a forward-looking and ultimately successful movement that dressed the part of neoleftism while limiting itself to reforms within the system.[101]

In France as in West Germany, social democratic modernization replaced supposedly obsolete Marxism with a post-ideological pragmatism. But intense disagreements lay behind this moderate push for consensus. The "end of ideology" discourse in the 1950s reflected the momentary boom of democratic capitalism and the seeming permanence of the welfare state. Just like Bernstein's revisionism at the turn of the twentieth century, post-ideological modernization fixated on a partial and fleeting moment of social transformation. This post-ideological turn actually represented the triumph of a new kind of ideology: rigid adherence to liberal democratic norms, denial of class conflict, obsession with totalitarian dictatorship as a foil, praise for free enterprise, and sacralization of individual liberties.

Of course, the modernizers did not think of themselves as cynical opportunists or traitors to left tradition. Their adaptation to the conditions of postwar capitalism seemed progressive and liberating. The Godesberg transformation of the SPD paid swift dividends. Brandt's Ostpolitik during the 1960s, which officially recognized the German-German border and sought "change

---

99. See Hauss, *New Left in France*; Jean-François Kesler, *De la gauche dissidente au nouveau Parti socialiste: Les minorités qui ont rénové le P.S.* (Toulouse: Privat, 1990); and Bernard Ravenel, *Quand la gauche se réinventait: Le PSU, histoire d'un parti visionnaire (1960–1989)* (Paris: La Découverte, 2016).

100. Lichtheim, *Marxism in Modern France*, 166–67.

101. Cf. Gerd-Rainer Horn's interpretation of the PSU as belonging to a distinct Mediterranean New Left together with the Italian Socialist Party of Proletarian Unity and the Spanish Popular Liberation Front in *Spirit of '68*, 148–52. For a critique of Horn, see D. Gordon, "'Mediterranean New Left'?"

through rapprochement" with the Soviet bloc, followed logically from the Godesberg moment. And in 1966 the SPD succeeded in appealing to a middle-class electorate. That year, for the first time since 1930, it gained power at the federal level as part of the Grand Coalition. Social Democrats solidified those gains in 1969 when they finally defeated the CDU/CSU under the chancellor-ship of Brandt, himself a prominent neoleftist turned modernizer. However much Marxist left socialists might have complained, the Godesberg conven-tion proved a boon for German Social Democracy.

The Godesberg program placed an emphasis on higher education and vocational training. Modernizers knew that they needed to win over the young generation. Giving young people diverse employment opportunities and mak-ing them co-responsible citizens was necessary for stabilizing the democratic system. Schools must strengthen young citizens' "power of resistance against the conformist tendencies of our time," the program declared.[102] For the six-ties youth, however, the twin precepts of co-responsible citizenship and non-conformist resistance would come into open contradiction. Young people began to feel alienated from the institutions of the welfare state. And material conditions changed as Western European countries transitioned into a postin-dustrial society. A generational revolt was in the making.

While employing the rhetoric of modernization, postwar Social Democrats undertook renewal mainly at the level of ideals, policies, and messaging. The minimal organizational reforms adopted by German Social Democrats at their Stuttgart and Godesberg conventions shifted power away from local and re-gional functionaries toward the parliamentary faction and party leadership, as the next chapter will discuss.[103] Perhaps even because of its electoral success, social democratic modernization failed as neoleftism: it did represent a kind of postwar new left, but one that adapted its organizational form to the re-quirements of electoral democracy within existing capitalist welfare states. The modernizers' plan after Godesberg was to marginalize Marxist left socialists and the militant youth. The next chapter will explain how conflict with the SPD leadership pushed those two groups together into a neoleftist community of the expelled. A grassroots movement and extraparliamentary left soon took shape. The task of redefining the left fell to the anti-authoritarian youth, who rediscovered the organizational forms of radical antifascism.

102. SPD (Vorstand), *Grundsatzprogramm der Sozialdemokratischen Partei*, 20–23.
103. See also Klotzbach, *Der Weg zur Staatspartei*.

7

Left Socialism

IN THE MID- TO LATE 1950S, moderate left parties and unions in most Western European countries became reliable partners in the democratic capitalist order.[1] This process of social democratic modernization shifted the political terrain most clearly in West Germany, where the SPD after Godesberg eliminated class struggle from its party program. But foreign policy conditioned that process from the start, as memories of the Berlin fusion struggle and mounting Cold War tensions hardened Social Democrats' stance against Communism and any perceived leftist deviations. Pushed out of mainstream politics, a band of defiant intellectuals and students laid the groundwork for a new left.

External pressures also shaped two other neoleftist phenomena, the British New Left and the French *Nouvelle gauche*. In both cases, the year 1956 was crucial. The Hungarian Revolution against bureaucratic Communism witnessed a remarkable confluence of student protests, workers' councils, and grassroots militias. Its crushing defeat by Soviet troops embittered a number of British Communist intellectuals against their party.[2] That same year the British military cooperated in an invasion of Egypt in order to prevent Gamal Abdel Nasser from nationalizing the Suez Canal. As the prominent neoleftist Stuart Hall put it, those events of 1956 "unmasked the underlying violence and aggression latent in the two systems that dominated political life at the

---

1. This chapter includes excerpts from Terence Renaud, "German New Lefts: Postwar Socialists between Past and Future," *New German Critique*, no. 137 (Aug. 2019), pp. 117–143. © 2019. Reproduced with permission of *New German Critique*.

2. For postwar Communists, it became increasingly difficult to justify Stalinism. See Thomas Kroll, *Kommunistische Intellektuelle in Westeuropa: Frankreich, Österreich, Italien und Grossbritannien im Vergleich (1945–1956)* (Cologne: Böhlau, 2009). On the Hungarian return of the council form in 1956, see Oskar Anweiler, "Die Räte in der ungarischen Revolution 1956," *Osteuropa* 8, no. 6 (1958): 393–400: "Hungary in 1956 showed very clearly that Lenin's slogan of 1917, 'All power to the soviets,' forty years later had become the most dangerous battle cry against Communism" (399–400).

time—Western imperialism and Stalinism—and sent a shock wave through the political world."[3] Renegade Communists, nonconformist intellectuals, and the independent socialist youth came together to carve out "a third political space" beyond Stalinism and Labour Party reformism. People like Hall, John Saville, E. P. Thompson, Raphael Samuel, and Raymond Williams contributed to a new brand of cultural Marxism and anti-imperialism in the pages of two journals, *Universities and Left Review* and the *New Reasoner*, which merged in 1960 into the *New Left Review*.[4] That year the US sociologist C. Wright Mills wrote his famous "Letter to the New Left" to this British group, insisting on the interrelation of form and content in the development of neoleftism: "If there is to be a politics of a New Left, what needs to be analysed is the structure of institutions." Riffing on the title of an essay collection by British neoleftists, *Out of Apathy*, Mills concluded his letter by declaring, "Let the old men ask sourly, 'Out of Apathy—into what?' The Age of Complacency is ending. Let the old women complain wisely about 'the end of ideology.' We are beginning to move again."[5] Although Mills spoke of old men and old women, suggesting that generational consciousness catalyzed this new left, its gender was definitely masculine.

In their twenties or thirties and mostly male, British militants and their American admirers did not invent the name New Left. They adopted it after hearing about developments in France from the Resistance veteran and anticolonial journalist Charles Bourdet. In his 1957 article for *Universities and Left Review*, Bourdet described the progress of the nonaligned French left over the past few years. Dissident Communists, left Catholics, and independent socialists had coordinated their opposition to the government and major workers' parties.[6] Around 1954, the left wing of the SFIO began protesting party leader Guy Mollet and his Algeria policy. The Independent Lefts Action Center (Centre d'action des gauches indépendantes) was established by members of the defunct RDR;[7] a series of New Left Workshops (Journées d'études de la Nouvelle gauche) took place over the course of 1954; and a National

3. Hall, "Life and Times," 177.

4. See Hamilton, *Crisis of Theory*; D. Thompson, *Pessimism of the Intellect?*; Paul Blackledge, *Perry Anderson, Marxism and the New Left* (London: Merlin, 2004); Michael Newman, *Ralph Miliband and the Politics of the New Left* (London: Merlin, 2002); Dworkin, *Cultural Marxism*; Kenny, *First New Left*; and Chun, *British New Left*.

5. Mills, "Letter to the New Left," 21 and 25, emphasis removed. See E. Thompson, *Out of Apathy*, and also Nehring, "'Out of Apathy,'" and Daniel Geary, "'Becoming International Again': C. Wright Mills and the Emergence of a Global New Left, 1956–1962," *Journal of American History* 95, no. 3 (2008): 710–36.

6. Bourdet, "French Left."

7. Birchall, "Neither Washington nor Moscow?" 397.

Committee of the New Left (Comité national de la Nouvelle Gauche) formed at the end of that year. Bourdet's newspaper, *France-Observateur*, agitated for this band of politically homeless left socialists, who were mainly in their forties or fifties. They included veterans of radical antifascism such as Colette Audry, Daniel Guérin, Michel Collinet, and Gilles Martinet. A contributor to Emmanuel Mounier's left Catholic journal *Esprit* asked in 1955, "By whom and how will the New Left be made, if it should be made someday?"[8] The problems of finding a social base and figuring out the best organizational form preoccupied French left socialists during this decade.

For the emerging *Nouvelle gauche*, the issue of imperialism was paramount. The French Empire underwent a violent process of decolonization. It had already lost its colony Indochina in 1954 after a humiliating military defeat at Điện Biên Phủ. In May 1958, a moment that people frequently invoked ten years later, rebellious French generals in Algeria attempted a coup d'état that failed but resulted in the return of Charles de Gaulle to power and the establishment of a new republic. Three years later, in October 1961, French police at the command of Maurice Papon brutally suppressed a protest demonstration in Paris by Algerian supporters of the National Liberation Front. The massacre left dozens dead and a public weary of France's colonial project. Algeria won its independence the next year.

This was the turbulent backdrop for the formation of what one historian has called France's new radical left against imperialism.[9] A catalyst for later activism was the Manifesto of the 121, or Manifesto of Insubordination, which leading intellectuals and left socialists signed in 1960 in support of French students who refused the military draft and the Algerian War. Immediately the government censored the manifesto and the old left parties condemned it, which of course made it into an underground sensation.[10] Thus left socialists of the antifascist generation declared solidarity with the nonconformist youth.

Although French left socialists were the first to identify as a "new left," they and their successors in the radical student movement did not develop a lasting association with the term and had all but abandoned it by the late 1960s. The

8. Louis Bodin, "Qui fera la nouvelle gauche?" *Esprit*, no. 224 (March 1955): 456–75. Editors of *Esprit* had long called for an assembly of left forces that might oppose party sclerosis and dogmatic ideology. As far as I can tell, the first uses of the term *nouvelle gauche* to describe a distinct political current appeared in the pages of this journal. For example, see Emmanuel Mounier, "L'opération 'titisme français,'" *Esprit*, no. 166 (1950): 660–62 (at 660). The young sociologist Michel Crozier also used the term there: "Vue d'ensemble," *Esprit*, no. 196 (1952): 570–87. See also Crozier, *Bureaucratic Phenomenon*.

9. Kalter, *Discovery of the Third World*.

10. "Le Manifeste des 121," archived at https://web.archive.org/web/20041030212203 /http://www.lecri.net/liste_noire/manifeste_121.html, accessed February 2019.

editors of one journal in 1968 even seemed unsure of the correct grammar, alternating between *nouvelle gauche* and *gauche nouvelle*.[11] Some reasons for why the name did not stick in France the same way that it did elsewhere will be given in the next chapter.

But first, this chapter defines the characteristics of 1950s left socialism in Western Europe. French and British left socialists were diverse in ideology and social background. While their countries' political contexts differed, their emerging projects offered a similar generational blend of former radical anti-fascists and a new generation of discontents. In Britain and France, left socialists of the 1950s served as a bridge between past and future radicalisms. They created space for an autonomous left politics, and they incubated Western Marxism in a public climate inhospitable to emancipatory critiques of capitalism or imperialism. I have chosen to call these nonaligned groups "left socialist" in order to indicate their ideological position as well as their transitional role between radical antifascism and sixties anti-authoritarianism. I do not consider this term a party label, since as such it would have meant different things, for example, in France versus Britain.[12]

The term left socialism does have a specific history in Germany. It goes back to the Austromarxist Max Adler, who in 1932 used it to define a third way between Soviet communism and the reformism of the Social Democratic parties. Left socialism (*Linkssozialismus*) arose as a new concept and basis for organization amid the global crisis of capitalism and the confusion that accompanied the rise of fascism.[13] It resurfaced in postwar Europe among people on the left who criticized both Stalinism and official Social Democracy. In West Germany, where the Communist Party lacked mass support and was even banned in 1956, left socialism signified the dissident currents inside and outside the Social Democratic Party. Studies of postwar left socialism have appeared only recently.[14] They tend, however, to focus on one narrow milieu.

11. "Une nouvelle gauche est-elle née?" *Le Cri du monde*, no. 19 (May–June 1968), Hoover, French Subject Collection, 86.

12. George Lichtheim interpreted the general history of socialism in this nonpartisan way. He argued that "cleavages separating communists from democratic socialists, and both from anarchists or anarchosyndicalists, occur within what may broadly be termed the socialist movement. . . . Socialism in this sense is not a party label, but the designation of a historically conditioned response to a particular challenge." Lichtheim, *Short History of Socialism*, x. He also distinguished analytically between the history of socialist thought and the history of the workers' movement, which overlapped but did not always align.

13. Adler, "Die historische Funktion des Linkssozialismus" and *Linkssozialismus*.

14. The best study of German left socialism is Kritidis, *Linkssozialistische Opposition*. See also Jünke, *Linkssozialismus in Deutschland*; Diers, "Linkssozialismus"; Kufferath, "Das linkssozialistische Milieu"; and Oertzen, "Behelfsbrücken."

This chapter broadens the definition of left socialism by situating the phenomenon within a longer history of new lefts.

As the missing link between German new lefts in the 1930s and the 1960s, left socialists fostered an alternative theory and practice in the 1950s, when such an alternative was not fashionable. Having come of age during the interwar years, they worried about the authoritarian restoration of capitalism in West Germany and doubted the ability of existing left organizations to resist it. So, left socialists laid the groundwork for an extraparliamentary opposition and helped mobilize the youth as the vanguard of a new left. They encouraged the same organizational and theoretical creativity that they had practiced in the struggle against fascism. Because they were excluded from the political establishment, they could approach the youth as trustworthy stewards of a radical tradition. In the late 1950s, West Germany's nascent New Left was thus suspended between socialisms past and future.

German New Lefts

In July 1967, students at the Free University of Berlin would organize a panel discussion about the crisis in the Federal Republic. Watching the auditorium overflow with young people, the panelists themselves represented several generations. Besides the Frankfurt School celebrity Herbert Marcuse and the scholar of religion Jacob Taubes, they included the sixty-year-old Social Democrat Richard Löwenthal and the student leader Rudi Dutschke.

A fiery debate ensued. Dutschke claimed that modern technology had enabled humans to overcome material scarcity and live free from domination, so long as one abolished the capitalist class. Löwenthal disagreed. He too wished to end domination, but wishes alone offered no solutions. Romantic revolutionaries like Dutschke, he thought, failed to account for the realities of politics and rational administration. With his long hair, tattered sweater, and angry demeanor, "Red" Rudi was a poster boy for rebellion. He responded to Löwenthal by pulling a pamphlet from his pocket and reading aloud a quote: "'In order for the next German revolution to succeed, the revolutionary party must be created so as to prepare in equal measure for organizing mass action and running the economic apparatus.'" Those words sounded familiar to Löwenthal. Their author was Paul Sering, the alias he had used thirty years ago as a member of New Beginning.[15]

---

15. Paul Sering [Richard Löwenthal], "Anstelle eines Vorwortes: Ein Auszug aus eine[r] Podiumsdiskussion . . . (Berlin, Juli 1967)," in *Faschismus und Monopolkapitalismus*.

By summoning this ghost from the past, Dutschke reminded his antagonist that he too once believed in a revolutionary movement with realistic aims. He too once identified with a radical new left. Since the 1930s, however, Sering had evolved into Löwenthal, a loyal member of the Social Democratic Party and defender of the welfare state. He replied ironically that Dutschke had "proven himself to be my posthumous disciple," for Sering was long dead.[16]

Looking ahead, we might scale up Löwenthal's reply. The sixties New Left in general, with all its important national variations, was the posthumous disciple of the antifascist generation. Sixties radicals paid homage to their parents' younger selves. They faced organizational challenges and theoretical problems very similar to those of their forebears in the 1930s. Radicals in both decades rejected the status quo politics of existing Social Democratic and Communist parties. Both declared the bankruptcy of what they considered the old left. For many grassroots campaigns, extraparliamentary oppositions, and student factions in the 1960s, the Western Marxist theories and neoleftist small groups of the interwar years served as models. One could even hear the rhetoric of antifascism again.[17] But sixties radicals also rebelled against a political establishment ruled in part by those neoleftist pioneers, their parents' generation. Antifascism's children renounced their inheritance. The legacy of the antifascist new left would haunt the 1960s as a specter of attraction and aversion.[18]

Recent transnational studies of West Germany and the Global Sixties have expanded our understanding of German new lefts across space.[19] But the theories and political activism of two exemplary left socialists illustrate the continuity of new lefts across time. Ossip K. Flechtheim (1909–1998) and Wolfgang Abendroth (1906–1985) transmitted their experiences of antifascism to a new, decidedly postwar generation. Both helped build the academic discipline of political science in West Germany. Like their counterpart Löwenthal, they belonged to the antifascist generation born roughly between 1905 and 1915, that is, after the First World War "front generation" that led the Weimar-era workers' parties but before the "Forty-fivers," who entered adulthood during postwar reconstruction.[20] Unlike Löwenthal, however, they

---

16. Paul Sering [Richard Löwenthal].

17. Mercer, "Specters of Fascism."

18. Cf. Derrida, *Specters of Marx*. See also Rabinbach, "Legacies of Antifascism," and Eley, "Legacies of Antifascism." Dan Stone agrees about the dual nature of antifascist memory during the 1960s. Stone, *Goodbye to All That?* 113.

19. For a recent example, see Chen, *Routledge Handbook of the Global Sixties*. See also Brown, *West Germany and the Global Sixties*.

20. Ample scholarship exists on German generations. For example, see Moses, *German Intellectuals*; Herwig, *Die Flakhelfer*; Arndt Weinrich, *Der Weltkrieg als Erzieher: Jugend zwischen*

refused to rally behind the SPD, which in 1959 abandoned Marxism and declared its commitment to welfare politics within a regulated capitalist system. As mainstream Social Democrats pursued modernization, Flechtheim and Abendroth criticized the conformist tendencies in the party, defended a critical form of Marxism, and built solidarity through causes such as decolonization and antinuclear activism. Their respective theories of futurology and antagonistic society transposed radical antifascism into a new key of social protest.

Around 1960 the crisis of the West German left came to a head in the controversy over the Socialist German Student League (SDS).[21] As will be shown, Social Democrat leaders distanced themselves from these radical students and eventually declared their organization irreconcilable with party membership. Flechtheim and Abendroth, by contrast, helped form the Socialist Sponsors' Association on the students' behalf. In the winter of 1961–62, they and a number of other left socialists either resigned or were expelled from the party. Young and middle-aged militants together began debating how to reorganize the West German left, as the Sponsors' Association transformed into a more permanent forum called the Socialist League. Amid concern about creeping authoritarianism and disillusionment with electoral politics across Western Europe, the sixties New Left anxiously took shape.

Ossip K. Flechtheim and Futurology

After returning briefly to Germany as an adviser during the Nuremberg Trials, the émigré Flechtheim resumed his career as a political scientist at Bates College and Colby College in Maine. There he grappled with cultural isolation, skepticism about the future of socialism, and his Jewish wife Lili's reluctance to return to the country that perpetrated the Holocaust.[22] Although beset by personal and political uncertainty, Flechtheim's years in US exile from 1939 to

---

Weimarer Republik und Nationalsozialismus (Essen: Klartext, 2013); Kohut, *German Generation*; Barbara Stambolis, *Töchter ohne Väter: Frauen der Kriegsgeneration und ihre lebenslange Sehnsucht* (Stuttgart: Klett-Cotta, 2012); Fulbrook, *Dissonant Lives*; Wierling, "Generations as Narrative Communities"; Michael Wildt, *An Uncompromising Generation: The Nazi Leadership of the Reich Security Main Office* [2002], trans. Tom Lampert (Madison: University of Wisconsin Press, 2009); Sigrid Weigel, "'Generation' as a Symbolic Form: On the Genealogical Discourse of Memory since 1945," *Germanic Review* 77, no. 4 (2002): 264–77; and Weisbrod, "Generation und Generationalität."

21. In this chapter, SDS is used only for the Socialist German Student League.

22. Ossip was Jewish too, but he was more willing to distinguish between Germans and Nazis. See L. Flechtheim, "Emigration und Remigration," and Keßler, *Ossip K. Flechtheim*, ch. 2.

1951 allowed him to generate his main contribution to postwar intellectual history: a brand of critical utopian studies he called futurology.

Already in Geneva, just before emigrating to the United States, he had written a critique of Marx's teleological concept of history that emphasized instead the open-endedness of human action. Marx, whose work Flechtheim otherwise revered, defined social totality according to a goal of human emancipation that lay in the distant future. That end of history amounted to "a metaphysically contradictory utopia." History was essentially directionless, Flechtheim claimed, and no social order represented a higher stage relative to any other. Every society, regardless of how just or unjust, was scientifically equal. He warned that such historical relativism should not, however, lead to political resignation. Between the "optimistic dogmatism" of Hegel or Marx and the pessimistic historicism of someone like Arnold J. Toynbee, who introduced a popular theory of the rise and fall of civilizations, Flechtheim sketched out an alternative philosophy of history. Cautiously optimistic, he took into account the shifting nature of one's present standpoint and the possibility of futures that looked radically different from the past. In addition to highlighting "futures past" as evidence of historical contingency, he interpreted the present's own future visions as a factor that shapes our shared reality.[23]

As the Cold War developed, forecasting the future through statistical models, doomsday scenarios, and game theory became a lucrative industry in service of the great-power rivalry.[24] Increasingly Flechtheim considered it his duty as a political scientist to "save the future" from present geopolitical and socioeconomic determinations. He hoped to conduct a critical investigation of alternative futures in the name of socialist humanism.

He introduced the term "futurology" in his 1945 essay "Teaching the Future," which appeared in the *Journal of Higher Education*. Listing ancient prophets such as Cassandra and Renaissance prognosticators such as Nostradamus, he observed that thinking about the future had "been both the sacred preserve of the genius and the happy hunting ground of the charlatan." But he was careful to historicize the prophetic imagination. In the "relatively static age" before the bourgeois revolutions, social change proceeded so slowly that past, present, and future appeared as "basically identical, each constituting

23. O. Flechtheim, "Kritik der Marxschen Geschichtskonzeption." Cf. Arnold J. Toynbee's critique of "futurism" in *A Study of History*, abr. D. C. Somervell (New York: Oxford University Press), 515–26. On the Hegelian origins of the longitudinal concept of totality, which essentially was Flechtheim's target of critique, see Jay, *Marxism and Totality*, chs. 1–2. Cf. Koselleck, *Futures Past*.

24. See J. Andersson, *Future of the World*; Radkau, *Geschichte der Zukunft*; and Seefried, *Zukünfte*.

but a link in the endless chain of repetitious events which makes up the whole of human development." In the modern age of crisis and rapid change, however, "the future appears to be basically different from the past." The advance of secularization, rationalization, and technological progress had enabled people of Flechtheim's day, "for the first time in human history, to attempt what might be called a scientific prognosis": neither idle speculation nor positivist projection of present conditions into the future, but an evaluation of all possible scenarios and a determination of the most likely course of events. "Instead of consulting the stars," he proclaimed, "the 'futurologist' of 1945 can get his clews [sic] from historians and sociologists, from philosophers and psychologists, from political scientists and economists." Futurology should constitute an interdisciplinary field of research that drew on an array of authorities from G.W.F. Hegel to Johan Huizinga.[25]

The teacher of futurology, Flechtheim stipulated, must be "a truly creative scholar with a wide socio-cultural background and a vital interest in the forces of our age." For their part, students of futurology must learn to either "adapt themselves with a sense of responsibility to the historically and culturally inevitable or withstand it individually with knowledge and personal conviction."[26] Flechtheim's own commitment to antifascist resistance and revolutionary socialism during his youth might suggest that he preferred withstanding injustice rather than adapting or resigning oneself to it.

He edited a textbook called the *Fundamentals of Political Science* in 1952 that integrated his futurological ideas into the categories of a nascent discipline. Flechtheim described the political scientist's main object of inquiry, the polity, as "the realm of today and tomorrow, not that of eternity or the remote future." One should beware thinking "what happened in the past or what is happening in the present is all that is possible." Even while studying harsh political realities, cool-headed statesmanship, and the tragic dilemma of politics versus ethics, students of political science must entertain the possibility of a postpolitical society in which rational consent to expert guidance takes the place of government: "Then, and only then, would political power vanish from the earth"— and presumably also political science.[27]

25. O. Flechtheim, "Teaching the Future," 460 and 461. He first mentioned the term "futurology" in 1943 in a footnote to his essay "Toynbee and the Webers," *Phylon* 4, no. 3 (1943): 248–64 (at 248n2).

26. O. Flechtheim, "Teaching the Future," 465.

27. O. Flechtheim, *Fundamentals of Political Science*, iv, 9, 11, 19, and 25. It is unclear whether he actually desired such a postpolitical society or only identified it as the hypothetical limit of political science. For a later critique of postpolitics, see Rancière, *Disagreement*. On Abendroth's recommendation, a German edition of Flechtheim's textbook appeared under the title

Flechtheim liked thinking in counterfactuals and posing speculative alternatives. The "past does not predetermine the future," he wrote, and indeed if anything it was the other way around: awareness of possible futures may influence both our interpretations of the past and our decisions in the present. The final part of the *Fundamentals* textbook bore the portentous title "Utopia or *1984*." Like many people of his generation, Flechtheim viewed the midcentury moment as a crisis of civilization. As wars persisted, the threat of atomic bombs grew, and society underwent constant upheaval, two alternatives to the status quo had arisen: totalitarianism and a "third force." He claimed that communism and fascism both functioned as totalitarian secular religions that threatened further descent into barbarism. In the case of communism, at least, an originally emancipatory movement had degenerated into an authoritarian dystopia. That was ostensibly what George Orwell had in mind when he wrote his novel *Nineteen Eighty-Four* (1949). Flechtheim's antitotalitarian alternative, the third force, encompassed instead all "dynamic, democratic, and humanist movements." Hearkening back to the Popular Front, he admitted that his vision of a progressive coalition lacked the "clear-cut and unequivocal" ideology of fascism or communism. But for that reason, the third force's diverse components offered the best response to the crisis. Only the third force could realistically avoid the dystopia of "extreme affirmation of power" and the utopia of "its total rejection."[28]

Trying to popularize futurology among scholars in the United States, Flechtheim circulated a manifesto to leading intellectuals there, such as the writers Aldous Huxley and Thomas Mann, the scholar Lewis Mumford, and the sociologist Pitirim Sorokin. It did not meet with enthusiasm. Huxley, who wrote the dystopian novel *Brave New World* (1932), replied that any futurology should be accompanied by what he called eternitology: "It is not much use knowing what is likely, given present circumstances, to happen, unless one has clear ideas about man's Final End, in the light of which those tendencies and their probable outcome can be evaluated."[29] By that time Huxley had also written a book on mysticism, *The Perennial Philosophy* (1945), which might explain his skepticism of Flechtheim's plan for rational prognoses. Despite such rebuffs, futurology's Final End had not yet come into view. It would take twenty years for the new science to break through to a wider audience.

Grundlegung der Politischen Wissenschaft (Meisenheim am Glan, Germany: A. Hain, 1958). See Flechtheim to Abendroth, October 7, 1953, IISG, Abendroth Papers, 77.

28. O. Flechtheim, *Fundamentals of Political Science*, 38 and 551–55.

29. Quoted in Keßler, *Ossip K. Flechtheim*, 80.

In 1952 Flechtheim returned from exile to accept a job at the German Academy for Politics, which soon transformed into the Otto Suhr Institute at the Free University. Working in West Berlin, he published a compendium of documents and analyses of the German party system since 1945 and would go on to edit a nine-volume book on the subject. He also researched the history of world communism. In the mid-1960s, he returned to the subject of futurology, sometimes in collaboration with his friend Robert Jungk.[30] Futurology would finally resonate with the utopian sensibilities of the sixties generation. The young intellectuals of the West German New Left found futurology attractive not because of its theoretical novelty, but because it combined social critique and political engagement. Flechtheim later wrote that futurology "must try to merge prognosis, planning, and philosophy of the future into a new unity in which the philosophy of the future includes the politics and pedagogy of the future."[31] Reminiscent of the Brazilian theorist Paulo Freire's influential work *The Pedagogy of the Oppressed* (1968), Flechtheim's fusion of philosophy, politics, and pedagogy meant transforming left theory and practice. In reorienting the West German youth away from stagnant party politics and hierarchical learning environments and toward new organizational forms, Flechtheim had an ally in the Marburg political scientist Abendroth.

Wolfgang Abendroth and Antagonistic Society

If Flechtheim looked to the future for inspiration, Abendroth sought to redeem the socialist past. The philosopher and Abendroth's postdoctoral advisee Jürgen Habermas once described how he "lives in a consciousness that relentlessly makes the past present," treating the events of the 1920s and 1930s as if the newspapers reported them just a moment ago. For a recent scholar, Abendroth was also a forerunner and "political pedagogue" of the sixties New Left.[32] His dual role as redeemer of the past and forerunner of the future made Abendroth a symbolic figure for neoleftism in Europe.

His wartime odyssey involved serving in a German penal battalion, defecting to the Greek Resistance, doing time as a British prisoner of war in Egypt, and undergoing democratic "reeducation" in England. He returned to Germany in 1946 and settled in the Soviet occupation zone. After brief stints as a

30. For example, see Jungk's foreword to O. Flechtheim, *History and Futurology*.

31. O. Flechtheim, *Futurologie*, 9.

32. Jürgen Habermas, "Partisanenprofessor im Lande der Mitläufer: Der Marburger Ordinarius Wolfgang Abendroth wird am 2. Mai sechzig Jahre alt," *Die Zeit*, April 29, 1966, and Heigl, *Oppositionspolitik*.

professor of jurisprudence in Halle, Leipzig, and Jena, he grew disillusioned with Communism and even came to fear for his life. At the end of 1948, he fled to the West in the middle of the night along with his wife Lisa and their one-year-old daughter.[33] But those travails did not weaken his socialist convictions.

Eventually he secured a position as professor of political science at the University of Marburg. There he challenged the majority conservative and often ex-Nazi faculty by introducing a curriculum that featured left-wing perspectives. He defined politics more broadly than Flechtheim as "each social activity that either wants to change the structure of society (and thus the distribution of power among social groups in society) or to stabilize it through the exercise of power." Because politics referred to "a specific form of social behavior," Abendroth argued, political science constituted "a special discipline of the science of society, political sociology."[34] This methodological stance enabled him to develop the concept of antagonistic society, which applied a Marxist critique to the legal and political institutions of the Federal Republic of Germany.

Political sociology combined theory and practice and required a certain partisanship in its approach. Abendroth welcomed controversy: scholars could approach objectivity only through debate with others and reflection on their own subjective viewpoints. He echoed his friend Flechtheim's preoccupation with futurology when he described political sociology's "maximum approximation of objective knowledge and actual comprehension of the political process in its historicity and directedness toward the future." Such an understanding derived from Abendroth's commitment to a "socialist and democratic humanism" based on "a critically renewed Marxism."[35]

He supervised dissertations in a research program designed to expand scholarship on and public awareness of working-class resistance to Nazism. Like other veterans of the antifascist new left such as Fritz Erler, he lamented West Germans' limited understanding of the anti-Nazi resistance. The public did commemorate the attempt by military officers to assassinate Hitler on July 20, 1944, but paid less attention to the widespread and more enduring resistance by socialists. Abendroth's students produced a remarkable body of

33. L. Abendroth, "Die Flucht." See also the various books by Andreas Diers and Uli Schöler. Hardly any scholarship on Abendroth exists in English.

34. Wolfgang Abendroth, "Politische Wissenschaft als politische Soziologie" [1966], in *Antagonistische Gesellschaft*, 9–13 (at 10).

35. W. Abendroth, 12, emphasis removed. The Marburg School distilled this approach to political sociology into a textbook edited by Abendroth and Kurt Lenk, *Einführung in die politische Wissenschaft* (Bern: Francke, 1968).

scholarship on that and related themes. During the 1950s and 1960s, the so-called Marburg school of political science curated the heritage of the antifascist generation. These young scholars commemorated and critically evaluated the history of the divided workers' movement, the struggle against fascism, and the postfascist renewal of the left.[36]

In a 1957 lecture series on Marxist political theory, Abendroth suggested that a moment of unity recurred in the history of the left whenever the Hegelian roots of Marx's and Engels's idea of totality were rediscovered. One such Hegel revival occurred in the 1920s, when Georg Lukács and Karl Korsch published their classic works of Marxist humanism and scholars in Moscow, Frankfurt, and elsewhere delved into the early works of Marx.[37] Unity of Marxist thought across national divides paved the way for international unity of action, Abendroth claimed, especially during economic crises like the Great Depression. The rise of fascism and the suppression of dissent in the Soviet Union prevented that interwar Hegelian consensus from amounting to much: its progenitors either fell victim to the purges (e.g., David Riazanov), recanted (Lukács), or went into exile (the Frankfurt School).[38]

According to Abendroth, another chance at unity occurred immediately following World War II. A consensus in favor of socialism or some form of planned economy existed in occupied Germany and most of Europe from 1945 to 1948. But conservative elites and Cold War geopolitics nipped that chance at socialism in the bud. He elaborated on this idea of Germany's missed chance in his studies of the constitutional development of the Federal Republic. The occupation powers, he claimed, had suppressed genuine democratic forces in postwar Germany. A twin process of Stalinization in the East and authoritarian restoration in the West stifled hopes for both democratic socialism and German national unity.[39]

36. See Wolfgang Abendroth, "Der deutsche politische Widerstand gegen das 'Dritte Reich'" [1964], in *Antagonistische Gesellschaft*, 518–33. From 1954 to 1976, Abendroth's doctoral students included Rüdiger Altmann, Arno Klönne, Reinhard Kühnl, Hans Manfred Bock, Frank Deppe, and Georg Fülberth. This Marburg school should not be confused with the homonymous revival of neo-Kantian philosophy at the turn of the twentieth century.

37. See Jay, *Marxism and Totality*, ch. 2, and P. Anderson, *Considerations on Western Marxism*, ch. 2. Another Hegel revival took place in France during the 1940s. See Mark Poster, "The Hegel Renaissance," *Telos*, no. 16 (1973): 109–27, and *Existential Marxism*.

38. Lectures on "Die politische Theorie des Marxismus," University of Marburg, Summer 1957 and Winter 1957–58, IISG, Abendroth Papers, 365–367.

39. Wolfgang Abendroth, "Die verfassungspolitische Entwicklung des Bundes" [1957], in *Antagonistische Gesellschaft*, 48–61. See also the interview transcript "Versäumter Sozialismus"

Abendroth thought that the Federal Republic harbored a contradiction between its political form of democracy and its material basis as an antagonistic society. Real social inequalities belied the constitutional ideal of civil equality. That contradiction was expressed in the Basic Law itself, which enshrined the right to private property (Article 14) alongside the possibility of nationalizing land, natural resources, and other means of production (Article 15).[40] One of the Basic Law's redeeming qualities, according to the Marburg school, was that it did not define the future character of Germany's social order. None of its articles guaranteed capitalism. The nationalization provision of Article 15 (*Vergesellschaftung*) could be interpreted as a legal anticipation of socialism. Given the description of "a democratic and social federal state" in Article 20, Abendroth pointed out that the Basic Law "reckons instead with a long period of transformation of existing society into one of social democracy and therefore has opened the lasting constitutional possibility of an ever more social intervention into the order of property."[41]

Abendroth anticipated objections by liberal critics who feared the power of an overbearing state. The alternative lay not between the individual and the state, he explained, but rather between multiple social groups, all vying for political power. For him, the liberal rule of law (*Rechtsstaat*) did not contradict the idea of a welfare state (*Sozialstaat*). In fact, "equality before the law" (Article 3.1) could be fully realized only through greater social equality. He interpreted the legal contradiction between Articles 14 (private ownership) and 15 (public ownership) as justifying the role of an interventionist state that may steer society toward democratic socialism.

But to describe this argument as "the legal road to socialism," as does the historian Jan-Werner Müller, risks missing Abendroth's point.[42] The Basic Law provided a framework for socialist politics in West Germany, but laws alone would never suffice for a new social order. "The mere fact of the

---

in the radio series *Unter uns gesagt* on Bayerischer Rundfunk, July 30, 1962, IISG, Abendroth Papers, 712.

40. Abendroth, "Verfassungspolitische Entwicklung," 58–59. He drew on the arguments of several Weimar-era scholars: the historian Arthur Rosenberg and the legal philosophers Hermann Heller and Hugo Sinzheimer.

41. Wolfgang Abendroth, "Zum Begriff des demokratischen und sozialen Rechtsstaates im Grundgesetz der Bundesrepublik Deutschland" [1954], in *Antagonistische Gesellschaft*, 109–38 (at 119). On Abendroth's role in the debate over "the social *Rechtsstaat*," see Caldwell, *Democracy*, ch. 2. See also John P. McCormick, *Weber, Habermas, and Transformations of the European State: Constitutional, Social, and Supranational Democracy* (New York: Cambridge University Press, 2007).

42. J.-W. Müller, "1968 as Event," 21–23.

existence of a democratized parliamentary constitution," he wrote in 1954, "offers no guarantee for peaceful further development into a democratic society."[43] In an antagonistic society, one could never trust the ruling class to respect the law and not rely on violence in an emergency. Abendroth and his students thought that the only guarantee of democracy was extraparliamentary action inspired by a unity of theory and practice.

Beyond Social Democracy

Before they developed a radical praxis for the postwar era, Flechtheim and Abendroth had to free themselves from political and ideological association with Social Democracy. The position of left socialists within the SPD had grown weaker since the defeat of the factory codetermination movement in 1951–52, the death of the charismatic party leader Kurt Schumacher, and the consolidation of Christian Democratic hegemony after the 1953 federal elections.[44] As discussed in the previous chapter, the SPD executive board voted in 1954 to revise the party program. It soon became clear to left socialists on the program committee, such as Abendroth, that the party leadership favored the anti-Marxist modernizers and, if necessary, would use illiberal means to ensure their success.

In response to the SPD's electoral defeats, Flechtheim and Abendroth proposed strengthening the party base, continuing to expose the authoritarian tendencies of West German society, and mobilizing outside of parliament through labor actions and mass demonstrations on the model of England's antinuclear Aldermaston marches (called Easter marches in West Germany).[45] The SPD leadership decided on the opposite course: leaving the party base alone, tolerating the Federal Republic's authoritarian tendencies, attracting more middle-class voters, and enlarging the parliamentary faction through state and federal elections. The history of Social Democracy encompassed diverse activities organized by trade unions, benefit societies, choirs, sports clubs, youth leagues, reading groups, and of course the mass party itself. By

43. Wolfgang Abendroth, "Demokratie als Institution und Aufgabe" [1954], in *Gesammelte Schriften*, 2: 407–16 (at 412), emphasis removed.

44. On the general history of German Social Democracy, see Grebing, *Geschichte der deutschen Arbeiterbewegung*; Potthoff and Miller, *Social Democratic Party of Germany*; and Klotzbach, *Der Weg zur Staatspartei*.

45. See Holger Nehring, "Demonstrating for 'Peace' in the Cold War: The British and West German Easter Marches, 1958–1964," in *The Street as Stage: Protest Marches and Public Rallies since the Nineteenth Century*, ed. Matthias Reiss (London: Oxford University Press, 2007), 275–93.

transitioning to what the British Marxist Ralph Miliband called parliamentary socialism, the modernizers wanted to make electoral campaigns predominate over all other activities.[46]

Never having shared the party leadership's faith in parliament, Abendroth worried that too much focus on attracting voters and winning elections would distract from the structural transformation of society. As a result, left politics might degenerate into "mere ad campaigns."[47] For him, elections served only as a guarantor of democratic pluralism, not an end in themselves. So long as the economy continued to grow, the SPD could safely function as one democratic party among others. But should an economic crisis like the Great Depression happen again, he warned, fickle voters would switch allegiances to totalitarian parties. By providing a clear alternative to existing capitalist society, the SPD had in the past and would again in the future transform into "the center of attraction for the broad masses."[48]

After the SPD's defeat in the 1957 election, a seven-person commission undertook organizational reforms. They restructured the party by expanding the influence of the parliamentary faction. Local decision making was subsumed under provincial (*Land*) control in an effort to better coordinate campaign strategy at all levels. In Abendroth's interpretation, the reforms signaled a transfer of power from the party's grass roots and middle levels to the professional politicians at the top. A key figure behind these organizational reforms was the ex-Communist leader Herbert Wehner, whose involvement in Stalinist intrigues during the 1930s would never be forgotten by people like Abendroth. The "de-democratizing effect" of the reforms also favored social liberals in the party such as Heinrich Deist and Willy Brandt. Abendroth claimed that these modernizers wanted the "de-politicization of party debate" and the watering-down even of traditional Social Democratic reformism.[49]

---

46. Miliband, *Parliamentary Socialism*.

47. W. Abendroth, "Demokratie als Institution," 413. His remark about ad campaigns referred specifically to capitalist interest groups in league with the CDU. But clearly he viewed the tendency as dangerous for the SPD too. For Flechtheim's critique of CDU campaign finance, see "Politische Entwicklung und Finanzierung der CDU," *Die Neue Gesellschaft* 5, no. 3 (1958): 182–89.

48. Wolfgang Abendroth, "Warum Parteiprogramm?," *Die Neue Gesellschaft* 3, no. 4 (1956): 283–91 (at 288).

49. Wolfgang Abendroth, "Die Diskussion in der deutschen Sozialdemokratie nach der Bundestagswahl 1957" [1958], in *Gesammelte Schriften*, 3: 222–25. See Gary Roth's review of Christoph Meyer's 2006 biography of Wehner, "Roth on Meyer, 'Herbert Wehner: Biographie,'" H-Net, H-German, November 2008, https://networks.h-net.org/node/35008/reviews/45590/roth-meyer-herbert-wehner-biographie.

He expressed disdain for the SPD's program draft. It failed to expose the "class nature and class structure" of West Germany, he complained. In bourgeois society, "only the workers, their unions, and their political parties embody democracy to its full extent, and through their struggle against the class domination of finance capital only they could . . . fill democratic constitutional norms with vital content." Democracy on paper was not safe from authoritarian and often ex-Nazi bureaucrats. What the program draft lacked and desperately needed was a historical critique of state power that went beyond humanistic platitudes.[50] Flechtheim echoed his friend's concerns when he described the program discussions as "long-winded [and] insufficiently concrete."[51]

The status of Marxism caused the most controversy. Already in 1954 with the founding of the party's theoretical journal, *Die Neue Gesellschaft*, Abendroth had to defend the continued viability of Marxism. He took an immediate dislike to the journal's young editor Ulrich Lohmar, a leader of the nascent SDS and doctoral student of the sociologist Helmut Schelsky. Lohmar aligned himself with the party's right wing and set about attacking Social Democracy's Marxist heritage. In answering these attacks, Abendroth insisted that "Marxism is not a dogma but rather a social scientific method." He admitted that the viability of Marxism did pose a problem worthy of discussion, but Lohmar seemed to prefer "that kind of 'discussion' which threatens to invalidate the . . . loyalty of comrades who are [simply] mistaken and which endangers the party as well as the future of socialism and democracy." Misrepresenting Marx's class analysis and hounding Marxists in the party, as Lohmar had allegedly done, created a witch-hunt atmosphere that corrupted internal party democracy.[52]

In 1958 Abendroth published an article dedicated to the question: Is Marxism obsolete? Several areas of Marx's and Engels's thought had come under attack in the 1950s during West Germany's economic boom, including the concepts of alienation, totality, and class struggle. Drawing on Lukács and the Western Marxist tradition, Abendroth demonstrated how the basic problem of alienation remained relevant as a framework for interpreting both the worker's separation from the means of production and the individual's isolation in

50. Wolfgang Abendroth, "Arbeiterklasse, Staat und Verfassung: Kritisches zum Programmentwurf der SPD," *Die Neue Gesellschaft* 6, no. 1 (1959): 42–45 (at 44).

51. Ossip K. Flechtheim, "Zur Grundsatzdebatte: Langatmig—zu wenig konkret," *Berliner Stimme*, March 28, 1959.

52. Wolfgang Abendroth, "'Ethischer' Sozialismus, Marxismus und Demokratie: Eine sozialdemokratische Antwort an Gerhard Weißer und Ulrich Lohmar" [1955], in *Gesammelte Schriften*, 2: 580–83 (at 581).

modern society. Nuclear armament and other technological advances worsened the alienation already inherent in capitalism by turning man-made destruction of the world into a very real possibility. As for the concept of totality,
he supplemented Lukács by observing that postwar concerns such as decolonization and the Cold War made a global perspective on social totality even
more necessary. Marxist method provided a means of explaining isolated
events in terms of their global and social significance.[53]

One of the chief theoretical challenges to Marxism was Schelsky's model
of a leveled middle-class society. For adherents of that model like Lohmar, the
postwar era of capitalist prosperity negated the Marxist premise of an antagonistic society riven by class conflict. The bourgeoisie and proletariat had supposedly dissolved into a single, amorphous middle class. But Abendroth cited
several factors that belied that argument. Drawing on the US sociologist
Mills's popular book, *The Power Elite* (1956), he observed that the tendency
toward centralization of power in the hands of elites had accelerated. The "new
middle class" of technicians and administrative personnel in fact constituted
an enlarged working class, which Abendroth labeled jobholders (*Arbeitnehmer*). He used this label differently than the drafters of the SPD's Godesberg
program, where jobholders appeared as a euphemism for middle-class consumers. In his definition, everyone who worked for a salary or wage and did
not own the means of production (or earn income from stock dividends, like
managing executives) was a jobholder. Contrary to theorists of a managerial
revolution such as James Burnham, Abendroth argued that the functional divide between managers and owners did not change the essence of class struggle. Advanced capitalism was structured differently than the capitalism of
Marx and Engels's day, he conceded, but its essence of class conflict remained
the same. Marxist method always grappled with new phases of capitalist development. Insisting on the reality of social antagonisms, Abendroth portrayed Schelsky's model of a leveled middle-class society as an ideology of
classless society—a caricature of Marx's own future vision. In the grips of such
an ideology, citizens of an antagonistic society blinded themselves to real
divisions.[54]

While left socialists like Abendroth and Flechtheim tried to show the ap-
plicability of Marxist method to advanced capitalism, they lamented the SPD's

53. Wolfgang Abendroth, "Ist der Marxismus 'überholt'?" [1958], in *Antagonistische Gesellschaft*, 347–63. The Marxist economist Fritz Sternberg argued that capitalism had materially
unified the globe, allowing local crises to assume cataclysmic proportions as they reverberated
through world markets. See Renaud, "Sternberg in Amerika."

54. W. Abendroth, "Ist der Marxismus 'überholt'?" Cf. Ossip K. Flechtheim, "Über Marx
hinaus?" *Vorwärts*, June 26, 1959.

conformity to prevailing economic and political norms. In a critique published just before the 1959 party convention, Abendroth contrasted the Social Democratic tradition of robust party programs with the new program of "assimilation and resignation." By switching allegiance from the working class to the middle class—or by disavowing class entirely—the program broke with tradition. He accused the drafters of the Godesberg program, most of whom also belonged to the antifascist generation, of forgetting the key experiences of their youth: the interwar crisis, the collapse of the Weimar Republic, the division of the workers' movement, and its defeat by fascism. Their "neoliberal pipe dreams [neoliberale Wunschträume]" and lip service to freedom ("for whom?" he asked) did nothing to combat capitalism; they even helped it.[55] He sneered at the friendly echo that the program draft received in the mainstream press. Pandering to "the illusions of the average voter" in West Germany during a period of economic growth, the program "obscures and flattens" the differences between the political parties, making the SPD essentially the same as the CDU or the Free Democratic Party. Social Democracy's program should offer voters a real alternative, Abendroth believed. Instead it renounced the working class and welcomed a free-market economy. Any future success by the party of democratic socialism, he predicted, would occur not because but in spite of the program.[56]

Although he had previously avoided open conflict with the party leadership, preferring instead to keep a foothold within the SPD, Abendroth's frustration with the modernizers led to more provocative behavior. Just before the Godesberg convention he published an alternative program. In contrast to the modernizers' program, which began with a poetic list of hopes, fears, and core values, Abendroth's counterprogram began with an analysis of "the social situation in the capitalist-organized part of the world." The picture he painted was dire: monopolization, centralization, concentration of power into the hands of elites, neocolonialism, endless preparation for war, and a looming descent into barbarism. To avoid catastrophe, industrialized countries had to rein in the chaos of the market through democratic planning. Aside from state intervention in the economy, Abendroth's counterprogram called for participatory democracy that went beyond mere electoral participation. The SPD and trade unions were ideally situated to foster the development of a healthy,

---

55. Wolfgang Abendroth, "Ein Programm-Entwurf der Anpassung und Resignation," *Sozialistische Politik* 6, no. 10 (1959): 1–2 (at 2).

56. W. Abendroth, 2. He later provided historical background for his theory of Social Democratic assimilation in the short book *Aufstieg und Krise*. Flechtheim picked up on the theme in his article "Die Anpassung der SPD."

extraparliamentary opposition. Direct political action outside the halls of parliament would sustain the democratic citizenry against reactionary forces.[57]

Abendroth thought that the SPD should also focus on redressing inequalities in the education system. From the Basic Law's norm of equality and democracy's need for a citizenry capable of critical thought, he derived a model of higher education freed from financial dependence on the market. He called for more socialist or progressive faculty appointments to counteract the conservative mandarins, who by and large had discredited themselves under the Nazi regime. For him, freedom of scholarly opinion meant freedom *from* the conformist and restorationist tendencies of the Federal Republic. Likewise, he understood freedom of the press as freedom from usurpation by corporate mass media, an argument that aligned closely with the 1962 book by his postdoctoral advisee Habermas, *The Structural Transformation of the Public Sphere*. Abendroth's counterprogram promised that a democratically controlled media would enable public discussion and rational debate.[58]

Although the counterprogram may have rallied left socialists who opposed social democratic modernization, it did not alter the fact that by the time of the Godesberg convention in November 1959 they constituted an isolated minority. Out of hundreds of votes cast, the left socialists mobilized just sixteen against the adoption of the new program. After losing that battle, they tried to survive as an oppositional wing based on their assumption of internal party democracy. Their only remaining allies were the socialist youth. Around 1960, however, the SDS diverged from the party mainstream. Together with their left socialist mentors, members of the SDS moved beyond social democratic modernization to embrace neoleftism.

Community of the Expelled

Most left socialists wanted to remain in the party at all costs. They bitterly recalled their experience of sectarianism and isolation during the 1930s. But the transformation of Social Democracy after Godesberg made the task of internal opposition more difficult. Looking to capitalize on the momentum generated by the new program, the party leadership started to censure all perceived manifestations of radicalism. What began as a manageable if heated rivalry developed after 1959 into open conflict between the anti-Marxist

---

57. Wolfgang Abendroth, "Aufgaben und Ziele der deutschen Sozialdemokratie. Programmentwurf 1959" [1959], in *Antagonistische Gesellschaft*, 407–28.

58. See Habermas, *Structural Transformation*, which quotes Abendroth on pp. 226–27. On the relationship between Abendroth and Habermas, see Specter, *Habermas*.

majority and the recalcitrant Marxist minority. For the latter, the problem of renewing the left within existing party and union organizations turned into a question of building a new left outside them.

In May 1959, the chairman of the SDS Oswald Hüller organized an event in Frankfurt called "Congress for Democracy—Against Restoration and Militarism." Abendroth, Flechtheim, and other left socialists were invited to address hundreds of enthusiastic delegates from a range of youth groups on the subjects of West German rearmament, militarism, NATO, and authoritarian restoration. Unanimously the speakers denounced the policies of Konrad Adenauer's government and by implication the SPD's own pragmatic overtures to the CDU. The SPD leadership had not authorized the congress, which involved several groups sponsored by the party. It strongly disapproved of the event's critical tone and even suspected that some SDS members wanted to manipulate the party youth by Communist means. One of the keynote speakers was incredibly Ruth Fischer, the former ultra-leftist leader of the German Communist Party in the mid-1920s who turned virulently anti-Communist in the 1940s but now, after the Khrushchev Thaw, again identified herself with the radical left.[59] A far-left faction around the magazine *Konkret* that included Ulrike Meinhof, the journalist and later terrorist outlaw, did in fact maneuver behind the scenes.[60] Meinhof had studied pedagogy and psychology at the University of Marburg from 1955 to 1957 in the same building as Abendroth's lectures on Marxism and antifascism, which she occasionally attended. There her political ideas matured as she absorbed the left socialist critique of West German authoritarianism.[61]

Social Democrat leaders' frustration with the radical students prompted calls for the creation of a rival student organization loyal to the party. Chaos resulted in the SDS. Hüller was voted off the executive board, and the remaining student leaders distanced themselves from Meinhof and the *Konkret* gang. The SPD considered these measures satisfactory for the moment, but some party leaders continued to lobby for a new organization to replace the renegade SDS. In May 1960 they got their wish when students loyal to the party founded their own Social Democratic Collegiate League. A minority of SDS members voted to dissolve into the rival group. Party leaders took the next logical step that July, when they cut off funding to the SDS and demanded that

59. See Keßler, *Ruth Fischer*.

60. For summaries of the congress, see Fichter, *SDS und SPD*, 274–77, and Albrecht, *Der Sozialistische Deutsche Studentenbund*, 325–30.

61. See Ditfurth, *Ulrike Meinhof*, 91, and Alois Prinz, *Lieber wütend als traurig: Die Lebensgeschichte der Ulrike Marie Meinhof* (Frankfurt am Main: Suhrkamp, 2012), 80.

all its members join the Social Democratic Collegiate League. Relations between the party and the radical students were officially broken off.[62] The young generation on the left was now divided between modernizers loyal to the party and radicals aligned with the Marxist left socialists.

Over the next year, the SDS struggled financially but succeeded in developing an independent theoretical and political line. Older left socialists stepped up during this time of need. They functioned as gurus who mentored SDS circles in various cities throughout West Germany. Most belonged to the antifascist generation and transmitted their experiences of interwar politics to this new generation of militants. Through their mediation, a student leader later recalled, "the roughly 20 SDS university groups adopted—at first still quietly—the mostly forgotten left theories and utopias of the Weimar period."[63]

In October 1961, several hundred supporters of the SDS gathered in Frankfurt to found the Socialist Sponsors' Association of Friends, Patrons, and Former Members of the Socialist German Student League, known simply as the Sponsors' Association (Förderergesellschaft). Abendroth was elected chairman, and Flechtheim sat on its board of trustees. The former considered it his duty "not to abandon the most important social force at German universities, the SDS, and thereby put students tending toward socialism at risk of slipping into sectarian trains of thought or being influenced by Stalinist-influenced forces." Without support, he reasoned, the students might fall under Communist influence or drift into ineffectual anarchism. The Sponsors' Association, which consisted of trade unionists, academics, and other intellectuals dissatisfied by Social Democrat leaders' "misguided" policy, would help the SDS pursue an autonomous socialist course.[64]

The next month, party leaders passed a resolution that decided the issue once and for all. "Membership in the Socialist Sponsors' Association," they declared, "is irreconcilable with membership in the German Social Democratic Party, as it is also irreconcilable to be both a member of the SDS and of the [party]."[65] Irony seems to have been lost on Social Democrats like Erler and Waldemar von Knoeringen, who now undertook the same disciplinary measures used by the party in the 1930s against their former selves, the young militants of the antifascist new left.[66] In the early 1960s, the newest militants

62. Albrecht, *Der Sozialistische Deutsche Studentenbund*, 330–34 and 389–90.

63. Fichter, *SDS und SPD*, 18 and 244, and Brown, *West Germany and the Global Sixties*, 90.

64. Wolfgang Abendroth to Erich Ollenhauer, October 13, 1961, quoted in Fichter, *SDS und SPD*, 346.

65. Quoted in Fichter and Lönnendonker, *Kleine Geschichte des SDS*, 69.

66. See Erich Schmidt, *Meine Jugend in Groß-Berlin*, 125–31.

were allegedly Leninists, Trotskyists, Stalinists, and Titoists—all at once. According to a former student leader, the Social Democrats' resolution owed to "a growing intolerance in the SPD executive board for leftist intellectuals" of any kind.[67]

As the Sponsors' Association's chairman, Abendroth was immediately expelled from the party. Flechtheim resigned two months later along with several other left socialists. "We do not identify ourselves with every step taken by the SDS," they explained, but "the expulsion of the SDS members and sponsors establishes in itself both a failure to recognize the principles of academic freedom and an injury to the internal party democracy demanded by the Basic Law [Art. 21.1]."[68] Flechtheim and his comrades could not tolerate the party's heavy-handed treatment of dissidents within its ranks.

The SDS and Sponsors' Association now stood outside the only purportedly socialist party in West Germany. Moreover, expulsion from the SPD made it nearly impossible for socialists to get jobs in SPD-affiliated unions. After choosing to remain in the SDS after the irreconcilability resolution, the theorist Oskar Negt for example could no longer teach at union academies: only a university career remained open to Marxist intellectuals like him.[69] Together, the SDS holdouts and their left socialist backers formed a community of the expelled. They developed a cross-generational consciousness of working against the current of existing society. Under the mantra "The critical intelligentsia must get out of the party!"[70] the expellees moved toward a new left.

Students for a New Left

During the lean period of 1961–64, radical young intellectuals and older left socialists alike struggled to find new languages and organizational forms to counter what they perceived as the growing authoritarianism of West

---

67. Fichter, *SDS und SPD*, 345 and 351.

68. Quoted in Fichter, *SDS und SPD*, 352–53. See also O. Flechtheim, "Zur Frage der innerparteilichen Demokratie," and Flechtheim, "Gedankenfreiheit in Parteien bedroht? Führungsgremium strafen abweichende Meinungsäußerungen und Kritik oft mit dem Ausschluß," *Westdeutsches Tageblatt*, January 8, 1962. For news coverage of the expulsions and resignations, see for example "Sind unbequem: SPD-Führung schließt SDS-Anhänger aus," *Berliner Zeitung*, November 8, 1961, and "Geist und Macht," *Der Spiegel*, December 13, 1961.

69. Negt, *Erfahrungsspuren*, 108 and 264–65. Despite having quit the SPD, Negt writes in retrospect that "My whole life I have remained a Social Democrat by constitution" (265).

70. Fichter, *SDS und SPD*, 69. For more on the history of the SDS, see Andrea Wienhaus, *Bildungswege zu "1968": Eine Kollektivbiografie des Sozialistischen Deutschen Studentenbundes* (Bielefeld, Germany: Transcript, 2014).

Germany. Amid controversies surrounding the government's plan for emergency laws and the 1962 *Spiegel* affair involving the CDU's illegal reprisal against a media outlet, Abendroth wrote of the "de-liberalization of the Federal Republic" and Flechtheim of "emergency: a cement bunker for our government."[71]

In the late summer of 1962, members of the Sponsors' Association discussed the possibility of expanding their activity beyond moral and material support for the students. Heinz Brakemeier and Heinz-Joachim Heydorn in particular wanted to formalize the Association into an alternative left organization that might recruit a broader membership. Not everyone agreed. Flechtheim told Abendroth that he thought such "an expansion of the activity of the Sponsors' Association should have no success and indeed could probably even do harm." Given that the SPD had gained votes relative to the CDU in the 1961 federal election, left socialists' previous thesis that the Godesberg program would weaken the party had proven false. "In this situation," he wrote in an explicit allusion to the antifascist splinter groups of the 1930s, "work only makes sense if it occurs in the most intimate of circles. Quality, not quantity!" Despite his sympathy for militant members who wanted to engage in direct action, Flechtheim thought that the Sponsors' Association should stick to its original goal of supporting the students and fostering public enlightenment.[72]

By that October, however, advocates of expanding the Association's activity won out. Brakemeier and Heydorn proposed a new name for the organization that included the term "New Left," but other members including Abendroth decided on something less antagonistic to the old left: the Socialist League.[73] Abendroth still thought of himself as representing "the left within the left" in the spirit of Rosa Luxemburg, Karl Liebknecht, and other early Communists who remained "at first totally isolated" within existing socialist organizations

---

71. Wolfgang Abendroth, "Die Entliberalisierung der Bundesrepublik und der politische Funktionswandel des Bundesverfassungsgerichts" [1961], in *Arbeiterklasse, Staat und Verfassung: Materialien zur Verfassungsgeschichte und Verfassungstheorie der Bundesrepublik*, ed. Joachim Perels (Frankfurt am Main: Europäische Verlagsanstalt, 1975), 166–69, and Ossip K. Flechtheim, "Notstand—ein Zementbunker für unsere Regierung," *Westdeutsches Tageblatt*, October 29, 1962.

72. Ossip K. Flechtheim to Wolfgang Abendroth (Marburg), August 20, 1962, DNB, NL Flechtheim, EB 98/179.

73. Ossip K. Flechtheim to Wolfgang Abendroth (Marburg), October 1, 1962; Abendroth to Flechtheim (Berlin-Dahlem), October 11, 1961; and Fritz Lamm (Stuttgart) to Abendroth, November 1, 1962; all DNB, NL Flechtheim, EB 98/179. On the origins of the Socialist League, see Negt, *Erfahrungsspuren*, 265–69.

before finding a mass base outside them.[74] Abendroth wrote in 1963 that the radical students of "a new left" (still lowercase with an indefinite article: *eine neue Linke*) should not sever themselves from all that seemed old in the socialist movement. If they did that, then SDS members risked losing valuable assets from a radical tradition. The students needed to learn from the antifascist generation. Abendroth called for generational cooperation between the Socialist League and the SDS in order to maintain the continuity of German new lefts. In this partnership, older left socialists would act as transmitters of the antifascist tradition. The sixties New Left, he concluded, needed both historical consciousness and a real social base in order to transform society.[75]

The biggest problem for any new left, Abendroth claimed, was that fascism and the conservative Federal Republic had decimated working-class consciousness. Contrary to what sociologists like Schelsky claimed, this lack of class consciousness did not mean that there were no more antagonistic classes. Ideology, repression, and compromise accounted for why working people either accepted class divisions as a natural fact or did not themselves feel oppressed. Having lived through Nazism and Stalinism, Abendroth understood why many young people wrote off the workers as a lost cause. Instead of abandoning them, however, he proposed that a new left should focus on reawakening working-class consciousness.[76]

Abendroth stayed true to the formula of critical intellectuals plus reawakened workers, but Flechtheim imagined alternative modes of organization. Observing the civil rights movement in the United States and decentralized citizens' campaigns such as the antinuclear Aldermaston marches in Britain, he reevaluated the relationship between party, movement, and pressure group in the early 1960s. Single-purpose movements enlisted diverse sectors of the population in typically short-term manifestations of grassroots democracy. Most importantly, through direct action, social movements liberated themselves from the monopoly exercised over left politics by the parties and unions of the working class.[77] Flechtheim urged the burgeoning new left to examine

74. Wolfgang Abendroth, "Aufgaben einer deutschen Linken," in Horst Krüger, ed., *Was ist heute Links? Thesen und Theorien zu einer politischen Position* (Munich: P. List, 1963), 130–57 (at 134).

75. Wolfgang Abendroth, "'Alte' und 'neue' Linke" [1963], in *Gesammelte Schriften*, 3: 557–62. See also Fichter, *SDS und SPD*, 18 and 244.

76. See Wolfgang Abendroth, "Die gegenwärtige Situation und die Aufgaben des SB" [1963], in *Gesammelte Schriften*, 3: 567–74, and "Die Aufgaben der jungen Intelligenz im Klassenkampf" [1963], in *Gesammelte Schriften*, 3: 595–600. On the need for partnership between workers and intellectuals, see Abendroth's only book translated into English, *European Working Class*.

77. Ossip K. Flechtheim, "Partei, Bewegung, Pressure Group" [1962], in *Zeitgeschichte und Zukunftspolitik*, 59–78. Martin Klimke highlights the role of the political scientist Michael Vester

the history of radical antifascism, which provided examples of small groups and communities of progressive action.[78] By exposing the limits of the West German party system, he prompted student organizations like the SDS and social movements like the peace movement to form an extraparliamentary opposition. This opposition would comprise informal clubs, public demonstrations, and associations for all oppressed people.[79]

Flechtheim's thinking about alternative forms of organization was influenced by his expanded concept of the proletariat, which included many more people than just workers in economically developed countries. He argued that only in the underdeveloped Third World could one still find those pariahs with nothing to lose and everything to gain whom Marx and Engels had identified as the proletariat. If the agents of emancipatory politics included postcolonial workers and peasants, then a nascent new left in Europe might look there for innovative models of nonviolent, nonconformist, and extraparliamentary opposition.[80] The high number of Third World foreign students in West Germany helped realize Flechtheim's vision by radicalizing German students, building anti-imperialist solidarity, and proving that militant young people could make a difference.[81]

The jurist and political scientist Jürgen Seifert argued in 1963 that the term "new left" caught on so quickly because it was not organizationally hardened like "social democracy" or "democratic socialism" or "communism," which were inseparable from existing parties and unions. A new left stood for the renewal of forces both inside and outside the old organizations of the left.[82]

---

in forging ties between the American and West German student movements. Vester promoted the US civil rights tactic of nonviolent direct action in articles such as "Die Strategie der direkten Aktion." See Klimke, *Other Alliance*, ch. 1, and Hanshew, *Terror and Democracy*, 90–92. On the role of transnational social movements in the formation of the sixties New Left, see Horn, *Spirit of '68*; Nehring, *Politics of Security*; and Brown, *Sixties Europe*.

78. O. Flechtheim, "Die neue Linke." See also Flechtheim's review of several books by Abendroth's doctoral students about the antifascist small groups, "Sekte oder politische Kraft?" *Die Zeit*, November 12, 1965.

79. Fichter and Lönnendonker, *Kleine Geschichte des SDS*, 73–77.

80. O. Flechtheim, "Die neue Linke." See also Christoph Kalter, "From Global to Local and Back: The 'Third World' Concept and the New Radical Left in France," *Journal of Global History* 12, no. 1 (2017): 115–36; Robert Gildea, James Mark, and Niek Pas, "European Radicals and the 'Third World': Imagined Solidarities and Radical Networks, 1958–73," *Cultural and Social History* 8, no. 4 (2011): 449–71; and B. R. Tomlinson, "What Was the Third World?" *Journal of Contemporary History* 38, no. 2 (2003): 307–21.

81. See Slobodian, *Foreign Front*.

82. Seifert, "Die Neue Linke." The aforementioned article by Flechtheim, "Die neue Linke in der neuen Welt," was a response to Seifert. Cf. Wolfgang Abendroth, K. Graf Moltke, and

Especially in West Germany, however, the mid-1960s saw a gradual shift in terminology from an indefinite new left (*eine neue Linke*) to the proper name New Left (*die Neue Linke*). That shift symbolized how a dynamic process of renewal could give way to a fixed identity. Despite its historical roots and its association with left socialists and older theorists such as Marcuse, the New Left in the late 1960s would become identified exclusively with the youth.

The links between postwar and interwar radical theory nevertheless endured. For most scholars, a classical place for such links was the Frankfurt School. Indeed, some of the most prominent SDS members like Hans-Jürgen Krahl studied at the Institute for Social Research and radicalized the brand of critical theory they learned there. Thus it is fair to state that "West German students with little or no personal memory of the Nazi period encountered the early works of Georg Lukács, Karl Korsch, and others, as well as the still-evolving thought of the Institute's own faculty. As such the Frankfurt School was a living connection to a Weimar-era left that had been utterly destroyed under Hitler."[83] While valid, such a statement about the Frankfurt School's influence on the New Left neglects to mention the equally important contributions by left socialists like Flechtheim and Abendroth. The latter two in fact provided a more actionable political critique than the cultural and aesthetic theory of Max Horkheimer and Theodor W. Adorno.[84] Unlike left socialists, Adorno for example abandoned emancipatory politics in the late 1960s for fear of renewed totalitarian violence.[85]

Between 1966 and 1970, Flechtheim and Abendroth joined the political theorist Iring Fetscher to edit a book series, Political Texts, with the European Publishing House in Frankfurt. Titles included Luxemburg's *Political Writings*, Franz L. Neumann's *The Democratic and Authoritarian State*, Korsch's *Marxism and Philosophy*, Auguste Blanqui's *Instructions for an Armed Uprising*, and a widely shared volume on interwar theories of fascism.[86] In addition to their

---

Lelio Basso, *Für eine neue linke sozialistische Bewegung* (Frankfurt am Main: Sozialistischer Bund, 1964).

83. Spaulding and Boyle, "Hans-Jürgen Krahl." See also Demirović, *Der nonkonformistische Intellektuelle*, 856.

84. Cf. Demirović, who claims that Horkheimer's and Adorno's seminars imbued students with a lasting commitment to uniting theory and practice in their everyday lives, whereas Abendroth at Marburg supposedly "separated his own political-theoretical position more strictly from his academic work." *Der nonkonformistische Intellektuelle*, 478n413.

85. See Adorno and Marcuse, "German Student Movement," and Wiggershaus, *Frankfurt School*, 609–36.

86. W. Abendroth, *Faschismus und Kapitalismus*. On the popularity of this book, see Frei, *1968*, 242n19.

participation in campaigns against nuclear weapons, emergency laws, and the Vietnam War, left socialists helped write the sixties radical curriculum.[87]

The mid- to late 1960s also saw a renaissance of futurology. Flechtheim accounted for this new interest by observing that the Federal Republic otherwise lacked "an antenna into the future." He presented futurology as a compendium of theories developed by the antifascist generation, including social democratic modernizers alongside their left socialist critics. Noting that a futurology club had cropped up during the Prague Spring in 1968, Flechtheim considered the critical study of utopias and dystopias the logical accompaniment of what the Czechoslovak leader Alexander Dubček called socialism with a human face.[88]

Futurology appealed to West German students not only because their appetite for theory was insatiable. It also expanded their horizon of possibility by making alternative futures an object of scholarly analysis. Enthusiasm for futurology did lead to a great deal of skepticism in the mainstream press: "Are futurologists charlatans?" asked Die Zeit, for example.[89] Animated by their utopian imagination, young neoleftists were eager to preempt the charge of charlatanry without adopting the adult attitude of sober realism. Flechtheim's new science offered them one way of pulling that off, but there were other ways. As the next chapter will show, the history of the sixties New Left resembled one protracted search for a method.[90]

87. Besides editing book series, left socialists contributed regularly to radical journals such as Das Argument and Neue Kritik. See Brown, West Germany and the Global Sixties, 90–91. On Abendroth's participation in the Club Voltaire and the Republican Club, see Heigl, Oppositionspolitik.

88. Flechtheim, Futurologie, 15, 64, 162, 195–98, and 300. Flechtheim's 1972 book Futurologie was dedicated to Abendroth and included praise for Löwenthal's 1946 book Jenseits des Kapitalismus. For Flechtheim's earlier forays into futurology, see the 1966 collection History and Futurology. Cf. Erik Olin Wright, Envisioning Real Utopias (London: Verso, 2010), which unfortunately does not reference Flechtheim's pioneer work.

89. Claus Grossner, "Sind Futurologen Scharlatane? Zukunftsforschung ohne Zukunft," Die Zeit, November 21, 1969. See also Von Dirke, "All Power to the Imagination!"

90. Cf. Sartre, Search for a Method. In his related work, the formidable Critique of Dialectical Reason, vol. 1, Sartre analyzed at an abstract level the processes by which individuals form "practical ensembles." He dwelled on the way that "groups die and disintegrate, . . . ossify, become stratified and return into more general socialities" (254). For example, organizational phases of the workers' movement could be understood according to his theory as passive series, active fused groups, or institutions, all flowing back into each other (678–710). With its attention to organizational form and bureaucratic hardening, Sartre's critique was a recognizably neoleftist project. See Thomas R. Flynn, Sartre: A Philosophical Biography (Cambridge: Cambridge University Press, 2014), ch. 13.

8

The Sixties New Left

WHAT LINKED INTERWAR and postwar new lefts was a shared approach to organizational form. Continuities in the content of neoleftist politics certainly existed across the decades: radical democracy, cultural experimentation, sexual liberation, anticolonial solidarity, and so on. But it was its form of spontaneous collective action, or at least the attempt to create such a form, that made neoleftism recognizable as a long-term phenomenon. Parties, unions, and any sort of institutionalized politics would accordingly appear obsolete to radicals in the 1960s. They knew that emancipatory parties or unions could degenerate into bureaucratic apparatuses. In West Germany, France, and elsewhere in Europe, the dramatic events around 1968 turned on the issue of how to organize. Specifically, how could the new radicals mobilize without resorting to the sort of hierarchical leadership and bureaucratic control that soured them on previous left politics? In a prefigurative way, the new radicals believed that the means they chose for practicing left politics now—that is, the organizational forms they adopted—would determine the ends of the movement. For the sixties New Left, the movement itself was the revolution.

This final chapter presents the anti-authoritarian New Left of the 1960s as the culmination of a dynamic process of midcentury neoleftism. It focuses on two prominent sixties radicals who always put organizational problems first and grappled with the neoleftist dilemma. In West Germany, Rudi Dutschke was keenly aware of the neoleftist tradition. He wrote his doctoral dissertation on the early Georg Lukács after himself having tested the limits of Leninist modes of organization within the SDS. In the late 1960s, he became the leading spokesman of the West German extraparliamentary opposition. His counterpart in France was Daniel Cohn-Bendit, who helped start the student revolt at the University of Paris at Nanterre in the fall of 1967. Campus activism eventually snowballed into the popular uprising of May 1968. A massive general strike amalgamated students and workers. For a few weeks of exuberant anarchy, a Western European new left came as close to seizing power as one would ever get. The tandem history of Dutschke and Cohn-Bendit, whose temperaments diverged widely, brings the sixties New Left into focus. Both militants looked to new lefts past in order to chart a course for the future movement.

Rudi Dutschke and Subversive Action

To place Dutschke and Cohn-Bendit at the center of this chapter does uphold a tired scholarly convention. Historians of the sixties and the student movement in particular tend to privilege the perspective of leading male intellectuals. The most exciting new scholarship corrects that imbalance by foregrounding "the other '68ers": women, conservative students, older people, and people living outside the major cities.[1] Nonetheless, the two main leaders of the West German and French student movements, respectively, play a key role in the argument of this book. Through his study of Marxist theory and the history of the left, Dutschke consciously broke from old forms of organization and tried to construct new forms calibrated to the postindustrial society and global entanglements of postwar Europe.

Consideration of Dutschke's East German background and his university studies does challenge other conventions. First, books by Hans Kundnani, Dirk Moses, and others treat the postwar youth's response to the Nazi past and their parents' complicity in it as the catalysts of the sixties New Left's social critique. The Nazi past certainly did influence the young generation's opposition to "fascistic" tendencies, but it was not the whole story. Dutschke's path is typical for many neoleftists who sought mainly to break away from traditional party politics and overthrow the capitalist and imperialist structure of existing society. Relitigating the Nazi past was not their priority. As important as the Frankfurt Auschwitz trials and other reckonings with Nazism were, it would be a mistake to conceive of the German New Left solely as "part of the family drama of post-Nazi reconstruction."[2]

Second, surveys of the 1960s in Europe and North America tend to place more emphasis on countercultural rebellion, which succeeded in weakening some conservative values, than on political revolt, which failed completely.[3] As spokesman for a social movement, Dutschke combined the heritage of the antifascist new left with an anti-authoritarian politics based on a radical

1. For example, see Hodenberg, *Das andere Achtundsechzig*; Siegfried, *1968*; and Von der Goltz, "Other '68ers in West Berlin."

2. Neaman, *Free Radicals*, 4. See also Kundnani, *Utopia or Auschwitz*, and Moses, *German Intellectuals*.

3. See the classic study by Arthur Marwick, *Sixties*. See also Von Dirke, *"All Power to the Imagination!"*

reading of Frankfurt School critical theory. This combination had organizational consequences inside the SDS and, after 1966, in the loosely defined Extraparliamentary Opposition (APO). For the New Left across Europe, counterculture was inseparable from politics. Just as for Lukács during Central Europe's revolutionary crisis around 1918–19, the problem of organization in the 1960s merged cultural, aesthetic, and political forms.

Dutschke was born in 1940 in a small Brandenburg town south of what would become East Berlin. He grew up as the son of a postal official in the German Democratic Republic. He did well in school and excelled at sports, becoming a star decathlete. Significantly for his later career, young Dutschke was a devout Christian and participated actively in the local Protestant community. His earliest political stance derived from a fusion of his religious faith and the Marxist-Leninist ideology he absorbed as a member of the Free German Youth. While contradictory in some respects, such religious socialism was not unusual in the former Prussian lands. For example, the New Beginning group had included members of the League of Religious Socialists, such as Erich Kürschner. The East German regime meanwhile tolerated the churches so long as they did not interfere in politics.

Dutschke underwent a conversion at the age of sixteen when he heard about the Soviet invasion of Hungary. Like heterodox Communists in Western Europe, he could not reconcile the revolutionary rhetoric of state socialism with its counterrevolutionary actions. Out of personal conviction, he declared himself a pacifist and conscientious objector when the National People's Army instituted the draft. This dissident act was tolerated, but it did prevent him from getting his high school diploma on time and enrolling in college to study sports journalism as planned. Instead he entered vocational training in industrial business management. In 1960 he traveled to West Berlin to attend high school and finish his diploma requirements. After that, in his first brush with the Axel Springer media company, he took a job at the tabloid *B.Z.* Sensing which way the wind was blowing, he decided to move permanently to West Berlin in August 1961, just three days before the border closed and construction on the wall began. In his second political act, Dutschke protested the Berlin Wall and declared himself a political refugee.

He began studies at the Free University that winter, where he concentrated on sociology, history, and philosophy. He read the German and French existentialists, the young Marx, Frankfurt School critical theory, and crisis theology. That last subject he pursued at the urging of the American theology student Gretchen Klotz, whom he would marry a few years later. Although he never totally lost his Christian faith, Dutschke did trade the religious socialism of his adolescence for Marxist humanism. He also forged a link in the neoleftist chain by taking courses with the political scientist and former New Beginning leader Richard Löwenthal. From Löwenthal he learned about Leninist strategy, the Bolshevik one-party state, and Soviet development policy in the Third World.[4] After completing an undergraduate degree, Dutschke received a stipend for graduate studies and was hired as a research assistant at the Free University's Eastern Europe Institute. He would remain at the university through the late 1960s.

But Dutschke's radicalism unfolded outside the seminar room. He fell in with an eclectic band of militants that called itself Subversive Action. In Munich, the bohemian prankster Dieter Kunzelmann, along with Frank Böckelmann, Rodolphe Gasché, and several others, founded the group in 1963. They wanted to start "a wave of micro-rebellions" that would unsettle the genteel norms of West German society.[5] Even the fascist-sounding abbreviation for the group, SA, was meant as an ironic provocation (SA was also the abbreviation used for the Nazi Storm Detachment, Sturmabteilung, also known as the brownshirts). Kunzelmann has been described as "one of the most scintillating, intriguing, controversial, and in many ways repugnant figures of the youth rebellion of the 1960s." He published pirate editions of Wilhelm Reich's books on sexual liberation and put Situationist ideas into practice while a member of the avant-garde artist collective SPUR.[6] SA reached beyond Munich to set up discussion circles in Frankfurt, Stuttgart, and West Berlin. Drawn especially to Herbert Marcuse's critique of one-dimensional society, members of SA read and intensely debated Frankfurt School critical theory. They also sought ways to translate their theoretical debates into direct action. SA members adopted the persona of *Homo subversivus*, or the subversive human who transforms old values into new values at the vanguard of a cultural revolution. The group named its journal *Anschlag*, a word that meant either a public notice or an assassination attempt.

Dutschke joined the West Berlin section of SA along with his friend Bernd Rabehl, another militant student originally from the East. These two did the most to bridge the gap between SA and the SDS, which since its expulsion from the SPD in 1961 had operated as an autonomous organization. Collaboration between the two groups was tense. At first SA wanted to infiltrate the SDS and steer its politics in a more radical direction. In that respect, SA conspirators operated much as the Org and early New Beginning group had when

4. Rudi Dutschke, Studienbücher 1961–69, HIS, NL Rudi Dutschke, RUD 110.2.

5. Reimann, *Dieter Kunzelmann*, 97.

6. Neaman, *Free Radicals*, 24–26. See Jacopo Galimberti, "The Spur Group, *Détournement* and the Politics of Time in the Adenauer Era," *Oxford Art Journal* 39, no. 3 (December 2016): 399–419.

they entered the Social Democratic and Communist parties in the 1930s. But in 1965, Dutschke and Rabehl abandoned that tactic and decided to openly join the SDS, effectively merging the two organizations. SA members brought to the SDS experience in civil disobedience and public disruption, which they had learned from the French Situationists and Dutch Provos. The SDS provided the SA with access to a wider base of students and an opportunity to trade conspiratorial methods for an open strategy of grassroots mobilization.

The merger of SA and the SDS immediately brought organizational questions to the fore. Dutschke was elected to the SDS political advisory board. He quickly rose to prominence within the group owing to his public-speaking ability and fluency in Marxist theory. Along with Rabehl, he pushed the SDS in a more anti-authoritarian and anti-imperialist direction. Kunzelmann and Böckelmann were opposed to joining a larger organization. They worried that SA would lose its autonomy as an avant-garde. Dutschke and the pro-SDS faction began to suspect that Kunzelmann was plotting a challenge to the group. After an SA conference in April 1965, from which Dutschke was absent, the majority decided to expel Kunzelmann, Böckelmann, and Marion Steffel-Stergar for "unsolidary and contemptible behavior."[7] For his own part, Kunzelmann was happy to leave a group that he now considered dogmatic and beholden to revolutionary fantasy. "The metaphysics of revolution must finally land in the dustbin of history," he declared, "because it has nothing to do with Marxism." He also criticized Dutschke's obsession with Third World liberation movements: "Their struggle is our struggle, but we must not mistake their tasks for ours."[8] Although the characters were different, this whole episode seemed to replay the Org's 1935 schism and reconstitution as New Beginning.

The former SDS member Christian Riechers was a scholar of council communism and the work of Antonio Gramsci. He wrote to Dutschke in June 1965 about the organizational problems facing the student movement. Riechers wondered "how long groups like yours can last, because there must certainly be definite organizational crystallizations in order to practice long-term, transformative politics." The existing parties and unions of the left offered no possibilities for transformative action. The present situation, Riechers thought, seemed to require "a type of organization that—in order to be effective—must immediately disintegrate into its individual components." That indeed was the

---

7. Minutes of the Munich "Konzil," HIS, NL Dutschke, RUD 210.04.

8. Dieter Kunzelmann (Munich) to Rudi Dutschke, September 21, 1965, HIS, NL Dutschke, RUD 151.06.

neoleftist dilemma, and it is fitting that a scholar of historical leftism should have recognized it. Social transformation required a disciplined political movement capable of sustaining action over the long term. But traditional modes of organization tended to obstruct internal democracy: sustained action would become coordinated, controlled, and directed from above. For Riechers, the danger of bureaucratic sclerosis loomed large. Dutschke made a note to himself to reread the letter, and he highlighted the phrases "organizational crystallizations" and "organizational forms."[9]

A core group of SDS theorists met regularly in West Berlin from 1965 to 1967 to discuss matters of organization. Minutes from a May 1966 meeting referred to the situation of the SDS as it transitioned "into an independently functioning socialist organization after the break from the SPD." Amid that transition, the SDS must evolve into a new form. No longer could it rely on the structure of a traditional party, with a national leadership committee, dedicated officers, and local branches conforming to a central party line. Since no revolution seemed imminent in the advanced capitalist world, the minutes recounted, the SDS must focus on developing an analysis of capitalist contradictions, raise consciousness of socialism, and explore possibilities for supporting anticolonial struggles in the Third World. Its organization should decentralize and expand outward, encompassing a range of marginalized groups beyond students and industrial workers. Those at the meeting called repeatedly for an "autonomous organizational form" but never specified what that might look like.[10]

Rabehl thought that the task for the New Left in general was to preserve Marxist theory and utopian sensibilities for a time when objective forces were more favorable for revolution. For the moment, therefore, members of SA and the SDS should remain "sectarians" and undertake actions aimed at internal bonding rather than external influence.[11] The leftist lawyer and SDS counsel Horst Mahler agreed, but he also proposed building a network of small groups across the country. Through such a leftist network, mass action might eventually become possible. His plan resembled the underground strategy of radical antifascists inside Nazi Germany: according to New Beginning, for example, a committed minority should survive and prepare to assume leadership positions in the coming revolutionary crisis. Stressing the primacy of organization,

9. Christian Riechers to Rudi Dutschke, June 14, 1965, HIS, NL Dutschke, RUD 151.05.

10. Meeting minutes, "Betrifft Arbeitskreis Verhältnis von Theorie und Organisation. Dutschke, [Hansmartin] Kuhn, [Horst] Kunitzky, Rabehl," May 19, 1966, HIS NL Dutschke, RUD 210.08.

11. Bernd Rabehl to Dieter Kunzelmann, March 9, 1965, HIS, NL Dutschke, RUD 151.06.

Mahler tried to explain why the left faced a dilemma unlike anything faced by the right (an ironic point given his later conversion to the far right): "The right can always rely on the default state and social structures of capitalist society. The right can limit itself to integrating the masses into these default structures. . . . Through these power structures, social and political controversies are broadly institutionalized." By contrast, a new left must prepare the masses "to organize outside the bourgeois power structures."[12] In other words, new lefts, unlike new rights, had to invent democratic forms that countered the hierarchical, inegalitarian, and disenfranchising institutions of existing society. He hinted at a growing awareness among West German radicals of the neoleftism dilemma.

They cultivated that awareness by studying the history of antifascism and reading the interwar Western Marxists. Going to the source of this lost tradition, the newly married Dutschke and Klotz traveled to Hungary for their honeymoon in 1966 in order to meet Lukács. With him they discussed revolution in general and the 1920s in particular. Afterward Dutschke wrote Lukács a letter that connected West Germany's lack of revolutionary theory to its lack of new organizational forms. "The basic difference between Lenin, the 1920s, and today," he claimed, is "that today we can no longer proceed from the dialectical identity of socioeconomic processes and sociopolitical revolution." Dutschke might have been showing off here, but his rendezvous with Lukács did coincide with the latter's reexamination of his own leftist past during the years 1918–21.[13]

The Dutschke couple also cultivated ties with Karola and Ernst Bloch, who had played a key role in the development of Marxist humanism. Karola wrote to say that "meeting with you and the revolutionary youth meant for me a meeting with my own youth."[14] Such encounters between the sixties generation and interwar Western Marxists were frequent. SDS members such as Hans-Jürgen Krahl studied directly with the Frankfurt School luminaries Theodor W. Adorno and Max Horkheimer. Through encounters like these, the

---

12. Horst Mahler, "Anmerkungen aus der Sicht des Jahres 1966," addendum to "Die Aufgaben der sozialistischen Linken in Westdeutschland" (1962), HIS, NL Dutschke, RUD 210.08. Both Mahler and Rabehl belonged to a number of left radicals who, after supporting far-left terrorism during the 1970s, ended up supporting neo-Nazis and the far right. See Wagner, *Die Angstmacher*, and Seitenbecher, *Mahler, Maschke & Co.* Cf. Weiß, *Die autoritäre Revolte.*

13. Rudi Dutschke (West Berlin) to Georg Lukács, March 31, 1967, HIS, NL Dutschke, RUD 151.09. See chapter 1. Dutschke's dissertation would focus on Lenin, Lukács, and early debates in the Comintern: Dutschke, *Lenin auf die Füsse.*

14. Karola Bloch (Tübingen) to Rudi Dutschke, February 5, 1968, HIS, NL Dutschke, RUD 152.01.

concepts of alienation, reification, culture industry, and authoritarian personality came to serve more radical ends than their creators presently wished: Jürgen Habermas claimed for example that Horkheimer kept copies of the interwar journal *Zeitschrift für Sozialforschung* locked away in the basement of the Institute for Social Research, lest students read it and draw dangerous conclusions.[15] Marcuse was the only affiliate of the Frankfurt School to expressly identify with the New Left.

The previous chapter mentioned an event hosted by the Free University's student government in July 1967. Panel discussions accompanied two keynote lectures by Marcuse, who was visiting from his home university in California. He traveled widely and, to his occasional embarrassment, was fêted as the gray eminence of a global new left.[16] Other speakers at the event included the student activists Dutschke, Peter Furth, Wolfgang Lefèvre, Peter Gäng, René Mayorga, and Bahman Nirumand. The professors who participated were Löwenthal, Jacob Taubes, Alexander Schwan, and Dieter Claessens. They discussed the postwar affluent society, violent and nonviolent resistance, differences between opposition movements in Europe and anticolonial struggles in the Third World, and whether the New Left needed a concrete plan for a liberated society.

In these discussions before a packed auditorium, the problem of organization came up repeatedly. The main point of disagreement between the neoleftists Marcuse, Dutschke, and Furth and the social democratic modernizers Löwenthal and Schwan was the extent to which human emancipation could occur within the existing capitalist system. And if emancipation were impossible through the existing system, then should not neoleftists explain how to build an alternative? Löwenthal and Schwan believed that without a plan detailing the transition from capitalism to socialism and explaining how revolutionaries would deal with the complex problems of governmental administration and Cold War geopolitics, the student movement indulged in fantasy, or worse, nihilism. That is, if they could not design something better than the existing system, then young militants should work with the one they had. Liberal democracy was infinitely better than fascist or Stalinist dictatorship, Löwenthal advised. Marcuse countered that no concrete program could be formulated in advance. To do so would be just as hopelessly utopian as the modernizers' belief in gradual improvements. Within a culture of total affirmation, he argued, the opposition must take the form of total negation: antiwar, anti-imperialism, anti-capitalism, anti-establishment. This politics of negation

---

15. Wiggershaus, *Frankfurt School*, 544.
16. See Kellner, *Herbert Marcuse*, ch. 9.

was a process of creative destruction. For example, the antiwar struggle against a society that sends young people off to fight in imperialist wars already contains a positive vision of a peaceful, liberated society. Marcuse believed that such "negative" movements would figure out the details along the way.[17]

The discussants used the Canadian-American economist John Kenneth Galbraith's concept of the affluent society to describe the social conditions of North America and Western Europe since the 1950s: highly industrialized, technologically advanced, privately wealthy, but publicly poor.[18] Marcuse claimed that the affluent society had the capacity to provide abundant material goods and services for its entire population. It failed to do so because of political, cultural, and class-based obstructions. Specifically, decisions about investments and distribution were not made democratically but rather by technocratic administrators in service of capitalist class interests. The formal institutions of liberal democracy such as voting, free speech, and an impartial judiciary were subsumed under an illiberal technocracy.

In his most widely read book of the time, *One-Dimensional Man* (1964), Marcuse described the effects of mass consumer culture on individuals' psychological development. Technocratic society sustained itself, he argued, by reproducing the kind of human being whose desires conformed to a single, homogeneous mass culture. Freedom in capitalist democracies was limited to choices circumscribed by a fixed frame of possibilities. The American dream of owning a house and a car (or multiple cars) defined freedom in general as individualized suburban consumer freedom. And even that was deceptive. Although we may think that choosing between Coke or Pepsi makes us free, Marcuse might have said, we are actually one-dimensional humans who cannot *not* desire soft drinks. Consumer choice is a control mechanism. Through the compound desires that condition our everyday life, or what later theorists inspired by Freud called the libidinal economy, we undergo forms of repression that do not manifest as obvious material scarcity. Quite the opposite: sodas for everyone, but nobody is free to live differently. Likewise, free speech reinforces one-dimensional society when it permits us to voice our crazy opinions without ever challenging the system. In another widely read text, Marcuse called this latter phenomenon repressive tolerance.[19]

---

17. Marcuse, *Das Ende der Utopie.* See also the full text of one of Marcuse's lectures, "Das Problem der Gewalt in der Opposition," under the title "Ziele, Formen und Aussichten der Studentenopposition," *Das Argument* 9, no. 45 (1967): 398–407. For his critique of positive thinking, see Marcuse, *One-Dimensional Man*, chs. 6–7.

18. Galbraith, *Affluent Society.*

19. Marcuse, "Repressive Tolerance."

Against such insidious and even totalitarian conformity, Marcuse imagined what it might mean to live differently. He sympathized with the sixties counterculture whose motto "turn on, tune in, drop out," regardless of its psychedelic connotation, acknowledged the need for a new way of life. The early Lukács had shown that creating a new culture was a revolutionary political task. Soviet experiments in socially engineering "the new man" also proved this, sometimes with bad results. In any case, Marcuse and the young neoleftists knew the political stakes of counterculture.

A distinctive feature of the new culture was its rebellion against authority. Löwenthal accused neoleftists of wanting to dispense with all forms of authority: organizational hierarchy, technical-scientific expertise, parental responsibility, democratic leadership, and so on. Marcuse countered that the New Left did not (or should not) desire an anarchist rejection of authority as such. He distinguished between, on the one hand, rational authority directed toward freedom and, on the other, irrational or excess authority directed toward domination. The new culture must realize freedom against domination, but not against all kinds of authority. The way he interpreted rational authority made room for the creation of new forms of social and political organization that might sustain progressive action. He understood liberation in dialectical terms: not as something abstract and absolute, but something relative to existing forms of domination.[20]

Marcuse also redefined the collective agent of social transformation. For the old left, that agent had been the industrial working class. For social democratic modernizers, it was the undifferentiated middle class. But Marcuse had lost faith in industrial workers and expected nothing but conformity from the middle class. So he looked to the diverse array of socially unintegrated people: outsiders and racial minorities in the European and American metropoles and anticolonial resisters in the Third World. On a global scale, these marginal groups (*Randgruppen*) shared the same interest in overthrowing capitalism, imperialism, and bureaucratic communism. Marcuse explained, however, that the struggles of marginal groups in different places would vary in tactics. The enemy of anticolonial movements was clearly foreign imperialists or a native oligarchy in league with foreign capital, both of which must be confronted by armed resistance. But the metropoles lacked a clear-cut enemy and need for such naked violence. Instead, the New Left in advanced capitalist parts of the

20. See Christopher Connery, "The Dialectics of Liberation: The Global 1960s and the Present," in Chen Jian et al., *Routledge Handbook of the Global Sixties*, 575–88, and Sonja Levsen, "Authority and Democracy in Postwar France and West Germany, 1945–1968," *Journal of Modern History* 89, no. 4 (2017): 812–50.

world should develop tactics for refusing the "affirmative culture" that preached consumerism at home and imperialism abroad. Industrial workers, who historically engaged in antisystemic opposition, were now mostly integrated into the capitalist way of life. According to Marcuse's pessimistic view, one should not bother following the advice of left socialists such as Abendroth, who wanted the students to reawaken workers' class consciousness. The New Left should ally with militant workers whenever possible, but it should not expect much from that assimilated class. As he put it bluntly, "There are broad sectors of the population with whom any discussion is hopeless. It is a waste of time and energy to talk to these people. . . . One simply avoids talking to them because one knows that nothing will come of it."[21] In that broad category of deplorables, he included the leadership of the SPD.

Löwenthal was of course a social democratic modernizer. In a rhetorical move that was risky given his opponent's expertise in psychoanalytic theory, Löwenthal invoked Freud to argue that neoleftists suffered from a narcissistic discontent with civilization. If rational adaptation to industrial society yielded economic growth, full employment, and social welfare, he claimed, then it was worth the price of repression. Marcuse countered that even materially secure life in advanced capitalism, which certainly was not guaranteed for large sectors of the population, required an unnecessarily high degree of cultural and psychological misery. In other words, the Freudian scheme of civilization and its discontents must be historicized. Here in agreement with Wilhelm Reich, Marcuse suggested that repression under capitalist civilization was more intense than under prior (and perhaps future) modes of social organization: capitalism mutilated human sensibilities in a historically specific way.

The affirmative culture of advanced capitalism, he thought, obstructed critical debate and democratic decision making. Owing to the power of corporate media, consumer advertising, and law-and-order politics, the electoral strategy of the old left was inadequate. Winning power by amassing votes seemed to involve accommodating the desires of an existing majority rather than building support for social change. Periodic elections might be formally democratic and useful, Marcuse suggested, but on their own they failed to challenge the hegemonic way of life that propped up capitalist society. Electoral campaigns catered to the masses rather than transformed them. Because he considered the electoral party form insufficient on its own, he focused on "the underlying

---

21. Marcuse, *Das Ende der Utopie*, 67–68. Elsewhere he did remark that "In spite of everything that has been said, I still cannot imagine a revolution without the working class." Interview of Marcuse by Jean-Louis Ferrier, Jacques Boetsch, and Françoise Giroud, "Marcuse Defines His New Left Line," trans. Helen Weaver, *New York Times*, October 27, 1968, SM29.

population" (to use Thorstein Veblen's term) rather than eligible voters in an existing majority.[22]

Besides critiquing the limits of electoral democracy, Marcuse put forward a principle, echoed by Dutschke, that the New Left must articulate global aims. The Vietnam War loomed large in the sixties imagination. For American students, who would enter the draft after graduation, the stakes were real and immediate. But for Western Europeans, too, the war symbolized the injustice of US imperialism and the ongoing Cold War. Aside from the David-versus-Goliath framing of the Vietnamese anticolonial struggle, the thing that appealed most to militants in the metropoles was a new organizational form visible in Southeast Asia, Latin America, and Africa: the guerrilla unit. Guerrillas dated back to the early nineteenth century and the Spanish "small wars" against Napoleon, but only in the decades following World War II did guerrillas take the lead in a global war against imperialism. Of course, the guerrilla form was grounded in Third World agrarian struggles. It appealed to neoleftists because it nevertheless responded to a similar situation of asymmetrical power that they experienced under heavily policed capitalist democracies.

For understanding the dynamics of guerrilla movements and how the guerrilla form might function in urban metropoles, neoleftists turned to Che Guevara as their go-to theorist and revolutionary guru. In April 1967, Guevara famously spoke of opening up "two, three or many Vietnams" as multiple fronts in the anti-imperialist struggle.[23] The Bolivian student Mayorga quoted this phrase at the Free University event three months later, endorsing the idea of a guerrilla network of global confrontations as the organizational form that marginal groups should adopt everywhere. The guerrilla form destabilized state sovereignty, erased borders, and even mimicked the decentralized flow of capital itself. Guevara died in October of that year while coordinating rural and urban guerrillas in Bolivia.[24]

22. Marcuse, *Das Ende der Utopie*, 53. See Veblen, *Engineers and the Price System*. For Marcuse's critique of law-and-order politics, see *Essay on Liberation*, 49–55.

23. Guevara, "Message to the Tricontinental." Neoleftists tended to downplay the violence of guerrilla resistance. See Hosek, "'Subaltern Nationalism.'"

24. On the destabilizing effects of this political form, see Mao, *On Guerrilla Warfare*; Guevara, *Guerrilla Warfare*; and Schmitt, *Theory of the Partisan*. See also Robert V. Daniels, *Year of the Heroic Guerrilla: World Revolution and Counterrevolution in 1968* [1989] (Cambridge, MA: Harvard University Press, 1996). Dutschke's understanding of the urban guerrilla, the related theory of "focuses" (*focos*), and the image of a long march through the institutions owed a debt to the French philosopher and activist Régis Debray. See Debray, "Latin America," and Dutschke's foreword to Debray, *Der lange Marsch*.

West German protests against the Vietnam War started in earnest in 1966. It was during such antiwar demos that the students had their first serious run-ins with the police. Tensions mounted inside the SDS about the use of violence. University administrators began to treat every demo as a potential riot. Controversies over campus free speech had helped launch the US New Left a year before, and now the same debates came to Western Europe. In 1967 the Free University rector Hans-Joachim Lieber grew tired of Dutschke's activism and, in a petty but symbolic act, decided not to renew his assistantship.

The precarity of many students like Dutschke, who himself was a political refugee from the East and financially dependent on his university job, prompted the New Left to explore sustainable forms of solidary living. A subset of militants tried to build working communes that could survive outside the capitalist market. Communal living supposedly broke down habits of individualist consumption as well as patriarchal family structures. After being ousted from SA, Kunzelmann helped found the fabled Kommune I in West Berlin. Dutschke and Klotz considered joining him but decided against it, since the communards opposed all kinds of fixed relationship including a monogamous partnership.

If the commune was a way of living differently from the bourgeoisie, then the counteruniversity emerged as an alternative form of higher education. Radical students wanted to seize control of the curriculum. For that purpose, Dutschke edited a bibliography of texts on revolutionary socialism that included work by early utopian socialists, syndicalists, anarchists, Bolsheviks, Lukács, Korsch, Reich, and the Frankfurt School.[25] He visited the International Institute of Social History in Amsterdam and bookstores in New York City in order to acquire copies of texts from the interwar years, many of which the Nazis had banned and thus were still difficult to find in West Germany. These texts were then republished in pirate editions. Like the antifascist new left during the 1930s, Dutschke and the sixties New Left reshaped their country's intellectual terrain by smuggling in radical texts. The hunger for alternative literature in the counteruniversity also reflected neoleftists' poor opinion of Social Democratic culture, the only other source of literature on the left.

Critical or counteruniversities also emerged elsewhere. In October 1967, Italian students at the University of Trento issued a "Manifesto for a Negative University" that demanded alternative syllabi and seminars.[26] American

---

25. Dutschke, "Literatur des revolutionären Sozialismus." This bibliography appeared in several editions. On the alternative publishing scene, see Brown, *West Germany and the Global Sixties*, 146–52.

26. Stone, *Goodbye to All That?* 116. See also Horn, *Spirit of '68*, ch. 2.

students and radical faculty at Columbia University sought to develop new modes of behavior and organization "not burdened with policy commitments and patterns of operation inherited from the past."[27] But the campus revolts that occurred across Western Europe and North America were not insular phenomena. On the contrary, the creation of counteruniversities reflected the politicization of students and the entanglement of higher education in a broader social crisis.

With the formation of the Grand Coalition between Social Democrats and Christian Democrats in December 1966, the disillusionment of West German neoleftists with the SPD was complete. To make matters worse, one of the priorities of that government was to pass emergency laws that would suspend constitutional liberties in the event of a national crisis. The New Left and some Social Democrats, too, viewed the emergency laws as a threat to democracy that replayed Hitler's Enabling Act of 1933. To oppose them, Dutschke and the SDS called for the creation of an Extraparliamentary Opposition (APO). As the historian Elliot Neaman writes, "the ostracized SDS leaders launched the same critique, with the same political categories, against their elders, namely, party sclerosis and abandonment of the working class, which in their youth they had employed to critique the Stalinism of the 1940s." The SDS critique also resembled left socialist opposition to Social Democracy in the 1950s. The fact that the students repeated this midcentury critique of party sclerosis was not a paradox, as Neaman calls it, but rather the constitutive irony of historical new lefts.[28]

According to the political sociologist Karl A. Otto, the APO represented a "self-organized, collective, and political learning process, that was independent of the established organizations of the workers' movement and had deep animosity toward the structures of domination representing the 'establishment.'"[29] Dutschke encouraged those who identified with the APO to continue experimenting with organizational forms. "We are not just thirty or forty cranks anymore," he said, alluding perhaps to SA's conspiratorial past. "Here in the university we have an anti-authoritarian camp of 4,000 to 5,000 students," and that camp could run campaigns to reach a broader public.[30] He challenged his fellow students to break free from their self-imposed isolation and join with underprivileged groups outside the university. Not only did he

27. "AFT-ACSCP Joint Committee on a New Organization," n.d., Hoover, New Left Collection, 30/12.

28. Neaman, *Free Radicals*, 35. For contemporary critiques of the emergency laws, see Kogon et al., *Der totale Notstandsstaat*.

29. Paraphrased in Heigl, *Oppositionspolitik*, 13. See Otto, *Vom Ostermarsch zur APO*.

30. Quoted in Marcuse, *Das Ende der Utopie*, 72–73, 81, and 116.

want to expand the New Left's social base, he also wanted to sustain extraparliamentary opposition after students finished their degrees and exited the institutional framework of the university. The APO contained a contradiction between anti-authoritarian ideology and the need for stable organization.[31]

In a way, working within the university inhibited militant students from thinking seriously about how to organize. They would gather dependably in the cafeterias, sit together in lecture halls, debate each other in seminars, volunteer for the student government, and pursue courses of study prescribed from above. While the counteruniversity subverted that framework, it did not solve the problem of what to do when classes ended or after students graduated. Dutschke thought that the best way to ensure continuity in the opposition was to establish a system of democracy from below. Grassroots action committees need not be confined to the university.

Against the structural violence of a police state, he claimed, the APO needed to mobilize in swarms, demos, riots, and what today one might call flash mobs. Some neoleftists referred to such public disruptions as revolutionary counterviolence. The form of extraparliamentary opposition described by Dutschke broke with liberal norms and included the possibility of violence against property. When confronting the police, militants also risked suffering violence against themselves. For these reasons, Habermas accused radical students of flirting with "left fascism."[32] Given the social conditions of Western Europe at the time, however, participatory democracy and direct action were the only ways to create a situation of dual power: the power of the people versus the power of the state and its formally democratic institutions. Dutschke and his allies wagered that this extraparliamentary strategy might win popular support owing to the alienation that many citizens felt toward their political representatives. In mobilizing outside the university, workplace, and party, the APO pointed beyond existing institutions. The apparent formlessness of the APO masked its negation of all prior organizational forms. What gave it power was not outright physical violence or terrorism, but coercion exerted by bodies in the street, occupying public space.

Dutschke helped plan a street demo against a visit to West Berlin by the shah of Iran, whose authoritarian regime had originated in a US-backed coup.

---

31. Brown, *West Germany and the Global Sixties*, 243–44. Brown interprets this contradiction within the APO as the origin of the movement's later split into centralized K-Groups and decentralized Spontis. See also Kasper, *Spontis*.

32. Habermas used the term *Linksfaschismus* only once. It was in a heated moment at a public congress in Hannover on June 9, 1967, one week after the shooting of Benno Ohnesorg. While debating Dutschke and Krahl, he referred to the theoretical foundations of Dutschke's voluntarist ideology as "left fascism." Within a month or so, Habermas yielded to criticism and recanted. See Negt, *Die Linke antwortet Jürgen Habermas*.

At the demo on June 2, 1967, the student Benno Ohnesorg was shot by the policeman Karl-Heinz Kurras. Protests against Ohnesorg's killing continued over the next few days. Despite the risks of confronting police, Dutschke organized similar actions against the Vietnam War. But he devoted the most energy to a campaign against the Axel Springer media company, which published a number of right-wing tabloids. Aside from boycotts and calls to "expropriate Springer," this campaign involved zealous destruction of property: throwing stones through Springer windows, setting fire to newspaper stacks, and overturning delivery trucks.

In reading chronicles of 1960s protest actions, such as those compiled by Wolfgang Kraushaar, one gets a sense of spontaneity, fluid motion, rapid assembly then dispersal, condensation then evaporation. But to speak of the New Left as "not organizationally defined" because it appeared variously in many places, as does one historian,[33] misses the bigger picture: various new lefts constituted a rebellion against the organizational definition of the old left. The New Left was organizationally defined, but negatively so. There was form to its formlessness. Neoleftist anti-organization in the 1960s makes sense as a historical process of decoupling antisystemic opposition from the existing left parties and trade unions. That process often goes unnoticed, because the anti-authoritarian ideas that predominated among SDS leaders did not grow out of the workers' movement. Students like Krahl and to a lesser extent also Dutschke developed their anti-authoritarianism through intellectual dialogue with the Frankfurt School, rather than through internal debates within the old left. This relative separation from working-class organizations helps explain why neoleftism became hardened into a nominalized identity (the New Left) in its 1960s anti-authoritarian phase, but not in earlier phases.

By contrast, left socialists very much engaged in debates internal to the old left. A left socialist current persisted within the SDS, drawing inspiration chiefly from Social Democracy's left-wing expellees like Abendroth and Communism's anti-Stalinist expellees like the sociologist Leo Kofler, rather than the politically unattached Frankfurt School. For example, an important SDS group in Frankfurt around the journal *Neue Kritik*, which consciously used the name New Left, insisted on avoiding Frankfurt School jargon. One of the journal's editors wanted to translate critical theory into readable and actionable prose. "'Adornism' as an end in itself should be absent," he wrote in reference to Adorno's notoriously dense style.[34]

---

33. Heigl, *Oppositionspolitik*, 26–27.

34. Jürgen Schaltenbrand, "Ein paar Bemerkungen zur publizistischen Arbeit der neuen linken" [mid-1962], FU, APO Archive, 22 (old number). Situated between anti-authoritarianism

Dutschke seemed most able to unite the anti-authoritarian and left socialist currents, which is perhaps why he became the most prominent German student leader of those years. In February 1968, while debating the SPD politician Johannes Rau on the limits of parliamentary reforms, he called for an alliance of workers and students. Events happening abroad encouraged the formation of such an alliance. In March, Dutschke and Klotz traveled to Czechoslovakia and witnessed the Prague Spring firsthand. Although short-lived, this united front of Czechoslovak workers, students, and intellectuals answered Alexander Dubček's call to build "socialism with a human face." Dutschke then planned to take an extended trip to the United States, where he would start a research project on Latin American liberation movements. His reasons for wanting to leave West Germany at such a crucial moment were twofold. First, he had become a celebrity after doing a television interview with Günter Gaus. That drew unwanted attention from conservative and far-right trolls, who directed their anger at him personally. Hate graffiti, smoke bombs outside his apartment building, and assorted death threats prompted him and Klotz to seek temporary safety abroad, especially after their first child was born.

Second, Dutschke recognized that his fans and the media had anointed him leader of the New Left, a paradoxical position for an anti-authoritarian and supposedly leaderless movement. By leaving West Germany, he hoped to dampen that reputation and preserve the grassroots character of the APO. His decision to abdicate leadership owed to his awareness of the neoleftist dilemma of sustaining new forms. In the meantime, he was invited by French students to speak at the upcoming May Day events in Paris. Neither that engagement nor his trip to the United States would come to pass, as will be discussed later.

Daniel Cohn-Bendit and the May Movement

The most consequential event in the history of new lefts was the combined French student revolt and workers' strike of May–June 1968. The upheaval of that spring occurred during a period of economic prosperity in France, the peak of the "Thirty Glorious Years" after the end of World War II. However, such growth in national economies across Western Europe masked rising unemployment, currency devaluation, and diminished career prospects for the young generation still in school or just entering the workforce. Anxiety mounted about nuclear war and the uncertain future of humanity. The French

---

and left socialism was Wolfgang Fritz Haug's important journal *Das Argument* (est. 1959). See Kufferath, "Das linkssozialistische Milieu," ch. 3.

university became a battleground for radical politics because the postwar youth came to regard it as a factory for the reproduction of consumers and "the managing elites [cadres] that society demands of it."[35] On top of that, universities allegedly reproduced the militarist and imperialist ideology of the Cold War. The philosopher Louis Althusser remarked that, by means of controlling knowledge, the bourgeoisie built its "true fortress of class influence in the university."[36]

By the late 1960s, the atmosphere was thick with unease among young people, anger at imperialism kindled by Algeria and stoked by Vietnam, and disgust with the cultural values of modern consumer society. Some French students decided to stage a revolt. It kicked off at Nanterre, a new suburban campus of the University of Paris. There in 1967, the French-German sociology student Cohn-Bendit started a movement to challenge the university's repressive structures. Specifically, he and his friends wanted access to the women's dormitories, which officially barred male visitors. Campus social life was perhaps more important there than at other French universities, since the Nanterre neighborhood at the time lacked many cultural amenities. Mirroring Kunzelmann's antics in West Germany, Cohn-Bendit's cabal appealed to "the political, social and revolutionary theories of Wilhelm Reich, [and] started a sex-education campaign on campus." As a step toward sexual revolution, male students occupied the female dorms. Today that may appear like male aggression, and indeed it was. According to Cohn-Bendit's own analysis, however, the female students welcomed a rebellion against "the petty restrictions surrounding these bastions of French purity and chastity." Breaking those restrictions supposedly enabled "the warmth of human companionship" and subverted the puritan morals that officially undergirded university culture.[37]

35. Commission nationale inter-disciplines, "Pour une réflexion sur la mutation de l'université" (June 6, 1968), Hoover, French Subject Collection, 85/21.

36. Althusser, "Student Problems," 13.

37. Cohn-Bendit and Cohn-Bendit, *Obsolete Communism*, 29 and 55. West German students expressed similar desires. See Herzog, *Sex after Fascism*, ch. 4. The decision to occupy the women's dorms came after Boris Fraenkel gave a lecture on campus about the ideas of Reich. Touraine, *May Movement*, 138. Fraenkel was an important popularizer of Reich, Marcuse, and Lukács in France. Gombin, *Origins of Modern Leftism*, ch. 5. One year earlier, students at Strasbourg launched a similar campaign of sexual liberation inspired by the Situationist text "On the Poverty of Student Life" [1966], in Knabb, *Situationist International Anthology*, 408–29. See also Sarah Fishman, *From Vichy to the Sexual Revolution: Gender and Family Life in Postwar France* (New York: Oxford University Press, 2017), and Richard Ivan Jobs, *Riding the New Wave: Youth and the Rejuvenation of France after the Second World War* (Stanford, CA: Stanford University Press, 2007).

In the winter of 1967–68, students succeeded in having dorm restrictions lifted at Nanterre and several other campuses. But their political aims were more ambitious. Protest against the US war in Vietnam situated the local student revolt within a global anti-imperialist context, which again followed the West German example. In February 1968, students at Nanterre formed a Grassroots Vietnam Committee that declared its support for the Vietnamese people and protested in front of the American embassy. The Tet Offensive by the Viet Cong and North Vietnamese People's Army, which had begun in January, intensified the students' frustration at the war. The fact that the Vietnamese were actually beating the most technologically advanced and well-funded military in the world, and that Cuban revolutionaries had likewise resisted American power, proved the vulnerability of the capitalist world system.[38]

Thousands of students at Nanterre went on strike. In his own reconstruction of events, Cohn-Bendit recalled that the existing student union tried to take over leadership. He and his fellow "ultra-Leftists" refused, which "simply reflected our determination to reject all bureaucracy." The movement at Nanterre, wrote the sociologist Alain Touraine, "was entirely unbalanced; it had no organization, no doctrine, and no program. It was condemned either to exhaust itself where it was or to throw itself into more and more general activity."[39] The first strikes did not last long, but they started a crescendo of protest actions. In mid-March, sociology students voted to boycott exams and "sealed their decision by singing the Internationale."[40] In addition to the repressive culture of the university in general, these students rejected tendencies within the discipline of sociology itself; namely, its subsumption by positivist methods and ties to the advertising industry. They rejected the functionalism of the leading US sociologist Talcott Parsons, which downplayed social conflict, as well as the discipline's increasing reliance on statistics. Quantifying phenomena without relating them to the social totality seemed like the methodological equivalent of capitalism's elevation of exchange value over any qualitative use value. Professionalized and highly specialized, mainstream sociology appeared to militant students as conformist. Instead, sociologists like Althusser and Touraine who used qualitative methods of critical theory came into vogue.[41]

38. See Mohandesi, "Bringing Vietnam Home."

39. Touraine, *May Movement*, 151.

40. Cohn-Bendit and Cohn-Bendit, *Obsolete Communism*, 34–35. Often students with little or no exposure to the old left had to "relearn" the words of the Internationale. Touraine, *May Movement*, 164.

41. At Nanterre, at least four professors declared solidarity with the students: the sociologist Touraine, the philosophers Henri Lefebvre and Paul Ricœur, and the literature scholar Guy Michaud.

This revolt against positivism recalled the intellectual mood at the turn of the century, when "life philosophy" and other vitalist theories became popular.[42] It also echoed the romantic anti-capitalism of the early Lukács. Many adherents of the sixties New Left shared the turn-of-the-century anxiety about modern life and its iron cage of rationality. Radical students in France and elsewhere came to believe that the universities offered only dead knowledge. Living knowledge, by contrast, required permanent reflection and ideological contestation. All received beliefs were subject to critique. Militant students rejected the government and university administrators' own proposals for reform because those were clearly meant to strengthen the status quo of the technocratic university.[43]

The postwar youth came of age in a society that was functionally unable to integrate it. For the French students and young workers who spearheaded the uprisings of 1967–68, the universities and vocational schools failed to provide an education that guaranteed living wages and satisfying jobs. Moreover, higher education seemed to erect barriers against the advancement of working-class youth. Universities thus served to reinforce class hierarchy. Quality of life and access to education were themes that brought bourgeois college kids together with young factory workers. What soon became known as the May Movement began as a revolution of the youth, whose generational solidarity cut across class lines.[44]

Rather than "the New Left," French radicals preferred to call themselves "the Movement." The latter term appeared all over the place in May and June 1968: audibly in the slogans and visually on the walls and in the ad hoc publications of the ubiquitous action committees. The May Movement was the French equivalent of the West German APO, but on a much larger scale. Across Western Europe the sixties New Left stressed decentralized decision making, spontaneity, and the ephemerality of political forms. Neoleftists believed that their movement must replenish itself constantly, lest it perish. As the Austrian-French theorist André Gorz put it, neoleftists must undertake "the repeated liquidation of the hierarchic structure and bureaucratic rigidities which tend to re-emerge."[45] Ironically, the New Left ended up radicalizing

---

42. Hughes, *Consciousness and Society*, ch. 2.

43. Cf. Clark Kerr's analysis of the technocratic university and its ties to the US military-industrial complex, *Uses of the University*.

44. "La révolution de la jeunesse," *Le Cri du monde*, no. 19 (May–June 1968), Hoover, French Subject Collection, 86.

45. Gorz, *Socialism and Revolution*, 177. Hannah Arendt described movement politics pejoratively as "planned shapelessness" in *Origins of Totalitarianism*, chs. 11–12. Cf. Andrew Denning,

Eduard Bernstein's revisionist dictum: the ultimate aim of the revolution is nothing (or at least something), but the movement is everything.[46]

On March 22, 1968, after students from a Vietnam Committee at Nanterre were arrested, several hundred people assembled to demand their release. The assembly decided collectively to occupy a university building. Debates took place through the night about strategy and tactics. The occupiers wrote a statement and distributed five thousand copies the next day. It protested police brutality and harassment of demonstrators, and it called for a permanent occupation of the university. The students plastered the walls with anti-authoritarian slogans. Working groups germinated. The March 22 Movement was born. Much as forerunners of the US New Left had done with the 1962 Port Huron Statement, the Nanterre students adopted a common program that broke with the verbiage of the old left.[47] They set their own curriculum, and through the remainder of March and April they actively debated means of overthrowing capitalism and imperialism. Administrators decided to close down the university on May 2, so the radical students of Nanterre flocked into central Paris.

With his striking hair color and irreverent antics, Dany "The Red" Cohn-Bendit quickly became the most famous student leader in Europe. His parents were German-Jewish refugees who had settled in Montauban in the South of France. He lived there as a stateless person until 1958, when at the age of thirteen he moved to Germany to attend high school and claim West German citizenship. In 1966, he returned to France to study sociology at Paris-Nanterre. There he studied with the young Spanish sociologist and antifascist Manuel

---

"'Life Is Movement, Movement Is Life!': Mobility Politics and the Circulatory State in Nazi Germany," *American Historical Review* 123, no. 5 (2018): 1479–1503.

46. Cf. Eduard Bernstein, *Evolutionary Socialism* [1899], trans. Edith C. Harvey (Independent Labour Party, 1907), Marxists' Internet Archive, https://www.marxists.org/reference/archive/bernstein/works/1899/evsoc/index.htm: "To me that which is generally called the ultimate aim of socialism is nothing, but the movement is everything" (Conclusion).

47. Cohn-Bendit and Cohn-Bendit, *Obsolete Communism*, 48–53. See Howard Brick and Christopher Phelps, *Radicals in America: The U.S. Left since the Second World War* (Cambridge: Cambridge University Press, 2015), ch. 3. The closest US equivalent to the March 22 Movement was probably not the Students for a Democratic Society, which authored the Port Huron Statement, but the Yippies. While technically belonging to a so-called Youth International Party (YIP), these radicals, such as Abbie Hoffman and Jerry Rubin, detested the traditional party form. They preferred countercultural rebellion, provocations, and pranks. Most famously, they nominated a 145-pound pig named Pigasus for president in 1968. The title of a report in the *Village Voice* by Sally Kempton says it all: "Yippies Anti-Organize a Groovy Revolution" (March 21, 1968).

Castells and became involved in anarchist politics, all while staying in touch with West German students. The left socialist Edgar Morin praised his audacity and gift for strategy, observing that in May 1968 "this 'German Jew' [became] the most remarkable French political personality of the hour."[48] That April, a police report singled out Cohn-Bendit as the leading protestor, "simultaneously cutting a figure of agitator and playing the role of moderator."[49] Noting his charisma, easy laughter, and talent for public speaking, Touraine claimed that his "role was to break down structures," including those of the old left.[50] Cohn-Bendit's immigrant background, international contacts, and extroverted personality made him a key figure for the sixties New Left.[51]

Like Dutschke, he helped articulate the anti-authoritarian sentiment that had grown among students over the past several years. The March 22 Movement believed in spontaneous, direct action against the Gaullist regime, consumer society, and imperialism. It refused any organization imposed from outside, opting instead for student self-organization. The Movement's preferred tactic was the occupation of symbolic buildings. It entrusted decisions to general assemblies, eschewing any formal leadership. Cohn-Bendit and company also engaged in playful provocations like those practiced by the Situationists and Dutch Provos. They used these subversive tactics to upset the decorum of electoral politics. As Cohn-Bendit put it, provocations aimed to "unmask the true nature of the State, in practice rather than by means of theoretical analyses the State can safely ignore." Thus unmasked, he claimed, the capitalist state looked no different from Franco's dictatorship in Spain or the bureaucratic regimes of the Eastern bloc.[52]

The March 22 Movement emerged partly out of a feud within the Socialist and Communist Party camps, like all new lefts. Young radicals challenged the authority of older pragmatists, most of whom had cut their teeth in the Popular Front struggles of the 1930s or the wartime Resistance. Despite important divisions in age, experience, and temperament, almost the entire French left agreed that Gaullism posed the most immediate threat. De Gaulle's government had actually implemented a number of reforms to appease the working

48. Edgar Morin, "La commune étudiante," in Morin, Castoriadis, and Lefort, *Mai 1968*, 11–33 (at 20).

49. Paris Préfecture de Police, "La situation estudiantine dans la région parisienne," April 29, 1968, Hoover, French Subject Collection, 84/2.

50. Touraine, *May Movement*, 142.

51. On the role of non-European immigrants in the French New Left, see D. Gordon, *Immigrants and Intellectuals*. Greek immigrants also played an outsized role in French left socialism and the New Left—e.g., Cornelius Castoriadis, Kostas Axelos, and Nicos Poulantzas.

52. Cohn-Bendit and Cohn-Bendit, *Obsolete Communism*, 165.

class. Just after the war he founded a short-lived populist movement called Assembly of the French People (RPF), which opposed the constitution of the Fourth Republic. The RPF fizzled out, but De Gaulle himself returned to power in 1958 with a patriotic promise to restore order and transcend partisan strife. The inventiveness of Gaullist populism was undeniable. He remained popular despite the tumult of May–June 1968, winning another election later that year.[53]

Gaullism proved formidable. The French left disagreed on the best strategy for combatting it. As in the 1930s, ideological divisions between Socialists, Communists, anarchists, and syndicalists gave way to a crosscutting division between new and old. The militant youth often presented problems of organization in generational terms. Spatial distribution across the political compass, a model that typically includes an x-axis of economics (left vs. right) and a y-axis of politics or culture (authoritarian vs. libertarian), acquired a third dimension: a z-axis of age.[54] The greatest ambition of the sixties New Left was to forge an alliance between students, young workers, and anticolonial resisters in the Third World. Such an alliance seemed possible partly because of that decade's temporalization of left politics: each of those groups made some claim on the New and shared similar horizons of expectation. That simple (and even simplistic) fact made it possible to imagine untried coalitions across university, factory, and colony.[55]

On May 6, the day after Marx's 150th birthday, tens of thousands of students, faculty, and their allies marched on the Sorbonne to liberate it from police occupation. National riot police (the Republican Security Companies, CRS) had moved in three days earlier to enforce the official closure of the university. Now the police faced a determined crowd that wanted them gone. A violent clash occurred as waves of protestors broke against shields and batons in a cloud of tear gas. The struggle reached a climax on the night of May 10–11. Recalling the grand *journées* of France's revolutionary past, thousands of protestors erected barricades in defensive positions throughout the city. The protestors consciously drew on a revolutionary tradition associated with the general strike of 1936 and especially the Paris Commune of 1871. Red

---

53. See Julian Jackson, *De Gaulle* (Cambridge, MA: Harvard University Press, 2018); Grey Anderson, *La guerre civile en France, 1958–1962: Du coup d'État gaulliste à la fin de l'OAS* (Paris: La fabrique, 2018); and Suri, *Power and Protest*, ch. 2.

54. For example, see "Les jeunes et la révolution," *Front 1: Bulletin des Comités d'Initiative pour un Front Révolutionnaire de la Jeunesse*, no. 1, n.d., Hoover, French Subject Collection, 86. See also Wikipedia contributors, "Political Spectrum," *Wikipedia*, accessed May 2020, https://en .wikipedia.org/w/index.php?title=Political_spectrum&oldid=992344162.

55. Cf. Koselleck, *Futures Past*, ch. 14.

flags were easy to find, since all one had to do was tear off the blue and white stripes from the national tricolor.[56]

The confrontation with the CRS proved a watershed. Young factory workers and high school students (*lycéens*) joined the uprising. Over the next few days, mass protest actions escalated. The CRS crackdown was so harsh that some apolitical French citizens began to sympathize with the protestors. Soon the crisis reached the point where two of the largest unions, Workers' Force and the Communist-aligned General Confederation of Labor (CGT), called for a general strike on May 13. Millions of people answered that call. Thus began the largest strike in French history: shops closed, transit stopped, work ceased. It lasted for two weeks, and the revolution imagined by neoleftists nearly came to pass.

During the strike, the student-specific March 22 Movement morphed into the general May Movement. Although its social base widened, the latter's organizational form remained varied and amorphous. Cohn-Bendit observed that the May Movement initially "took the form of unofficial strikes, student unrest, [and] the activity of tiny left-wing splinter groups, the so-called *groupuscles* [grouplets]."[57] The proliferation of grouplets followed the same splintering pattern as the antifascist new left. Touraine downplayed their significance, claiming that they were "outflanked by the collective action" of the Movement. When the Trotskyist or Maoist grouplets cooperated with the decentralized May Movement, the relationship was tense. The former wanted to impose the sort of ideological homogeneity and rigid organization that the latter rejected. While the grouplets and the Movement never fused organizationally, they were united "in the active expression of revolt, indignation, and resentment and in the push toward social transformation."[58]

Like the antifascist network of the interwar years, the sixties New Left experimented with new forms of communication. Newspapers, broadsheets, and placards were rapidly screen printed and posted. Many new magazines and journals were so ephemeral that they lasted for just one issue. Spray-painted graffiti were the Movement's transgressive medium of choice. More so than disseminating the printed word, claimed Touraine, spray-painting functioned as a creative rejection of existing social norms: it delivered a pithy message and also defaced capitalist property. Besides the government's monopoly on the

---

56. Touraine, *May Movement*, 164. See "Paris 1968 or Paris 1871?" *Barricades*, no. 1 (June 1968), Hoover, French Subject Collection, 86, and also Provenzano, "Beyond the Matraque."

57. Cohn-Bendit and Cohn-Bendit, *Obsolete Communism*, 13.

58. Touraine, *May Movement*, 162. According to Morin, the grouplets "regulate and channel the movement without ever taming it." *Mai 1968*, 19.

radio, mainstream media consisted of several leading newspapers controlled by private companies or political parties. One of the largest professional strikes was organized by journalists and technicians working at the French Radio and Television Broadcasting Office, who mobilized against state censorship of nonprint media.

Students performed teach-outs, turned the Latin Quarter into an open forum, and experimented with forms of direct democracy. They created child-care centers in the occupied buildings, "ate and slept, took care of their needs, organized themselves, and debated—in other words, they lived there."[59] The French counteruniversity posed as a complete alternative society. "Even the football clubs were taken over by their players!" exclaimed Cohn-Bendit: "new forms of organization of society were being discussed everywhere."[60] Discussion, experimentation, revision, repeat: it was a time of radical creativity in which everything seemed possible. Giant murals were painted on the walls of the Sorbonne, depicting excerpts from a 1936 essay by Reich, "Sexuality and Repression." Student occupiers literally surrounded themselves with the words of the antifascist new left.[61] The invention of new forms was accompanied by the rediscovery of old ones, such as workers' councils. Debates occurred everywhere, and workers' control was at the top of the agenda.

One important difference between French and West German neoleftists was their respective views on students' economic role. While Marcuse and Dutschke associated students with an intelligentsia at the margins of mainstream society, Touraine placed them right at the center of an emerging postindustrial society. This concept, which Touraine invented and other sociologists such as Daniel Bell elaborated, referred to the shift in advanced industrial economies toward highly skilled, technical, and service-oriented work. The postindustrial society elevated software above hardware, creativity above inventions, technology over machinery, and cybernetics over markets. In the global north, technicians, engineers, and highly educated specialists displaced industrial workers from the center of production. Touraine used the Marxist argument that while capitalism had already evolved into this postindustrial stage, social relations lagged behind. This accounted for the feeling among students and young skilled workers that they inhabited an outdated social structure. Sociologically speaking, the May–June uprising was a crisis of modernization.[62]

59. Touraine, *May Movement*, 245.

60. Cohn-Bendit and Cohn-Bendit, *Obsolete Communism*, 67.

61. Gombin, *Origins of Modern Leftism*, ch. 5.

62. Touraine, *Post-Industrial Society*. See also Bell, *Coming of Post-Industrial Society*.

Postindustrial class conflict no longer pitted owners against workers, Touraine claimed. Instead, a technocratic bureaucracy contended with the specialists, professionals, and white-collar workers who actually ran the productive apparatus. That shift in social forces explained the conservatism of the old left parties and unions. The Communist unions in particular were entrenched in the industrial mode of production. For Touraine, May 1968 marked the ascent of a new working class, which included the young intelligentsia. Demoting the factory, he believed that social struggles would now take place outside traditional sites of production: in everyday life, on the streets, in the universities, and at the marketplace. These new struggles would no longer be driven by traditional wage demands. "The struggle was not against capitalism," he went so far as to say, "but first and foremost against technocracy."[63]

The idea of a new working class preoccupied the sixties New Left. Along with others, Touraine tried to explain why postwar technicians and their university education mattered. The sixties crisis represented "the first time that education in the economically advanced countries has become a factor of production and decisive growth, not merely the transmission of a cultural heritage."[64] He framed this shift toward highly educated specialists as "a generational change in class conflicts," which showed both a continuity with past workers' struggles and a rupture with old left politics. As "children of the bourgeoisie [and] future 'professionals' confronting the technostructure," he wrote, students stood between two worlds.[65] In their role as future technicians, they formed the core of the postindustrial society. The uprisings of 1968 were not carried out by irresponsible intellectuals and privileged students, but by young professionals raging against an authoritarian state in league with the corporate machine.

Action Committees Everywhere

The French economy was conducive to such a social uprising, but not a political revolution in the traditional sense. Touraine recognized what I call the neoleftist dilemma of organization. The May Movement, he wrote, "was

63. Touraine, *May Movement*, 28. His analysis drew on the pioneering work by Serge Mallet, *New Working Class*.

64. Touraine, *May Movement*, 355. Cf. the concept of knowledge economy developed by Peter Drucker and others around that time. Drucker, *The Age of Discontinuity: Guidelines to Our Changing Society* [1969], 2nd ed. (Abingdon, UK: Routledge, 2017), ch. 12.

65. Touraine, *May Movement*, 27. See the epic historical and ethnographic survey of the French '68er generation by Hervé Hamon and Patrick Rotman, *Génération*, 2 vols. (Paris: Seuil, 1987–88).

creative only in what prevented it from succeeding, its spontaneity." Its real problem was organization: "revolutionary action will be pursued only if it destroys what gave strength to the uprising, only if imaginary possession of power is replaced by political organization and strategy."[66] He predicted the entropy of a movement based solely on spontaneous, direct democracy. It would inevitably collapse through a combination of outside pressure and internal discord.

In examining documents from May–June 1968, one is immediately struck by the ubiquity of one organizational form in particular: action committees. They sprang up like mushrooms.[67] Action committees were organized by district, apartment building, place of work, and place of study. Unlike trade unions, action committees eschewed particular demands such as better wages in favor of total demands for popular control. They emerged as a practical response to the state of emergency created by the general strike. Each locality now needed to manage its own mundane affairs like trash cleanup, and action committees met that need. But in a broader sense, this new form eroded bourgeois norms of political representation and private property. The committees' antithesis, the Gaullist state, embodied the rule of corporate capital. Political parties normally mediated between the state and the people, but parties were remarkably absent from everyday life during the general strike.[68]

On the ground, action committees handled administrative tasks and disseminated revolutionary propaganda. Neighbors, coworkers, and fellow students collectively debated programs and manifestos. They also created a range of smaller propaganda, including slogans and stickers. For example, some stickers read:

> The consumer society should die a violent death.
> CRS = SS.
> Enragés of all countries, unite.
> Learn how to sing the International.
> Treat your desires like realities.
> Young people make love, old people make obscene gestures.[69]

The slogans of May worked like memes: catchy, applied to any surface, fleeting, but far from meaningless. They mirrored the form of the action committee

---

66. Touraine, *May Movement*, 62 and 63–64.

67. Gombin, *Origins of Modern Leftism*, ch. 4a.

68. See Ross, *May '68*, ch. 2.

69. Copy of assorted stickers and labels in Hoover, French Subject Collection, 84/4.

itself. As open laboratories for a new culture, action committees reflected a widespread hostility toward bureaucratic procedure and indirect political representation. Their organizational form encouraged direct participation by the greatest number of people. Constant rotation and turnover of administrative roles would guarantee that a high number of people held positions of responsibility.[70]

The militants of May knew that this was a novel form. One declaration included a section called "Action Committees Everywhere." It predicted that immediate tasks for the committees would grow while those for electoral parties diminished.[71] Decentralized power did not exactly promote efficiency, however. Committee debates were "long, loaded with repetitions, tortured, and often gave a strong impression of not getting anywhere; after an hour's absence, one could pick up the thread with no trouble." Touraine first offered the standard explanation that these debates were more about liberated self-expression than pragmatic deliberation. But then he asked, "can anyone who has heard union meetings or sessions of a faculty council forget the much greater richness of the May debates?" In their very disorder, he wrote, "they committed each one who spoke, not to an established body, but to a collectivity of individuals." Those individuals differed from one another much more than bourgeois representatives did in a parliamentary assembly, but their common commitment to liberation created a sense of solidarity.[72] Participants knew that the rambling discussions lacked efficiency. That was a price they were willing to pay for avoiding indirect representation and bureaucratic procedure.

Nonetheless, some militants tried to coordinate the work of the committees. One group called itself the Movement of Action Committees, combining at least conceptually the fluid spontaneity and the distinctive organizational form of May. There was even a Coordinating Committee of Contesting Cadres, known as C4. But the sheer multiplicity of grassroots gatherings exceeded all attempts at control. In almost every major French city there were occupation committees, strike committees, popular action committees, high school action committees, worker-student-peasant liaison committees, defense committees against police repression, committees for initiating a revolutionary movement, and so on. Writing about high school action committees, one

70. Comité de grève, "Qu'est-ce qu'un Comité de base?" n.d., Hoover, French Subject Collection, 85/31. Cf. Yves Sintomer, "From Deliberative to Radical Democracy? Sortition and Politics in the Twenty-First Century," *Politics and Society* 46, no. 3 (2018): 337–57.

71. La coordination des comités d'action, "Appel," n.d., Hoover, French Subject Collection, 84/5. See also Glucksmann, "Strategy and Revolution."

72. Touraine, *May Movement*, 251.

militant included a poem inspired by a verb conjugation exercise: "I organize myself / You organize yourself / One organizes oneself / We organize ourselves / You structure yourselves and / They will fail."[73] Despite the apparent formlessness of the Movement, the committees imagined themselves as forming counterstructures against an authoritarian police state.

The action committee form briefly became hegemonic when De Gaulle himself called on the Parisian bourgeoisie to organize civic action committees (CACs) in defense of the Republic. A few cropped up here and there, and like their revolutionary counterparts they were organized locally. According to one CAC, it represented "the near totality of the economic, cultural, and social civic associations of our district." But in representing already existing social institutions, these state-sanctioned committees only gave local expression to the Gaullist establishment. Their well-to-do participants assumed official duties and titles as if they had just joined a social club. Never widespread, the CACs were still a grassroots phenomenon. Unlike the neoleftist action committees, they made no effort to preserve internal democracy or deepen democracy in society at large. They faced no organizational dilemma.[74]

When De Gaulle announced new elections for June, the neoleftist action committee of the Sixth District issued a statement in opposition. Reminiscent of council communists earlier in the century, the statement called for extraparliamentary opposition and denounced electoral participation as an act of submission.[75] Everywhere the committees rejected the election, because they thought it would symbolize a compromise with the Gaullist regime, restore normality, and threaten the committees' continued existence. Only outside parliament could the people directly challenge the power of employers and the state. Power is not to be found in ballot boxes (*les urnes*), one flier read, but in the factories (*les usines*).[76] Although their strategy may seem formally undemocratic, action committees decided that opposing the official election was their only way of expressing popular democracy. In another verb conjugation meme, the action committee of the Odéon Theater wrote: "I participate / you participate / he participates / we participate / you all participate / *they*

73. "Structurer les C.A.L.," *Barricades*, no. 2 (n.d. [1968]), Hoover, French Subject Collection, 86.

74. CAC document, Hoover, French Subject Collection, 84/14.

75. Comité d'action du 6ᵉ Arrondissement, "Élections: Arme de la bourgeoisie," Hoover, French Subject Collection, 84/5.

76. La coordination des comités d'action, "Élections—cadeau empoisonné," n.d., Hoover, French Subject Collection, 84/5.

profit." Participatory democracy in that moment, oddly enough, meant not voting.[77]

Tension between the grouplets and the action committees mounted. One high school action committee declared, "The term grouplet has had its day!!!" as if it could wish out of existence the many sectarian grouplets that the emergency had spawned.[78] A prominent Trotskyist grouplet called Revolutionary Communist Youth (JCR) threw the criticism back at the spontaneist Movement, accusing Cohn-Bendit of spreading a "groupuscular attitude" among the students.[79] For his part, Cohn-Bendit celebrated the fact that in the committees "we suddenly saw thousands of militants joining together without any outside prompting, all of them active, informed, aware and responsible." What Hannah Arendt called revolution's lost treasure of collective action was located there in the action committee, that soviet redux. "Thousands of people discussed democracy, the class struggle, the next action," Cohn-Bendit rhapsodized, "and all this without having learned to recite the magic spells put out by the Central Committee of the Communist Party; without even knowing there are five different wings to the Fourth International, or whether the PCMLF or the UJC(M-L) support Mao Zedong."[80] While the grouplets engaged in old practices of vanguardism and sectarian infighting, the Movement, according to Cohn-Bendit, broke free.

Action committees propagated locally without any central plan or leaders. Ordinary citizens, students, and workers participated in them on terms of equality. As in the Commune of 1871, barriers between people that existed in class society came crashing down. Most participants agreed that the chief goal of these assemblies was to preserve autonomy. According to Cohn-Bendit, the action committees gave the Movement "a foretaste of what self-government can achieve in practice." He extended this idea into the postcapitalist future: "Social relationships will no longer be vertical—from top to bottom, from director to worker—but horizontal, between equal producers working in harmony."[81]

77. *CAR* [Comité d'action révolutionnaire] *Odéon*, no. [4?], Hoover, French Subject Collection, 86.

78. Untitled document by Comité d'action lycéen, n.d., Hoover, French Subject Collection, 84/20.

79. "L'enjeu des comités d'action," *La voie: Bulletin d'action communiste*, no. 23 (December 1968), Hoover, French Subject Collection, 88.

80. Cohn-Bendit and Cohn-Bendit, *Obsolete Communism*, 77–78. See Arendt, *On Revolution*, ch. 6.

81. Cohn-Bendit and Cohn-Bendit, *Obsolete Communism*, 83 and 106.

The Movement's leaderless ethos annoyed the French Communist Party (PCF), which denounced street violence as the work of irresponsible leftists and false revolutionaries. Marching under the anarchist banner of "no bureaucracy, no masters," the students and young workers considered party and union leaders out of touch. Cohn-Bendit claimed that the PCF and its affiliated unions lagged behind the events of May–June. Despite his obvious bias in favor of the Movement, his interpretation largely agrees with the facts. The PCF scrambled to co-opt and defuse the wildcat protests, and that effort explains the party's decision to call a general strike. Viewed through a neoleftist filter, the general strike takes on a different hue than how historians typically view it. Instead of a demonstration of workers' power—which it surely was, also—the general strike seemed to neoleftists like a rearguard action by the old left. Militants in the action committees felt betrayed by the PCF and CGT. Official Communism, observed Touraine, was "more determined to destroy deviations on its left than on its right in order to maintain the unity and power of the party." He was in tune with the neoleftist temporalization of politics. He suggested replacing "spatial metaphors—extreme left, center, right—with a more historical view." In that scheme, Communists represented the interests of organized workers under industrial conditions. No wonder a new left should rise up at the dawn of postindustrial society. "The May Movement is not to the left of the Communist Party but ahead of it," he claimed: "it belongs to the next generation."[82] And the Movement's youthfulness was determined not by its average age, but by its adherents' novel economic role in the postindustrial society.

Cohn-Bendit described Communist union leaders as "generals of a counterrevolution," viewing the CGT's policy as a repeat of the PCF's braking maneuver in June 1936, when party leader Maurice Thorez had quipped, "You have to know how to stop a strike."[83] The Maubert-Langevin section of the Paris PCF issued a statement on June 10 that described its two-front war "against the Gaullists and technocrats, and against the adventurers."[84] As for the factory occupations that paralleled the student strikes, the PCF tried to steer workers' energy toward particular demands like better wages. The party had no patience for people who called for total revolution or an unlimited general strike. It

82. Touraine, *May Movement*, 232 and 235.

83. Quoted in Cohn-Bendit and Cohn-Bendit, *Obsolete Communism*, 61 and 158. This Thorez quote was mockingly cited by the JCR journal *Avant-garde jeunesse* along with an accompanying photo of a CRS agent. Hoover, French Subject Collection, 86.

84. PCF, Section Maubert-Langevin, Comité de parti, "Sur les deux fronts: Contre les gaullistes et technocrats, contre les aventuriers," June 10, 1968, Hoover, French Subject Collection, 84/17.

hoped to use the uprising as leverage in negotiations with employers and the government, and it expected to win politically in the next election. From a neoleftist perspective, the PCF aimed to reshuffle personnel within the existing social and political hierarchy. Communist political ambitions did enable De Gaulle to change the terms of the struggle from anti-capitalist resistance to an anti-Communist defense of democracy.

Militants of the Movement tried to bypass Communist organizations by reaching out directly to workers. Specialists from the chemical industry, engineers from the automotive industry, and school teachers actually did join the Movement.[85] Older workers in traditional industries, such as mining and the railways, were less sympathetic. Despite simmering class resentments, the students and many young workers agreed on the principle of workers' control. Gorz argued that this desire for self-management was a revolt against all forms of bureaucracy. Technocratic management regimented the labor process more than even the original Taylorist or Fordist methods. Workers in industrial and postindustrial sectors alike faced a stark alternative: conformity or autonomy. Only by wresting control away from technocratic managers, he believed, could workers achieve autonomy. Rising up from the factory floor, through the unions, and through a new revolutionary party: that was Gorz's bottom-up path to overcoming capitalist alienation. For him, as for Italian autonomists around Mario Tronti, Antonio Negri, and the journals *Quaderni Rossi* and *Classe Operaia*, there was no such thing as top-down democratization. Gorz firmly believed that radical students needed to embed themselves at sites of production. Workers' autonomy was a positive expression of the New Left's negative, anti-authoritarian impulse.[86]

But neoleftists often betrayed a poor understanding of working-class behavior. For example, Cohn-Bendit chided the shop floor committee of the Rhône-Poulenc pharmaceutical factory for playing cards and boules after getting bored with the endless debates over strategy. Leisure activity by French workers was just as "spontaneous" as student occupations, although it may have derived from what Lenin called trade-union consciousness. Cohn-Bendit tried to account for the passivity of most workers and the outright hostility of

85. Touraine, *May Movement*, 202 and 220.

86. Gorz, *Socialism and Revolution*, 95. See also Wright, *Storming Heaven*, and the novel by Nanni Balestrini, *We Want Everything* [1971], trans. Matt Holden (London: Verso, 2016). The chief Western Marxist interpreter of Frederick Winslow Taylor's and Henry Ford's methods of industrial production was Antonio Gramsci. See the collection of Gramsci's writings on this subject, "Americanism and Fordism," in *Prison Notebooks*, 277–322. On the influence of Gramsci on Tronti's emerging workerism, see Andrew Anastasi, "A Living Unity in the Marxist: Introduction to Tronti's Early Writings," *Viewpoint Magazine*, October 3, 2016.

some. When workers assumed political responsibility themselves, he wrote, "they came alive and took an active part in making important decisions." But when union bureaucrats or outside activists such as students assumed that responsibility on their behalf, workers lost interest.[87]

At the core of neoleftism's dilemma lay the problem of spontaneity: who decided to act on their own, what for, and how long they could sustain action before yielding to external control or internal hierarchy. Cohn-Bendit noted that CGT leaders such as Georges Séguy repeatedly denied the spontaneous character of the May uprising. Their reason seemed simple: "spontaneity is the chief enemy of all bureaucrats—it challenges their very existence." Of course, Cohn-Bendit admitted that no social movement had ever been totally spontaneous. Concrete historical circumstances conditioned every collective action taken by workers or any other class. Plus, the revolutionary tradition would always offer social movements a repertoire of slogans, models, and martyrs. Neoleftist spontaneity for him meant the Movement's capacity "to develop its own methods of struggle irrespective of, or even against, the wishes of all those great or petty 'vanguards' who proclaim themselves leaders of the proletariat." Direct action and self-organization do not occur "'without precedent,' but simply 'without official blessing.'" He also linked spontaneity to anonymity, insofar as a movement without figureheads has no official name.[88] This implied that new lefts, once they give themselves a name (especially "the New Left"), lose both their anonymity and their spontaneity. Naming the Movement may be the first step toward freezing it into an institution.

Frozen or not, the Movement never occupied government ministries and public buildings, took over radio stations, or in any way smashed the state. It failed to take power. Following De Gaulle's speech on May 24, government representatives met with leaders of big business and the trade unions to negotiate an end to the strike. While making important concessions to workers, the resulting Grenelle Agreements killed the Movement's momentum. Cohn-Bendit called it a sordid deal between bureaucrats "Right, Left, and Centre."[89] Even the concessions fell far short of the Matignon Agreements of 1936, which had included phenomenal gains like the forty-hour working week, paid vacations, and collective bargaining rights.

87. Cohn-Bendit and Cohn-Bendit, *Obsolete Communism*, 102–3. For a skeptical account of students' overtures to the workers, see Seidman, *Imaginary Revolution*, ch. 4. Cf. Cole Stangler's article on historiographical and popular disregard for worker militancy, "The Neglected History of the May '68 Uprising in France," *Nation*, August 3, 2018.

88. Cohn-Bendit and Cohn-Bendit, *Obsolete Communism*, 154, 157, and 207.

89. Cohn-Bendit and Cohn-Bendit, 124.

The left parties' counterpart to Grenelle was a mass meeting held at Charléty Stadium on May 27. There, representatives from Édouard Depreux's Unified Socialist Party (PSU) addressed a crowd of about forty thousand people. The main speakers included the rising PSU star Michel Rocard as well as Pierre Mendès France, a well-known leader of the Radical Party and the anti-imperialist left.[90] Although the PSU was among the few parties to openly support the Movement, Cohn-Bendit and company remained skeptical of its aims. Its call for market-socialist modernization, electoral democracy, and left unity closely resembled the PCF line. The Charléty meeting seemed to neoleftists like "a great salvage operation by the official parties of the Left." Cohn-Bendit claimed that the meeting gave the French bourgeoisie a chance to use its Trojan horse of institutionalized politics, which would channel the energy of the masses into a predictable pattern of electoral participation. Oddly enough, the activist Alain Krivine and his Trotskyist grouplet, the JCR, had a hand in organizing the Charléty meeting. They hoped to use the occasion to create an umbrella group for the countless action committees and thus centralize the Movement. The JCR invoked the legacy of Marceau Pivert, repeating his cry, "Everything is possible!" and equating May 1968 with June 1936. According to Cohn-Bendit, the crowd rejected the JCR plan as "the old Bolshevism adorned with a liberal sash": militant students and young workers preferred their own committees to new parties like the PSU.[91]

Three days later, May 30, marked a turning point. The CGT held a mass demo in Paris against De Gaulle, who earlier had fled to West Germany in order to prepare military options in the case of an armed uprising. De Gaulle returned on the day of the CGT demo and delivered a speech over radio announcing the new election for June 23. An even larger demo in support of De Gaulle—actually the largest ever in France—took place that evening after the speech. Many thousands of Gaullists waved tricolor flags and chanted hymns to the Republic. The general strike was over and, according to Cohn-Bendit, "the bourgeoisie took a deep breath of relief."[92]

After that, bands of students set off to aid worker holdouts who continued to occupy their factories. Student-worker committees and "support and

90. Parti socialiste unifié, "Objectif 1972: Pour une société nouvelle," May 22, 1968, Hoover, French Subject Collection, 84/15.

91. Cohn-Bendit and Cohn-Bendit, *Obsolete Communism*, 73; "Tout est possible," *Avant-garde jeunesse*, no. 14 (May 27, 1968); and "Compte rendu de l'Assemblée générale," May 28, 1968, Hoover, French Subject Collection, 85/23. On the JCR and French Trotskyism in general, see Daniel Bensaïd, *An Impatient Life: A Memoir* [2004], trans. David Fernbach (London: Verso, 2014).

92. Cohn-Bendit and Cohn-Bendit, *Obsolete Communism*, 74.

solidarity" groups formed at the Renault and Peugeot car plants. If Paris and other French cities seemed impossible to win for the revolution, the students wagered, then at least worker-controlled factories in the suburbs might survive as "islands of resistance." Guerrilla battles with riot police broke out along the factory perimeter fences. Meanwhile the CGT denounced these wildcat actions. Most older workers sided with the union.[93]

De Gaulle's election announcement basically deactivated the Movement. Workers drifted back to work, and parties reasserted control over politics as usual. Cohn-Bendit described the parties as "monopolizing all discussion, excluding the masses, and speaking in order to dissemble." Even if the old left parties won the June elections, which they would not, they probably would have pursued the same policy as the Gaullist regime: quell the spontaneous uprising and stabilize the existing technocratic system. At least that was how defeated militants like Cohn-Bendit interpreted the situation.[94] Rather than a conservative backlash, the Gaullist retrenchment starting in the fall of 1968 represented for them the flip side of old left obsolescence.

Leftism's Revenge or Romantic Regression?

Just like the soviets in 1917–21, the action committees of 1968 challenged the control exercised by parties and unions over left politics. Lenin fended off the grassroots challenge to his vanguardist party by painting his leftist opponents as naïve and inexperienced idealists who suffered from an "infantile disorder." Amid the Stalinization of Communist parties across Europe and the malaise of Cold War geopolitics, however, the vanguardist party form lost its luster. This reversal in the form's revolutionary potential provided the occasion for Cohn-Bendit and his brother Gabriel to parody the old party line in *Leftism: Remedy for the Senile Disorder of Communism* (1969), a book already cited at length in this chapter.[95]

Lenin called leftists childish because he thought that they lacked discipline, tactical flexibility, and commitment to a long and difficult struggle. Now

93. Cohn-Bendit and Cohn-Bendit, 74. See Xavier Vigna, *L'insubordination ouvrière dans les années 68: Essai d'histoire politique des usines* (Rennes: PUR, 2007).

94. Cohn-Bendit and Cohn-Bendit, *Obsolete Communism*, 127.

95. The title of the English edition, *Obsolete Communism: The Left-Wing Alternative*, loses both the emphasis on historical leftism and the allusion to Lenin conveyed by the original French title, *Le Gauchisme: Remède à la maladie sénile du communisme*, as well as the title of the German translation, *Linksradikalismus—Gewaltkur gegen die Alterskrankheit des Kommunismus*. The book was also translated into Italian and Spanish. Although he coauthored the book with his brother Gabriel, Daniel Cohn-Bendit was responsible for most of its content.

Cohn-Bendit turned the tables. By the late 1960s, he guessed that people plainly saw the "senile" Communists as stuck in obsolete and unrealistic modes of struggle. He wrote that "Leftism is everything that is new in Revolutionary history, and is forever being challenged by the old." Radical students across France protested alongside young workers without authorization from the PCF and CGT, not to speak of the moribund SFIO. "Let the dead bury their dead," he wrote, quoting Marx on the need for revolutionaries to draw their poetry from the future, not the past.[96]

The purpose of the book *Leftism* was not simply to explain the rise and fall of the May Movement. Cohn-Bendit wrote it explicitly as "an attempt to participate in a continuing scene, with all its remarkable spontaneity." The hastily written work stoked the intellectual embers of the Movement after the fire burned out. But some left socialists criticized Cohn-Bendit's celebration of leftism. A guiding spirit of the *Socialism or Barbarism* group, Claude Lefort, claimed that the book's recipe combined "a pinch of realism and a large dose of impudence." In response, Cohn-Bendit used Lefort's own past words against him, claiming that he based his neoleftist stance "on the theses which Lefort (among others) published in *Socialisme ou Barbarie*." Here was another irony of midcentury new lefts. The irreverent Cohn-Bendit declared that "I am not, and do not want to be, anything but a plagiarist when it comes to the preaching of revolutionary theory and practice." He added that the May events, while certainly a "rupture [brèche]" in postwar history, also renewed a lost tradition of leftism that existing organizations had allegedly betrayed.[97]

Unlike Lefort and company, Cohn-Bendit thought that the Movement belonged to a history of grassroots actions that either created new organizational forms or rendered old ones obsolete: "during the Paris Commune of 1871, during the Russian Revolutions of 1905 and 1917, during the Spanish Revolution of 1936, and finally during the Hungarian Revolution of 1956."[98] Insofar as his book tried to connect its readers to a broader neoleftist community, it functioned analogously to the Miles pamphlet *Neu beginnen!* published three decades earlier. Like the Org founder Walter Loewenheim, Cohn-Bendit wanted readers to overcome their sense of isolation by realizing "that hundreds of thousands of others have had identical experiences." Such a realization might build generational consciousness, just as it might help radical students

---

96. Cohn-Bendit and Cohn-Bendit, *Obsolete Communism*, 18. The Marx quote comes from *The Eighteenth Brumaire of Louis Napoleon* (1852).

97. Cohn-Bendit and Cohn-Bendit, *Obsolete Communism*, 16–19. Cf. Morin, Castoriadis, and Lefort, *Mai 1968*.

98. Cohn-Bendit and Cohn-Bendit, *Obsolete Communism*, 16. For a survey of historical leftisms, see Mattick, *Anti-Bolshevik Communism*.

and young workers recover from the apathy that set in after the Movement's collapse.[99]

Unlike Loewenheim, who used the alias Miles, Cohn-Bendit published under his own name, alongside his older brother Gabriel. He knew that the book would reinforce the personality cult that the police and media had created for him in order to put a face on the anonymous Movement. Encouraging that cult would contradict the leaderless spirit of the sixties New Left. In West Germany, Dutschke planned to solve this same problem by escaping the media on a trip abroad. Cohn-Bendit's opposite solution owed to his different temperament and the fact that on May 21, French authorities issued an expulsion order against him: originally stateless but by then a West German citizen, he was denied reentry into France after a visit to Frankfurt. Rather than reject the personality cult entirely, he styled himself an ironic leader of a leaderless movement. He played the role that the authorities and media demanded of him but with a smirk that signaled an inside joke to comrades. After returning to France in disguise, he attended a press conference at the Sorbonne, where journalists were greeted by a crowd of students chanting, "We are all Cohn-Bendit."[100]

In *Leftism*'s final pages, the author outlined what he expected from a future new left. It would have to respect diversity within the movement; oppose privileged expertise; share ideas freely; resist hierarchy; abolish divisions within the working class, including those based on gender; and demand workers' control over factories and businesses. "What we need," he wrote, "is not organization with a capital O, but a host of insurrectional cells, be they ideological groups, study groups—we can even use street gangs." Cohn-Bendit grasped at any means necessary to keep the Movement alive during an era of authoritarian retrenchment. At the same time, his call for a "multiplication of nuclei of confrontation" seemed to offer a recipe for disintegration, not coordinated action. In hoping that every radical group would "find its own form, take its own action, and speak its own language," the iconic left-libertarian Cohn-Bendit unknowingly described the exhaustion of new lefts over the next decade.[101]

99. Cohn-Bendit and Cohn-Bendit, *Obsolete Communism*, 194–95.

100. Touraine, *May Movement*, 248. The more famous slogan in support of Cohn-Bendit was "We are all German Jews. We are all foreigners." See Kalter, *Discovery of the Third World*, 180–82, and Andrew Feenberg and Jim Freedman, *When Poetry Ruled the Streets: The French May Events of 1968* (Albany: SUNY, 2001), 50–52. The 1960 film *Spartacus* (Beverly Hills: Bryna Productions; directed by Stanley Kubrick and starring Kirk Douglas) popularized this dramatic scene, in which the protagonist's comrades declare one after another, "I'm Spartacus."

101. Cohn-Bendit and Cohn-Bendit, *Obsolete Communism*, 255–56.

The social democratic modernizer Richard Löwenthal knew that the sixties New Left would disintegrate. Published together under the title *The Romantic Regression: Normality and Pathology of a Revolution Turned Backwards*, two lectures he delivered in 1967 and 1969 represent a counterpoint to Cohn-Bendit's revenge of leftism. Löwenthal likely borrowed his subtitle from Anna Freud's book *Normality and Pathology in Childhood*, whose German edition appeared in 1968.[102] Just like in his debate with Marcuse at the aforementioned Free University event, he invoked Freud's idea that modern civilization (or industrial society) required an array of repressions in order to sustain itself: sexual repression, familial and institutional hierarchy, moral discipline, labor specialization, and even a social class system. Löwenthal claimed that instead of facing the reality of this civilization and improving it, as did modernizers like him, neoleftist discontents rejected modernity altogether. Their fantasy was actually a premodern community based on unmediated relations and the minimal repression appropriate to a low level of social complexity. He described this fantasy as Romantic nostalgia.[103]

The main goal for postfascist Germany, he claimed, should be the anchoring of democratic institutions in all social areas. As a further goal, the democratic left ought to humanize industrial society and the modern state. Löwenthal reserved his greatest praise for the generation of Germans who came of age right after the fall of Nazism. Instead of becoming responsible democrats like those "45ers," he thought, the '68er generation nihilistically seceded from existing society.[104]

Löwenthal presented the youth revolt as a pathological deviation from normal social integration. He faulted his own antifascist generation for failing to pass down its democratic values to its children and prepare them for the realities of the modern world. The nihilism of the sixties youth, he believed, had precedents dating back to the nineteenth century. He drew connections between "our radical nonconformists" and early utopian socialists like Charles

---

102. Löwenthal, *Der romantische Rückfall*. Cf. Anna Freud, *Wege und Irrwege in der Kinderentwicklung* (Stuttgart: Klett, 1968), published originally in English in 1965. The second of Löwenthal's lectures appeared in English as the mimeographed booklet *Unreason and Revolution* and the essay "Unreason and Revolution," *Encounter*, November 1969, 22–34, which was reprinted in Howe, *Beyond the New Left*, 55–84.

103. This critique of neoleftism's alleged premodernity contrasts with analyses that treat the sixties New Left as a forerunner of postmodernism. For example, see Felsch, *Der lange Sommer der Theorie*; Carl Boggs, *The Socialist Tradition: From Crisis to Decline* (New York: Routledge, 1995), ch. 6; and, most pejoratively, Roger Scruton, *Fools, Frauds and Firebrands: Thinkers of the New Left* [1985] (London: Bloomsbury, 2015), ch. 7.

104. See Moses, *German Intellectuals*, ch. 3. See also Forner, *German Intellectuals*.

Fourier, nationalists like Richard Wagner, anarchists like Mikhail Bakunin, left-wing Nazis like Otto Strasser, and all those "leftist guys on the right" so prevalent in the interwar years.[105] Apart from Fourier, the past nonconformists and cultural pessimists listed by Löwenthal either condoned or encouraged violence. Sixties neoleftists shared with their forerunners a "virulently destructive" nature, he thought. Their politics were voluntarist, elitist, and irresponsible. Like children, they foreshortened their time horizon, expecting immediate social transformation regardless of circumstances: they wanted utopia now.[106]

Löwenthal's book *The Romantic Regression* drew on the standard repertoire of antileftist insults. The student movement was accordingly naïve, impatient, irrational, escapist, dogmatic, and even authoritarian. By contrast, he advocated realism, concrete planning, healthy skepticism, liberal tolerance, compromise, and scientific objectivity. He even dissociated the New Left from the ideas of Marx and Lenin, who for all their faults at least had constructive projects. While Western Europe had its problems, he thought, certain realities of industrial society were inescapable both in the capitalist West and the communist East. As a result of such thinking, he framed Third World problems in terms of modernization and economic development rather than imperialism.[107]

Neoleftists' rejection of democratic institutions, insistence on direct action, and dream of bringing the anticolonial war home posed a threat to the welfare state that veteran antifascists like Löwenthal had fought so hard to create. In his view, the New Left was dangerous because it subverted Western humanistic values, promoting instead "destruction, decay and barbarization." For this former neoleftist grown old, civilization must be defended. Löwenthal's cultural defensiveness helps explain why in 1970 he joined the mostly conservative League for Academic Freedom, which opposed the alleged threat to objective scholarship posed by radical leftists. That decision cost him several friendships, including his former comrades Abendroth and Flechtheim.[108]

---

105. Löwenthal, *Der romantische Rückfall*, 24. See Kurt Hiller's essay on the National Bolsheviks, "Linke Leute von rechts."

106. Löwenthal, *Unreason and Revolution*, 22. Löwenthal twice acknowledged his debt to Raymond Aron for associating the sixties youth with the nihilist tradition. Cf. Aron, *Elusive Revolution*. The source of this idea was possibly Hermann Rauschning's book about the Nazi regime, *The Revolution of Nihilism: Warning to the West* [1938], trans. E. W. Dickes (New York: Alliance, 1939).

107. Löwenthal, *Unreason and Revolution*, 10 and 32–33.

108. Ossip K. Flechtheim to Richard Löwenthal, November 23, 1970, DNB, NL Flechtheim, EB 98/179, and Flechtheim to Wolfgang Abendroth, November 24, 1970, IISG, NL Abendroth,

Ultimately he was correct that the sixties youth sought warm communitarian bonds as a palliative against cold, rationalistic modernity. But Löwenthal's defense of technocratic modernity had its own problems. The writer Johano Strasser claims that *The Romantic Regression* exposed, among other things, the environmental blindness of social democratic modernizers. Decades after the fact, the New Left critique of industrial society looked less like irrational romanticism than "the anticipation of a modern, entirely rational ecological consciousness."[109]

Despite its weaknesses, Löwenthal's critique of the New Left still has its proponents. The US historian Neaman, for example, describes the student movement as "a late form of German romanticism" that "mirrored the romantic-nationalist reaction from the post-Napoleonic period." The German historian Götz Aly makes a similar argument. Looking back in irritation at his own radical past, Aly now views the New Left as another symptom of Germany's totalitarian century. He indicts the anti-authoritarian youth for repeating all the mistakes of the Nazi youth.[110] Across decades, the consistency between these antileftist critiques is remarkable.

In addition to Romanticism and totalitarianism, some critics have interpreted the New Left as a secular religion. Löwenthal saw in Marcuse's negative utopianism a revival of messianic redemption combined with philosophical existentialism. Likewise, the French political theorist Raymond Aron thought that the militant students and intellectuals were in search of a new religion after the death of god. The Polish philosopher Leszek Kołakowski detected a revolutionary eschatology within the neo-Marxist movements of the 1960s. In basic agreement, the political scientist Kurt Sontheimer brought the antileftist critique full circle by interpreting the students' dreams of liberation as "products of a fantasy that is understood better as the consequence of a revolutionary neurosis promoted by group-inbreeding than as the result of a rational assessment of political circumstances."[111] When confronted with slogans like "Be realistic, demand the impossible," antileftist critics pathologized new lefts.

---

96. See Nikolai Wehrs, *Protest der Professoren: Der "Bund Freiheit der Wissenschaft" in den 1970er Jahren* (Göttingen: Wallstein, 2014).

109. Johano Strasser, "Streitschrift wider die Studentenbewegung," *Deutschlandfunk*, January 10, 2011, https://www.deutschlandfunk.de/streitschrift-wider-die-studentenbewegung.1310.de.html?dram:article_id=194276.

110. Neaman, *Free Radicals*, 14–15, and Aly, *Unser Kampf 1968*.

111. Sontheimer, *Das Elend unserer Intellektuellen*, 169; Aron, *Elusive Revolution*; and Kołakowski, *Main Currents of Marxism*, 3: chs. 11–13. Cf. Kołakowski's more sympathetic appraisal, "Concept of the Left."

Neoleftism's Moveable Feast

The fact that such criticisms were formulated by people of Löwenthal's generation and milieu is of course ironic: they targeted young people who spoke and acted the same way many of them had at that age. The organizational forms and theoretical consciousness developed by the sixties New Left resembled to a remarkable degree those of the antifascist new left. The myriad subversive groups, extraparliamentary oppositions, and action committees—despite their various compositions and goals—copied the decentralized style of the interwar small groups such as New Beginning, Socialist Battle, and the Spanish antifascist militias.

Besides a similar phenomenology of organization, midcentury new lefts all experienced a revolutionary suspension of time. An amazing thing about May 1968 was the extent to which participants chronicled the daily and hourly events as they happened. Contemporary journals and magazines printed detailed chronologies in every issue. Often those chronologies were accompanied by tables of acronyms (CAR, JCR, PCF, etc.) and glossaries of keywords (autonomy, reification, alienation, etc.). Already in the June issue of a journal called the *Event* one could read a collectively authored "First History of the Revolution."[112] Activists felt compelled to write the history of events that were still unfolding, as if time were compressed or suspended. Despite the attention paid by people like Cohn-Bendit to leftist tradition, "1968" was actually experienced as historic rather than historical—that is, as a qualitative rupture in time rather than part of a sequence or process.[113] The revolutionary tradition in general was lived as a simultaneity of historic ruptures; that is why activists in 1968 found it easy to conjure up 1936 or 1917 or 1871 or 1789. Only after the event and at the level of analysis do historical processes come into view.

Militants who experienced "1968" as a revolutionary suspension of time were thus able to recall those events in memory decades later as if they were happening now. Christians refer to holy days that are not affixed to specific dates as moveable feasts. The events of May represented a moveable feast that the '68er generation would relive again and again, even to the point of traumatic repetition.

112. *L'événement*, no. 29 (June 1968).

113. Here I agree with Morin, Castoriadis, and Lefort in *Mai 1968*. On "divine" revolutionary time versus "mythic" ordinary time, see Walter Benjamin, "Critique of Violence" [1921], in *Reflections: Essays, Aphorisms, Autobiographical Writings*, trans. Edmund Jephcott and ed. Peter Demetz (New York: Harcourt Brace Jovanovich, 1978), 277–300. Benjamin also distinguished between an emergent "now-time [Jetztzeit]" and homogeneous empty time in his "Theses on the Philosophy of History." Cf. Badiou, *Being and Event*, bk. 5.

In the wake of the events themselves, observers quickly noted the political failure of the New Left. Nowhere did its adherents seize power. In fact, nowhere did neoleftists dislodge the hegemony of traditional left parties and unions, which in some places enjoyed electoral success into the 1970s. As this book has shown, however, political power was never the main goal for new lefts. Young militants who went underground, studied theory, or took to the streets were not interested in building a new parliamentary coalition. Seizing the state was peripheral to the neoleftist project, despite what antileftists might have feared. "For uncompromised as they were by the exigencies of power," the historian Martin Jay has written about the soviets, "they could remain the repository of phantasmic hopes rather than betray the promise of socialism. Their prefigurative function was thus ironically enhanced by their practical defeat."[114] The same could be said about the action committees of May and all other neoleftist forms.

The goal for new lefts was internal: to create a self-perpetuating movement and, through historic ruptures, to preview life in a free and egalitarian society. To make that feeling last was the affective dimension of the neoleftist dilemma. New lefts looked inward in an attempt to sustain their own capacity to begin anew, keep the revolution going, and enjoy their moveable feast. A fixation on permanent renewal helps explain the multiplication of small groups in the 1930s, the postwar years, and the late 1960s. It also accounts for the centrality of debates about new forms of collective action, debates that link Western Europe's midcentury new lefts to our own era of global uprisings. Then as now, organization is back on the agenda.

114. Jay, "No Power to the Soviets," 65.

Epilogue

Everything changes. You can
Begin anew with your last breath.
But what happened has happened. And the water
You poured into the wine, you can
Never pour out again.

What happened has happened. The water
You poured into the wine, you can
Never pour out again, but
Everything changes. You can
Begin anew with your last breath.

—BERTOLT BRECHT, "EVERYTHING
CHANGES [ALLES WANDELT SICH],"
MY TRANSLATION

THIS BOOK HAS ANALYZED the historical continuities between radical antifascism in the 1920s and 1930s, left socialism in the 1940s and 1950s, and antiauthoritarianism in the 1960s.[1] Historians of the German and Western European left usually treat those periods as separate. The interwar period concerns the crisis of the old left, as the divided workers' movement suffered defeat at the hands of fascism. And the postwar period concerns social democratic modernization, the welfare state, and the sixties New Left. In actual left theory and practice, however, the contrast between interwar and postwar lefts was not so stark. This book has shown how intergenerational transmission and

1. This epilogue includes excerpts from Terence Renaud, "Assembling a New Left," *Los Angeles Review of Books* (Aug. 16, 2018). © 2018. Reproduced with permission of *Los Angeles Review of Books*.

organizational imitation, or the dialogue between younger and older militants and the copying of past alternatives to the party form, forged a link between radical antifascists, left socialists, and anti-authoritarians.

Historians of antifascism tend to look backward to the revolutionary crisis of 1918–19 and earlier in order to explain the fratricidal conflict between Social Democrats, Communists, anarchists, and other lefts. The underlying claim is usually that division on the left enabled fascists to seize power, a claim that this book does not dispute. Historians of the sixties meanwhile tend to look forward to ways in which the anti-authoritarian revolt of that decade anticipated the new social movements and culture of the 1970s through the present day, another claim that this book does not dispute. Instead, I have turned the gazes of both bodies of scholarship around to face each other: antifascism looking forward, anti-authoritarianism looking backward. This introversion brings the phenomenon of neoleftism into focus. Left socialism sits at the center of this field of vision.

Both the interwar and the postwar periods witnessed a struggle on the fringes of official Social Democratic and Communist parties over the issue of internal democracy. The German term captures the meaning more precisely: *innerparteiliche Demokratie*, or intraparty democracy. Over several decades, young militants repeatedly challenged the bureaucratic and authoritarian tendencies that they detected in the large parties and unions of the left. In today's language, one might describe this as a populist revolt against party elites.[2] The leading militants were intellectuals of diverse backgrounds who, under conditions of political and cultural repression, imagined alternative ways of organizing movements to transform society. Radical antifascists, left socialists, and anti-authoritarians built "new lefts" out of the defeated or obsolete remnants of what they considered the old left. They fought a two-front war against conservatism, capitalism, and imperialism at large and against oligarchy within the left itself. Despite different circumstances, neoleftists consciously faced the same dilemma: How do you sustain internal democracy and achieve social change without resorting to hierarchy, delegation, and other institutionalized forms of politics? In other words, how do you keep your new left forever young?

Only in the 1950s did militants in Western Europe start giving a proper name to this fringe phenomenon. The New Left formalized a long-term process and radical tradition of breaking free from Social Democratic and

---

2. For example, see Jake Watts and Tim Bale, "Populism as an Intra-party Phenomenon: The British Labour Party under Jeremy Corbyn," *British Journal of Politics and International Relations* 21, no. 1 (October 2018): 99–115.

Communist institutions. The various neoleftists examined in this book—from New Beginning to the May Movement—failed to solve the dilemma of sustaining internal democracy. Recognizing failure was a symbolic act of maturity for many radicals who later gave up on new lefts. Some exited politics altogether, but most ex-neoleftists "grew up" by accommodating themselves to pragmatic reforms within the framework of democratic capitalism. Thus representatives of a formerly neoleftist generation often found themselves targeted by a rising new left, which again demanded total transformation and a radical break from existing society.

This book's main trope, as Hayden White would interpret it, is irony. New lefts were constantly evolving into old lefts, and the cornerstones of one generation turned into stumbling blocks for the next. In White's terms, this book's mode of emplotment is tragicomedy: tragic, because midcentury neoleftists believed that they acted freely, even though their actions were caught in a cycle of renewal-obsolescence from which historically no one seemed to escape; and comic, because they did enjoy temporary triumphs and occasional reconciliations of their desires with the opposing forces of the social world.[3] This book does not impose a contrived narrative on its subjects. Many neoleftists themselves showed an ironic awareness of their tragicomic emplotment. That awareness influenced their response to the neoleftist dilemma.

The irony of neoleftism was often most visible in members of the antifascist generation who engaged in self-criticism during the tumultuous 1960s. Fritz Erler, whose prestige in the German Social Democratic Party (SPD) was surpassed only by that of the future chancellor Willy Brandt, reflected that "just as in my youth I stood somewhat to the left of my father, so my children even today would stand within the general spectrum of Social Democracy rather somewhat to the left of me." Reflecting further on the generational divide, he lamented the fact that members of Social Democratic youth organizations no longer addressed older party members as "comrade" or with the familiar *Du*. The shift to the formal *Sie* indicated a real problem. The gap of experience that separated the antifascist generation from the discontented youth had grown too wide. Erler observed that "one cannot simply transplant the traditions of the youth movement of the Twenties into the Sixties."[4]

3. White, *Metahistory*, 9.

4. Interview of Fritz Erler by Günter Gaus, ZDF broadcast on January 7, 1965, transcript in Erler, *Politik für Deutschland*, 19–44 (at 25–26). It is also worth noting that in the 1960s few members of the antifascist generation shared the youth's taste for recreational drugs, free love, and rock music.

The twin tasks of renewing the left and preserving the socialist tradition came into contradiction during that decade. The SPD leader Waldemar von Knoeringen launched an effort in 1966 called Mobilization of Democracy, which anticipated Brandt's later campaign slogan, "Let's take a chance on more democracy [Mehr Demokratie wagen]." This effort sought to revive the kind of discussions about democratization that had occurred in the early years of postwar reconstruction. Knoeringen enlisted former members of the interwar small groups such as Erler and Richard Löwenthal in a public speaking tour.[5] But he worried that mainstream Social Democrats had already lost touch with the burgeoning New Left. "What should you say to young people when you want to convince them that they should join the cause of Social Democracy," he wondered anxiously, "and they ask about 'socialism'?" Increasingly pessimistic about the work of his own generation, he thought that the SPD, despite its recent electoral success, no longer had an answer.[6]

Löwenthal was more optimistic. He remembered himself in his fifties as advocating "a newer politics, a freer politics, a more active politics" in the context of West Germany's return to the world stage through Brandt's Ostpolitik. While he could not countenance the harsh tone of debate adopted by young people "who wanted to talk about Vietnam at every assembly," he did think that there were some "personally very decent and very qualified" people among the radical young intellectuals.[7] Chief among them was his former student Rudi Dutschke, who took courses with him at the Free University. On April 11, 1968, a right-wing extremist named Josef Bachmann tried to assassinate Dutschke, shooting him in the head. The resulting anger felt by students as well as Social Democrats like Löwenthal prompted a truce between the warring anti-authoritarian and antifascist generations. Spending that year as a visiting scholar at the Hoover Institution in Stanford, California, Löwenthal offered to help Dutschke find a quiet academic home in the United States where he could convalesce and finish his PhD. The ex-firebrand of the antifascist new left wrote to the anti-authoritarian spokesman, "I have always appreciated you a lot despite our often sharp political disagreements—not only because of your intellectual qualities and your seriousness about facts, but also

5. Knoeringen, *Mobilisierung der Demokratie*. See Mehringer, *Waldemar von Knoeringen*, 384.

6. Waldemar von Knoeringen to Richard Löwenthal (Berlin-Schöneberg), November 2, 1966, FES, NL Knoeringen, 84, and Mehringer, *Waldemar von Knoeringen*, 384. See also Knoeringen and Lohmar, *Was bleibt vom Sozialismus?*

7. Interview of Richard Löwenthal by Hans-Christoph Knebusch on *Zeugen des Jahrhunderts* (1989), YouTube, Zeitzeugen-portal, accessed May 2018, www.youtube.com/watch?v=rbLO3xKC2rA.

because of your honesty and fairness in disputes."[8] Dutschke would not return to the United States, however, despite his earlier research plans and Löwenthal's offer. Recovering from a gunshot wound to the head required extensive physical and speech therapy. He never fully recovered. In 1979 he died of a wound-related seizure.

Germans were central to the history of new lefts. From their experiences of mass socialist politics and two world wars emerged radical antifascism, left socialism, and anti-authoritarianism in a neoleftist continuity more pronounced than elsewhere in Europe. This book's central example, the group New Beginning and its afterlives, demonstrates the transnational connections forged between German and other European new lefts. New Beginning's members routinely crossed borders in their fight against fascism. Their revolutionary ambitions and arena for political action were international. And their years of exile in Czechoslovakia, France, Spain, Britain, the United States, and beyond made a lasting impression. New Beginning was both generative and representative of midcentury new lefts, whose specific politics did of course vary country by country.

The poem by Bertolt Brecht at the head of this epilogue conveys the idea of renewal that informs this book's interpretation of new lefts. Brecht wrote "Everything Changes" in 1944 while in Californian exile, a moment at which that greatest of all German left dramatists reflected on his own damaged life against the backdrop of revolutionary history. Everything changes and you can begin anew with your last breath: this expression of hope begins and ends the palindromic poem. But the water you poured into the wine you can never pour out again: this expression of despair at irreparable loss, compromise, and dilution of the historic cause operates as the poem's fulcrum. What happened has happened, so you never start again with a blank slate. When applied to this book's narrative, the poem suggests that midcentury new lefts always bore within them remnants of past defeats. The organizational experimentation and theoretical self-critique practiced by new lefts did the work of mourning, as the historian Enzo Traverso has powerfully suggested.[9] New lefts' creativity in moments of crisis also entailed a knowing *trotzdem*, a *malgré tout*, or a "nevertheless and despite-it-all" commitment to change everything.[10] An awareness of possible futility belonged to the neoleftist dilemma. It was even a sign

---

8. Richard Löwenthal (Stanford, CA) to Rudi Dutschke, August 19, 1968, HIS, NL Dutschke, 152/11.

9. Traverso, *Left-Wing Melancholia*.

10. Cf. the title of an autobiography by the futurologist and one-time New Beginning member Robert Jungk, *Trotzdem: Mein Leben für die Zukunft*.

of maturity, which reinforces this book's effort to debunk the myth of young radicals' naiveté.

In addition to its historical argument, this book defines neoleftism as a political phenomenon whose relevance extends beyond the mid-twentieth century. Much as one can write a history of liberalism or conservatism that includes people and movements that did not always call themselves liberal or conservative,[11] I have framed this book as an attempt to rethink neoleftism as a theory and a practice that transcend actual usage of the term "new left." However, neoleftism differs from other ideologies such as liberalism or conservatism in its determination by organizational form. It involves a total commitment to synchronize revolutionary means and ends. On the broad historical spectrum of the left, it represents the most prefigurative position: the desired future society must be modeled now in the presently existing movement.[12] And rather more than Social Democrats or Communists or anarchists, neoleftists worried about the paradox of their own enterprise.[13] The inability to sustain new forms, the ephemerality of grassroots action, the challenge of internal democracy: this book has described the neoleftist dilemma in several ways. It entails a preoccupation with organization among militants struggling to achieve radical democracy within their own movement and in society at large. Once-radical forms can and do change into routinized forms. Militants' resistance to routinization often translates into self-conscious nonconformism. Because it unfolds over time as militants realize the limits of their own organizational forms, neoleftism must be understood as a process—a dialectical succession of new lefts—rather than a stable political ideology. This book pushes back against any definition of "the New Left" derived from characteristics of just one historical phase in that succession, such as sixties counterculture. A processual concept of neoleftism also opposes any psychologization of individual or group trajectories from far left to moderate center and sometimes to far right. While it is true that sixties neoleftists such as Bernd Rabehl and Horst Mahler turned into far-right figures, the explanation for that turn lies not in some eternal psychology of rebellion. Psychobiographical explanations for ideology and organizational form often culminate in the pathologization of politics. Such explanations are historically blind.

---

11. For example, see Helena Rosenblatt, *The Lost History of Liberalism: From Ancient Rome to the Twenty-First Century* (Princeton, NJ: Princeton University Press, 2018), and Russell Kirk, *The Conservative Mind: From Burke to Santayana* (Chicago: H. Regnery, 1953).

12. On prefigurative politics, see Raekstad and Gradin, *Prefigurative Politics*; U. Gordon, "Prefigurative Politics"; W. Breines, *Community and Organization*; and Boggs, "Marxism."

13. A possible exception is Peter Gay's classic interpretation of Eduard Bernstein's revisionism, *Dilemma of Democratic Socialism*.

For example, after evolving from a vanguardist cadre group, New Beginning in the mid-1930s reorganized itself as an internally democratic but still elite group that tried to transform the parties and unions of the left from within. The pressures of underground resistance, survival in exile, and collaboration in the Allied war effort caused that "democratic elite" organization to implode. Many of New Beginning's former members nonetheless carried the idea of a democratic elite forward into their plans for postwar reconstruction. That was most apparent during the fusion struggle in Allied-occupied Berlin, when former New Beginning members plotted behind the scenes to resist the Soviet-sponsored push for a Socialist Unity Party. The idea of a democratic elite was also apparent in the 1950s during the modernization of the SPD, which shifted authority away from the base and middle echelons to the parliamentary faction and party leaders at the top (several of whom were former New Beginning members). The party officially abandoned Marxism, and its leaders interpreted that move as a progressive step toward modernization. Left socialist opponents of the modernizers interpreted the organizational and ideological reforms as bureaucratic measures for suppressing internal dissent and accommodating Social Democracy to the West German status quo. Out of that context arose the sixties youth revolt against authority and the turn toward extra-parliamentary, nonparty action.

There were surely elitist tendencies in the West German New Left, too, especially within Subversive Action and the leadership of the Socialist German Student League. But that decade's moment of ironic reversal occurred when the decentralized action favored by anti-authoritarians proved unable to revolutionize society or even bring about radical reforms. The events of May 1968 in France preoccupy the last chapter of this book, mainly because the action committees represented the apotheosis—or *reductio ad absurdum*—of new lefts' organized spontaneity. It was the emergence of this organizational form in the French May rather than the explicit name New Left (French militants called themselves the Movement) that marked that moment as a culmination of midcentury new lefts. The French-German neoleftist Daniel Cohn-Bendit was almost immediately critical of the Movement after its defeat in the summer of 1968. "Once again," he wrote, "the bands of hope stand at the corners chanting their old litanies, telling the workers that only by heeding the call of the 'vanguard' will they ever achieve their emancipation. Words are apparently more important than deeds once again."[14] The Movement disintegrated into vanguardist cells shouting tired slogans, once again alienated from any industrial or postindustrial base.

14. Cohn-Bendit and Cohn-Bendit, *Obsolete Communism*, 83.

Precisely because of its structurelessness, or its constitutive lack of formal organization, the French Movement and its global analogues had nowhere to go after the immediate revolutionary situation ended. Restructuring after defeat proved impossible for a structureless movement. Whereas an "organized political movement can make a retreat, go underground, work out new forms of action, and plan its strategy," wrote the sociologist Alain Touraine, the Movement "was pure offensive; it could not make a successful retreat."[15] This was a paradox of sixties anti-authoritarianism: movements that resisted formal political institutions seemed destined to burn out rather than fade away.

Besides May 1968 in France, other candidates for peak neoleftism in that decade include the Italian activism that began in 1966 and culminated in the so-called Hot Autumn of wildcat industrial strikes in 1969–70. And there were numerous examples of neoleftism in Japan, Mexico, the Middle East, and elsewhere.[16] Perhaps the most obvious candidate is the US New Left, which formed in the early 1960s in association with the Students for a Democratic Society, the campus free speech movement, and the Black civil rights movement. Historians such as Gerd-Rainer Horn have noted the transnational links between US and Western European new lefts, particularly in their exchange of protest tactics like sit-ins and occupations.[17] The historian Peter Linebaugh was a graduate student at Columbia University, then the most militant East Coast campus. He and his comrades enthusiastically saluted Paris: "With a wide brush I painted *Dessous les pavés c'est la plage* [Beneath the cobblestones, the beach] on the wall. And Paris saluted us." On both sides of the Atlantic, militants "took up the slogan *l'imagination prend le pouvoir*": all power to the imagination.[18] But critics at the time observed an important difference between American militants and their Western European counterparts: organizationally the US New Left had not emerged out of an "old left" of workers' parties and trade unions.[19] Even the most organized part of the manifold New Left, the Students for a Democratic Society, was at first a youth arm of the League for Industrial Democracy, itself a creation not of the workers' movement but of left-liberal intellectuals. Except for "red-diaper babies" who grew up in Communist families during the McCarthy era—and many of those were

15. Touraine, *May Movement*, 316.

16. On global new lefts and protest movements in the 1960s, see Chen et al., *Routledge Handbook of the Global Sixties*.

17. Horn, *Spirit of '68*.

18. Peter Linebaugh, "Be Realistic: Demand the Impossible," *Boston Review*, August 1, 2018.

19. For example, see Howe, *Beyond the New Left*. Howe and other contributors to this volume repeated the same antileftist rhetoric used by social democratic modernizers in Western Europe.

immigrant families with roots in the European workers' movement—the US New Left developed primarily among unorganized middle-class youth who were disillusioned with New Deal liberalism, a welfare state that condoned racism and poverty, and the war in Vietnam.[20]

Nevertheless, internal critiques of the US New Left often centered on organizational form. In the early 1970s, the feminist scholar and activist Jo Freeman (alias Joreen) published several versions of an essay titled "The Tyranny of Structurelessness." She argued that structurelessness had become an anti-organizational fetish for the women's liberation movement. In reaction to patriarchal capitalism in general and the misogynist behavior of male New Left leaders in particular, radical feminists understandably promoted leaderless collectives, open discussion in "rap sessions," and a communal lifestyle. But any collection of people who gather together for a cause, Freeman observed, implicitly adopts some kind of group structure. Only an anarchy of isolated individuals can properly be called structureless in the absolute sense. In practice, structureless movements just mean those that are organized informally. Her critique proceeded from there. Informal organization often functions as "a way of masking power," she argued, because a lack of rules or formal procedures results in the creation of an in-group with special privileges. Unstructured groups foster elitism, since newcomers or less active participants have no way of accessing the group's informal decision-making process. De facto leadership by an unelected and unaccountable minority Hannah Arendt had once associated with the "structurelessness of the totalitarian state."[21] Freeman had in mind something more like a sorority clique. Aside from the exclusivity of such informal leaderships, she claimed, unstructured groups are useless for accomplishing political tasks. According to her, only structured groups are capable of running a national campaign or planning large-scale action. So she called instead for "democratic structuring" as a progressive alternative to the ideology of structurelessness, the hierarchical form of male-led New Left

20. On the experience of red-diaper babies, see the memoir by Bettina Aptheker, *Intimate Politics: How I Grew Up Red, Fought for Free Speech, and Became a Feminist Rebel* (New York: Basic Books, 2011), and the collection edited by Judy Kaplan and Linn Shapiro, *Red Diapers: Growing Up in the Communist Left* (Urbana: University of Illinois Press, 1998). On alliances that did occur between US New Left activists and organized labor, see Van Gosse, *Rethinking the New Left: An Interpretative History* (New York: Palgrave Macmillan, 2005), ch. 3; Jeffrey W. Coker, *Confronting American Labor: The New Left Dilemma* (Columbia: University of Missouri Press, 2002); Peter B. Levy, *The New Left and Labor in the 1960s* (Urbana: University of Illinois Press, 1994); and Maurice Isserman, *If I Had a Hammer: The Death of the Old Left and the Birth of the New Left* (New York: Basic Books, 1987).

21. Arendt, *Origins of Totalitarianism*, 418.

cadres, or the bureaucracy of electoral parties. Among her recommendations, she included assigning tasks by lot (sortition), distributing authority as much as possible, delegating tasks as little as possible, rotating responsibilities, keeping the flow of information transparent, and ensuring equal access to the group's material resources. Her concept of democratic structuring resembled the action committee form of May 1968. Even in her astute critique of structurelessness, however, Freeman did not acknowledge the neoleftist dilemma of bureaucratic hardening over time.[22]

Few radical groups in the United States or elsewhere adopted Freeman's recommendations. The first half of the 1970s saw a gradual disintegration of the New Left in Western Europe. Every student magazine, discussion group, commune, and Maoist cell practiced its own, idiosyncratic leftism. Dutschke had foreseen this possibility already in November 1967, when he sat down with Günter Gaus for a widely watched television interview. The only way to avoid splintering and a loss of momentum was "to structure the transformation process, a prolonged process, as a process of developing the consciousness of participants in the movement." Only then, he said, would it become "impossible for the elites to manipulate us."[23] Structuring a resilient militant consciousness amounted to what the Italian theorist Antonio Gramsci had called a war of position, as opposed to a war of maneuver that directly confronts the state and ruling classes. Dutschke claimed that such indirect consciousness-building would be "a long march," further alluding to the French theorist Régis Debray's survey of guerrilla wars in Latin America.[24] Without an appropriate structure, militant consciousness could easily dissipate. After the failures of 1967–68 and during his own long recovery from a gunshot wound, Dutschke reformulated this concept as a march *through* the institutions of existing society. He encouraged the anti-authoritarian generation to transform its revolutionary energies into pragmatic work within a capitalist and liberal democratic framework. Neoleftists should become teachers, civil servants, and even politicians. Their goal should not be to assimilate or give up on the revolution, but rather to build up antisystemic capacities over time.[25]

22. Freeman, "Tyranny of Structurelessness."

23. Quoted in "Der lange Marsch," *Der Spiegel*, December 11, 1967, 52–66 (at 53).

24. Gramsci, *Prison Notebooks*, 106–20 and 229–43, and Dutschke, foreward to Debray, *Der lange Marsch*. The long march also refers to the Chinese Red Army's strategic retreat in 1934–35 from the nationalist Kuomintang army, during which Mao Zedong rose to prominence. See Slobodian, "Meanings of Western Maoism." See also Lovell, *Maoism*.

25. The idea of a march through the institutions became Dutschke's leitmotif. See his posthumous memoirs *Mein langer Marsch*.

The sixties New Left split in three directions. One group matured into anticommunist pragmatists who accepted the framework of Western democratic capitalism. A number of West German militants rejoined the SPD, which showed vitality under the leadership of Brandt and Helmut Schmidt. Some in this group consciously followed Dutschke's call to work through the institutions. Others bitterly rejected the whole tradition of new lefts.[26] In France, a few veterans of May were influenced by Alexander Solzhenitsyn's exposé of the Soviet gulags, which turned them definitively against Marxism. Championing human rights and liberal internationalism, these "new philosophers" included André Glucksmann, Alain Finkielkraut, and other modish television personalities who repurposed neoleftist theory to denounce totalitarianism. One scholar has summarized the intellectual history of France since 1968 as a shift from revolution to ethics.[27]

A second group hardened its opposition to capitalism and the democratic state, organized conspiratorial cadres, and even engaged in terrorism. The far left in the 1970s was characterized by sensational acts of violence committed by an almost religiously committed minority. In the spring of 1967, Dutschke befriended the far-left journalist Ulrike Meinhof, whose magazine *Konkret* paired intelligent essays on Marxism with pornographic images of women—a sort of *Playboy* for radicals. Meinhof underwent a process of radicalization after 1967–68. Along with Mahler and a few Socialist German Student League stalwarts, she cofounded the Red Army Faction in 1970, which over the next few years carried out a series of terrorist acts. The historian Karrin Hanshew argues that people on the left could apologize for Red Army Faction terrorism into the mid-1970s because of the prevalent concept of counterviolence. According to that concept, targeted coercion or destruction of property merely countered the systemic violence of imperialist war and the capitalist state. But after a few kidnappings and murders that culminated in the German Autumn of 1977, former neoleftists abandoned the concept of counterviolence and condemned far-left terrorism as

26. For example, the former student activist Michael Schneider published an essay in 1971 that skewered the Maoist cadre culture to which he once belonged and reasserted Social Democratic virtues of sobriety, pragmatism, and party discipline. The essay title played on Cohn-Bendit's "senile disorder" trope. Schneider, "Gegen den Linken Dogmatismus, eine 'Alterskrankheit' des Kommunismus."

27. Bourg, *From Revolution to Ethics*. See also Eleanor Davey, *Idealism Beyond Borders: The French Revolutionary Left and the Rise of Humanitarianism, 1954–1988* (Cambridge: Cambridge University Press, 2015); Michael Christofferson, *French Intellectuals against the Left: The Antitotalitarian Moment of the 1970's* (New York: Berghahn, 2004); and Ross, *May '68*.

illegitimate. Nonviolence became an essential condition of democratic contestation. Similar turns occurred in Italy and France, launching what another
historian has called the era of nonviolence.[28]

Partly in reaction to far-left terrorism and partly out of frustration at Social
Democracy, a third group of former neoleftists broke with working-class tradition entirely. They funneled into the new social movements, which concentrated on issues such as women's rights, disability rights, gay rights, and human
rights. The growing environmentalist movement drew on a tradition of anti-
nuclear protests that dated back to the 1950s and had real democratic potential.[29] Participants in these movements were the chief constituency of another
political force that came on the scene at the end of the 1970s: the Greens.
Ideologically neither right nor left (though leaning left), the West German and
European Greens nevertheless experienced a neoleftist dilemma in terms of
organization. A factional battle broke out between a fundamentalist wing (in
German, known as the Fundis), which wanted decentralized action and absolute commitment to principle, and a realistic wing (the Realos), which wanted
to transform the grassroots movement into a stable party and eventually participate in government. The Realos won.[30]

The West German Greens accepted a degree of institutionalization when
they entered parliament in 1983 as the first new party with sufficient electoral
backing since the founding of the Federal Republic. There they joined Social
Democrats in the opposition against the center-right coalition of conservative
Christian Democrats and liberal Free Democrats. With the exception of
France, where a center-left government took shape around François Mitter-
rand's Socialist Party, the 1980s witnessed conservative retrenchment at the
national level across Western Europe and the United States. Welfare states
crumbled, the Cold War intensified, and those who stayed true to leftism

28. Hanshew, *Terror and Democracy*, and Nehring, "Era of Non-violence." See also Hanno
Balz, *Von Terroristen, Sympathisanten und dem starken Staat: Die öffentliche Debatte über die RAF
in den 70er Jahren* (Frankfurt am Main: Campus, 2008), and Alessandro Orsini, *Anatomy of the
Red Brigades: The Religious Mind-Set of Modern Terrorists* [2010], trans. Sarah J. Nodes (Ithaca,
NY: Cornell University Press, 2016).

29. See Milder, *Greening Democracy*, and Tompkins, *Better Active than Radioactive!*

30. On the relationship between the New Left and the Greens, see the "from-red-to-green"
biographies by Hockenos, *Joschka Fischer*, and Stamer, *Cohn-Bendit*. See also Markovits and
Gorski, *German Left*, and Carl Boggs, "Rethinking the Sixties Legacy: From New Left to New
Social Movements," in *Breaking Chains: Social Movements and Collective Action*, ed. Michael
Peter Smith (New Brunswick, NJ: Transaction, 1991), 50–68.

tended to leave the traditional political arena, adopt alternative lifestyles, and withdraw into autonomist communes.[31]

Traces of the New Left and its anti-authoritarian sensibility remained in the 1980s and 1990s. At the level of theory, post-Marxists tried to articulate a program of radical democracy that could mobilize "the people" beyond identification with any particular class. Post-Marxism has lately inspired a revival of left populism in Europe.[32] A more militant legacy of neoleftism materialized in the alter-globalization movement, which came to a head in the remarkable protests in Seattle against the World Trade Organization in 1999. Cohn-Bendit's description of how the action committees of May 1968 organized previously apolitical people into a community of solidarity could just as well apply to the Seattle protests. As a background for the tentative new lefts of the 1990s, one must keep in mind the thorough capture of European center-left parties and the US Democratic Party by corporate interests and neoliberal economic policy. The political scientist Peter Mair referred to the hollowing out of Western democracy, as technocratic party leaders operated without accountability to any member or voter base.[33] With no place for them in the established left parties and little chance of integration into a declining labor movement, latter-day neoleftists engaged in sporadic environmentalist actions, sectarian disputes in fringe parties, and tentative efforts to build a new movement around twenty-first-century concerns.

The 2008 financial crisis sparked a renewal of the alter-globalization movement, transposing it into new forms of action. Mass protests against austerity and inequality, left populist movements, and growing unrest in the eurozone resuscitated the socialist idea.[34] The year 2011 was miraculous in this respect. First, millions of young people, workers, and citizens in Arab countries took to the streets in protest against authoritarian regimes and flagging economies. As this Arab Spring bloomed, anti-austerity protests swept through Spain,

31. See Reichardt, *Authentizität und Gemeinschaft*; Häberlen, *Emotional Politics*; and Katsiaficas, *Subversion of Politics*.

32. See Laclau and Mouffe, *Hegemony and Socialist Strategy*, and more recently Mouffe, *For a Left Populism*. See also Breckman, *Adventures of the Symbolic*, and Therborn, *From Marxism to Post-Marxism?* For a critique, see Anton Jäger, "We Bet the House on Left Populism—and Lost," *Jacobin*, November 25, 2019.

33. Mair, *Ruling the Void*. The neoliberalization of center-left parties peaked in the 1990s, especially with New Labour in the UK and "third way" Social Democracy across Continental Europe. But the process started in the 1950s during the first era of social democratic modernization. See chapter 6 and Mudge, *Leftism Reinvented*.

34. See Honneth, *Idea of Socialism*, and Hägglund, *This Life*. For a survey of post-2008 new lefts, see Susan Watkins, "Oppositions," *New Left Review*, no. 98 (March–April 2016): 5–30.

Portugal, and Greece; riots shook London; and Occupy Wall Street shut down Lower Manhattan. Despite different national circumstances, participants imagined themselves as taking part in a common enterprise: the democratic revolt of the "99 percent" against oligarchical elites. These uprisings scaled up the Seattle protests against the World Trade Organization twelve years earlier: they involved the same mixture of planning and spontaneous assembly at symbolic sites of finance and trade. In his sweeping chronicle *Why It's Kicking Off Everywhere* (2012), the journalist Paul Mason described the situation as "a revolution caused by the near collapse of free-market capitalism combined with an upswing in technical innovation, a surge in desire for individual freedom and a change in human consciousness about what freedom means." He highlighted the role of young activists using social media as a catalyst for the uprisings. These millennials had only ever experienced economic precarity and downward social mobility, which Mason likened to the experience of drifters during the Great Depression. He argued that technological innovations and the conditions of casualized labor in the gig economy caused a change in generational consciousness, which so far has not found expression in changed social relations. The global uprisings represented "the networked individual colliding with the economic crisis."[35]

The theorists Michael Hardt and Antonio Negri have gone further than most in linking these latest new lefts to problems of organization. From their breakout collaboration *Empire* (2000) through their book *Assembly* (2017),[36] this pair of autonomist Marxists has underscored the uprisings' leaderless mode of organization. One of their guiding concepts, horizontalism, refers to social movements that categorically reject vertical hierarchies. Such movements radicalize the demand for internal democracy that animated a broad range of new lefts in the past. The global uprisings around 2011 featured a prefigurative politics that dispensed with leaders, hierarchy, and the party form.

The best example was Occupy Wall Street's general assembly. In that alternative form of collective decision making, participants used hand signals to communicate feelings (agreement, disagreement, soft opposition, firm opposition) and desire to speak (new comment, direct response, clarification, point of order). Such mechanisms reduced the noise that ordinarily drowns out speakers in a crowd. The general assembly also used a human microphone system, which involved people repeating in chorus what a nearby speaker said in order to amplify that person's voice. Images of Occupy protestors twinkling

35. P. Mason, *Why It's Kicking Off*, 3 and 292. He drew heavily on the sociologist Manuel Castells, a teacher of Cohn-Bendit in the 1960s. See Castells, *Networks of Outrage*.

36. Cf. Hardt and Negri, "Empire, Twenty Years On."

their upraised hands in agreement invited a fair amount of ridicule in the media. But they did prefigure the kind of participatory democracy and popular control that the militants hoped to exercise in a future, postcapitalist society.

While Hardt and Negri have foregrounded horizontalism as the main feature of the 2011 uprisings, they immediately noted the tendency of such movements to break down over time. Occupy Wall Street lasted only two months, and other uprisings likewise faded rapidly. Today's new lefts thus face the dilemma of how to extend the lifespan of spontaneous assemblies. Like Freeman, Hardt and Negri have warned against the absolute rejection of structure as such, or what they call a fetish of horizontality. But they have recommended overturning the traditional division of labor between leaders and led. While the most active militants will gravitate toward positions of leadership and make necessary tactical decisions, they should refer strategic decisions to the multitude. Whether it meets in person or virtually, the assembly should be trusted to provide programmatic goals, peer education, chants, memes, and crowdsourced knowledge.[37]

In terms of what could actually be implemented, Hardt and Negri's ideas seem best suited to periods of low mobilization on the left. During such periods of capitalist stability, domestic political reaction, or foreign military distraction (e.g., the early years of the war on terror), the anti-capitalist left must rely on immanent resistance and gradual changes to the social terrain. This is not so different from what Dutschke had in mind with his march through the institutions, or what Gramsci meant by a war of position. During periods of crisis and instability, however, new lefts must become more maneuverable by building coalitions and adopting more structured forms of organization. Even anarchists at the turn of the twentieth century recognized the need to pose as a rational order against the irrational disorder of existing society.

Still, Hardt and Negri have done a good job of demystifying the apparent spontaneity of recent uprisings. The social and economic terrain created by neoliberalism has already produced the new multitude, a potentially revolutionary subject in search of political form. Several other left theorists have revisited the question of organization in the wake of the 2011 uprisings. In *Crowds and Party* (2016), Jodi Dean stressed the inability of horizontalist movements like Occupy to sustain their momentum. She diagnosed the left with an organizational deficit, and she claimed that only a new communist party could fill the gap. Like fellow neocommunists Alain Badiou, Bruno Bosteels, and Slavoj Žižek, she has proposed reviving the vanguard party form as

---

37. On inclusion of participants not able to be physically present and on ways of sustaining collective action beyond the radical event, see Butler, *Performative Theory of Assembly*.

a means of channeling, organizing, and prolonging assemblies after the radical event. She has rejected Hardt and Negri's theory of immanent resistance, whose hybrid and mobile manifestations she thinks concede too much ground to neoliberal decentralization. Historically, she has argued, only centralized parties proved capable of building solidarities that last. At times Dean's book sounds like Lenin's critique of leftism's infantile disorder: let the Bolshevik adults in the room do the organizing.[38]

Such disagreements between defenders of party discipline versus spontaneous assemblies fit squarely in the history of new lefts. Neoleftists today would do well to confront the legacy of new lefts past. In breaking from existing modes of left politics, anti-authoritarians in the 1960s likewise confronted the legacy of radical antifascism in the 1930s. They engaged consciously with historical texts and imitated past models.

For a while, scholarship on the sixties was done by participants in that decade's struggles. The French general strike of 1968, university occupations across Western Europe, antiwar demos, democratic reforms in Czechoslovakia and Poland: all those events never ended for the '68ers, who continuously reflected on and reassessed them.[39] In the late 1990s, the historian Ingrid Gilcher-Holtey challenged that mode of participant scholarship. Much as François Furet once declared "The Revolution is over" as a way to end ideological disputes dating back to the original French Revolution, Gilcher-Holtey declared "1968" finally over so that we might move beyond partisan testimonials to objective history.[40] She also had a political agenda insofar as she criticized the "internal tension and limited effectiveness of the New Left," which "could not assume power without destroying itself."[41] I do not dispute the need to treat 1968 and other key moments in the history of the left as objects of critical analysis rather than commemoration. It is also true, however, that past actors experienced those moments as radical events, or ruptures in the historical continuum. An objective history must include and interpret that level of experience. Another historian of 1968 observes that we often look back on grand evenings from the wee hours of the morning. Surely historians

38. Dean, *Crowds and Party*. See also her more recent book *Comrade*.

39. For example, see the study by Gitlin, *Sixties*. Cohn-Bendit is also haunted by those formative moments of 1967–68. See Daniel Cohn-Bendit, *Forget 68*, ed. Stéphane Paoli and Jean Viard (La Tour-d'Aigues: Éditions de l'Aube, 2008).

40. Gilcher-Holtey, *1968*. Cf. François Furet, "The Revolution Is Over" [1978], in *Interpreting the French Revolution*, trans. Elborg Forster (Cambridge: Cambridge University Press, 1981), 1–79.

41. Quoted in Stone, *Goodbye to All That?*, 114.

require a measure of sobriety and distance. But the grand evenings happened and will happen again.[42]

Touraine expressed it well when he wrote that the week of the barricades in May 1968 "did not overturn the world; it was not the political achievement of decades of revolutionary analysis and practice. But it created, beyond protests, revolts, and sects, a new social movement that will perhaps be dismembered, disorganized, or repressed but which will mark . . . the social history of the years to come."[43] Less optimistically, some critics have claimed that while the New Left lost politically, it managed over time to win the culture war. For example, American conservatives and the alt-right today use this often antisemitic argument in order to discredit "cultural Marxists" who allegedly pervade universities, mainstream media, and the entertainment industry. For conservatives who seem to overlook the function of law and business schools, college campuses are sites of leftist indoctrination.[44] By contrast, critics on the left claim that the anti-authoritarianism of the New Left foreshadowed the individualist ethos, antistatist animus, and decentralizing drive of neoliberalism. From that perspective, too, the sixties New Left ironically succeeded in its project of cultural and aesthetic liberation.[45]

While the history of new lefts may help make sense of today's struggles, the specific forms of neoleftist organization from the 1930s through the 1960s may not offer good models to emulate. Their breakaway from the party form occurred in the context of a well-developed labor movement, socialist mass parties, and a high degree of organization on the old left. The present situation in advanced capitalist countries involves none of those things. Until a recent wave of strikes in the United States and renewed labor militancy in Europe, organized labor had declined everywhere in the global north. It makes no sense today to speak of "the old left" as something that exists at all, much less something that bureaucratically represses radicals. Unlike in the middle of last century, young people today who identify as leftist or progressive probably find themselves organizationally adrift. Our own ironic reversal may involve a

42. Bantigny, *1968*. Kristin Ross insists on preserving the radical event and not commemorating or normalizing it as part of a unifying national story. See her interview "Against Commemoration: What Happened after May 1968," *New Frame*, February 1, 2019, and her book *May '68*.

43. Touraine, *May Movement*, 186.

44. See Tanner Mirrlees, "The Alt-right's Discourse on 'Cultural Marxism': A Political Instrument of Intersectional Hate," *Atlantis* 39, no. 1 (2018): 49–69, and Noah Berlatsky, "The Lethal Antisemitism of 'Cultural Marxism,'" *Jewish Currents*, May 3, 2019.

45. On the New Left's "aesthetic critique" of capitalism, see Boltanski, "Left after May 1968." See also Boltanski and Chiapello, *New Spirit of Capitalism*, pt. 2.

return to the party form. Either expansion and transformation of existing parties such as Die Linke in Germany or the formalization of electoral coalitions
such as La France insoumise seem like the best options for leftists who want
to challenge liberal-conservative centrism and an emboldened far right. If the
party form does make a comeback, then Europe's next left will look a lot like
the historical old left.

In the United States, the newfound popularity of democratic socialism
among young people reflects this antiquarian revival. The leading socialist
magazine *Jacobin* may be aesthetically hip, but it trades in older ideas about
union organizing, working-class consciousness, and socialist tradition. In
April 2020, former leaders of the Students for a Democratic Society published
an open letter in the *Nation* "to the New New Left from the Old New Left." Its
purpose was to chastise supporters of the democratic socialist Bernie Sanders,
who lost the presidential primary, and persuade them to back his Democrat
rival Joe Biden in the upcoming general election.[46] In calling for unity against
the fascist threat embodied by Donald Trump and the Republican Party, these
boomer-generation radicals seem to have missed a dual irony. First, their letter
repeats the same "face the facts" rhetoric that their politically moderate parents
used against them when they were young and did not listen. And second, what
they call the New New Left actually supports conventional democratic socialism rather than the anti-authoritarian radicalism of the 1960s. That is, today's
militants are already a great deal more "pragmatic" than their parents' or
grandparents' generations were in their youth. In mobilizing for things such
as universal health care, a Green New Deal, debt cancellation, and decom-
modified housing, the millennial and postmillennial left thinks in terms of
institutions and an expansion of democratic state power. The missed ironies
in this confrontation between past and present generations of radical protest
are typical of this book's history of new lefts. But history never repeats itself
exactly: today's new left will surely move beyond the strategies and tactics of
new lefts past.

Shortly after that letter appeared in the *Nation*, millions of Americans took
to the streets in protest against systemic racism. Black Lives Matter (BLM)
originated in 2013 and became a popular movement in late 2014 after Michael
Brown was shot and killed by the police officer Darren Wilson in Ferguson,
Missouri. As the scholar Keeanga-Yamahtta Taylor wrote in late 2019, BLM
emerged as a spontaneous movement "to end the reign of police terror in black
poor and working-class communities." That original movement had no leaders
and kept its organization decentralized. Taylor observed that over the next few

---

46. Former leaders of the Students for a Democratic Society, "Open Letter."

years, BLM lost momentum as activists fought among themselves over whether to create a more structured organization that could channel popular energy into institutional reforms. Radicals worried about "movement capture" by insider politicians from the Democratic Party and progressive philanthropists from the Ford Foundation. Moderates worried about a "tyranny of structurelessness" not unlike what Freeman criticized in the feminist movement of the 1970s. For her part, Taylor claimed that BLM's strength lay in its grassroots character and the "transformative power in the assembly and collective action required to demonstrate together."[47] BLM regained this grassroots power in late May 2020, when demonstrations against the police killings of George Floyd and Breonna Taylor overtook cities all over the United States and the world. This second wave of BLM protests differed from the first wave in its larger size, broader participation of non-Black supporters, and incredible longevity: in some places protests occurred every day for months on end.

Already this amazing horizontal movement of the early twenty-first century has matched or surpassed the accomplishments of the historical new lefts described in this book. Regardless of how one labels it politically, BLM is neoleftist in terms of its organizational form and the dilemmas of internal democracy that it surely does or will face. This century's new lefts will undoubtedly combine party forms and nonparty forms. For all of them, a popular slogan and graffiti from the 1960s may serve as inspiration: "The struggle continues."

---

47. Keeanga-Yamahtta Taylor, "Five Years Later, Do Black Lives Matter?" *Jacobin*, September 30, 2019. See also her book *From #BlackLivesMatter to Black Liberation* (Chicago: Haymarket, 2016).

ACKNOWLEDGMENTS

I WRITE THESE LINES at the concurrence of at least four crises. First, the COVID-19 pandemic and resulting economic collapse have thrown all our lives into disarray, and some lives more than others. Amid quarantines, social distancing, needless deaths, and unanswered questions about the nature of the disease, it feels like everything is uncertain. Second, after the police killings of George Floyd and Breonna Taylor, millions of people have filled the streets to protest police brutality and insist that Black lives matter. In the United States and abroad, this is one of the biggest uprisings in decades. It feels like everything is possible. But a third crisis gives cause for pessimism: as global temperatures rise and nothing is done to slash carbon emissions, we hurtle toward a climate catastrophe and further immiseration of life on this planet. During recent protests, graffiti appeared that encapsulates these desperate yet defiant times: "Another end of the world is possible."

By comparison, the fourth crisis might seem minor, but it directly affects me and many others in my profession. Every page of this book was written in the shadow of a worsening academic job market in the humanities and social sciences. The pandemic only accelerates a long-term process, prompting colleges and universities to impose austerity cuts on the ranks of already precarious non-tenure-track faculty. Higher education depends on contingent faculty to teach the majority of students. Contingent faculty are disposable, however, like the "essential" workers who sustain our economy and infrastructure. This untenable situation poses a legitimation crisis for academia no less than a labor crisis.

Without my doctoral stipend, supplemental funding through fellowships, and then a rare full-time lectureship, this book would not exist. Without challenging corporate administrators, refunding public universities, and overhauling the tenure system, entire disciplines will soon no longer exist. History and the related humanities fields in which I work cannot reproduce themselves equitably unless their practitioners demand better working conditions, especially for scholars who have trained and entered the workforce after the 2008 recession. The disembodied life of the mind is a lie: scholarship is embodied intellectual work that requires access to resources, professional networks, and

295

stable employment. While earning a PhD qualifies you as a professional, the current odds of landing a decent job in your field are like those of becoming a professional athlete. This situation cannot continue if history is to have a future.

There are many people and institutions without whom I could not have written this book. The final product was ushered into the world by my editors Eric Crahan, Thalia Leaf, and Priya Nelson, my copy editor Maia Vaswani, and the superb staff at Princeton University Press. In the years prior to publication, I thank those who read and commented on my dissertation, book proposal, or book manuscript in whole or part. They include Ian Beacock, Timothy Scott Brown, Eliah Bures, Sarah Cramsey, Carolyn J. Dean, Sean A. Forner, Udi Greenberg, Scott Krause, Tobias Kühne, Samuel Moyn, Sophia Rosenfeld, and the two anonymous readers for the Press. Besides those colleagues and friends, my PhD advisers at the University of California, Berkeley, guided the conception and execution of the work. Thank you, John Connelly, Stefan-Ludwig Hoffmann, Robert Kaufman, and Martin Jay. I am especially indebted to Marty, whose generosity and scholarly example I can only hope to emulate. He taught me that "if the study of intellectual history is to have any ultimate justification, it is its capacity to rescue the legacy of the past in order to allow us to realize the potential of the future." In addition to them, other faculty in Berkeley's history department provided me advice, housing, bar talk, and cats to sit. They include Margaret L. Anderson, Carla Hesse, Thomas W. Laqueur, and Jonathan Sheehan. My graduate student and postdoctoral friends made those years in the Bay Area magical, and I learned perhaps more from them than anyone else. Thank you, Daniela Blei, Chris Church, Alice Goff, Peggy O'Donnell, Tehila Sasson, Ilan Tojerow, Gene Zubovich, Katherine Zubovich, the Kroužek and Kreis working groups, and members of the Program in Critical Theory.

Libraries and archives are the lifeblood of my profession. This book benefitted greatly from the cataloguing, curation, conservation, reference assistance, and deep knowledge of staff at the UC Berkeley Library, Yale University Library, Hoover Institution Archive in Stanford, Berlin State Library (StaBi), Berlin State Archive, German Federal Archive in Berlin-Lichterfelde, Archive of the German Democratic Republic Opposition at the Robert Havemann Society in Berlin, Archive of Social Democracy at the Friedrich Ebert Foundation in Bonn, German National Library in Frankfurt am Main, and Hamburg Institute for Social Research. Above all I look forward to returning to my favorite archive, the International Institute of Social History in Amsterdam, whose endless material on the history of the left, smart and solidary staff, and reading room that overlooks Robert Jasper Grootveld's floating gardens in the Zeeburg waterway are about as close as I will get to research utopia.

The funding for my research stays in Germany and the Netherlands came from the Volkswagen Foundation, Alexander von Humboldt Foundation, Central European History Society, Berkeley Institute for European Studies, and Yale MacMillan Center. As a visiting scholar, I had the good fortune to be hosted by two excellent research groups: Thomas Lindenberger, Jens Gieseke, and Mario Keßler at the Leibniz Centre for Contemporary History in Potsdam, and Thomas Mergel and Malte Zierenberg in the Department of History at the Humboldt University of Berlin. They gracefully tolerated my spoken German and steered my project clear from some obvious errors. For that they have my gratitude.

The person who set me on the path to research New Beginning was James Schmidt at Boston University. His seminar "Refugee Intellectuals" introduced me to the Frankfurt School of critical theory, which ended up being fate. And he supervised my gargantuan task of writing an undergraduate thesis. I remember what Jim said when I told him years ago that I was finally done researching those German émigrés: "We'll see about that." I can only hope that the courses I teach at Yale will make as lasting an impression on my students in Directed Studies, the Humanities Program, and the Department of History.

My first encounter with a historian happened in seventh grade, when Ms. Sharon Kolodny revealed to me the infinite worlds of the past. I am forever grateful to her and all my teachers in the public schools of East Greenbush, New York.

For my friends and family who have loved and entertained me and kept me sane over the past ten years of working on this book, nothing I write here will be adequate. To name a few: Eric Borden, Tina Borden, Barbara Bray, Sage Bray, Philippe Male, the San Francisco Pacifics, Mike Steinke, and Danny Steinmetz-Jenkins. I owe a special thanks to Jenni Allen, who was there for much of the joy and sorrow. My brothers Dan and Kevin and my sisters-in-law Molly and Erica have kept it real. My nieces Lucy and Millie have shown me what literal new beginnings look like. My wonderful partner Kate Brackney has encouraged me, cracked me up, and made me feel lucky every single day. My parents Dave and Pat have supported me always. And finally, my loving grandparents Rene, Jeannette, Robert, and Marilyn live on in memory.

New Haven, Connecticut, September 2020

SELECT BIBLIOGRAPHY

Archives

August Bebel Institute (ABI, Berlin)
    Nachlass (personal papers) Eberhard Hesse
Berlin State Archive/Landesarchiv (LArch)
    Nachlass Ernst Reuter
    Nachlass Gustav Klingelhöfer
    Nachlass Otto Suhr
Federal Bureau of Investigation (FBI), FOIA Requests
    Emergency Rescue Committee
    Karl B. Frank
Free University of Berlin (FU), University Archive
    APO-Archiv
Friedrich Ebert Foundation, Archiv der sozialen Demokratie (FES, Bonn)
    Nachlass Erwin Schoettle
    Nachlass Fritz Erler
    Nachlass Georg Eliasberg
    Nachlass Karl Elgaß
    Nachlass Kurt Mattick
    Nachlass Kurt Schumacher
    Nachlass Paul Hertz
    Nachlass Richard Löwenthal
    Nachlass Waldemar von Knoeringen
    Sammlung Personalia
    Willy-Brandt-Archiv
Gedenkstätte Deutscher Widerstand (GDW, Berlin)
German Federal Archives/Bundesarchiv (BArch, Berlin-Lichterfelde)
    RY 1: Kommunistische Partei Deutschlands
    RY 2: Sozialdemokratische Partei Deutschlands
    R 58: Reichssicherheitshauptamt
German National Library, Exile Collections (DNB, Frankfurt am Main)
    Nachlass Ossip K. Flechtheim
Hamburg Institute for Social Research (HIS)
    Nachlass Rudi Dutschke
    Graue Literatur

Hoover Institution Archives (Stanford, California)
    French Subject Collection
    Horst Mendershausen Papers
    Karl B. Frank Papers
    New Left Collection
International Institute of Social History (IISG, Amsterdam)
    Friedrich Adler Papers
    Labour and Socialist International Archives
    Neu Beginnen (NB) Archives
    Paul Hertz Papers
    Wolfgang Abendroth Papers
Robert Havemann Society, Archiv der DDR-Opposition (RHG, Berlin)
    Nachlass Harold Hurwitz
    Nachlass Robert Havemann
University at Albany, SUNY (UAlbany), M. E. Grenander Department of Special
    Collections and Archives, German and Jewish Intellectual Émigré Collection
    Emergency Rescue Committee Records
    Karl M. Otto Paetel Papers
    Reinhard Bendix Papers
University of Oregon, Special Collections (U of O, Eugene)
    Maurice J. Goldbloom Papers
University of Vienna, University Archive
    Frank, Karl
Wiener Library (London)
    Julia Rahmer Papers
    Vicky Abrams Papers

Primary Sources and Theory

Abendroth, Lisa. "Die Flucht: Warum Wolfgang Abendroth die sowjetische Besatzungszone verließ." *Sozialismus* 16, no. 2 (1996): 24–27.

Abendroth, Wolfgang. *Antagonistische Gesellschaft und politische Demokratie: Aufsätze zur politischen Soziologie.* Berlin: Luchterhand, 1967.

———. *Aufstieg und Krise der deutschen Sozialdemokratie: Das Problem der Zweckentfremdung einer politischen Partei durch die Anpassungstendenz von Institutionen an vorgegebene Machtverhältnisse.* Frankfurt am Main: Stimme, 1964.

———. ed. *Faschismus und Kapitalismus: Theorien über die sozialen Ursprünge und die Funktion des Faschismus.* Politische Texte. Frankfurt am Main: Europäische Verlags-Anstalt and Europa, 1967.

———. *Gesammelte Schriften.* 4 vols. Edited by Michael Buckmiller, Joachim Perels, and Uli Schöler. Hannover: Offizin, 2006–2014.

———. *A Short History of the European Working Class* [1965]. Translated by N. Jacobs and B. Trench. New York: Monthly Review, 1972.

Adler, Max. "Die historische Funktion des Linkssozialismus." *Der Kampf*, no. 2 (1932): 71–76.

————. *Linkssozialismus: Notwendige Betrachtungen über Reformismus und revolutionären Sozialismus*. Carlsbad: Graphia, 1933.

Adorno, Theodor W., and Herbert Marcuse. "Correspondence on the German Student Movement" [1969]. *New Left Review*, no. 233 (January–February 1999): 123–36.

Agnoli, Johannes. *Subversive Theorie: "Die Sache selbst" und ihre Geschichte*. Freiburg: Ça ira, 1996.

Alsen, Fritz. *See* Ehrmann, Henry W.

Althusser, Louis. "Student Problems" [1964]. Translated by Dick Bateman [1967]. *Radical Philosophy*, no. 170 (November–December 2011): 11–15.

American Association for a Democratic Germany, ed. *Der neue Kampf um Freiheit: Briefe und Dokumente Berliner Sozialisten*. New York: American Association for a Democratic Germany, 1946.

Anderson, Evelyn. *Hammer or Anvil: The Story of the German Working-Class Movement*. London: Gollancz, 1945.

———— [Evelyn Lend, alias]. *The Underground Struggle in Germany*. London: Fact, 1938.

Arbeitskreis Revolutionärer Sozialisten [RSD], "Der Weg zum sozialistischen Deutschland: Eine Plattform für die Einheitsfront." *Zeitschrift für Sozialismus* 1, no. 12/13 (September/October 1934): 375–409.

Arendt, Hannah. *The Human Condition*. Chicago: University of Chicago, 1958.

————. *The Origins of Totalitarianism* [1951]. Cleveland: Meridian, 1958.

————. *On Revolution*. New York: Viking, 1963.

Aron, Raymond. *The Elusive Revolution: Anatomy of a Student Revolt* [1968]. Translated by Gordon Clough. New York: Praeger, 1969.

Badiou, Alain. *Being and Event* [1988]. Translated by Oliver Feltham. London: Bloomsbury, 2013.

Bell, Daniel. *The Coming of Post-Industrial Society: A Venture in Social Forecasting*. New York: Basic Books, 1973.

————. *The End of Ideology: On the Exhaustion of Political Ideas in the Fifties*. Glencoe, IL: Free Press, 1960.

Bendix, Reinhard. *From Berlin to Berkeley: German-Jewish Identities*. New Brunswick, NJ: Transaction, 1986.

Benjamin, Walter. "Theses on the Philosophy of History" [1940]. In *Illuminations*, edited by Hannah Arendt, 253–64. New York: Schocken, 1968.

Bernstein, Eduard. *The Preconditions of Socialism* [1899]. Cambridge: Cambridge University Press, 1993; also published as *Evolutionary Socialism*.

Bloch, Ernst. *The Principle of Hope*. 3 vols. [1954–59]. Translated by Neville Plaice, Stephen Plaice, and Paul Knight. Cambridge, MA: Harvard University Press, 1986–95.

Boltanski, Luc. "The Left after May 1968 and the Longing for Total Revolution." *Thesis Eleven* 69, no. 1 (2002): 1–20.

Boltanski, Luc, and Ève Chiapello. *The New Spirit of Capitalism* [1999]. Translated by Gregory Elliott. London: Verso, 2005.

Borkenau, Franz. *The Spanish Cockpit: An Eye-Witness Account of the Political and Social Conflicts of the Spanish Civil War*. London: Faber and Faber, 1937.

Bourdet, Claude. "The French Left: Long-run Trends." *Universities and Left Review* 1, no. 1 (Spring 1957): 13–16.

Brandt, Willy. *In Exile: Essays, Reflections and Letters, 1933–1947* [1966]. London: Wolff, 1971.

Brill, Hermann. *Gegen den Strom*. Offenbach am Main: Bollwerk-Verlag K. Drott, 1946.

Bry, Gerhard. *Resistance: Recollections from the Nazi Years*. West Orange, NJ: self-pub., 1979.

Bürger, Peter. *Theory of the Avant-Garde* [1974]. Translated by Michael Shaw. Minneapolis: University of Minnesota, 1984.

Burnham, James. *The Managerial Revolution: What Is Happening in the World*. New York: John Day, 1941.

Butler, Judith. *Notes toward a Performative Theory of Assembly*. Cambridge, MA: Harvard University Press, 2015.

Buttinger, Joseph. *In the Twilight of Socialism: A History of the Revolutionary Socialists of Austria*. Translated by E. B. Ashton. New York: F. A. Praeger, 1953.

Cardan, Paul. *See* Castoriadis, Cornelius.

Castells, Manuel. *Networks of Outrage and Hope: Social Movements in the Internet Age*. Cambridge, MA: Polity, 2012.

Castoriadis, Cornelius [Paul Cardan, alias]. "Prolétariat et organisation." 2 pts. *Socialisme ou barbarie*, nos. 27–28 (April–May and July–August 1959).

Clover, Joshua. *Riot. Strike. Riot.: The New Era of Uprisings*. Brooklyn: Verso, 2016.

Cohn-Bendit, Daniel, and Gabriel Cohn-Bendit. *Obsolete Communism: The Left-Wing Alternative*. Translated by Arnold Pomerans. New York: McGraw-Hill, 1968.

Crosland, C.A.R. *The Future of Socialism*. London: Jonathan Cape, 1956.

Crozier, Michel. *The Bureaucratic Phenomenon* [1963]. Chicago: University of Chicago, 1964.

Dahrendorf, Gustav. *Der Mensch, das Maß aller Dinge: Reden und Schriften zur deutschen Politik 1945–1954*. Edited by Ralf Dahrendorf. Hamburg: Verlagsgesellschaft deutscher Konsumgenossenschaften, 1955.

Dean, Jodi. *Comrade: An Essay on Political Belonging*. Brooklyn: Verso, 2019.

———. *Crowds and Party*. Brooklyn: Verso, 2016.

Debord, Guy. *The Society of the Spectacle* [1967]. Translated by Donald Nicholson-Smith. New York: Zone Books, 1994.

Debray, Régis. "Latin America: The Long March." *New Left Review*, no. 33 (1965): 17–58.

Depreux, Édouard. *Renouvellement du socialisme*. Paris: Calman-Lévy, 1960.

Derrida, Jacques. *Specters of Marx: The State of the Debt, the Work of Mourning, and the New International*. Translated by Peggy Kamuf. New York: Routledge, 1994.

Dietrich, Barbara, and Wolfgang Abendroth, eds. *Wolfgang Abendroth. Ein Leben in der Arbeiterbewegung: Gespräche*. Frankfurt am Main: Suhrkamp, 1977.

Djilas, Milovan. *The New Class: An Analysis of the Communist System*. New York: Praeger, 1957.

Dutschke, Rudi. Foreword to Régis Debray, *Der lange Marsch*. Munich: Trikont, 1968.

———. *Mein langer Marsch: Reden, Schriften und Tagebücher aus zwanzig Jahren*. Edited by Gretchen Dutschke-Klotz, Helmut Gollwitzer, and Jürgen Miermeister. Reinbek bei Hamburg: Rowohlt, 1980.

———. *Versuch, Lenin auf die Füsse zu stellen. Über den halbasiatischen und den westeuropäischen Weg zum Sozialismus: Lenin, Lukács und die Dritte Internationale*. Berlin: K. Wagenbach, 1974.

———. "Zur Literatur des revolutionären Sozialismus von K. Marx bis in die Gegenwart." *SDS-Korrespondenz*, October 1966.

Ehrmann, Henry W. [Fritz Alsen, alias]. "Napoleon III. und Hitler: Bonapartismus und Faschismus." *Zeitschrift für Sozialismus* 3, no. 31 (April 1936): 989–94.

Eiber, Ludwig, ed. *Die Sozialdemokratie in der Emigration. Die "Union deutscher sozialistischer Organisationen in Grossbritannien" 1941–1946 und ihre Mitglieder: Protokolle, Erklärungen, Materialien.* Bonn: J.H.W. Dietz Nachf., 1998.

Erler, Fritz. *Politik für Deutschland.* Edited by Wolfgang Gaebler. Stuttgart: Seewald, 1968.

———. "Die Rolle der Gruppe Neu Beginnen." *Politiche Studien* 6, no. 69 (January 1956): 43–45.

———. *Sozialismus als Gegenwartsaufgabe.* Schwenningen am Neckar: Neckar, 1947.

Esping-Andersen, Gøsta. *Social Foundations of Postindustrial Economies.* Oxford: Oxford University Press, 1999.

Flechtheim, Lili. "Emigration und Remigration." In *Heimat und Heimatlosigkeit,* edited by Christa Dericum and Philipp Wambolt, 33–38. Berlin: K. Kramer, 1987.

Flechtheim, Ossip K. "Die Anpassung der SPD: 1914, 1933 und 1959." *Kölner Zeitschrift für Soziologie und Sozialpsychologie* 17, no. 3 (1965): 584–604.

———. *Bolschewismus 1917–1967: Von der Weltrevolution zum Sowjetimperium.* Vienna: Europa, 1967.

———, ed. *Dokumente zur parteipolitischen Entwicklung in Deutschland seit 1945.* 9 vols. Berlin: Herbert Wendler, 1962–1971.

———. *Eine Welt oder keine? Beiträge zur Politik, Politologie und Philosophie.* Frankfurt am Main: Europäische Verlagsanstalt, 1964.

———, ed. *Fundamentals of Political Science.* New York: Ronald, 1952.

———. *Futurologie: Der Kampf um die Zukunft.* Frankfurt am Main: Fischer-Taschenbuch, 1972.

———. *History and Futurology.* Meisenheim am Glan: Hain, 1966.

———. *Die Kommunistische Partei Deutschlands in der Weimarer Republik.* Offenbach am Main: Bollwerk-Verlag K. Drott, 1948.

———. "Die neue Linke in der neuen Welt." *Frankfurter Hefte* 18, no. 3 (March 1963): 148–50.

———. "Teaching the Future: A Contribution to the Intellectual and Moral Growth of the Participants." *Journal of Higher Education* 16, no. 9 (1945): 460–65.

———. *Zeitgeschichte und Zukunftspolitik.* Hamburg: Hoffmann und Campe, 1974.

———. "Zur Frage der innerparteilichen Demokratie." *neue kritik* 2, no. 8 (November 1961): 19–22.

———. "Zur Kritik der Marxschen Geschichtskonzeption" [1939]. *Cahiers Vilfredo Pareto* 3, no. 5 (1965): 141–58.

Frank, Karl B. [Paul Hagen, alias]. *Erobert, nicht befreit! Das deutsche Volk im ersten Besatzungsjahr.* New York: American Association for a Democratic Germany, 1946.

——— [Willi Müller, alias]. "Gegen Argumente des Konservatismus!" *Zeitschrift für Sozialismus* 1, no. 7 (April 1934): 226–34.

——— [Paul Hagen, alias]. *Germany after Hitler.* New York: Farrar and Rinehart, 1944.

——— [Willi Müller, alias]. "Hitlers fait accompli." *Zeitschrift für Sozialismus* 3, no. 30 (March 1936): 945–50.

——— [Paul Hagen, alias]. "Integraler Sozialismus." *Zeitschrift für Sozialismus* 3, 34/35 (July–August 1936): 1099–104.

——— [Paul Hagen, alias]. *Will Germany Crack? A Factual Report on Germany from Within.* Translated by Anna Caples. New York: Harper, 1942.

Franz, Leopold. *See* Neumann, Franz L.

Freeman, Jo. "The Tyranny of Structurelessness" (1971–73, some as alias Joreen). Jo Freeman's website, n.d., accessed September 2020. https://www.jofreeman.com/joreen/tyranny.htm.

Fromm, Erich. *Escape from Freedom* [1941]. New York: Henry Holt, 1994.

Galbraith, John Kenneth. *The Affluent Society*. Boston: Houghton Mifflin, 1958.

Glucksmann, André. "Strategy and Revolution in France 1968." *New Left Review*, no. 52 (1968): 67–121.

Gniffke, Erich W. *Jahre mit Ulbricht*. Cologne: Verlag Wissenschaft und Politik, 1966.

Gordon, Uri. "Prefigurative Politics between Ethical Practice and Absent Promise." *Political Studies* 66, no. 2 (2018): 521–37.

Gorz, André. *Socialism and Revolution* [1967]. Translated by Norman Denny. Garden City, NY: Anchor, 1973.

Gramsci, Antonio. *Selections from the Prison Notebooks* [1929–35]. Edited and translated by Q. Hoare and G. N. Smith. New York: International, 1971.

———. "Soviets in Italy" [1919–20]. *New Left Review*, no. 51 (September–October 1968): 28–58.

Grotewohl, Otto. *Otto Grotewohl und die Einheitspartei: Dokumente*. 2 vols. Edited by Hans-Joachim Fieber, Maren Franke, and Wolfgang Triebel. Berlin: Edition Luisenstadt, 1994.

Groys, Boris. *On the New* [1992]. Translated by G. M. Goshgarian. New York: Verso, 2014.

Guevara, Ernesto Che. *Guerrilla Warfare*. New York: Monthly Review Press, 1961.

———. "Message to the Tricontinental" (Havana, April 16, 1967). Marxists Internet Archive, n.d., accessed September 2020. https://www.marxists.org/archive/guevara/1967/04/16.htm.

Habermas, Jürgen. *The Structural Transformation of the Public Sphere: An Inquiry into a Category of Bourgeois Society* [1962]. Translated by Thomas Burger. Cambridge, MA: MIT Press, 1989.

Hagen, Paul. *See* Frank, Karl B.

Hägglund, Martin. *This Life: Secular Faith and Spiritual Freedom*. New York: Pantheon, 2019.

Hall, Stuart. "Life and Times of the First New Left." *New Left Review*, no. 61 (January–February 2010): 177–96.

Hanisch, Carol. "The Personal Is Political" [1969]. In *Notes from the Second Year: Women's Liberation*, edited by Shulamith Firestone and Anne Koedt, 76–78. New York: Radical Feminism, 1970.

Hardt, Michael, and Antonio Negri. *Assembly*. New York: Oxford University Press, 2017.

———. *Empire*. Cambridge, MA: Harvard University Press, 2000.

———. "Empire, Twenty Years On." *New Left Review*, no. 120 (November–December 2019): 67–92.

Heideking, Jürgen, and Christof Mauch, eds. *American Intelligence and the German Resistance to Hitler: A Documentary History*. Boulder, CO: Westview, 1996.

Hellmann, Henry [Ernst Schlosser, alias]. "Fünfzig Jahre 'Neu Beginnen!'" *Internationale Wissenschaftliche Korrespondenz zur Geschichte der Deutschen Arbeiterbewegung* 19, no. 3 (1983): 491–93.

Hiller, Kurt. "Linke Leute von rechts." *Die Weltbühne* 28, no. 31 (August 2, 1932): 153–58.

Historikus. *See* Rosenberg, Arthur.

Honneth, Axel. *The Idea of Socialism: Towards a Renewal* [2015]. Translated by Joseph Ganahl. Cambridge, MA: Polity, 2017.

Horkheimer, Max. *A Life in Letters: Selected Correspondence*. Edited and translated by M. R. and E. M. Jacobson. Lincoln: University of Nebraska, 2007.

Howe, Irving, ed. *Beyond the New Left*. New York: Horizon, 1970.

Jansen, Jon B., and Stefan Weyl. *See* Taurer, Bernhard, and Georg Eliasberg.

Jungk, Robert. *Trotzdem: Mein Leben für die Zukunft*. Munich: C. Hanser, 1993.

Kerr, Clark. *The Uses of the University*. Cambridge, MA: Harvard University Press, 1963.

Kirchheimer, Otto. "The Transformation of Western European Party Systems." In *Political Parties and Political Development*, edited by Joseph LaPalombara and Myron Weiner, 177–200. Princeton, NJ: Princeton University Press, 1966.

Koestler, Arthur. *The Invisible Writing: An Autobiography*. New York: Macmillan, 1954.

———. *Spanish Testament*. London: Gollancz, 1937.

Kofler, Leo. *Marxistischer oder ethischer Sozialismus?* Bovenden bei Göttingen: Verlag Sozialistische Politik, 1955.

Kogon, Eugen, Wolfgang Abendroth, Helmut Ridder, Heinrich Hannover, and Jürgen Seifert. *Der totale Notstandsstaat*. Frankfurt am Main: Stimme, 1965.

Kołakowski, Leszek. "The Concept of the Left" [1968]. In *Marxism and Beyond: On Historical Understanding and Individual Responsibility*, translated by Jane Zielonko Peel, 87–103. London: Pall Mall, 1969.

———. *Main Currents of Marxism* [1976]. 3 vols. Translated by P. S. Falla. Oxford: Oxford University Press, 1978.

Koselleck, Reinhart. *Futures Past: On the Semantics of Historical Time* [1979]. Translated by Keith Tribe. New York: Columbia University Press, 2004.

———. *The Practice of Conceptual History: Timing History, Spacing Concepts*. Stanford, CA: Stanford University Press, 2002.

Klotzbach, Kurt, ed. *Drei Schriften aus dem Exil*. Berlin: J.H.W. Dietz Nachf., 1974.

Kluge, Alexander, and Oskar Negt, *History and Obstinacy* [1981]. Edited by Devin Fore. Translated by Richard Langston, Cyrus Shahan, Martin Brady, Helen Hughes, and Joel Golb. Brooklyn: Zone Books, 2014.

Knabb, Ken, ed. *Situationist International Anthology*. Rev. ed. Berkeley, CA: Bureau of Public Secrets, 2006.

Knoeringen, Waldemar von. *Mobilisierung der Demokratie: Ein Beitrag zur Demokratiereform*. Munich: Bavaria-Druck, 1966.

Knoeringen, Waldemar von, and Ulrich Lohmar, eds. *Was bleibt vom Sozialismus?* Hannover: Verlag für Literatur und Zeitgeschehen, 1968.

Korsch, Karl. *Marxism and Philosophy* [1923]. New York: Monthly Review, 1971.

Laclau, Ernesto, and Chantal Mouffe. *Hegemony and Socialist Strategy: Towards a Radical Democratic Politics* [1985]. 2nd ed. London: Verso, 2001.

Laudani, Raffaele, ed. *Secret Reports on Nazi Germany: The Frankfurt School Contribution to the War Effort*. Princeton, NJ: Princeton University Press, 2013.

Lefebvre, Henri. *Critique of Everyday Life*. 3 vols. [1947, 1961, and 1981]. Translated by John Moore and Gregory Elliott. London: Verso, 2014.

Lefort, Claude. "Organisation et parti." *Socialisme ou barbarie*, no. 26 (November 1958).

Lend, Evelyn. *See* Anderson, Evelyn.

Lenin, V. I. *Collected Works*. Moscow: Progress Publishers, 1960–1970.

———. *Essential Works of Lenin*. Edited by H. M. Christman. New York: Dover, 1987.

Leonhard, Wolfgang. *Child of the Revolution* [1955]. Translated by C. M. Woodhouse. Chicago: H. Regnery, 1958.

Loewenheim, Walter [Miles, alias]. *Eine Welt im Umbruch: Zur Auseinandersetzung um die Krise unserer Zeit*. Bremen: Verlag Der Werktag, 1961.

———. *Geschichte der Org 1929–1935*. Edited by Jan Foitzik. Berlin: Gedenkstätte Deutscher Widerstand and Edition Hentrich, 1995.

——— [Miles, alias]. *Neu beginnen! Faschismus oder Sozialismus: Diskussionsgrundlage zu den Streitfragen unserer Epoche*. Carlsbad: Graphia, 1933.

——— [Miles, alias]. *Socialism's New Beginning: A Manifesto from Underground Germany*. New York: Rand School and League for Industrial Democracy, 1934.

Löwenthal, Richard [Paul Sering, alias]. "Der Faschismus." 2 pts. *Zeitschrift für Sozialismus* 2, no. 24/25 and 26/27 (September–October and November–December 1935): 765–87 and 839–56.

———. *Faschismus—Bolschewismus—Totalitarismus: Schriften zur Weltanschauungsdiktatur im 20. Jahrhundert*. Edited by Mike Schmeitzner. Göttingen: Vandenhoeck und Ruprecht, 2009.

——— [Paul Sering, alias]. *Faschismus und Monopolkapitalismus: 6 frühe Aufsätze*. Berlin: Guhl, 1979.

——— [Paul Sering, alias]. "Historische Voraussetzungen des deutschen Nationalsozialismus." *Zeitschrift für Sozialismus* 3, no. 30 (March 1936): 959–75.

——— [Paul Sering, alias]. *Jenseits des Kapitalismus: Ein Beitrag zur sozialistischen Neuorientierung*. Nuremberg: Nest, 1946.

———. "Konflikte, Bündnisse und Resultate der deutschen politischen Emigration." *Vierteljahrshefte für Zeitgeschichte* 39, no. 4 (October 1991): 626–36.

———. *Der romantische Rückfall: Wege und Irrwege einer rückwärts gewendeten Revolution*. Stuttgart: W. Kohlhammer, 1970.

———. "Die Schrift 'Neu Beginnen' 50 Jahre danach." *Internationale Wissenschaftliche Korrespondenz zur Geschichte der Deutschen Arbeiterbewegung* 19, no. 4 (1983): 561–70.

———. "Sozialismus ohne Utopie." *Die Neue Gesellschaft* 1, no. 2 (September–October 1954): 50–59.

———. *Unreason and Revolution: Reflections on the Dissociation of Revolutionary Practice from Marxist Theory* [February 28, 1969]. Santa Monica, CA: RAND Corporation, 1969.

——— [Paul Sering, alias]. "Die Wandlungen des Kapitalismus." *Zeitschrift für Sozialismus* 2, no. 22/23 (August 1935): 704–25.

——— [Paul Sering, alias]. "Was ist der Volkssozialismus?" *Zeitschrift für Sozialismus* 3, no. 36 (September 1936): 1105–36.

———. *Die Widerstandsgruppe "Neu Beginnen."* Berlin: Gedenkstätte Deutscher Widerstand, 1981.

———. *World Communism: The Disintegration of a Secular Faith* [1963]. New York: Oxford University Press, 1966.

Lukács, Georg. "Aesthetic Culture" [1910]. Translated by Rita Keresztesi-Treat. Edited by Tyrus Miller. *Yale Journal of Criticism* 11, no. 2 (1998): 365–79.

————. "Bolshevism as a Moral Problem" [1918]. Translated by Judith Marcus Tarr. *Social Research* 44, no. 3 (1977): 416–24.

————. *A Defence of "History and Class Consciousness": Tailism and the Dialectic* [1925–26]. London: Verso, 2000.

————. *History and Class Consciousness: Studies in Marxist Dialectics* [1923]. Translated by R. Livingstone. Cambridge, MA: MIT Press, 1971.

————. *Lenin: A Study on the Unity of His Thought* [1924]. Translated by Nicholas Jacobs. London: New Left Books, 1977.

————. "The Old Culture and the New Culture" [1919–20]. Translated by Paul Breines. *Telos*, no. 5 (Spring 1970): 21–30.

————. "Party and Class" [1919]. in *Tactics and Ethics*, 28–36.

————. "The Question of Parliamentarism" [March 1, 1920]. In *Tactics and Ethics*, 53–63.

————. *Record of a Life: An Autobiographical Sketch*. Translated by Rodney Livingstone. Edited by István Eörsi. London: Verso, 1983.

————. *Soul and Form* [1911]. Translated by Anna Bostock. Cambridge, MA: MIT Press, 1974.

————. *Tactics and Ethics: Political Essays, 1919–1929* [1972]. Translated by Michael McColgan. London: Verso, 2014.

————. *The Theory of the Novel: A Historico-Philosophical Essay on the Forms of Great Epic Literature* [1916]. Cambridge, MA: MIT Press, 1971.

————. *The Young Hegel: Studies in the Relations Between Dialectics and Economics* [1938]. Translated by Rodney Livingstone. Cambridge, MA: MIT Press, 1976.

Luxemburg, Rosa. *The Accumulation of Capital* [1913]. Translated by Agnes Schwarzschild. London: Routledge and Kegan Paul, 1951.

————. *The Rosa Luxemburg Reader*. Edited by Peter Hudis and Kevin B. Anderson. New York: Monthly Review, 2004.

Mair, Peter. *Ruling the Void: The Hollowing of Western Democracy*. London: Verso, 2013.

Mallet, Serge. *The New Working Class* [1963]. Translated by Andrée Shepherd and Bob Shepherd. Nottingham, UK: Spokesman, 1975.

Mannheim, Karl. *Ideology and Utopia: An Introduction to the Sociology of Knowledge* [1929]. Translated by Louis Wirth and Edward Shils. New York: Harcourt, Brace, 1936.

————. "The Problem of Generations" [1928]. In *Essays on the Sociology of Knowledge*, edited by Paul Kecskemeti, 276–320. New York: Oxford University Press, 1952.

————. "Soul and Culture" [1918]. Translated by Anna Wessely. *Theory, Culture and Society* 29, no. 7/8 (2012): 286–301.

Mao Zedong. *On Guerrilla Warfare* [1937]. Translated by Samuel B. Griffith. Mineola, NY: Dover, 2005.

Marcuse, Herbert. *Counterrevolution and Revolt*. Boston: Beacon, 1972.

————. *Das Ende der Utopie*. Edited by Horst Kurnitzky and Hansmartin Kuhn. Berlin: Maikowski, 1967.

————. *Eros and Civilization: A Philosophical Inquiry into Freud*. New York: Vintage, 1955.

————. *An Essay on Liberation*. Boston: Beacon, 1969.

————. "On the New Left" [1968]. In *The New Left: A Documentary History*, edited by Massimo Teodori, 468–73. Indianapolis: Bobbs-Merrill, 1969.

————. *One-Dimensional Man: Studies in the Ideology of Advanced Industrial Society*. Boston: Beacon, 1964.

Marcuse, Herbert. "Repressive Tolerance." In *A Critique of Pure Tolerance*, by Robert Paul Wolff, Barrington Moore Jr., and Marcuse, 95–137. Boston: Beacon, 1965.

Maurín, Joaquín. *Hacia la segunda revolución: El fracaso de la República y la insurrección de octubre*. Barcelona: Gráficos Alfa, 1935.

Merleau-Ponty, Maurice. *Adventures of the Dialectic* [1955]. Translated by Joseph Bien. London: Heinemann, 1974.

Michels, Robert. *Political Parties: A Sociological Study of the Oligarchical Tendencies of Modern Democracy* [1911]. Translated by Eden and Cedar Paul. New York: Collier, 1962.

Miles. *See* Loewenheim, Walter.

Miliband, Ralph. *Parliamentary Socialism: A Study in the Politics of Labour*. New York: Monthly Review, 1961.

———. *The State in Capitalist Society*. New York: Basic, 1969.

Mills, C. Wright. "Letter to the New Left." *New Left Review*, no. 5 (September–October 1960): 18–23.

———. *The Power Elite*. New York: Oxford University Press, 1956.

Morin, Edgar, Cornelius Castoriadis [Jean-Marc Coudray, alias], and Claude Lefort. *Mai 1968: La Brèche*. Paris: Fayard, 1968.

Mouffe, Chantal. *For a Left Populism*. London: Verso, 2018.

Mounier, Emmanuel. *A Personalist Manifesto* [1936]. Translated by Monks of St. John's Abbey. London: Longmans, Green, 1938.

———. *Révolution personnaliste et communautaire*. Paris: F. Aubier, 1935.

Müller, Willi. *See* Frank, Karl B.

Negt, Oskar. *Erfahrungsspuren: Eine autobiographische Denkreise*. Göttingen: Steidl, 2019.

———, ed. *Die Linke antwortet Jürgen Habermas*. Frankfurt am Main: Europäische Verlagsanstalt, 1968.

Neu Beginnen. *Klare Fronten: Die deutschen Sozialisten und Hitlers Überfall auf die Sowjet-Union*. London: Auslandsbüro Neu Beginnen, 1941.

———. *Materialien zur sozialistischen Konzentration: Zur Information der Mitglieder der Sozialdemokratischen Partei Deutschlands*. Prague: Auslandsbüro Neu Beginnen, 1938.

———. *Neu Beginnen: Was es will, was es ist und wie es wurde*. London: Auslandsbüro Neu Beginnen, 1939.

———. *Wandlungen der Sowjet-Union: Zur Neubeurteilung der russischen Frage nach dem Achtzehnten Parteitag*. London: Auslandsbüro Neu Beginnen, 1940.

Neu Beginnen, Sozialistische Arbeiterpartei Deutschlands (German Socialist Workers' Party), and Revolutionäre Sozialisten Österreichs (Austrian Revolutionary Socialists). *Der kommende Weltkrieg. Aufgaben und Ziele des deutschen Sozialismus: Eine Diskussionsgrundlage*. Paris: self-pub., 1939.

Neumann, Franz L. *Behemoth: The Structure and Practice of National Socialism* [1942]. Chicago: Ivan R. Dee, 2009.

——— [Leopold Franz, alias]. "Rechtsstaat, Gewaltenteilung und Sozialismus." *Zeitschrift für Sozialismus* 1, no. 8 (May 1934): 254–61.

——— [Leopold Franz, alias]. "Zur marxistischen Staatstheorie." *Zeitschrift für Sozialismus* 2, no. 26/27 (November/December 1935).

Orwell, George. *Homage to Catalonia* [1938]. New York: Harcourt, Brace, 1952.

Pieck, Wilhelm. *Reden und Aufsätze: Auswahl aus den Jahren 1908–1950*. 4 vols. East Berlin: Dietz, 1951.

Pivert, Marceau. "Everything Is Possible." Translation of "Tout est possible!" *Le Populaire* (May 27, 1936). Marxists Internet Archive, accessed December 2017. https://www.marxists .org/archive/pivert/1936/everything-possible.htm.

Polanyi, Karl. *The Great Transformation* [1944]. Boston: Beacon, 1957.

Popp-Madsen, Benjamin. "Between Constituent Power and Political Form: Toward a Theory of Council Democracy." *Political Theory*, May 23, 2020. https://doi.org/10.1177 /0090591720925435.

Preston, Paul, ed. *Leviatán: Antología*. Madrid: Ediciones Turner, 1976.

Raekstad, Paul, and Sofa Saio Gradin. *Prefigurative Politics: Building Tomorrow Today*. Cambridge, UK: Polity, 2020.

Rancière, Jacques. *Disagreement: Politics and Philosophy* [1995]. Translated by Julie Rose. Minneapolis: University of Minnesota, 1998.

Reich, Wilhelm. *Massenpsychologie des Faschismus*. Copenhagen: Verlag für Sexualpolitik, 1933.

———. *The Mass Psychology of Fascism* [1933]. New York: Farrar, Straus and Giroux, 1970.

———. *Sex-Pol: Essays, 1929–1934*. Translated by Anna Bostock, Lee Baxandall, and Tom Du-Bose. Edited by Lee Baxandall. New York: Random House, 1972.

Reichhardt, Hans J., Hanns U. Treutler, and Albrecht Lampe, eds. *Berlin: Quellen und Dokumente 1945–1951*. Berlin: H. Spitzing, 1964.

Rosenberg, Arthur [Historikus, alias]. *Der Faschismus als Massenbewegung: Sein Aufstieg und seine Zersetzung*. Carlsbad: Graphia, 1934.

Rühle, Otto. *Die Revolution ist keine Parteisache*. Berlin-Wilmersdorf: Die Aktion, 1920.

Sartre, Jean-Paul. *Critique of Dialectical Reason*. Vol. 1 [1960]. Translated by Alan Sheridan-Smith. Edited by Jonathan Rée. London: New Left Books and Humanities, 1976.

———. *Search for a Method* [1957]. Translated by Hazel E. Barnes. New York: Knopf, 1963.

———. *What Is Literature?* [1948]. Translated by Bernard Frechtman. Abingdon, UK: Routledge, 2001.

Schelsky, Helmut. *Die skeptische Generation: Eine Soziologie der deutschen Jugend*. Düsseldorf: Diederichs, 1957.

———. *Wandlungen der deutschen Familie in der Gegenwart*. Stuttgart: Enke, 1953.

Schlosser, Ernst. *See* Hellmann, Henry.

Schmidt, Erich R. *Meine Emigrantenjahre 1933–1940: Berlin-Bern-Paris*. Rostock: Verlag Jugend und Geschichte, 1994.

———. *Meine Jugend in Groß-Berlin: Triumph und Elend der Arbeiterbewegung 1918–1933*. Bremen: Donat, 1988.

Schmitt, Carl. *The Theory of the Partisan: A Commentary/Remark on the Concept of the Political* [1963]. Translated by A. C. Goodson. East Lansing: Michigan State University Press, 2004.

Schneider, Michael. "Gegen den Linken Dogmatismus, eine 'Alterskrankheit' des Kommunismus." *Kursbuch* 25 (October 1971): 73–121.

Schoettle, Erwin. "Die unerwartete Revolution und ihre Folgen: Die letzten 50 Jahre tätig mitgemacht." *Die Neue Gesellschaft* 15, no. 6 (November/December 1968): 469–72.

Schröder, Karl. *Vom Werden der neuen Gesellschaft (Alte und neue Organisationsformen)*. Berlin: Verlag der KAPD, [ca. 1920].

Schulz, Klaus-Peter. *Auftakt zum Kalten Krieg: Der Freiheitskampf der SPD in Berlin 1945/46*
Berlin: Colloquium, 1965.

Schumacher, Kurt. *Reden—Schriften—Korrespondenzen 1945–1952.* Edited by Willy Albrecht.
Berlin: J.H.W. Dietz Nachf., 1985.

Schumpeter, Joseph. *Capitalism, Socialism, and Democracy* [1942]. New York: Harper, 1947.

Students for a Democratic Society, former leaders of. "An Open Letter to the New New Left
from the Old New Left." *Nation*, April 16, 2020.

Seifert, Jürgen. "Innerparteiliche Opposition." *Frankfurter Hefte* 15, no. 11 (November 1960):
765–72.

———. "Die Neue Linke—Abgrenzung und Selbstanalyse." *Frankfurter Hefte* 18, no. 1 (January 1963): 30–40.

Serge, Victor. *Memoirs of a Revolutionary, 1901–1941* [1951]. Translated by Peter Sedgwick and
George Paizis. New York: NYRB Classics, 2012.

Sering, Paul. *See* Löwenthal, Richard.

Simmel, Georg. "On the Concept and Tragedy of Culture" [1911–12]. In *The Conflict in Modern
Culture and Other Essays*, translated and edited by K. Peter Etzkorn, 27–46. New York:
Teachers College, 1968.

———. "The Sociology of Secrecy and of Secret Societies." *American Journal of Sociology* 11,
no. 4 (January 1906): 441–98.

Sontheimer, Kurt. *Das Elend unserer Intellektuellen: Linke Theorie in der Bundesrepublik Deutschland.* Hamburg: Hoffmann und Campe, 1976.

Sopade. *Deutschland-Berichte der Sozialdemokratischen Partei Deutschlands.* Salzhausen: Petra
Nettelbeck, 1980.

———. "Kampf und Ziel des revolutionären Sozialismus: Die Politik der Sozialdemokratischen
Partei Deutschlands." *Neuer Vorwärts*, no. 33 (January 28, 1934).

Sorel, Georges. *Reflections on Violence* [1908]. Edited by Jeremy Jennings. Cambridge: Cambridge University Press, 1999.

———. "Le syndicalisme révolutionnaire." *Le mouvement socialiste*, no. 17 (1905): 265–80.

SPD (Vorstand), ed. *Grundsatzprogramm der Sozialdemokratischen Partei Deutschlands.* Cologne: Deutz, 1959.

———. *Protokoll der Verhandlungen des Außerordentlichen Parteitages der Sozialdemokratischen
Partei Deutschlands vom 13.–15. November 1959 in Bad Godesberg.* Hannover: Neuer Vorwärts,
1959.

Sternberg, Fritz. *Capitalism and Socialism on Trial.* London: Gollancz, 1951.

Stöver, Bernd, ed. *Berichte über die Lage in Deutschland: Die Lagemeldungen der Gruppe Neu
Beginnen aus dem Dritten Reich 1933–1936.* Bonn: J.H.W. Dietz, 1996.

Streeck, Wolfgang. *Buying Time: The Delayed Crisis of Democratic Capitalism* [2013]. Translated
by Patrick Camiller. London: Verso, 2014.

Taurer, Bernhard, and Georg Eliasberg [Jon B. Jansen and Stefan Weyl, alias]. *The Silent War:
The Underground Movement in Germany.* Philadelphia: Lippincott, 1943.

Thalheimer, August. "On Fascism" [1930]. *Telos*, no. 40 (1979): 109–22.

Therborn, Göran. *From Marxism to Post-Marxism?* London: Verso, 2008.

Thompson, E. P., ed. *Out of Apathy.* London: New Left Books, 1960.

Tönnies, Ferdinand. *Community and Society* [1887]. Translated by Charles P. Loomis. East Lansing: Michigan State University Press, 1957.

Touraine, Alain. *The May Movement: Revolt and Reform* [1968]. Translated by Leonard F. X. Mayhew. New York: Random House, 1971.

———. *The Post-Industrial Society: Tomorrow's Social History—Classes, Conflicts and Culture in the Programmed Society* [1969]. Translated by Leonard F. X. Mayhew. New York: Random House, 1971.

Trotsky, Leon. *The Revolution Betrayed* [1936]. Translated by Max Eastman. London: Faber and Faber, 1937.

Tucker, Robert C., ed. *The Marx-Engels Reader*. New York: Norton, 1972.

UDSO. *Die neue deutsche Republik*. London: UDSO, 1943.

———. *Zur Politik deutscher Sozialisten: Politische Kundgebungen und programmatische Richtlinien*. London: UDSO, 1945.

Vaneigem, Raoul. *The Revolution of Everyday Life* [1967]. Translated by Donald Nicholson-Smith. Oakland: PM, 2012.

Veblen, Thorstein. *The Engineers and the Price System*. New York: Huebsch, 1921.

Vester, Michael. "Die Strategie der direkten Aktion." *neue kritik*, no. 6 (1965): 12–20.

Weber, Max. "Politics as a Vocation" [1919]. In *The Vocation Lectures*, edited by David Owen and Tracy B. Strong, translated by Rodney Livingstone, 32–94. Indianapolis: Hackett, 2004.

Weil, Simone. *On the Abolition of All Political Parties* [1942–43]. Translated by Simon Leys. New York: New York Review Books, 2013.

Weiss, Peter. *The Aesthetics of Resistance*. Vol. 1. Translated by Joachim Neugroschel. Durham, NC: Duke University Press, 2005.

White, Hayden V. *Metahistory: The Historical Imagination in Nineteenth-Century Europe*. Baltimore: Johns Hopkins University Press, 1973.

Secondary Sources

Agocs, Andreas. *Antifascist Humanism and the Politics of Cultural Renewal in Germany*. Cambridge: Cambridge University Press, 2017.

Alba, Víctor, and Stephen Schwartz. *Spanish Marxism versus Soviet Communism: A History of the P.O.U.M.* New Brunswick, NJ: Transaction, 1988.

Albrecht, Willy. *Der Sozialistische Deutsche Studentenbund (SDS): Vom parteikonformen Studentenverband zum Repräsentanten der neuen Linken*. Bonn: J.H.W. Dietz Nachf., 1994.

Aly, Götz. *Unser Kampf 1968—ein irritierter Blick zurück*. Frankfurt am Main: Fischer, 2008.

Anderson, Perry. *Considerations on Western Marxism*. London: New Left Books, 1976.

Andersson, Jenny. *The Future of the World: Futurology, Futurists, and the Struggle for the Post Cold War Imagination*. Oxford: Oxford University Press, 2018.

Angster, Julia. *Konsenskapitalismus und Sozialdemokratie: Die Westernisierung von SPD und DGB*. Munich: Oldenbourg, 2003.

Anweiler, Oskar. *The Soviets: The Russian Workers', Peasants', and Soldiers' Councils, 1905–1921* [1958]. Translated by Ruth Hein. New York: Pantheon, 1975.

Arato, Andrew, and Paul Breines. *The Young Lukács and the Origins of Western Marxism*. New York: Seabury, 1979.

Bantigny, Ludivine. *1968: De grands soirs en petits matins*. Paris: Le Seuil, 2018.

Barclay, David E., and Eric D. Weitz, eds. *Between Reform and Revolution: German Socialism and Communism from 1840 to 1990*. New York: Berghahn, 1998.

Bergmann, Theodor. *"Gegen den Strom": Die Geschichte der KPD(Oppositon)*. 2nd ed. Hamburg: VSA, 2001.

Berliner Geschichtswerkstatt. *Widerstand in Berlin gegen das NS-Regime 1933–1945: Ein biographisches Lexikon*. 12 vols. Berlin: Trafo, 2004.

Berman, Sheri. *The Primacy of Politics: Social Democracy and the Making of Europe's Twentieth Century*. New York: Cambridge University Press, 2006.

Birchall, Ian H. "Neither Washington nor Moscow? The Rise and Fall of the Rassemblement Démocratique Révolutionnaire." *Journal of European Studies* 29, no. 4 (December 1999): 365–404.

———. *Sartre against Stalinism*. New York: Berghahn, 2004.

Bock, Hans Manfred. *Geschichte des "linken Radikalismus" in Deutschland: Ein Versuch*. Frankfurt am Main: Suhrkamp, 1976.

Boggs, Carl. "Marxism, Prefigurative Communism, and the Problem of Workers' Control." *Radical America* 11/12, nos. 6/1 (Winter 1977–78): 99–122.

———. "Revolutionary Process, Political Strategy, and the Dilemma of Power." *Theory and Society* 4, no. 3 (1977): 359–93.

Bourg, Julian. *From Revolution to Ethics: May 1968 and Contemporary French Thought*. Montreal: McGill-Queen's University Press, 2007.

Bourrinet, Philippe. *The Dutch and German Communist Left (1900–68): "Neither Lenin Nor Trotsky Nor Stalin!"—"All Workers Must Think for Themselves!"* [1995]. Leiden: Brill, 2017.

Breckman, Warren. *Adventures of the Symbolic: Post-Marxism and Radical Democracy*. New York: Columbia University Press, 2013.

Breines, Paul. "Young Lukács, Old Lukács, New Lukács." *Journal of Modern History* 51, no. 3 (September 1979): 533–46.

Breines, Wini. *Community and Organization in the New Left, 1962–1968: The Great Refusal*. New York: Praeger, 1982.

Bremer, Jörg. *Die Sozialistische Arbeiterpartei Deutschlands (SAP): Untergrund und Exil 1933–1945*. Frankfurt am Main: Campus, 1978.

Broué, Pierre. *The German Revolution, 1917–1923* [1971]. Translated by John Archer. Edited by Ian Birchall and Brian Pearce. Chicago: Haymarket, 2006.

———. *Staline et la révolution: Le cas espagnol (1936–1939)*. Paris: Fayard, 1993.

Brown, Timothy Scott. *Sixties Europe*. Cambridge: Cambridge University Press, 2020.

———. *Weimar Radicals: Nazis and Communists between Authenticity and Performance*. New York: Berghahn, 2009.

———. *West Germany and the Global Sixties: The Anti-Authoritarian Revolt, 1962–1978*. Cambridge: Cambridge University Press, 2013.

Caldwell, Peter C. *Democracy, Capitalism, and the Welfare State: Debating Social Order in Postwar West Germany, 1949–1989*. Oxford: Oxford University Press, 2019.

Carsten, F. L. *Revolution in Central Europe, 1918–1919*. Berkeley: University of California Press, 1972.

Chappel, James. *Catholic Modern: The Challenge of Totalitarianism and the Remaking of the Church*. Cambridge, MA: Harvard University Press, 2018.

Chen Jian, Martin Klimke, Masha Kirasirova, Mary Nolan, Marilyn Young, and Joanna Waley-Cohen, eds. *The Routledge Handbook of the Global Sixties: Between Protest and Nation-Building*. Abingdon, UK: Routledge, 2018.

Chun Lin. *The British New Left*. Edinburgh: Edinburgh University Press, 1993.

Congdon, Lee. *The Young Lukács*. Chapel Hill: University of North Carolina Press, 1983.

Copsey, Nigel. "Towards a New Anti-fascist 'Minimum'?" In *Varieties of Anti-Fascism: Britain in the Inter-War Period*, edited by Copsey and Andrzej Olechnowicz, xiv–xxi. Basingstoke, UK: Palgrave Macmillan, 2010.

Cox, John M. *Circles of Resistance: Jewish, Leftist, and Youth Dissidence in Nazi Germany*. New York: Peter Lang, 2009.

Demirović, Alex. *Der nonkonformistische Intellektuelle: Die Entwicklung der Kritischen Theorie zur Frankfurter Schule*. Frankfurt am Main: Suhrkamp, 1999.

Diers, Andreas. *Arbeiterbewegung—Demokratie—Staat: Wolfgang Abendroth, Leben und Werk 1906–1948*. Hamburg: VSA, 2006.

———. "Linkssozialismus: Ursprünge und Geschichte 1917–1989." *Jahrbuch für Forschungen zur Geschichte der Arbeiterbewegung*, no. 2 (May 2010): 47–65.

Ditfurth, Jutta. *Ulrike Meinhof: Die Biografie*. Berlin: Ullstein, 2007.

Doering-Manteuffel, Anselm. *Wie westlich sind die Deutschen? Amerikanisierung und Westernisierung im 20. Jahrhundert*. Göttingen: Vandenhoeck und Ruprecht, 1999.

Drechsler, Hanno. *Die Sozialistische Arbeiterpartei Deutschlands (SAPD): Ein Beitrag zur Geschichte der deutschen Arbeiterbewegung am Ende der Weimarer Republik*. Meisenheim am Glan: A. Hain, 1965.

Droz, Jacques. *Histoire de l'antifascisme en Europe 1923–1939*. Paris: La Découverte, 1985.

Düffler, Jost. "Bonapartism, Fascism and National Socialism." *Journal of Contemporary History* 11, no. 4 (October 1976): 109–28.

Duhnke, Horst. *Die KPD von 1933 bis 1945*. Cologne: Kiepenheuer und Witsch, 1972.

Dworkin, Dennis L. *Cultural Marxism in Postwar Britain: History, the New Left, and the Origins of Cultural Studies*. Durham, NC: Duke University Press, 1997.

Edinger, Lewis J. *German Exile Politics: The Social Democratic Executive Committee in the Nazi Era*. Berkeley: University of California Press, 1956.

———. *Kurt Schumacher: A Study in Personality and Political Behavior*. Stanford, CA: Stanford University Press, 1965.

Eley, Geoff. *Forging Democracy: The History of the Left in Europe, 1850–2000*. Oxford: Oxford University Press, 2002.

———. "Legacies of Antifascism: Constructing Democracy in Postwar Europe." *New German Critique*, no. 67 (Winter 1996): 73–100.

———. "Reviewing the Socialist Tradition." In *The Crisis of Socialism in Europe*, edited by Christiane Lemke and Gary Marks, 21–60. Durham, NC: Duke University Press, 1992.

Epstein, Catherine. *The Last Revolutionaries: German Communists and Their Century*. Cambridge, MA: Harvard University Press, 2003.

Feenberg, Andrew. *The Philosophy of Praxis: Marx, Lukács, and the Frankfurt School*. London: Verso, 2014.

———. "Post-Utopian Marxism: Lukács and the Dilemmas of Organization." In *Confronting Mass Democracy and Industrial Technology: Political and Social Theory from Nietzsche to Habermas*, edited by John P. McCormick, 45–69. Durham, NC: Duke University Press, 2002.

Felsch, Philipp. *Der lange Sommer der Theorie: Geschichte einer Revolte 1960 bis 1990*. Munich: C. H. Beck, 2015.

Fichter, Tilman. *SDS und SPD: Parteilichkeit jenseits der Partei*. Opladen: Westdeutscher, 1988.

Fichter, Tilman, and Siegward Lönnendonker. *Kleine Geschichte des SDS: Der Sozialistische Deutsche Studentenbund von 1946 bis zur Selbstauflösung*. Berlin: Rotbuch, 1977.

Foitzik, Jan. *Zwischen den Fronten: Zur Politik, Organisation und Funktion linker politischer Kleinorganisationen im Widerstand 1933 bis 1939/40 unter besonderer Berücksichtigung des Exils*. Bonn: Verlag Neue Gesellschaft, 1986.

Forner, Sean A. *German Intellectuals and the Challenge of Democratic Renewal: Culture and Politics after 1945*. Cambridge: Cambridge University Press, 2014.

Frei, Norbert. *1968: Jugendrevolte und globaler Protest*. Munich: Deutscher Taschenbuch, 2008.

Freyberg, Jutta von. *Sozialdemokraten und Kommunisten: Die revolutionären Sozialisten Deutschlands vor dem Problem der Aktionseinheit 1934–1937*. Cologne: Pahl-Rugenstein, 1973.

Fuechtner, Veronika. *Berlin Psychoanalytic: Psychoanalysis and Culture in Weimar Republic Germany and Beyond*. Berkeley: University of California Press, 2011.

Fulbrook, Mary. *Dissonant Lives: Generations and Violence through the German Dictatorships*. Oxford: Oxford University Press, 2011.

García, Hugo, Mercedes Yusta Rodrigo, Xavier Tabet, and Cristina Clímaco, eds. *Rethinking Antifascism: History, Memory and Politics, 1922 to the Present*. New York: Berghahn, 2016.

Gauchet, Marcel. "Right and Left." In *Realms of Memory: Rethinking the French Past* [1984–92], vol. 1, edited by Pierre Nora, translated by Arthur Goldhammer, 240–98. New York: Columbia University Press, 1996.

Gay, Peter. *The Dilemma of Democratic Socialism: Eduard Bernstein's Challenge to Marx*. New York: Columbia University Press, 1952.

Gilcher-Holtey, Ingrid, ed. *1968—Vom Ereignis zum Gegenstand der Geschichtswissenschaft*. Göttingen: Vandenhoeck und Ruprecht, 1998.

Gitlin, Todd. *The Sixties: Years of Hope, Days of Rage*. Toronto: Bantam, 1987.

Glees, Anthony. *Exile Politics during the Second World War: The German Social Democrats in Britain*. Oxford: Oxford University Press, 1982.

Gluck, Mary. *Georg Lukács and His Generation, 1900–1918*. Cambridge, MA: Harvard University Press, 1985.

Goebel, Michael. *Anti-imperial Metropolis: Interwar Paris and the Seeds of Third World Nationalism*. Cambridge: Cambridge University Press, 2015.

Goldberger, Samuel. "Ervin Szabó, Anarcho-Syndicalism and Democratic Revolution in Turn-of-the-Century Hungary." PhD thesis, Columbia University, 1985.

Gombin, Richard. *The Origins of Modern Leftism* [1971]. Translated by Michael K. Perl. Harmondsworth, UK: Penguin, 1975.

Goodstein, Elizabeth S. *Georg Simmel and the Disciplinary Imaginary*. Stanford, CA: Stanford University Press, 2017.

Gordon, Daniel A. *Immigrants and Intellectuals: May '68 and the Rise of Anti-racism in France.* Pontypool, UK: Merlin, 2012.

———. "A 'Mediterranean New Left'? Comparing and Contrasting the French PSU and the Italian PSIUP." *Contemporary European History* 19, no. 4 (2010): 309–30.

Graf, Rüdiger, and Moritz Föllmer. "The Culture of 'Crisis' in the Weimar Republic." *Thesis Eleven*, no. 111 (August 2012): 36–47.

Graf, William D. *The German Left Since 1945: Socialism and Social Democracy in the German Federal Republic.* Cambridge, UK: Oleander, 1976.

Graham, Helen. "The Eclipse of the Socialist Left: 1934–1937." In *Élites and Power in Twentieth-Century Spain: Essays in Honor of Sir Raymond Carr*, edited by Frances Lannon and Paul Preston, 127–51. Oxford: Oxford University Press, 1990.

Grebing, Helga. *Geschichte der deutschen Arbeiterbewegung: Von der Revolution 1848 bis ins 21. Jahrhundert.* Berlin: Vorwärts-Buch, 2007.

Greenberg, Udi. *The Weimar Century: German Émigrés and the Ideological Foundations of the Cold War.* Princeton, NJ: Princeton University Press, 2015.

Groppo, Bruno. "De Karl Frank à Paul Hagen: Itinéraire d'un exilé atypique." *Matériaux pour l'histoire de notre temps* 60, no. 1 (2000): 31–33.

Gross, Babette. *Willi Münzenberg: A Political Biography* [1967]. Translated by Marian Jackson. East Lansing: Michigan State University Press, 1974.

Grossmann, Kurt R. *Emigration: Geschichte der Hitler-Flüchtlinge 1933–1945.* Frankfurt am Main: Europäische Verlagsanstalt, 1969.

Grunewald, Michel, and Frithjof Trapp, eds. *Autour du "Front populaire allemand": Einheitsfront—Volksfront.* Bern: Peter Lang, 1990.

Häberlen, Joachim C. *The Emotional Politics of the Alternative Left: West Germany, 1968–1984.* Cambridge: Cambridge University Press, 2018.

Hamilton, Scott. *The Crisis of Theory: E. P. Thompson, the New Left and Postwar British Politics.* Manchester: Manchester University Press, 2011.

Hanshew, Karrin. *Terror and Democracy in West Germany.* Cambridge: Cambridge University Press, 2012.

Harsch, Donna. *German Social Democracy and the Rise of Nazism.* Chapel Hill: University of North Carolina Press, 1993.

Hauss, Charles. *The New Left in France: The Unified Socialist Party.* Westport, CT: Greenwood, 1978.

Hebel-Kunze, Bärbel. *SPD und Faschismus: Zur politischen und organisatorischen Entwicklung der SPD 1932–1935.* Frankfurt am Main: Röderberg, 1977.

Heigl, Richard. *Oppositionspolitik: Wolfgang Abendroth und die Entstehung der Neuen Linken (1950–1968).* Hamburg: Argument, 2008.

Hellman, John. *Emmanuel Mounier and the New Catholic Left, 1930–1950.* Toronto: University of Toronto Press, 1981.

Herwig, Malte. *Die Flakhelfer: Wie aus Hitlers jüngsten Parteimitgliedern Deutschlands führende Demokraten wurden.* Munich: Deutsche Verlagsanstalt, 2013.

Herzog, Dagmar. *Sex after Fascism: Memory and Morality in Twentieth-Century Germany.* Princeton, NJ: Princeton University Press, 2005.

Heywood, Paul. *Marxism and the Failure of Organised Socialism in Spain, 1879–1936.* Cambridge: Cambridge University Press, 1990.

Hobsbawm, Eric. *The Age of Extremes: A History of the World, 1914–1991* [1994]. New York: Vintage, 1996.

———. *How to Change the World: Reflections on Marx and Marxism*. New Haven, CT: Yale University Press, 2011.

———. "In the Era of Anti-fascism 1929–45" [1979]. In *How to Change the World*, 261–313.

Hockenos, Paul. *Joschka Fischer and the Making of the Berlin Republic: An Alternative History of Postwar Germany*. Oxford: Oxford University Press, 2007.

Hodenberg, Christina von. *Das andere Achtundsechzig: Gesellschaftsgeschichte einer Revolte*. Munich: C. H. Beck, 2018.

Hoffmann, Stefan-Ludwig. "Germany Is No More: Defeat, Occupation, and the Postwar Order." Translated by Christine Brocks. In *The Oxford Handbook of Modern German History*, edited by Helmut Walser Smith, 593–614. Oxford: Oxford University Press, 2011.

Hoffrogge, Ralf. *A Jewish Communist in Weimar Germany: The Life of Werner Scholem*. Chicago: Haymarket, 2018.

———. *Working-Class Politics in the German Revolution: Richard Müller, the Revolutionary Shop Stewards and the Origins of the Council Movement*. Chicago: Haymarket, 2015.

Horn, Gerd-Rainer. *European Socialists Respond to Fascism: Ideology, Activism, and Contingency in the 1930s*. New York: Oxford University Press, 1996.

———. *The Spirit of '68: Rebellion in Western Europe and North America, 1956–1976*. Oxford: Oxford University Press, 2007.

Hosek, Jennifer Ruth. "'Subaltern Nationalism' and the West Berlin Anti-authoritarians." *German Politics and Society* 26, no. 1 (2008): 57–81.

Howard, Dick. *The Marxian Legacy*. New York: Urizen, 1977.

Hughes, H. Stuart. *Consciousness and Society*. New York: Knopf, 1958.

Hunt, Richard N. *German Social Democracy, 1918–1933*. New Haven, CT: Yale University Press, 1964.

Hurwitz, Harold. *Demokratie und Antikommunismus in Berlin nach 1945*. 4 vols. Cologne: Verlag Wissenschaft und Politik, 1990.

Imlay, Talbot C. *The Practice of Socialist Internationalism: European Socialists and International Politics, 1914–1960*. New York: Oxford University Press, 2018.

Jackson, Julian. *The Popular Front in France: Defending Democracy, 1934–38*. Cambridge: Cambridge University Press, 1988.

Jacoby, Russell. *Dialectic of Defeat: Contours of Western Marxism*. Cambridge: Cambridge University Press, 1981.

———. *The Repression of Psychoanalysis: Otto Fenichel and the Political Freudians*. New York: Basic Books, 1983.

Jarausch, Konrad. *After Hitler: Recivilizing Germans, 1945–1995*. Oxford: Oxford University Press, 2006.

Jay, Martin. *The Dialectical Imagination: A History of the Frankfurt School and the Institute of Social Research, 1923–1950*. Boston: Little, Brown, 1973.

———. *Marxism and Totality: The Adventures of a Concept from Lukács to Habermas*. Berkeley: University of California Press, 1984.

———. "No Power to the Soviets." *Salmagundi*, nos. 88/89 (1990): 64–71.

————. "The Weimar Left: Theory and Practice." In *Weimar Thought: A Contested Legacy*, edited by Peter E. Gordon and John P. McCormick, 377–93. Princeton, NJ: Princeton University Press, 2013.

Jones, Mark. *Founding Weimar: Violence and the German Revolution of 1918–1919*. Cambridge: Cambridge University Press, 2016.

Jones, William David. *The Lost Debate: German Socialist Intellectuals and Totalitarianism*. Urbana: University of Illinois Press, 1999.

Judt, Tony. *Postwar: A History of Europe Since 1945*. New York: Penguin, 2005.

Jünke, Christoph, ed. *Linkssozialismus in Deutschland: Jenseits von Sozialdemokratie und Kommunismus?* Hamburg: VSA, 2010.

————. *Streifzüge durch das rote 20. Jahrhundert*. Hamburg: LAIKA, 2014.

Kaden, Albrecht. *Einheit oder Freiheit: Die Wiedergründung der SPD 1945/46*. Hannover: J.H.W. Dietz Nachf., 1964.

Kalter, Christoph. *The Discovery of the Third World: Decolonization and the Rise of the New Left in France, c. 1950–1976* [2011]. Translated by Thomas Dunlap. Cambridge : Cambridge University Press, 2016.

Kasper, Sebastian. *Spontis: Eine Geschichte antiautoritärer Linker im roten Jahrzehnt*. Münster: edition assemblage, 2019.

Katsiaficas, George. *The Imagination of the New Left: A Global Analysis of 1968*. Boston: South End, 1987.

————. *The Subversion of Politics: European Autonomous Social Movements and the Decolonization of Everyday Life*. Atlantic Highlands, NJ: Humanities, 1997.

Katz, Barry M. *Foreign Intelligence: Research and Analysis in the Office of Strategic Services, 1942–1945*. Cambridge, MA: Harvard University Press, 1989.

Kavoulakos, Konstantinos. *Georg Lukács's Philosophy of Praxis: From Neo-Kantianism to Marxism*. London: Bloomsbury Academic, 2018.

Kellner, Douglas. *Herbert Marcuse and the Crisis of Marxism*. Berkeley: University of California Press, 1984.

Kenny, Michael. *The First New Left: British Intellectuals after Stalin*. London: Lawrence and Wishart, 1995.

Keßler, Mario. *Kommunismuskritik im westlichen Nachkriegsdeutschland: Franz Borkenau, Richard Löwenthal, Ossip Flechtheim*. Berlin: Verlag für Berlin-Brandenburg, 2010.

————. *Ossip K. Flechtheim: Politischer Wissenschaftler und Zukunftsdenker (1909–1998)*. Cologne: Böhlau, 2007.

————. *Ruth Fischer: Ein Leben mit und gegen Kommunisten*. Cologne: Böhlau, 2013.

Kettler, David. *Marxismus und Kultur: Mannheim und Lukács in den ungarischen Revolutionen 1918/19*. Berlin: Luchterhand, 1967.

Kliem, Kurt. "Der sozialistische Widerstand gegen das Dritte Reich dargestellt an der Gruppe 'Neu Beginnen.'" PhD thesis, University of Marburg, 1957.

Klimke, Martin. *The Other Alliance: Student Protest in West Germany and the United States in the Global Sixties*. Princeton, NJ: Princeton University Press, 2010.

Klönne, Arno. *Gegen den Strom: Bericht über den Jugendwiderstand im Dritten Reich*. Hannover: O. Goedel, 1957.

Klotzbach, Kurt. *Der Weg zur Staatspartei: Programmatik, praktische Politik und Organisation der deutschen Sozialdemokratie 1945 bis 1965*. Berlin: Dietz, 1982.

Kohut, Thomas A. *A German Generation: An Experiential History of the Twentieth Century*. New Haven, CT: Yale University Press, 2012.

Krause, Scott H. *Bringing Cold War Democracy to West Berlin: A Shared German-American Project, 1940–1972*. London: Routledge, 2018.

Kritidis, Gregor. *Linkssozialistische Opposition in der Ära Adenauer: Ein Beitrag zur Frühgeschichte der Bundesrepublik Deutschland*. Hannover: Offizin, 2008.

Kuby, Emma. *Political Survivors: The Resistance, the Cold War, and the Fight against Concentration Camps after 1945*. Ithaca, NY: Cornell University Press, 2019.

Kufferath, Philipp. "Das linkssozialistische Milieu und die intellektuellen Traditionen der Neuen Linken vor 1968." MA thesis, University of Göttingen, 2008.

Kühne, Tobias. "Das Netzwerk 'Neu Beginnen' und die Berliner SPD nach 1945." PhD thesis, Technical University of Berlin, 2014.

———. *Das Netzwerk "Neu Beginnen" und die Berliner SPD nach 1945*. Berlin: Verlag Berlin Brandenburg, 2018.

Kundnani, Hans. *Utopia or Auschwitz: Germany's 1968 Generation and the Holocaust*. New York: Columbia University Press, 2009.

Langkau-Alex, Ursula. *Deutsche Volksfront 1932–1939: Zwischen Berlin, Paris, Prag und Moskau*. 3 vols. Berlin: Akademie, 2004.

Lichtheim, George. *George Lukács*. New York: Viking, 1970.

———. *Marxism in Modern France*. New York: Columbia University Press, 1966.

———. *A Short History of Socialism*. New York: Praeger, 1970.

Lih, Lars T. *Lenin Rediscovered: "What Is to Be Done?" in Context*. Leiden: Brill, 2006.

Link, Werner. *Die Geschichte des Internationalen Jugend-Bundes (IJB) und des Internationalen Sozialistischen Kampf-Bundes (ISK): Ein Beitrag zur Geschichte der Arbeiterbewegung in der Weimarer Republik und im Dritten Reich*. Marburger Abhandlungen zur politischen Wissenschaft vol. 1. Meisenheim am Glan: A. Hain, 1964.

Lönnendonker, Siegward, et al. *Die antiautoritäre Revolte: Der Sozialistische Deutsche Studentenbund nach der Trennung von der SPD*. Vol. 1, *1960–1967*. Wiesbaden: Westdeutscher, 2002.

Loubet del Bayle, Jean-Louis. *Les non-conformistes des années 30: Une tentative de renouvellement de la pensée politique française*. Paris: Éditions du Seuil, 1969.

Lovell, Julia. *Maoism: A Global History*. London: Bodley Head, 2019.

Löwy, Michael. *Georg Lukács: From Romanticism to Bolshevism* [1976]. Translated by Patrick Camiller. London: New Left Books, 1979.

Major, Patrick. *The Death of the KPD: Communism and Anti-Communism in West Germany, 1945–1956*. Oxford: Clarendon, 1998.

Malycha, Andreas, and Peter Jochen Winters. *Die SED: Geschichte einer deutschen Partei*. Munich: C. H. Beck, 2009.

Markovits, Andrei S., and Philip S. Gorski. *The German Left: Red, Green and Beyond*. New York: Oxford University Press, 1993.

Marwick, Arthur. *The Sixties: Cultural Revolution in Britain, France, Italy, and the United States, c. 1958–c. 1974*. Oxford: Oxford University Press, 1998.

Mason, Paul. *Why It's Kicking Off Everywhere: The New Global Revolutions*. 2nd ed. London: Verso, 2013.

Mason, Timothy W. *Nazism, Fascism and the Working Class*. Edited by Jane Caplan. Cambridge: Cambridge University Press, 1995.

———. *Social Policy in the Third Reich: The Working Class and the "National Community."* Edited by Jane Caplan. Providence, RI: Berg, 1993.

Matthias, Erich. *Sozialdemokratie und Nation: Ein Beitrag zur Ideengeschichte der sozialdemokratischen Emigration in der Prager Zeit des Parteivorstandes 1933–1938*. Stuttgart: Deutsche Verlagsanstalt, 1952.

Mattick, Paul. *Anti-Bolshevik Communism*. London: Merlin, 1978.

McDougall, Alan. *Youth Politics in East Germany: The Free German Youth Movement, 1946–1968*. Oxford: Oxford University Press, 2004.

Mehringer, Hartmut. *Waldemar von Knoeringen—Eine politische Biographie: Der Weg vom revolutionären Sozialismus zur sozialen Demokratie*. Munich: K. G. Saur, 1989.

Mercer, Ben. "Specters of Fascism: The Rhetoric of Historical Analogy in 1968." *Journal of Modern History* 88, no. 1 (March 2016): 96–129.

Meyer, Bernhard. *Sozialdemokraten in der Entscheidung: Biographien und Chronologie*. Berlin: Edition Luisenstadt, 1994.

Milder, Stephen. *Greening Democracy: The Anti-nuclear Movement and Political Environmentalism in West Germany and Beyond, 1968–1983*. Cambridge: Cambridge University Press, 2017.

Mohandesi, Salar. "Bringing Vietnam Home: The Vietnam War, Internationalism, and May '68." *French Historical Studies* 41, no. 2 (2018): 219–51.

Moraw, Frank. *Die Parole der "Einheit" und die Sozialdemokratie: Zur parteiorganisatorischen und gesellschaftspolitischen Orientierung der SPD in der Periode der Illegalität und in der ersten Phase der Nachkriegszeit 1933–1948*. Bonn–Bad Godesberg: Verlag Neue Gesellschaft, 1973.

Moses, A. Dirk. *German Intellectuals and the Nazi Past*. Cambridge: Cambridge University Press, 2007.

Mudge, Stephanie L. *Leftism Reinvented: Western Parties from Socialism to Neoliberalism*. Cambridge, MA: Harvard University Press, 2018.

Müller, Jan-Werner. "1968 as Event, Milieu and Ideology." *Journal of Political Ideologies* 7, no. 1 (2002): 15–37.

Müller, Reinhard. "Karl B. Frank alias Paul Hagen (1893–1969)." *Newsletter des Archivs für die Geschichte der Soziologie in Österreich (Graz)* 12 (November 1995): 11–19.

Müller, Tim B. *Krieger und Gelehrte: Herbert Marcuse und die Denksysteme im Kalten Krieg*. Hamburg: Hamburger Edition, 2010.

Neaman, Elliott. *Free Radicals: Agitators, Hippies, Urban Guerrillas, and Germany's Youth Revolt of the 1960s and 1970s*. Candor, NY: Telos, 2016.

Nehring, Holger. "The Era of Non-violence: 'Terrorism' and the Emergence of Conceptions of Non-violent Statehood in Western Europe, 1967–1983." *European Review of History* 14, no. 3 (2007): 343–71.

———. "'Generation' as Political Argument in West European Protest Movements in the 1960s." In *Generations in Twentieth-Century Europe*, edited by Stephen Lovell, 57–78. Basingstoke, UK: Palgrave Macmillan, 2007.

Nehring, Holger. "'Out of Apathy': Genealogies of the British 'New Left' in a Transnational Context, 1956–1962." In *Between Prague Spring and French May: Opposition and Revolt in Europe, 1960–1980*, edited by Martin Klimke, Jacco Pekelder, and Joachim Scharloth, 15–31. New York: Berghahn, 2011.

———. *Politics of Security: British and West German Protest Movements and the Early Cold War, 1945–1970*. Oxford: Oxford University Press, 2013.

Nicholls, Anthony J. *Freedom with Responsibility: The Social Market Economy in Germany, 1918–1963*. Oxford: Oxford University Press, 1994.

Niethammer, Lutz, Ulrich Borsdorf, and Peter Brandt, eds. *Arbeiterinitiative 1945: Antifaschistische Ausschüsse und Reorganisation der Arbeiterbewegung in Deutschland*. Wuppertal: Peter Hammer, 1976.

Nolan, Mary. "Antifascism under Fascism: German Visions and Voices." *New German Critique*, no. 67 (Winter 1996): 33–55.

Oertzen, Peter von. "Behelfsbrücken: Linkssozialistische Zeitschriften in der Ära der 'Restauration' 1950–1962." In *Opposition als Triebkraft der Demokratie. Bilanz und Perspektiven der zweiten Republik: Jürgen Seifert zum 70. Geburtstag*, edited by Michael Buckmiller and Joachim Perels, 87–100. Hannover: Offizin, 1998.

Olsen, Niklas. *The Sovereign Consumer: A New Intellectual History of Neoliberalism*. New York: Palgrave Macmillan, 2018.

Orlow, Dietrich. *Common Destiny: A Comparative History of the Dutch, French, and German Social Democratic Parties, 1945–1969*. New York: Berghahn, 2000.

Otto, Karl A. *Vom Ostermarsch zur APO: Geschichte der außerparlamentarischen Opposition in der Bundesrepublik 1960–1970*. Frankfurt am Main: Campus, 1977.

Overesch, Manfred. *Machtergreifung von Links: Thüringen 1945/46*. Hildesheim: Olms, 1993.

Palmier, Jean-Michel. *Weimar in Exile: The Antifascist Emigration in Europe and America* [1987]. Translated by David Fernbach. London: Verso, 2006.

———. *Wilhelm Reich: Essai sur la naissance du Freudo-marxisme*. Paris: Union Générale d'éditions, 1969.

Payne, Stanley G. *The Spanish Revolution*. London: Weidenfeld and Nicolson, 1970.

Peukert, Detlev J. K. *Inside Nazi Germany: Conformity, Opposition, and Racism in Everyday Life* [1982]. Translated by Richard Deveson. New Haven, CT: Yale University Press, 1987.

———. *Die KPD im Widerstand: Verfolgung und Untergrundarbeit an Rhein und Ruhr 1933 bis 1945*. Wuppertal: Hammer, 1980.

———. *The Weimar Republic: The Crisis of Classical Modernity* [1987]. Translated by Richard Deveson. New York: Hill and Wang, 1992.

Poster, Mark. *Existential Marxism in Postwar France: From Sartre to Althusser*. Princeton, NJ: Princeton University Press, 1975.

Potthoff, Heinrich, and Susanne Miller. *The Social Democratic Party of Germany, 1848–2005*. Bonn: Dietz, 2006.

Preston, Paul. *The Coming of the Spanish Civil War: Reform, Reaction, and Revolution in the Second Republic 1931–1936* [1978]. London: Routledge, 1994.

Prezioso, Stéfanie. "'Aujourd'hui en Espagne, demain en Italie': L'exil antifasciste italien et la prise d'armes révolutionnaires." *Vingtième Siècle*, no. 93 (2007): 79–91.

Pritchard, Gareth. *Niemandsland: A History of Unoccupied Germany, 1944–45*. Cambridge: Cambridge University Press, 2012.

Provenzano, Luca. "Beyond the Matraque: State Violence and Its Representation during the Parisian 1968 Events." *Journal of Modern History* 91, no. 3 (2019): 586–624.

Rabaut, Jean. *Tout est possible! Les "gauchistes" français, 1929–1944.* Paris: Denoël-Gonthier, 1974.

Rabinbach, Anson. *The Crisis of Austrian Socialism: From Red Vienna to Civil War, 1927–1934.* Chicago: University of Chicago Press, 1983.

———. *The Eclipse of the Utopias of Labor.* New York: Fordham University Press, 2018.

———. "Introduction: Legacies of Antifascism." *New German Critique*, no. 67 (Winter 1996): 3–17.

———. "Paris, Capital of Antifascism." In *The Modernist Imagination: Intellectual History and Critical Theory*, edited by Warren Breckman, Peter E. Gordon, A. Dirk Moses, Samuel Moyn, and Elliot Neaman, 183–209. New York: Berghahn, 2009.

———. "Staging Antifascism: *The Brown Book of the Reichstag Fire and Hitler Terror.*" *New German Critique* 35, no. 1 (Spring 2008): 97–126.

Radkau, Joachim. *Die deutsche Emigration in den USA: Ihr Einfluss auf die amerikanische Europapolitik 1933–1945.* Düsseldorf: Bertelsmann, 1971.

———. *Geschichte der Zukunft: Prognosen, Visionen, Irrungen in Deutschland von 1945 bis heute.* Munich: Carl Hanser, 2017.

Reichardt, Sven. *Authentizität und Gemeinschaft: Linksalternatives Leben in den siebziger und frühen achtziger Jahren.* Berlin: Suhrkamp, 2014.

Reichhardt, Hans J. "Neu Beginnen: Ein Beitrag zur Geschichte des Widerstandes der Arbeiterbewegung gegen den Nationalsozialismus." *Jahrbuch für die Geschichte Mittel- und Ostdeutschlands* 12 (1963): 150–88.

Reimann, Aribert. *Dieter Kunzelmann: Avantgardist, Protestler, Radikaler.* Göttingen: Vandenhoeck und Ruprecht, 2009.

Renaud, Terence. "Assembling a New Left." *Los Angeles Review of Books*, August 16, 2018.

———. "German New Lefts: Postwar Socialists between Past and Future." *New German Critique*, no. 137 (2019): 117–49.

———. "The German Resistance in New York: Karl B. Frank and the New Beginning Group, 1935–1945." BA thesis, Boston University, 2007. http://terencerenaud.com/german_resistance.htm.

———. "Insider Intellectuals and the Crisis of Democracy." *German History* 37, no. 3 (2019): 392–404.

———. "Sternberg in Amerika: Betrachtungen über die globale Krise 1939–1951." In *Streiten für eine Welt jenseits des Kapitalismus: Fritz Sternberg—Wissenschaftler, Vordenker, Sozialist*, edited by Helga Grebing and Klaus-Jürgen Scherer, 154–88. Paderborn: F. Schöningh, 2017.

Riley, Dylan. "Bernstein's Heirs." *New Left Review*, no. 76 (July–August 2012): 136–50.

Robinson, Paul A. *The Freudian Left: Wilhelm Reich, Géza Róheim, Herbert Marcuse.* New York: Harper and Row, 1969.

Rosenhaft, Eve. *Beating the Fascists? The German Communists and Political Violence, 1929–1933.* Cambridge: Cambridge University Press, 1983.

Ross, Kristin. *Communal Luxury: The Political Imaginary of the Paris Commune.* London: Verso, 2015.

———. *May '68 and Its Afterlives.* Chicago: University of Chicago Press, 2002.

Rota, Emanuel. *A Pact with Vichy: Angelo Tasca from Italian Socialism to French Collaboration.* New York: Fordham University Press, 2013.

Rycroft, Charles. *Wilhelm Reich*. New York: Viking, 1971.

Samuels, Stuart. "The Left Book Club." *Journal of Contemporary History* 1, no. 2 (1966): 65–86.

Sandvoß, Hans-Rainer. *Die "andere" Reichshauptstadt: Widerstand aus der Arbeiterbewegung in Berlin von 1933 bis 1945*. Berlin: Lukas, 2007.

Sassoon, Donald. *One Hundred Years of Socialism: The West European Left in the Twentieth Century*. New York: New Press, 1996.

Schildt, Axel. *Moderne Zeiten: Freizeit, Massenmedien und "Zeitgeist" in der Bundesrepublik der 50er Jahre*. Hamburg: Christians, 1995.

Schmeitzner, Mike. *Eine totalitäre Revolution? Richard Löwenthal und die Weltanschauungsdiktaturen im 20. Jahrhundert*. Bonn: Friedrich-Ebert-Stiftung, 2012.

Schmidt, Eberhard. *Die verhinderte Neuordnung, 1945–1952: Zur Auseinandersetzung um die Demokratisierung der Wirtschaft in den westlichen Besatzungszonen und in der Bundesrepublik Deutschland*. Frankfurt am Main: Europäische Verlagsanstalt, 1970.

Schmidt, Oliver. *"Meine Heimat ist—die deutsche Arbeiterbewegung": Biographische Studien zu Richard Löwenthal im Übergang vom Exil zur frühen Bundesrepublik*. Frankfurt am Main: Peter Lang, 2007.

Schneider, Michael. *Demokratie in Gefahr? Der Konflikt um die Notstandsgesetze, Sozialdemokratie, Gewerkschaften und intellektueller Protest (1958–1968)*. Bonn: Neue Gesellschaft, 1986.

Schöler, Uli. *Auf dem Weg zum Sozialismus—Wolfgang Abendroth: Streiflichter eines Lebenswegs aus dem Blickwinkel seiner Aktivitäten in der Jugendbewegung der Weimarer Republik*. Berlin: Helle Panke, 2007.

———. *Die DDR und Wolfgang Abendroth—Wolfgang Abendroth und die DDR: Kritik einer Kampagne*. Hannover: Offizin, 2008.

———. *Wolfgang Abendroth und der "reale Sozialismus": Ein Balanceakt*. Berlin: Verlag für Berlin-Brandenburg, 2012.

Schorske, Carl E. *German Social Democracy, 1905–1917: The Development of the Great Schism*. Cambridge, MA: Harvard University Press, 1955.

Schröter, Michael, Elke Mühlleitner, and Ulrike May. "Edith Jacobson: Forty Years in Germany (1897–1938)." *Annual of Psychoanalysis* 32 (2004): 199–215.

Scott, Holly V. *Younger than That Now: The Politics of Age in the 1960s*. Amherst: University of Massachusetts Press, 2016.

Seefried, Elke. *Zukünfte: Aufstieg und Krise der Zukunftsforschung 1945–1980*. Berlin: De Gruyter Oldenbourg, 2015.

Seidman, Michael. *The Imaginary Revolution: Parisian Students and Workers in 1968*. New York: Berghahn, 2004.

———. *Transatlantic Antifascisms: From the Spanish Civil War to the End of World War II*. Cambridge: Cambridge University Press, 2018.

Seitenbecher, Manuel. *Mahler, Maschke & Co. Rechtes Denken in der 68er-Bewegung?* Paderborn: F. Schöningh, 2013.

Sennett, Alan. *Revolutionary Marxism in Spain, 1930–1937*. Chicago: Haymarket, 2015.

Shore, Marci. *Caviar and Ashes: A Warsaw Generation's Life and Death in Marxism, 1918–1968*. New Haven, CT: Yale University Press, 2006.

Shubert, Adrian. *The Road to Revolution in Spain: The Coal Miners of Asturias, 1860–1934*. Urbana: University of Illinois Press, 1987.

Siegfried, Detlef. *1968: Protest, Revolte, Gegenkultur*. Ditzingen: Reclam, 2018.

Slobodian, Quinn. *Foreign Front: Third World Politics in Sixties West Germany*. Durham, NC: Duke University Press, 2012.

———. "The Meanings of Western Maoism in the Global 1960s." In Chen et al., *Routledge Handbook of the Global Sixties*, 67–78.

Smaldone, William. *Confronting Hitler: German Social Democrats in Defense of the Weimar Republic, 1929–1933*. Lanham, MD: Lexington, 2009.

Smith, Evan, and Matthew Worley, eds. *Against the Grain: The British Far Left from 1956*. Manchester: Manchester University Press, 2014.

———. *Waiting for the Revolution: The British Far Left from 1956*. Manchester: Manchester University Press, 2017.

Soell, Hartmut. *Fritz Erler—Eine politische Biographie*. 2 vols. Berlin: J.H.W. Dietz Nachf., 1976.

Solano, Wilebaldo. *Le POUM: Révolution dans la guerre d'Espagne*. Translated by Olga Balaguer and Manuel Perianez. Paris: Syllepse, 2002.

Söllner, Alfons. *Zur Archäologie der Demokratie in Deutschland*. 2 vols. Frankfurt am Main: Europäische Verlagsanstalt, 1982.

Spaulding, Daniel, and Michael Shane Boyle. "Hans-Jürgen Krahl: From Critical to Revolutionary Theory." *Viewpoint Magazine*, September 29, 2014.

Specter, Matthew G. *Habermas: An Intellectual Biography*. Cambridge: Cambridge University Press, 2010.

Stamer, Sabine. *Cohn-Bendit: Die Biografie*. Hamburg: Europa, 2001.

Sternhell, Zeev. *Neither Right nor Left: Fascist Ideology in France* [1983]. Translated by David Maisel. Berkeley: University of California Press, 1986.

Stoffregen, Matthias. "Kämpfen für ein demokratisches Deutschland: Emigranten zwischen Politik und Politikwissenschaft." PhD thesis, University of Frankfurt, 2002.

Stone, Dan. *Goodbye to All That? The Story of Europe since 1945*. Oxford: Oxford University Press, 2014.

Strote, Noah Benezra. *Lions and Lambs: Conflict in Weimar and the Creation of Post-Nazi Germany*. New Haven, CT: Yale University Press, 2017.

Struve, Walter. *Elites against Democracy: Leadership Ideals in Bourgeois Political Thought in Germany, 1890–1933*. Princeton, NJ: Princeton University Press, 1973.

Suri, Jeremi. *Power and Protest: Global Revolution and the Rise of Détente*. Cambridge, MA: Harvard University Press, 2003.

Thomas, Hugh. *The Spanish Civil War*. New York: Harper and Row, 1961.

Thompson, Duncan. *Pessimism of the Intellect? A History of "New Left Review."* Monmouth, UK: Merlin, 2007.

Tjaden, Karl Hermann. *Struktur und Funktion der "KPD-Opposition" (KPO): Eine organisationssoziologische Untersuchung zur "Rechts"-Opposition im deutschen Kommunismus zur Zeit der Weimarer Republik*. Meisenheim am Glan: A. Hain, 1964.

Tombs, Isabelle. "Une identité européenne assiégée? Les exilés socialistes à Londres, 1939–1945." *Revue d'histoire moderne et contemporaine* 46, no. 2 (April–June 1999): 263–79.

Tompkins, Andrew S. *Better Active than Radioactive! Anti-nuclear Protest in 1970s France and West Germany*. New York: Oxford University Press, 2016.

Traverso, Enzo. *Fire and Blood: The European Civil War, 1914–1945* [2007]. London: Verso, 2016.

———. *Left-Wing Melancholia: Marxism, History, and Memory.* New York: Columbia University Press, 2016.

Van der Linden, Marcel. "Socialisme ou Barbarie: A French Revolutionary Group (1949–65)." *Left History* 5, no. 1 (1997): 7–37.

Van Hook, James C. *Rebuilding Germany: The Creation of the Social Market Economy, 1945–1957.* Cambridge: Cambridge University Press, 2004.

Varon, Jeremy. *Bringing the War Home: The Weather Underground, the Red Army Faction, and the Revolutionary Violence in the Sixties and Seventies.* Berkeley: University of California Press, 2004.

Von der Goltz, Anna. "Other '68ers in West Berlin: Christian Democratic Students and the Cold War City." *Central European History* 50, no. 1 (2017): 86–112.

———, ed. *"Talkin' 'bout my generation": Conflicts of Generation Building and Europe's "1968."* Göttingen: Wallstein, 2011.

Von Dirke, Sabine. *"All Power to the Imagination!" The West German Counterculture from the Student Movement to the Greens.* Lincoln: University of Nebraska Press, 1997.

Vorholt, Udo. *Die Sowjetunion im Urteil des sozialdemokratischen Exils, 1933 bis 1945: Eine Studie des Exilparteivorstandes der SPD, des Internationalen Sozialistischen Kampfbundes, der Sozialistischen Arbeiterpartie und der Gruppe Neu Beginnen.* Frankfurt am Main: Peter Lang, 1991.

Wagner, Thomas. *Die Angstmacher: 1968 und die Neuen Rechten.* Berlin: Aufbau, 2017.

Walter, Franz. *"Republik, das ist nicht viel": Partei und Jugend in der Krise des Weimarer Sozialismus.* Bielefeld: Transcript, 2011.

———. *Die SPD: Vom Proletariat zur Neuen Mitte.* Berlin: Alexander Fest, 2002.

Weber, Hermann. *Die Wandlung des deutschen Kommunismus: Die Stalinisierung der KPD in der Weimarer Republik.* 2 vols. Frankfurt am Main: Europäische Verlagsanstalt, 1969.

Weisbrod, Bernd. "Generation und Generationalität in der neueren Geschichte." *Aus Politik und Zeitgeschichte,* no. 8 (2005): 3–9.

Weiß, Volker. *Die autoritäre Revolte: Die Neue Rechte und der Untergang des Abendlandes.* Stuttgart: Klett-Cotta, 2017.

Weitz, Eric D. *Creating German Communism, 1890–1990: From Popular Protests to Socialist State.* Princeton, NJ: Princeton University Press, 1997.

Westerman, Richard. *Lukács's Phenomenology of Capitalism: Reification Revalued.* Cham, Switzerland: Palgrave Macmillan, 2019.

Whitney, Susan B. *Mobilizing Youth: Communists and Catholics in Interwar France.* Durham, NC: Duke University Press, 2009.

Wichers, Hermann. *Im Kampf gegen Hitler: Deutsche Sozialisten im schweizer Exil 1933–1940.* Zürich: Chronos, 1994.

Wierling, Dorothee. "Generations as Narrative Communities: Some Private Sources of Official Cultures of Remembrance in Postwar Germany." In *Histories of the Aftermath: The Legacies of the Second World War in Europe,* edited by Frank Biess and Robert G. Moeller, 102–20. New York: Berghahn, 2010.

Wiggershaus, Rolf. *The Frankfurt School: Its History, Theories and Political Significance* [1986]. Translated by Michael Robertson. Cambridge, MA: MIT Press and Polity, 1995.

Wilkinson, James D. *The Intellectual Resistance in Europe*. Cambridge, MA: Harvard University Press, 1981.

Wolin, Richard. *The Wind from the East: French Intellectuals, the Cultural Revolution, and the Legacy of the 1960s*. Princeton, NJ: Princeton University Press, 2010.

Wright, Steve. *Storming Heaven: Class Composition and Struggle in Italian Autonomist Marxism*. London: Pluto, 2002.

Wurgaft, Lewis D. *The Activists: Kurt Hiller and the Politics of Action on the German Left, 1914–1933*. Philadelphia: American Philosophical Society, 1977.

Yusta Rodrigo, Mercedes. "La construcción de una cultura política femenina desde el antifascismo (1934–1950)." In *Feminismos y antifeminismos: Culturas políticas e identidades de género en la España del siglo XX*, edited by Ana Aguado and Teresa Ma. Ortega, 253–81. Valencia: Publicacions de la Universitat de València, 2011.

Zur Mühlen, Patrik von. *Spanien war ihre Hoffnung: Die deutsche Linke im Spanischen Bürgerkrieg 1936 bis 1939*. Bonn: Verlag Neue Gesellschaft, 1983.

A NOTE ON THE TYPE

This book has been composed in Arno, an Old-style serif typeface in the
classic Venetian tradition, designed by Robert Slimbach at Adobe.

Lightning Source UK Ltd.
Milton Keynes UK
UKHW042215151021
392282UK00003B/20